Education Matters
Readings in Pastoral Care for School Chaplains, Guidance Counsellors and Teachers

Dr James O'Higgins Norman is a Senior Lecturer and Researcher, and Director of the National Anti-Bullying Research and Resource Centre at the School of Education Studies, Dublin City University. Previous publications include *Ethos and Education in Ireland* (2003) and *Homophobic Bullying in Irish Secondary Education* (2008). His current research is focused on cyberbullying and social media.

EDUCATION
MATTERS

**Readings in Pastoral Care for
School Chaplains,
Guidance Counsellors
and Teachers**

Edited by James O'Higgins Norman

VERITAS

Published 2014 by
Veritas Publications
7–8 Lower Abbey Street
Dublin 1, Ireland
publications@veritas.ie
www.veritas.ie

ISBN 978 1 84730 569 5

10 9 8 7 6 5 4 3 2 1

A catalogue record for this book is available from the British Library.

Designed by Heather Costello, Veritas Publications
Printed by Watermans Printers Ltd, Cork

Veritas books are printed on paper made from the wood pulp of managed forests. For every tree felled, at least one tree is planted, thereby renewing natural resources.

Dedicated to my nephews
Braidin, Callum and Killian

CONTENTS

Foreword

For a number of years now there has been a significant reimagining of education systems in the USA, Ireland, the UK, Australia, and elsewhere. A common theme underpins the changes being introduced and the concerns expressed by theorists, policy makers and practitioners alike. This is a concern about the extent to which our school systems meet the personal and social needs of an increasingly diverse population. The extent to which schools can promote and achieve well-being among their students is increasingly becoming as important to parents and teachers as the role of schools in academic and vocational preparation.

Despite the desire on the part of parents in particular that schools should assist them in helping young people to grow to be happy, resilient and successful, research on schools and well-being has been slow to develop and to keep pace with the ever emerging needs of school communities. Consequently, this book makes a welcome contribution to our knowledge and understanding of pastoral care and well-being in school communities. The editor, Dr James O'Higgins Norman, is to be commended for his sustained commitment to research and writing on issues related to pastoral care in education. He has successfully identified appropriate individual researchers and practitioners in Ireland, the USA, the UK and Australia, and in doing so has created a critical mass of reflection upon the values and actions that make schools truly successful communities of growth for young people.

The research presented in this volume highlights the complex nature of the relationships that exist in our schools and the extent to which these contribute to how young people experience education.

Professor Thomas H. Groome
Boston College
October 2014

I. Humanistic Pastoral Care

Pastoral Care in Schools

James O'Higgins Norman

The changing sociology of family life in western societies, the emergence of new social problems within school environments, the ever-increasing social, personal and emotional developmental effect of young people living in cyberspace and the development of an intercultural and secular climate all pose a new series of pastoral issues in schools that need to be addressed: substance abuse, binge drinking, bullying, teenage pregnancy, suicide, changing sexual mores, racism. The teacher is a significant catalyst, among others, in enabling the school to address these urgent educational and pastoral challenges.

In recent years the curriculum in Ireland has seen many additions that have raised our expectations of the goals of education and the role of the teacher. This is reflected in the pastoral goals of recent legislation in Ireland, which oblige schools to promote the 'moral, spiritual and personal' development of the pupil.[1] Syllabi such as Social Personal and Health Education (SPHE), Civic Social and Personal Education (CSPE) and Relationships and Sexuality Education (RSE) have been previously introduced to promote pupils' social and personal development and to provide a balance to the pervading academic ethos of Irish schools.[2] The new framework for junior cycle is underpinned by a belief that a young person's well-being must be central to teaching and learning.[3] Despite the fact that these initiatives have been introduced in a relatively short period of time onto an already overloaded school experience, teachers in Ireland may be admired for having responded so wholeheartedly to them. Furthermore, the extent to which teachers in Ireland have embraced the pastoral dimension to education in schools can be admired even further when we compare them with their colleagues in other countries where the teacher's duty of care is not always interpreted so liberally.

Context of Pastoral Care

The roots of contemporary second-level schooling in Ireland can be traced back to two influential forces. First, in terms of philosophy or ethos, the voluntary secondary schools that were developed in the nineteenth century[4] and were mainly run by religious congregations were very much rooted in a vision of education which encompassed the whole person, body, mind and soul. This philosophy of education remains an influencing force in second-level schools today, and despite the increasing alliances between the economy and education,[5][6] most Irish second-level schools still at least aim to develop the whole pupil. Second, many of the structures that are used to organise learning and promote the holistic development of pupils in schools in Ireland today have been influenced by the English public school system, which was often centred around the maintenance of good discipline and learning. In the public schools of the nineteenth century, which were mainly for boarders, pupils were organised into 'houses' and each house had a 'dean of residence' who was responsible for the discipline and well-being of the pupils in his care.[7] The similarities of this system with the year head and tutor structures in Irish schools today are not hard to see.

Whatever the influences are from the past, in more recent times the development of government policy and legislation[8] has provided schools and teachers with a strong framework in which to address the pastoral needs of their pupils. In considering the strong commitment on the part of Irish teachers to pastoral care in second-level schools, it should also be noted that recent industrial problems between teachers unions and government did highlight some frustration on the part of teachers in Ireland at the lack of adequate training, resources and clarity of role where pastoral care is concerned. Just because there has been a strong tradition of liberally interpreting the duty of care and teaching, does not mean that we can expect teachers to continue to address pupils' personal difficulties without adequate training and support. There is an urgent need to investigate the pastoral dimension of education in order to assess the needs of teachers in supporting their pupils.

Although it is true that Irish second-level schools have always had a holistic understanding of education, it is also true that the implications of this understanding have not always been fully appreciated. The enormous amount of energy, time and resources that are required to provide a holistic education is only fully impacting on our minds since the decline in the number of religious in our schools and the transfer of the full burden of pastoral care to lay teachers has occurred. That is not to say that lay teachers are new to pastoral care but rather that in the past much of the extra time and services required to support pupils came from the religious personnel who often lived and worked on the school premises. The extent to which pastoral care was taken for granted as part of Irish schooling is manifest in the fact that pastoral care was almost absent from policy documents until the Report of the National Education Convention in 1995 and in the White Paper on Education of the same year. Since then, through the Education Act (1998) and the Education (Welfare) Act (2000), schools have been given a strong legal framework in which to address the provision of pastoral care to pupils.

Defining Pastoral Care

Every school in Ireland claims to offer pastoral care, but on many visits to schools around the country I have observed that schools realise their pastoral obligations in different ways. In some schools pastoral care is identified with activities such as breakfast clubs, in other schools it is identified with the activities of the guidance counsellor, tutor or chaplain, while in others again pastoral care is seen as the delivery of a particular syllabus. Pastoral care can be defined as the response of the school, through its teachers, chaplains, counsellors and parents, to the emerging personal needs of the pupils with a view to promoting teaching and learning. Pastoral care is complex, and relies on a variety of systems, personnel and approaches. It is possible to categorise pastoral care into three stages or dimensions: humanistic, programmatic and spiritual.

I call stage one *humanistic* as it refers to the way in which the school seeks to meet the basic bodily or physical needs of its pupils. This stage of pastoral care relates to the basic security (safety, food, shelter) and social needs (finding love, belonging, self-help) identified by Maslow.[9] The school addresses these needs through the provision of projects such as breakfast clubs and by liaising with local community care professionals as well as through the development of positive teacher–pupil relationships within the classroom. Apart from a basic concern for the well-being of the pupil, this stage of pastoral care does not require specific training or skills and can be offered by most teachers with some support from the Home-School-Community Liaison. Stage two, *programmatic*, relates to higher 'ego' needs which have to do with the development of pupils' self-esteem, confidence and life skills through self-actualisation programmes such as SPHE, CSPE, RSE and Religious Education (RE). This stage of pastoral care will require teachers who have been trained in appropriate strategies in teaching and learning about well-being. Guidance counselling also has a very specific contribution to make at this stage of pastoral care in empowering pupils to make decisions about their future. Stage three, *spiritual*, refers to the young person's need to search for meaning and to be able to deal with the deeper questions of life. The loss of a parent through death or separation, for example, can act as a catalyst in a young person's life, causing them to ask questions which they have not thought about previously. At this stage of pastoral care, the young person is helped to reflect on their relationships with self, others, God and the world. The contribution of the school chaplain is obvious here in that they will have been specifically trained in theology and spirituality and will also have the counselling skills required to accompany pupils in their search for meaning and purpose in life.

Pastoral Care and Roles of Responsibility

It can be helpful to identify different stages or dimensions in pastoral care because this allows school management to develop a whole school plan for guidance, chaplaincy and pastoral care. Although these areas tend to be treated as distinct within the culture of most Irish schools, I think the integration of them into one school plan will provide the greatest benefit to pupils. It would be a mistake to think that any one of the above stages is more important than another or that the mere provision of a breakfast club or SPHE, for example, amounts to the totality of pastoral care. The individual needs of each pupil will dictate what type of pastoral care is required and it is the role of school management to ensure that there are teachers, chaplains and counsellors on the staff with appropriate insight and skills to meet the needs of these pupils.

In collaboration, school personnel are required to focus on the pupil's needs ahead of any concern for professional recognition or dominance. In particular, for too long the relationship between guidance counsellors and school chaplains in some schools has been characterised by competition and a desire for dominance in pastoral work instead of a shared common concern for the pastoral needs of pupils. This situation was not helped by the government's decision to reduce the allocation of hours for guidance counsellors as a cost-saving measure in 2012. However, research reported elsewhere by Hayes and Morgan[10] and by Áine Moran and myself later in this book (see chapters 19 and 20) confirms that in Ireland the majority of guidance counsellors and school chaplains are highly qualified professionals who hold both basic and advanced qualifications appropriate to their roles in schools and that both have an educational and legal mandate for their work among young people in schools. While both of these roles of pastoral responsibility have important distinct elements, they also share commonalities that can be fused for the benefit of pupils in schools. The challenge is then for guidance counsellors and school chaplains along with home-school-community liaisons and teachers to develop systems that respect their distinct roles while providing an opportunity to work together towards the well-being of young people. In doing so, they should recall the view of the Department of Education which promotes an understanding of guidance as a whole school activity that is integrated into all school programmes.[11]

Pastoral Care in Teaching and Learning

Kevin Williams is correct when he warns that while 'good teaching involves caring, caring should never replace good teaching'[12] and, later in this book, that fundamentally it is the school's task to promote socialisation and cultural enrichment. This does not mean, however, that pastoral care should be seen as ancillary to teaching and learning. Through pastoral care, pupils are helped to be ready to learn and so it can be justly claimed that pastoral care is central to education. If a pupil's needs become so great to the extent that a teacher has to stop teaching, then the teacher should be able to refer the pupil to pastoral care professionals within the school such as the chaplain or counsellor or to other professionals outside of the school. This book is intended to be a resource for those who study and practice pastoral care in second-level schools. As much of the book is based on the contributors' research, the book will contribute to praxis within pastoral care in second-level schools by encouraging reflection on action and action as a result of reflection.

Conclusion

Pastoral care is an important dimension to schooling in Ireland that is exercised for the most part by teachers who understand that their role is more than about merely imparting knowledge. Teachers are supported in their teaching and learning activities by other members of the school staff including guidance counsellors and school chaplains as well as parents. The development of a pastoral care plan is the responsibility of the whole school community including pupils. Members of staff who work on SPHE, CSPE, RSE and RE programmes should work together with school chaplains and guidance counsellors as well as senior management teams to develop systems and resources that promote the personal and social well-being of pupils.

Notes

1. Education Act (1998), 9(d).
2. S. Boldt, 'A Vantage Point of Values – Findings From School Culture and Ethos Survey Questionnaires' in C. Furlong and L. Monahan, *School Culture and Ethos: Cracking the Code* (Dublin: Marino, 2000), 29–58.
3. A Framework for Junior Cycle (Dublin: Department of Education and Skills, 2012), 4.
4. See J. Coolahan, *Irish Education History and Structure* (Dublin: IPA, 1981) for a full history of second-level schooling in the nineteenth century.
5. J. Dunne, 'What's the Good of Education?' in P. Hogan (ed.), *Partnership and the Benefits of Learning* (Dublin: Educational Studies Association of Ireland, 1995).

6. K. Lynch and M. Moran, 'Markets, Schools and the Convertibility of Economic Capital: The Complex Dynamics of Class Choice' in *British Journal of Sociology of Education* (April 2006), 27, 2, 221–35.

7. For a more in-depth description of the influences of nineteenth-century English public school's influence on pastoral care in modern schools, see P. Lang, 'Pastoral Care: Some Reflections on Possible Influences' in *Pastoral Care in Education* 2, 2 (Oxford: Blackwell, 1983).

8. See Education Act (1998); Education (Welfare) Act (2000).

9. A. Maslow, *Towards a Psychology of Being* (Princeton, NJ: Van Nostrand, 1968).

10. C. Hayes and M. Morgan, *Research on the Practice of Counselling by Guidance Counsellors in Post-Primary Schools* (Dublin: National Centre for Guidance in Education, 2011).

11. Department of Education, Guidelines for Schools on the Implications of Section 9(c) of the Education Act, Relating to Students' Access to Appropriate Guidance (Dublin: Government Publications, 2005), 4.

12. K. Williams, 'Understanding Ethos: A Philosophical and Literary Exploration' in Furlong and Monahan (eds), *School Culture and Ethos*, 77.

Caring as an Educational Aim

Kevin Williams

Over the years, it has often struck me that some of the standard criticisms of schools (as being too examination-oriented and too competitive, for example) are based on a failure to recognise the school has multiple purposes and a failure to recognise the nature and limits of the notion of care and nurture in educational institutions. In this chapter I propose to identify the multiple aims of schools and show how care and nurture have a place as an aim of education.

Some Aims of the School and One Consequence of Schooling

The first explicit purpose of the school is utilitarian: to provide socialisation. This refers to preparation to live in society and to contribute to society. It is both realistic and defensible to expect that the school curriculum should embrace preparation for working life as one of its aims. Even if we lived in a country where no one had to work to earn a living, it would be appropriate to teach young people what it is like for those who have to work in order to survive. This would be a legitimate part of the understanding which school education should be expected to promote. As we do not inhabit this fictional country, the society which supports the institution of formal schooling can reasonably expect that young people should leave school not only with an understanding of the world of work but also with an enhanced capacity to earn a living. This will contribute to the good of society as well as to their own personal sense of well-being.

The second purpose of the school is to provide cultural enrichment, and this might be considered its most conspicuously educational dimension. This refers to the responsibility of schools to introduce young people to cultural activities of a theoretical and practical character capable of yielding satisfaction and fulfilment. The other aims of the school are to provide young people with a nurturing environment, to cultivate moral character and to offer spiritual and religious education. There is little need to labour the fact that these aims overlap considerably and that teachers and chaplains can make an important contribution to realising them.

But organised learning or schooling has another feature, which is an unavoidable consequence of the institution in almost any society. This is its facilitation of positional advantage, i.e. the labour market advantage conferred by the *exchange value* of education. Many negative manifestations of schooling derive from the consequence of its having an exchange value. These features underlie the 'hidden curriculum' of academic competitiveness that is supposed to be a major feature of school life today. The reason why there is such an emphasis on achievement in the academic sphere is due to the esteem attached to academic/professional work in this society. But the narrow focus of some pupils and their parents on academic success is not the direct fault of the school. In any case, I wonder if critics of narrowness of educational focus have different priorities themselves when it comes to the education of their own children. I wonder if those who preach high theories about the 'whole person', the 'disadvantaged' or 'social integration' put these theories into practice when choosing schools for their offspring. I have no evidence on the matter but I do have some uncomfortable intuitions. If medical faculties decided to accept only those who had done the Leaving Certificate Applied, we would see a transformation in the perception of the less academically oriented curriculum. But unless we have such a dramatic reversal in the requirements for university entrance, the priorities of parents, their children and teachers regarding school are unlikely to change.

I am not persuaded that we can do much about the high valuation placed by many people on the professions and the knowledge that secures access to them. But I do think that schools should not engage in exaggerated fine-tuning of their role in assessing pupil achievement. The impact of the pressure for schools to be 'effective' can have this result. Where examination results are the only criterion for judging the quality of schooling, schools may experience pressure to increase the number and degree of passes at all costs. As Geoffrey Walford points out, one outcome of this process is to make of the school 'an even more effective sorting machine' in respect of allocating to young people their future occupational destinations.[1] What can happen is that a C rather than a D grade in a particular subject can have a wholly disproportionate influence on a person's life chances. Society can justifiably expect schools to offer broad indications of achievement of learners but not fine-grained categorisation based on particular grade differences whose validity and reliability may be questionable.

There is a reprehensible view that where the school has fulfilled its function as a social filter, the kind of curriculum offered to those who do not aspire to university education is not of great importance. This cynical attitude is captured in the words of a teacher reported by Gervase Phinn, an English school inspector: 'They're not your grammar school highfliers ... These lads will end up in manual jobs, that's if they're lucky, and not become university professors and brain surgeons.'[2] The teacher in this case is relatively indifferent to what young people are taught but often such pupils can be offered what might be called a tabloid curriculum to keep them occupied and entertained.[3] One reason for this dismissive attitude towards the fate of these young people is due to a view of study at second level as an apprenticeship to further study at university. This is an unfortunate conception because it means that aims within school subjects tend to be intra-subject, that is, that study of a subject at junior cycle at second level is conceived as leading to its continued study at senior cycle and then at university.[4] It should be possible, by contrast, for a period of study within a subject to be conceived as self-contained and also as connecting with wider civic and personal aims than acquiring skills and knowledge within that subject. One of the problems with promoting too close a link between school subjects and universities is that many young people can see their future study and career options as related exclusively to the continued study of the subject they were good at in school. Rather than thinking of the whole range of possibilities, some school leavers can think, for example, only of doing more history or science.

Let us turn next to an examination of the notion of nurture in schools.

The School as a Nurturing Environment

Schools in the English-speaking world are usually conceived as nurturing environments grounded in a broad or thicker conception of children's welfare than that of mere academic achievement. As has been highlighted in the previous chapter, this is not the case elsewhere. Observing the education of his two children, British novelist Tim Parks has written with some bewilderment about what he perceives as the very different remit of the Italian school from that of its English counterpart:

> For school offers no games, no extracurricular activities. There are no music lessons, no singing lessons, no school choir ... no hockey, no cricket, no netball, no basketball, no football, no swimming, no athletics, no sports day, no school teams.[5]

Most of all, what strikes him is the absence of any attempt to induce a family atmosphere in the school.

> The school doesn't, as it does in England, pretend to offer a community that might in any way supplant the family, or rival Mamma. That's important. It doesn't, and later on

the university won't either, try to create in the child the impression of belonging to a large social unit with its own identity. There is no assembly in the morning, no hymn singing, no prayers, no speech day …[6]

For his two children of six and eight, school is 'no more and no less than reading and writing and mathematics' and other school subjects.[7] Somewhat ironically, though, in spite of the attenuated and circumscribed or thin conception of the school's remit, religion is also part of the curriculum.

The contrast with the spirit of schooling in the English-speaking world could not be more dramatic. Here the school is often perceived as an extension of the home in terms of providing personal support and overall care for young people. Traditionally schools in Ireland and other Anglophone countries are perceived both as complementing the work of the home in terms of religious or catechetical formation as well as extending the parents' remit of caring. The school and its teachers stand *in loco parentis*. A moving incident of which I was a witness communicates very well what this can mean in practice. In a school that I was visiting, which was attached to a convent, I was told that the police were searching for the body of a parent who had died tragically. There was a great sense of foreboding and sadness on the day of my visit and it came as a relief when the body was recovered. I learned that the religious of the community, who owned the school, had been helping to look after the family over the weekend. This is the kind of service of care, support and nurture that educators have given so generously in many different school contexts.

This conception of the caring school is most conspicuous in the case of boarding schools. Here is novelist Monk Gibbon's description of the school in England that features in his novel, *The Pupil*. The narrator experiences the school as a 'kind of miniature Plato's Republic', a 'cultured oasis' animated by the conviction of the principal that a 'school should be a large family – a small nation'.[8] The school also assumes a responsibility for character education. In the words of the principal, education is animated by the conviction 'that character is everything, and that everything without character is nothing'.[9] The theme of safety and security surfaces in reminiscence on his schooldays by the English philosopher Michael Oakeshott. The happiness that Oakeshott experienced at school was 'a kind of serenity' as well as a sense that 'growing up was something to be enjoyed, not merely got through'.[10] What the school provided 'was a feeling of safety and an immense variety of outlets'.[11] It was 'surrounded by a thick, firm hedge, and inside this hedge was a world of beckoning activities and interests'.[12] These emanated from the principal or 'were the private enterprise of members of staff, ... [or were] made for oneself. There was a great deal of laughter and fun; there was a great deal of seriousness.'[13] Notable also in these reflections is the wide compass of activities included within the school. The positive educational experiences to be found even in traditional schools are often much more embracing than those offered by the formal curriculum.

The non-elitist outreach of the impulse to care
Moreover, commitment to the quality of the experience of school is not confined to teachers in upper middle class schools. Christopher Winch refers to the 'heroic efforts made by many secondary modern teachers to give their children a worthwhile experience at school'.[14] Here is an account again by Gervase Phinn of the role of the school that would be shared by committed teachers in many schools in the English-speaking world. He arrives in a boys' school in a lower socio-economic area catering for children who have failed to get places in the traditional academic secondary school. By virtue of attending this school the boys are already 'deemed to be failures' and arrive 'under-confident, with low self-esteem'.[15] The task of the school, explains the principal, is:

> [F]irst and foremost ... to build up their confidence and self-esteem, continue to have high expectations for them and be sure they know, give them maximum support and encouragement, develop their social skills and qualities of character to enable them to enter the world feeling good about themselves ... so they develop into well-rounded young people with courage, tolerance, strong convictions, lively enquiring minds and a sense of humour ... I do really believe ... that those of us in education can really make a difference, particularly in the lives of less fortunate children, those who are labelled failures.[16]

He tries, he says, to make the school 'like the good home that I was brought up in, a place where there is work and laughter, honesty and fairness'.[17] Here we find the metaphor of the school as being like a 'good home', reflecting the metaphor of the family in the quotation from Monk Gibbon.

Most schools that I have the privilege of visiting are nurturing and protective environments. Especially, but not only, in lower socio-economic area, schools can allow young people to be children, secure for a while from the cramped toughness of their world outside the classroom where the demands of a precocious adulthood encroach so insistently upon them. This is captured succinctly in the description of the primary school in Roddy Doyle's *A Star Called Henry*, where the brother of the eponymous hero cries on being withdrawn from school, missing 'the warmth, the singing, making words, the chalk working across his slate, the woman who'd made him feel wanted'.[18] A positive experience of schooling is not the sole prerogative of the middle class and those bound for university.

Teaching and Nurture

Here I wish to draw attention to the teacher's principal task in nurturing pupils. Fundamentally it is to ensure that the pupils learn. Nurturing is a part of educating; it is not an activity in itself. The defining character of the teacher's job specification is to promote learning. A comparison can be made with the world of medicine. Holistic concern for the patient should be part of any regime of treatment but this concern should not be at the expense of competent administration of medical care. Indeed, if I had to choose, I would prefer to be treated by someone who was competent, although curt and brusque, rather than by a person who was 'nice' but unskilled in the practice of medicine. Likewise in education, 'niceness' is no substitute for competence. Indeed, 'niceness' on its own can frustrate efforts to reach pupils. In his autobiography, *Another Country: Growing Up in 1950s Ireland*, Gene Kerrigan writes of the torment that befell a young 'nice priest' chaplain-teacher.[19] Kerrigan describes him as having a 'fresh, open mind, a soul yearning to enhance our spirituality within a changing, questioning society'.[20] His aim was to get the boys 'talking in the vernacular of the day about eternal truths'.[21] Willing to mingle with the pupils, he sat on an empty desk in the middle of the classroom rather than behind the teacher's desk.

> Smiling, open to dialogue. He wanted to be our friend.
> We ate him alive …
> He wanted nothing but good for us, he wanted to approach
> us on our terms, he respected us. And we laughed in his
> face …
> He offered friendship, we smelled weakness …
> We mistook love for vulnerability and we seized him by the
> throat.[22]

What this young priest did not appreciate was that schools operate within a particular framework, and in order to function successfully, teachers must take account of this framework. An essential feature of the framework is an awareness of the adult-child and individual-group character of the teacher-pupil relationship. This requires the exercise of an institutionally appropriate form of authority and the imposition of a certain control. Within this framework, it is possible to provide the nurture that characterises good teaching.

I am not suggesting that all teaching conducted in this context will result in successful learning. Failure to ensure learning may be due to factors beyond the control of the teacher – for example, domestic disharmony or illness. Yet teachers' primary responsibility is to teach their subjects. In some cases, where the resistance of the pupils to school and to learning seems insurmountable, this may prove impossible. But it is simply not good enough to forgo the attempt to teach on the grounds that all efforts are doomed to failure unless we change the whole educational system or indeed the whole socio-economic system. Fashionable theories about re-defining what counts as intelligence may well be sustainable but they are not an excuse for giving up on trying to teach that constituency of the young population described by some as low achievers. The principal referred to previously invokes no highfaluting slogans about the 'failure of the system', 'narrow conception of intelligence' or the need for 'critical theory'.

In some research I have conducted into the conceptions of good teachers held by student teachers, admiration for structured, orderly and efficient teaching is striking.[23] Young people who experience imaginative, structured and committed teaching are in the process experiencing nurture. Moreover, those who do not aspire to attend university need not be precluded from engagement with the traditional areas of the school curriculum (literature, language, history and science). Here is an account by Phinn of a teacher giving a lesson based on a novel set during the Second World War to a group of non-academically inclined learners.

> She used well chosen illustrations and probing questions to develop understanding of ideas and motives ... She encouraged the boys to explore character in greater depth, whilst sensitively supporting the less able, helping them to stay interested and involved by the use of questions matched to their abilities and interests. She required them to justify a point of view, refer to the text, relate to their own experiences and examine the use of language.

> The atmosphere in the classroom was warm and supportive, and the boys responded well to the teacher, clearly enjoying

her touches of humour … [She] had a real empathy with, and respect for, the pupils and … had high expectations of their success. She encouraged, directed, suggested, questioned, challenged and developed the pupils' understanding in an atmosphere of good humour and enjoyment.[24]

The positive attitudes of the teacher are also reflected in the actual classroom environment: 'wonderfully bright and attractive with appropriate displays of posters, photographs and artefacts which gave the pupils a feel for the period in which the novel was set.'[25] Striking in Phinn's characterisation of the classroom is the reference to warmth and good humour – the former also occurring in the extract from Roddy Doyle and the latter in the comments of the principal and in the reference to laughter and fun in the reminiscence from Oakeshott. Regrettably these concepts are not sufficiently foregrounded in educational discourse.

On leaving this class, Phinn heads for the final lesson of the day through the school hall. There he finds two aggressive groups of boys shaping up to one another. So intense does their aggression become that Phinn intervenes, much to the surprise of the boys and indeed of their teacher, who stands up to inform him that he has been watching a rehearsal of *Romeo and Juliet*. He spends the next half an hour watching 'the most gripping opening' of the play he had ever seen.[26]

The teachers in the two examples provided by Phinn nurtured their pupils precisely by teaching with energy, commitment and imagination. Teaching of such a character is more important than add-on programmes of pastoral care. I have always been more impressed by careful, consistent and constructive correction of pupils' assignments than by facility at producing theories about holistic education. This kind of caring for the welfare of learners is part of what is involved in being an educator.

The Complexity of Caring
To be sure there is scope for nurturing activities of an explicit character within schools both on the part of teachers and on the part of counsellors and chaplains. Many teachers feel the impulse to nurture their pupils by having regard for their welfare. Many will have at some time in their careers felt like Prudie, the fictional French teacher in *The Jane Austen Book Club* by Karen Joy Fowler. She claims that the pastoral concern should supplant conventional teaching. 'Why bother,' she reflects,

to send teenagers to school at all? Their minds were so clogged with hormones they couldn't possibly learn a complex system like calculus or chemistry, much less the wild tangle of a foreign language. Why put everyone to the aggravation of making them try? Prudie thought she could do the rest of it – watch them for signs of suicide or weapons or pregnancy or drug addiction or sexual abuse – but asking her to teach them French at the same time was really too much.[27]

In the novella *Lipstick on the Host*, taken from a collection of the same name by the Irish writer and broadcaster Aidan Mathews, the teacher, Meggie, feels acutely the same passion to care for her pupils as Prudie.[28] For example, she reproves the male principal for his total lack of awareness of how period pain can impact on the examinations performance of female pupils. The reality of being 'a casualty of ... basic biology' seemed a 'complete mystery' to him.[29] A boy in her class turns up the collar of his jacket to prevent her from seeing the boils on his neck, and at this poignant gesture of adolescent vanity she says that she 'loved him for a moment'.[30] She pities a poor boy wearing socks on his hands instead of gloves and would have given him hers but realises that his parents would object and she would be reported to the board of management.[31] She is well aware of the need to curtail her impulse to care but cannot prevent herself from wishing to take home with her a boy with a chronic cough in order to look after him properly.

The absolute necessity that a teacher refrain from laying a hand on a child in anger or affection can sometimes give rise to a tension between maintaining professional distance and offering human support. In his wonderful reminiscence on his career as a teacher, Frank McCourt gives an account of an incident that captures this tension unforgettably. A female student reads to the class her recollection of the first moon landing. This coincided with the death of her father, and the memory of the juxtaposition of this great event for humankind and the loss of her beloved father causes her to sob in front of the whole class.[32] How did McCourt react? He took the girl in his arms and let her sob on his shoulder, and when she recovered her composure the whole class applauded. This very human response however was not, in my opinion, appropriate, in the context of McCourt's professional role as a teacher.

Conclusion: Intervention Beyond the Classroom

McCourt's autobiography also offers an example of an incident where the teacher's concern with the welfare of a pupil requires intervention at another level. In a school essay by a female student, McCourt is concerned about her comments regarding her stepfather. 'He's a bit too familiar with her. Invites her to movies and dinner when her mother works overtime. And there's the way he looks at her'.[33] What should he do? 'Is this a cry for help or another teenage fantasy?'[34] McCourt is acutely conscious of the possibility that in taking the matter further he may either be the conduit of a false allegation or in failing to act that he may be putting the child's welfare gravely at risk. This is where intervention at a different level is required and in the Irish context the information must be passed on to the relevant authorised staff member (designated liaison person) to whom any reasonable grounds for concern about child abuse must be referred.

Fortunately, however, not all issues regarding pupil welfare are of such a nature. Yet teachers may have concerns about students that they have neither the time nor the expertise to address. As James Norman puts it:

> [Although] all teachers will be pastoral in their approach to pupils, there is also a need to have professionally qualified pastoral carers such as chaplains and guidance counsellors who will possess the competence to promote the pupils' spiritual and emotional development, which ultimately promotes their ability to learn in the classroom.[35]

In this situation the teacher needs to refer the matter to the professional team in the school because this is the kind of area that is outside the remit of the classroom teacher. To be sure, as a wise and experienced teacher turned counsellor observed to me, the expression of sympathy and concern is not the exclusive prerogative of the professional. In cases where a teacher knows of some difficult domestic situation, what is needed at times may be a brief sympathetic word communicating awareness of the young person's situation and the stress they must be undergoing. For educators, it is a humbling privilege to be able to offer support and sympathy to young people in times of loss and grief and trauma and in helping students to cope with personal problems. Yet it is crucially important that teachers appreciate when it is time for professional intervention. In addressing personal issues, chaplains and guidance counsellors, who do not normally have the burden of a teaching time table, are qualified to assist young people who wish to speak about troubling situations within the school, the home or indeed in their relationships with others.[36] The professional role counsellors/ chaplains play in providing care complements the nurture that is part of the activity of every educator.

Notes

1. G. Walford, 'Redefining school effectiveness' in *Westminster Studies in Education*, 25 (2002), 47–58, 35.

2. G. Phinn, *Over Hill and Dale* (London: Penguin, 2000), 159.

3. See some of the contributions to A. Hargreaves and P. Woods (eds), *Classrooms and Staffrooms: The Sociology of Teachers and Teaching* (Milton Keynes: Open University, 1984).

4. See J. White, *Rethinking the School Curriculum: Values, Aims and Purposes* (London: RoutledgeFalmer, 2004).

5. T. Parks, *An Italian Education* (London: Vintage, 2000), 287.

6. Ibid.

7. Ibid.

8. M. Gibbon, *The Pupil* (Dublin: Wolfhound Press, 1981). The quotations are taken from 21, 75 and 14 respectively.

9. Ibid., 76.

10. This quotation is from a text entitled 'Oakeshott on his Schooldays' published as an appendix in R. Grant, *Thinkers of Our Time: Oakeshott* (London: Claridge Press, 1990), 120.

11. Ibid.

12. Ibid.

13. Ibid.

14. C. Winch, 'The Economic Ends of Education' in *The Journal of Philosophy of Education*, 36 (Oxford: Blackwell, 2002), 101–118, 115, note 20.

15. Phinn, *Over Hill and Dale*, 152.

16. Ibid.

17. Ibid., 171.

18. R. Doyle, *A Star Called Henry* (London: Jonathan Cape, 1999), 79.

19. G. Kerrigan, *Another Country: Growing Up in 1950s Ireland* (Dublin: Gill and Macmillan, 1998), 55.

20. Ibid., 56.

21. Ibid.

22. Ibid.

23. K. Williams, 'Student Teachers Remember Good Teaching in Their Schooldays', *Prospero*, 4 (1998), 31–4.

24. Phinn, *Over Hill and Dale*, 164.

25. Ibid.

26. Ibid., 167.

27. K. J. Fowler, *The Jane Austen Bookclub* (London: Penguin, 1995), 86.

28. A. Mathews, *Lipstick on the Host* (London: Vintage, 1998).

29. Ibid., 222.

30. Ibid., 229.

31. Ibid., 248.

32. F. McCourt, *Teacherman* (London: Harper Perennial, 2006), 244.

33. Ibid., 188–9.

34. Ibid., 189.

35. J. E. Norman, 'Personal Difficulties and Educational Underachievement: The Contribution of Pastoral Care and School Chaplaincy' in *Irish Educational Studies*, 21, 1 (Spring 2002), 34.

36. In Ireland only certain schools (Community schools and some Community colleges) have access to the services of a chaplain who enjoys a state salary and considerable freedom from teaching duties.

Towards an Understanding of the Adolescent Search for Identity

Finola Cunnane

Wayne is sixteen, one of the lads, and beginning to focus on what the future might hold for him. He wonders who he is and questions the meaning and purpose of his life. Sarah's mother died tragically. She is no stranger to suffering and she questions the purpose of suffering and evil in our world. Tracey's parents have separated and her father has entered into a second relationship. Feelings of abandonment, resentment and anger rise to the surface every so often and she wonders if anyone really cares about her. Damien's family are struggling to make ends meet. He desperately seeks to be like those who seem to have it all. Steve is grappling with his sexuality. He is afraid to 'come out' but the burden of keeping silent is becoming unbearable. Chloe experiences herself as a victim to peer pressure. She cannot find her voice to say no to drugs and unwanted sexual encounters.

My experience is that these stories are representative of some of the concerns, struggles and questions for today's adolescents. These young people seek to make sense of the paradoxes of life they see around them: the break-up of family life, the quest for recognition, power and wealth, pressures to be acceptable, to do what would not necessarily be their deepest choice, as well as the injustices in society and in the world. They yearn for identity and a sense of self-worth. Hungering for meaning and purpose, for recognition and connection, for justice and for the holy, they seek a vision that is inviting and deserving of their energy and commitment. Ultimately, they seek a relationship with the Creator and Source of their being and they desire to nourish that hunger for mystery they experience within. In other words, they seek what James Bacik calls 'a deeper way of living humanly'.[1]

The Season of Adolescence

There is, indeed, a season for everything, as the Book of Ecclesiastes notes, and there is a season for adolescence. Marking the period from 'puberty until full adult status has been attained', the season of adolescence is one of physical, emotional and psychological upheaval.[2] A more comprehensive definition describes the period of adolescence as:

a chronological period beginning with the physical and emotional processes leading to a sexual and psychosocial maturity and ending at an ill-defined time when the individual achieves independence and social productivity.[3]

Noting that various activities emerge at specific times during adolescent development, Harvard psychiatrist Armand Nicholi has determined that adolescence comprises three stages: early, middle and late adolescence.[4] Early adolescence generally spans the twelve–fourteen year-old age group and is usually associated with puberty. Here young people are concerned with their changing bodies and with the physical aspect of their lives. Emotions are in turmoil and are expressed erratically, while the capacity to reflect and think critically is developing at a rapid pace. It is at this stage that the religious and philosophical questions regarding the meaning and purpose of life begin to emerge and relationships become more significant.

Middle adolescence is commonly understood as spanning the fifteen–eighteen year-old age group. The sexual self is now experienced at a deeper level and emotional involvement is sought with significant others. While the young person becomes more involved with peers and, perhaps, with various causes, this can be a lonely and confusing time as they struggle to separate from the authoritarian in the quest for personal identity.

Late adolescence refers to the period from eighteen years until independence and social productivity have been achieved. Issues of identity and intimacy can be heightened at this stage, as energies are focused on college, career and, sometimes, marriage choices, as well as concern for the roles that the young person hopes to fulfil in the world. Psychologist Daniel Levinson names this period of adolescence as 'early adult transition' and notes two tasks encountered by adolescents as they embrace the adult world.[5] First, young people find it necessary to terminate adolescence and, second, young people need to take on the responsibilities of young adulthood. These tasks entail a rearrangement of existing relationships and redefinition of self, together with exploratory undertakings and provisional commitments to the adult world.

The Question of Identity

Identity is the term most commonly associated with the season of adolescence. This is a time when young people strive for an understanding of the self and question who they are in relation to themselves, to others and to the world. Struggling with such questions as 'who am I?', 'where am I going?', 'what is the meaning of my life?', adolescents wonder who they are as persons and who they will become. Aware that their self-concept is changing, they seek to harmonise who they were as children with who they are becoming as adolescents. Young people struggle to become comfortable with who they are physically, emotionally, sexually and spiritually and they long for a sense of harmony with themselves, with each other and with the world. They seek what Craig Dykstra calls 'a sense of personal identity and a way of life'.[6]

What is identity and why is it so important during the adolescent years? Identity occurs when the young person has an awareness of self that gives meaning to who they are as a person, to their way of engaging in the world and to the direction their life is taking. Several factors contribute to the importance of identity during the adolescent years. First, adolescence represents a crucial time in the cognitive development of the young person. This, according to Jean Piaget, is a time when formal operational thought gives way to a deepening cognitive enquiry which results in the ability to engage in abstract and reflective thinking. As a result, urgent, life-meaning questions seek answers. A second reason why the quest for identity is crucial for adolescents is that the developing ability for cognitive reflection brings the young person face to face with their own life story. Conscious of their ability to reflect on the past and present, there is a growing awareness of the need to find and take responsibility for the future direction of their own life, one that fosters personal meaning. Finally, the developing capacity for abstract thinking and reflection, together with the increasing amount of facts and information, leads the young person to experience the complexity of everyday life. There are no easy answers to life's questions and problems. The task now is to find a personally meaningful and ethical way of being in the world in the midst of this growing complexity.

In order to understand the season of adolescence and its impact on young people, it is helpful to explore Erik Erikson's psychosocial theory of development. However, it is important to place the generality of developmental theory in dialogue with the uniqueness of each individual, a uniqueness that demands recognition and respect. Adolescent developmental theory is integrative in nature, and an understanding of adolescents should attempt to integrate all aspects of adolescent growth. Erikson's theory of psychosocial development reveals the meaning of identity and illustrates the process of identity synthesis in adolescence. It is to this that we now turn.

Psychosocial Development

In this theory, Erik Erikson expands the Freudian theory of

psychosexual development and bases it on the epigenetic principle. Erikson tells us that the idea behind this principle is that:

> anything that grows has a ground plan, and that out of this ground plan the parts arise, each part having its time of special ascendancy, until all parts have risen to form a functional whole.[7]

This principle notes that the various bodily organs develop at specific times in the physical development of the human person. Erikson believes that ego development follows a similar pattern. There is a basic plan for the personality out of which the ego develops as it proceeds through a range of interrelated stages. Each individual stage presents a developmental task that requires successful negotiation, together with an inherent risk when negotiation is unsuccessful.

Erikson covers the life cycle by proposing eight developmental stages, each of which focuses on an important emotional and social crisis influenced by both biological and cultural factors. Each stage is foundational for and operational in subsequent stages and as the individual resolves each crisis they move to the next stage. Erikson's eight developmental stages are identified individually by a conflict with the possibility of two contrasting outcomes. As a result, each stage derives its name from the dual aspect of the pertinent social crisis. Resolving the conflict in a constructive way enables the positive quality presented by the crisis to become part of the ego, thereby promoting healthy development. If, on the other hand, the conflict continues or is resolved in an unsatisfactory manner, the resulting negative quality becomes part of the personality and influences further development.

Occurring in sequential order, the crisis or conflict presented at each stage is emphasised most at the age in which it is placed. While the identity crisis is crucial for adolescents, it is important to note that it is not appearing for the time in the life of the adolescent and it will continue to re-appear and be reshaped at other major points in life. Identity issues re-emerge during times of major change, changes, for example, that occur in relation to employment, marital status, illness or bereavement. The manner in which one embraces any issue concerning a re-definition of identity may well be influenced by the healthy or unhealthy way in which the adolescent crisis of identity was resolved.

The Adolescent Crisis of Identity
The crucial stage for adolescents is *identity versus identity confusion*. Erikson describes identity as follows:

The wholeness to be achieved at this stage I have called a sense of inner identity. The young person, in order to experience wholeness, must feel a progressive continuity between that which he has come to be during the long years of childhood and that which he promises to become in the anticipated future; between that which he conceives himself to be and that which he perceives others to see him and to expect of him.[8]

How, then, does identity develop during adolescence? The physiological changes experienced in early adolescence increase the young person's awareness of difference – the difference between who one was as a child, who one is right now and who one is becoming. This takes place in conjunction with the growing ability to question the meaning of self and life. Changes are also experienced in relationships, particularly in familial relations as the young person seeks to detach and separate in order to establish personal identity. In their quest for identity, young people experience more autonomy and freedom. However, the false sense of power that accompanies this stage may lead the adolescent to engage in annoying behaviours in order to be recognised as a distinct and separate entity.[9]

The adolescent dulls the pain of familial separation through attachment to the peer group. However, the sense of security acquired through the peer group can be counterproductive if dynamics within the group demand conformity. In this regard, stress and insecurity may increase if the adolescent attempts to move away from or disagree with the group.

In addition to the above, escalating demands, expectations and responsibilities punctuate the season of adolescence. With an increasing school workload, the responsibility of a part-time job and deepening intimate relationships, new questions, demands and anxieties are presented. The ever-present question of 'who am I?' is constantly in dialogue with the growing responsibility expected by parents, teachers, employers and friends and can frequently clash with internal questioning and self-doubt.

According to Erikson, the process of identity formation 'depends on the interplay of what young persons at the end of childhood have come to mean to themselves and what they now appear to mean to those who become significant to them.'[10] Thus, the task of adolescents in this crucial stage is to establish a sense of identity and to avoid the potential dangers offered by identity confusion and diffusion. Adolescents must work at achieving identity by striving to answer the pertinent questions they have been asking regarding their existence. They also must embrace such critical developmental issues as occupation and career choice, engaging in appropriate role behaviours, including sexual behaviours, and developing a meaningful ideology. Failure to answer these questions and address these issues leads not only to feelings of isolation and alienation, but also to role diffusion.

Aware of the crucial aspect of this stage, Erikson writes that 'in no other stage of the life cycle are the promise of finding oneself and the threat of losing oneself so closely allied'.[11] An explanation for this lies in the fact that:

> the changes in identity which take place during adolescence involve the first substantial recognition and restructuring of the individual's sense of self at a time when he or she has the intellectual capability to appreciate fully just how significant the changes are.[12]

The Resolution of the Identity v. Identity Confusion Crisis

Many factors influence the successful resolution of the *identity versus identity confusion* crisis. One such influence has to do with the manner in which the individual resolved the crises of the previous four stages. For example, if the adolescent does not have a healthy sense of trust, autonomy, initiative and industry, they may find it difficult to achieve a healthy sense of identity. Similarly, the way in which the young person resolves the identity crisis will influence the ways in which they will embrace the subsequent crises of later life.

A second factor that influences the successful resolution of the adolescent identity crisis involves a social process and concerns the young person's communication with others. Through interactions with significant others, young people adopt characteristics that they would like to incorporate as part of their own identity. This can account for the 'hero-worship' that oftentimes characterises adolescence. Similarly, the manner in which young people interpret others' responses to them enables them to identify the elements in their own identities that they would like to hold onto, as well as those elements that they would like to discard. Through this process of observation and reflection, the young person seeks to resolve internal questions with external realities.

Identity Achievement

The successful achievement of a sense of identity in any one area of life means that identity has been achieved. This can be manifested through career choice, relationship choice, political ideology or the value system that directs one's life. Once achieved, the young person accepts responsibility for a continually evolving self, situated in a relational world. The young adult can now make a commitment to self, others and the world. Once established, a sense of identity is consciously experienced.

> One knows when identity is present, in greater or lesser degree. For the individual, identity is partly conscious and partly unconscious; it gives one's life a feeling of sameness and continuity, yet also a 'quality of unselfconscious living' and is taken for granted by those in possession.[13]

Erikson continues that the most obvious concomitants of identity are 'a feeling of being at home in one's body', a sense of 'knowing where one is going' and an 'inner assuredness of anticipated recognition from those who count'.[14] Identity achievement, therefore, is characterised by such factors as maturity, stability, consistency in attitudes and behaviour and manifested in effective interpersonal relationships. It is achieved when individuals 'feel in harmony with themselves, accept their capacities, limitations and opportunities ... There is a sense of direction and a positive orientation toward the future'.[15] Identity achievers, therefore, have the ability to cope with the various crises they encounter, emerging, usually, with successful outcomes.

Identity Confusion
However, identity achievement may be too difficult a task for the adolescent, and thus the young person experiences identity confusion or diffusion. In an article entitled 'Life and the Life-Cycle', Erikson describes identity confusion as 'a split of self-images ... a loss of centrality, a sense of dispersion and confusion and a fear of dissolution'.[16] With identity confusion, young people have not made any commitments and are unconcerned about any. They appear to be ambivalent regarding the past, present or future and, as a result, tend to be aimless and disorganised. Identity-diffused adolescents have no desire to embrace the values and responsibilities of the adult world. Fuhrmann notes that these young people frequently experience poor family relationships and adopt a 'façade of bravado' in order to disguise their low self-esteem.[17] They feel out of tune with themselves, with others and with the world.

When no positive identity is offered or achieved, rather than have no identity at all, adolescents may adopt an identity that is in opposition to parental and social guidance and regarded as undesirable by the wider community. This is done in an attempt to develop an identity in an environment in which they find it difficult to do so. By adopting a negative identity, manifested perhaps through vandalism or criminal behaviour, the young person gains the recognition they desire, but not in a way that fosters positive growth.

Alternatively, the young person may develop an identity that is seemingly the opposite to that of the negative identity by behaving in a very acceptable manner. The aim here is to please whoever is in authority and to engage in whatever it takes to fulfil this aim. While this form of behaviour can be socially acceptable, it can be unacceptable if it is manifested in obedience to the leader of a gang. The problem with this kind of blind obedience is that it is another manifestation of a negative identity in that it is symptomatic of no identity at all.

A similar aspect of a negative identity concerns conformity, particularly conformity to the peer group. While the peer group offers security and a sense of belonging, the fact is that each member of the peer group is also seeking identity and, thus, conformity may not lead to identity achievement. In the event of the group's disbandment, the assumed identity of the young person is in danger of collapsing since it has not been built on a solid foundation.

Having differentiated between identity achievement and identity confusion, Erikson points out that:

> a sense of identity is never gained nor maintained once and
> for all ... it is constantly lost and regained, although more
> lasting and more economical methods of maintenance and
> restoration are involved and fortified in late adolescence.[18]

This being the case, the successful resolution of the adolescent identity crisis manifests itself in the young person's commitment to a meaningful ideology – an ideology that reflects their own values. This commitment is called fidelity and is the essence of identity. Such a commitment is essential for adolescents because it offers young people a clear worldview, a healthy regard for the future and a method of resolving their ideal world with the reality they encounter. In addition, it provides opportunities for young people to experiment with roles, identify with others and offers a rationale for the values they hold.

James Marcia's Extension of Adolescent Identity Formation
Identity v. Role Diffusion
Psychologist James Marcia extended Erikson's psychosocial theory and identified common factors operating in young people in their

search for identity during adolescence. Recognising that adolescent identity achievement rarely occurs without some experience of struggle, Marcia suggests two criteria essential for the achievement of a mature identity – *crisis* and *commitment*. He writes:

> crisis refers to times during adolescence when the individual seems to be actively involved in choosing, among alternatives, occupations and beliefs. Commitment refers to the degree of personal investment the individual expresses in an occupation or belief.[19]

As the adolescent experiences crises, the young person reassesses current viewpoints and modes of behaviour, explores numerous life choices and makes a plethora of decisions with regard to basic life issues. Commitment, then, refers to the personal self-investment that the young person gives to the choices made. Marcia applied these elements of *crisis* and *commitment* to Erikson's 'Identity v. Identity Confusion' and carried out some research on adolescent identity formation. His study of identity growth led him to identify four major categories in the development of adolescent identity:

1. *Identity Diffusion:* An identity-diffused person has not undergone a crisis of identity nor made any commitment to a system of beliefs or a way of life.
2. *Foreclosure:* Although not having experienced an identity crisis, foreclosure types have values and have made commitments. These values and commitments, however, have not emerged from personal exploration but have been handed on and accepted without question.
3. *Moratorium:* A moratorium is a period of time, devoid of adult responsibilities and obligations, in which the young person actively explores and searches for an identity and for a set of beliefs and values that will depict who they are in the world. While this young person may have made some temporary commitments, they have not made any permanent commitment to an ideology or a way of life.
4. *Identity Achievement:* Identity achievement has been reached when the young person has resolved the crises of adolescence and, as a result, has made a personal commitment 'to an occupation, a religious belief, and a personal value system and has resolved his attitude toward sexuality'.[20]

A deeper exploration of Marcia's four categories is helpful.

Identity Diffusion
The person living in the identity-diffused state has not experienced an identity crisis with regard to exploring and evaluating a way of life, religious beliefs and values, a political ideology or a consistent manner of sexual behaviour. As a result, no obvious personal commitment has been made with regard to these issues. What is important to note here is that the identity-diffused state is an important part of the adolescent developmental process and should not be cause for alarm. It is only when identity diffusion continues beyond adolescence that help should be sought.

While some form of identity diffusion is a normal aspect of early adolescence, identity diffusion can be narcissistic in character. When this is the case, young people view the world as revolving around them and may use other people in order to enhance their own pleasure and to promote feelings of well-being. According to Muuss, this mode of behaviour may be the result of 'an unresolved ego crisis of Erikson's first stage, *trust versus mistrust*, and being unable to trust people, they use them'.[21] Alternatively, however, there are defence mechanisms put in place by young people in order to avoid the pain of identity diffusion. In this regard, psychologist Richard Logan identifies some of the ways in which young people seek to dull the pain of identity diffusion and engage in palliative behaviour aimed at bringing immediate relief.[22] For example, the pain of embracing the identity crisis may be too great and, as a result, the young person may turn to alcohol, drugs or other forms of temporary escape in order to ease or deny the confrontation being presented. Temporary escapes may also appear to have a positive nature and may be manifested through over-identification with a specific cause or with a specific role, e.g. athlete, intellectual, leader.

Another approach to the identity-diffused space may be expressed through the young person's desire to become someone. This desire may find expression through activities such as reckless driving, drug-taking and sexual behaviour. It may also manifest itself through competition where the young person strives to become someone either intellectually or athletically. Still other forms include the criticism of others in order to build and enhance one's self-esteem and sense of well-being, the engagement in meaningless activities in an effort to confirm the meaninglessness of one's own existence and the adoption of ways of behaviour that are contrary to the expectations of those in authority.

It is true to say that the identity-diffused person is in a state of psychological uncertainty, with no commitment to a way of life or a personal value system. Subject to a plethora of influences and a myriad of opportunities, the identity-diffused person is liable to respond to the most attractive invitations without sufficient reflection. As a result, the voice that speaks the loudest can be the one that has the most influence, causing answers to the question 'who am I?' to become all the more compounded and confused.

Foreclosure

Committed to an occupation, a personal ideology and value system, foreclosure subjects have many of the appearances of identity-achievers. The difference lies, however, in the fact that they have not experienced an identity crisis nor have they explored alternative values for their lives. Rather, the goals directing their lives and the values they live by were designed by people other than themselves – by parents, friends or by religious authorities. Such an example can be seen in the son or daughter who follows in their parent's footsteps without exploring other possibilities or who is encouraged to become what the parent was unable to become. Indeed, it is not unknown for parents to live their own dreams through the lives of their son or daughter. In cases like this, it is difficult to differentiate between the young person's goals and those of the parents. The danger with foreclosed subjects is that they become so entrenched in this position that they never achieve identity. What is needed is sufficient challenge and guidance that will enable the young person to reassess their unquestioned values and assumptions, otherwise the foreclosed state may become a permanent fixture.

Identity for the foreclosed adolescent is gleaned through relationship with others or is lived as an attachment of another person. While parents are regarded as having the prevailing influence in the foreclosed state, the peer group is also a swaying force. When the young person yields readily to the role demanded by the peer group, behaviour and manner of engagement is determined by the demands, pressures and expectations devised by this group. This may result in the temporary handing over of a developing identity to the peer group. Consequently, foreclosure occurs as one unquestioningly adopts the role determined by others and allows one's own identity to become subsumed into the group. The young person now defines a way of life and mode of behaviour according to the standards, expectations and demands of the peer group.

Moratorium

However, some young people do experience difficulty in making a commitment or in ascertaining a direction in life. Erikson sees these difficulties as part of the identity crisis and proposes a psychosocial moratorium – a period of time, devoid of adult responsibilities and obligations, set aside for young people to develop fidelity and reflect on their identity in terms of beliefs, values and commitment. The word 'moratorium' refers to a time of postponement when a young person delays making a commitment or taking on a more permanent responsibility. But Erikson stresses it is not only a delay. It is:

> a period that is characterised by a selective permissiveness on the part of society and of provocative playfulness on the part of youth, and yet it often leads to deep, if not transitory, commitment on the part of youth, and ends in a more or less ceremonial configuration of commitment on the part of society.[23]

The moratorium period recognises that young people must grow towards adulthood rather than be forced prematurely. While Muuss describes this developmental state as 'the adolescent issue *par excellence*', it is not without its crises and soul-searching questions.[24] This is a time when the young person explores, searches, experiments and struggles for meaningful answers to their life. It is also a time when young people experience the world as unpredictable and undesirable. They seek to right the wrongs they perceive and, therefore, challenge existing structures. While good and effective criticisms may be provided, young people in the moratorium state are unable to furnish solutions due to lack of identity and permanent commitment.

Both Erikson and Margaret Mead describe this period as an 'as if' period when young people are enabled to experiment with different roles 'as if' they had made a commitment to these roles.[25] This has the advantage of affording young people the opportunity to try on various roles, make mistakes, gain experience, change their values and commitments, and become more mature in the process. Facilitating young people in this way contributes to a healthy development of identity, as well as commitments to a personal ideology, vocation and religious beliefs. It is interesting to note that the final commitments made at the end of this period can be less radical than some of the temporary ones experimented with during the moratorium.

The moratorium period, therefore, is a time when the young person psychologically steps aside and grapples with the invitations of the adult world. It is the season of becoming and is, according to Marcia, an essential and crucial requirement for identity achievement.

Identity Achievement

The successful outcome of the adolescent moratorium results in a resolution of the identity crisis, permanent personal commitments and the achievement of identity. Conclusions have been reached, decisions have been made and various choices and alternatives have been considered. While it is not uncommon for the conclusion and decisions of young identity achievers to resemble those of their parents, the essential part of the journey took place through the various options and alternatives that they explored and, consequently, accepted or rejected. In this way, they differ from their foreclosed counterparts whose values also resemble those of their parents but who did not seriously consider other choices or question these values before adopting them.

Individuals who have achieved identity have a sense of direction in life and feel at home with themselves. There is a sense of personal continuity as one emerges from the past and embraces the future. According to Keniston, identity represents a new-found synthesis that 'will link the past, the present and the future'.[26] A new sense of self has now been created providing inner harmony, continuity and consistent values, purposes and goals. Once achieved, identity contributes to 'an increase in self-acceptance, a stable self-definition, a willingness to make commitments to a vocation, a religion, a political ideology and also to intimacy, engagement and marriage.'[27]

Conclusion: Implications for School Chaplaincy and Guidance and Pastoral Care

Clearly, the search for identity is closely linked to the search for meaning and this has particular implications for the way that chaplains, guidance counsellors and pastoral carers relate professionally to young people. Charles Shelton, in his book *Adolescent Spirituality*, has made several observations in relation to developmental theory and adolescent spirituality.[28] First, it is important to recognise and respect the uniqueness of each adolescent, together with the uniqueness of the young person's relationship with God or *Transcendent*. Second, relationships are key in adolescence and through them adolescents glean a sense of self. The hunger for Mystery is central to all relationships. A third observation acknowledges that adolescence is a period characterised by change and that the young person's perception, understanding and relationship with God is part of that change. Fourth, the capacity to critically think and reflect develops dramatically during adolescence. Values, attitudes and ideas are questioned. It is not unusual, therefore, for a young person to question the existence of God nor to question and criticise the modes of Church practice. Finally, the integrative nature of adolescent developmental theory calls for a spirituality that invites the young person to 'integrate all aspects of adolescent growth in a self that is capable of making a commitment to the Gospel and the forming of a personal relationship with Jesus in the context of a growing sense of adulthood'.[29]

The adolescent search for identity, therefore, is a journey in search of self. To accompany a young person on part of this sacred journey is, indeed, a privileged position. The task of the accompanier is to be a presence and to model genuine ways of living. It is to recognise the uniqueness of each individual and to offer to that young person the accompanier's authentic self. It is to pay particular attention to and enable the young person to nourish the four key dimensions of the human person: the physical, emotional, intellectual and spiritual. In so doing, the young person strives to become the 'best version' of themselves and begins to catch a glimpse of their essential purpose. They are put in touch with possibility and with the person God is dreaming them to be. Now they experience meaning and belonging. This is, indeed, a sacred time.

As we leave these pages to journey with young people as chaplains, guidance counsellors and pastoral carers, may the words of Max Warren guide our steps:

> Our first task in approaching another people, another culture, another religion is to take off our shoes, for the place we are approaching is holy. Else we may find ourselves treading on another's dream. More serious still we may forget that God was there before our arrival.[30]

Notes

1. J. Bacik, *The Gracious Mystery* (Cincinnati, OH: St Anthony Messenger Press, 1987), 2.
2. R. E. Muuss, *Theories of Adolescence* (New York: McGraw-Hill, 1988), 22.
3. American Psychiatric Association, quoted in C. M. Shelton, *Adolescent Spirituality* (New York: Crossroad, 1983), 2.
4. A. M. Nicholi Jr, 'The Adolescent' in *The Harvard Guide to Modern Psychiatry* (Cambridge, MA: The Belknap Press, 1978), 520.
5. D. J. Levinson et al., *The Seasons of a Man's Life* (New York: Alfred A. Knopf, 1978), 56.
6. C. Dykstra, 'Agenda for Youth Ministry: Problems, Questions and Strategies' in M. Warren (ed.), *Readings and Resources in Youth Ministry* (Winona, MN: St Mary's Press, 1987), 75.
7. E. Erikson, *Identity: Youth and Crisis* (New York: W.W. Norton & Son, 1968), 92.

8. Ibid., 87.

9. R. Josselson, 'Ego Development in Adolescence' in J. Adelson (ed.), *Handbook of Adolescent Psychology* (Hoboken, NJ: J. Wiley & Sons, Inc., 1980), 194.

10. E. Erikson, *Toys and Reasons* (New York: W.W. Norton & Son, 1977), 106.

11. Erikson, *Identity: Youth and Crisis*, 244.

12. L. Steinberg, *Adolescence* (New York: McGraw-Hill, 1993), 255.

13. J. Kroger, *Identity in Adolescence* (London & New York: Routledge Press, 1989), 14.

14. Erikson, *Identity: Youth and Crisis*, 165.

15. Muuss, *Theories of Adolescence*, 74.

16. Quoted in B. Fuhrmann, *Adolescence, Adolescents* (Illinois: Scott, Foreman/ Little, Brown, 1990), 122–3.

17. Ibid., 314.

18. E. Erikson, 'Identity and the Life Cycle: Selected Papers' in *Psychological Issues Monographic Series 1*, No. 1 (New York: International Universities Press, 1959), 118.

19. J. E. Marcia, 'Ego Identity Status: Relationship to Change in Self-Esteem, "General Maladjustment" and Authoritarianism' in *Journal of Personality* (1967), 35, 119.

20. Muuss, *Theories of Adolescence*, 66.

21. Ibid., 68.

22. R. Logan, 'Identity Diffusion and Psycho-Social Defense Mechanisms' in *Adolescence* 13 (Fall 1978), 503–7.

23. Ibid., 157.

24. Muuss, *Theories of Adolescence*, 72.

25. Quoted in ibid.

26. K. Keniston, 'Social Change and Youth in America' in E. Erikson (ed.), *The Challenge of Youth* (New York: Doubleday/Anchor, 1965), 212.

27. Muuss, *Theories of Adolescence*, 74.

28. C. M. Shelton, *Adolescent Spirituality* (Chicago: Loyola University Press, 1983), 112.

29. Ibid., 113.

30. M. Warren, from his general introduction to the *Christian Presence* series in Kenneth Cragg, *Sandals at the Mosque* (London: SCM Press, 1959), 9–10.

The Period of Adolescence and School Discipline

Maeve Martin

For those who have chosen to work with young people in schools today, both the privileges and challenges associated with this work are considerable. As chaplains, guidance counsellors and teachers, we have the opportunity to play a central part in the lives of the young as they go about negotiating the important developmental period of adolescence. In this period of transition from childhood to adulthood, they are no longer afforded the indulgence of a young child nor are they given the freedom or autonomy of adulthood. The main tasks of this developmental period have been outlined in the previous chapter and are in summary: 1. the forging of a personal identity; 2. achieving independence from parents; 3. making vocational choices; and 4. relating to peers and adults in a mature and respectful manner.[1] As role models and mentors in the lives of pupils, school personnel are vital forces. This is a rare privilege indeed, as our role gives us the opportunity to influence the process of negotiating the developmental tasks, and to help determine the outcome. We have access to the bright minds of our pupils, to their many gifts and talents, access to their idealism, to their enthusiasm and to their energy. In our gift is the capacity to help them develop and go forth in a way that does justice to these attributes, but alongside that, in a subtler and more profound way, we can influence their value system, their sense of themselves, their choices and their priorities. Our pupils represent a source of inspiration and hope for us, their seniors. We in turn are significant others in their lives. This reciprocal obligation of influence in which both sets of players operate is indeed a sphere of privilege.[2]

But while there is abundant privilege as an integral part of our role in working with pupils, there is also formidable challenge. Pupils today live very action-packed lives, supplemented by and sometimes embedded in cyberspace. Consequently, if their life in school is not stimulating, then there is a strong likelihood that they will become disinterested, even alienated, and will detach from the central purpose of the school, namely teaching and learning. Of course there are considerable numbers of pupils who live passive lives that are bleak and barren and that may be devoid of any kind of social or cultural capital. In the confines of the school setting these pupils may not pose discipline problems. They drift through school in a reasonably

invisible way that may mirror how they will go on to drift through
life. In a sense their needs may not be detected in the hurly-burly
of a busy school. They get lost in the system as their behaviour does
not impact either academically or antisocially. Apart from designated
duties of a teaching and administrative nature, staff energies tend to be
devoted to dealing with problems of persistent disruption, and so the
passive, unobtrusive, non-participating pupil may slip through the net.

A Clash of Cultures – External and Internal Challenges

So while schools cater for pupils who live orderly, self-disciplined
lives in the security of their caring and responsible families, there
are still many pupils who adopt lifestyles that do not seem to be
age-appropriate. The out-of-school lives of considerable numbers
of our pupils are apt to be filled with the excitement that comes
from: connecting with peers, drinking alcohol, experimenting with
illegal substances, being sexually active, having disposable income
that comes from holding down part-time jobs, viewing questionable
video material, listening to music that may contain messages of a
violent or sexual nature, using language that is coarse or vulgar,
sending and receiving innumerable text messages, and existing as
much in cyberspace as outside of it. There is a real sense in which the
throbbing lives that some pupils live may constitute a counter-culture
when compared to the dominant culture of schools. School personnel
cannot assume automatically that they have a pupil population that is
highly motivated and eager to learn. They may find that the norms
of behaviour and values which they advocate and work towards
are at variance with those espoused by their young pupils in their
off-campus lives. The variation that exists within schools is great.
Many schools do trojan work in creating school environments that
are centres of care, compassion and empathy. They throw lifelines to
their pupils who may be battling with issues that could easily scupper
their personal development and career ambition. These schools find
ways to make school sufficiently attractive to pupils so that they
remain in the system until they are legally allowed to leave formal
education. In many countries schools are so successful that the
majority of students will remain on after the legal age to complete
a senior cycle programme, with the highest post-primary completion
rates in Finland (96 per cent) followed, among others, by Korea (93
per cent), Germany (92 per cent), Ireland (89 per cent) and the USA
(72 per cent).[3] This high participation figure is a tribute to schools
in how they respond to the challenges that face them.

Apart from the challenges from the outside world that are
influential in school life today, there are pressures within the school

that drive much of what happens there. Schools feel that they operate in a system that is very influenced by a mode of assessment that is 'points' driven. There has been a regrettable tendency in recent years among some of the national newspapers to publish what approximates to a set of league tables. Schools deemed most successful are those that deliver large numbers of their final year pupils to higher education institutions. Entry into the tertiary sector is but one measure of a school's success, and not all schools nor all parents, nor indeed all pupils, see that as the single most important measure of how schools perform. These published tables are not comparing like with like, nor are they tapping into the value-added that schools create for their pupils. Many schools that are meeting the needs of their pupils in an admirable way, and that are succeeding against considerable odds, may be disheartened by the publication of these league tables. There is scant regard for or recognition of their noble and painstaking work with often difficult cohorts of pupils in challenging and bleak neighbourhoods. Entry into college is a crude but oft-cited measure of school effectiveness. Schools that build the self-esteem of a floundering adolescent, that listen to them, that give their pupils a voice, that offer hope and courage, that provide the skills and dispositions that shape attainable ambitions and that offer support and guidance in the realisation of these ambitions – these are the undervalued schools of our education system. They often plough a lonely furrow, and they may not figure in the published league tables that track the numbers of their school leavers who go on to participate in third level formal education.

Added to the pressure of working within a points-driven system is the reality of the changing characteristics of the pupil population itself. Parts of our society has become strongly multicultural. This is a phenomenon that has crept up on us very quickly. Some schools that in the past catered for a homogeneous pupil cohort are now catering for a very diverse pupil intake. Schools welcome the diversity that is associated with our increasing multiculturalism, but it poses challenges for school staff as they strive to behave in an equitable and responsive manner in meeting the needs of all their pupils. Many of the new populations may need enhanced language skills in order to engage with the curriculum. Not all schools have teachers with competence in teaching English as a foreign language or teaching English for special purposes. For those pupils coming from different traditions, their culture may vary in many aspects from the dominant culture of which they are now part.

Another feature of the inclusive nature of schools today is the integration of pupils with special educational needs. These pupils who have the right to be educated alongside their peers may pose challenges for teachers and school personnel who have had little or no professional development in working with children with disabilities. The characteristics of the pupil cohort is changing before the eyes of long-standing staff members, and the attendant challenges of working effectively with them are indeed daunting. Add to this changing scenario the rapid and extensive changes in curricula, the centrality of technology with its infusion into the teaching and learning process, the new active methodologies that are being advocated, and one cannot but sympathise with teachers who may feel overwhelmed, at times, by what is coming down the tracks.

Developmental Challenges

Added to the clash of cultures that exists between the 'within and the without of school' factors, and the pressures of the system, there is the challenge that comes from the number of age-related issues with which adolescents may present.[4] These may include depression, eating disorders, teen parenthood, anti-social behaviour/ delinquency, anxiety, suicidal tendencies. If we think *systemically*, we cannot dismiss the seriousness of these issues. They impact on the well-being of our pupils and on their peer group. Schools that are bereaved following the tragic suicide of a pupil are schools that are altered in very fundamental ways. Many of our pupils experience some kind of loss. The fall-out from loss can have grave implications for how a young pupil progresses and adapts to life in school. Considerable numbers of pupils live in households that have experienced parental disharmony that may result in separation or break-up. The legacy of this kind of major disruption in the domestic life of a pupil is pervasive, and its impact may be evidenced in ways that violate aspects of the school's code of behaviour. Pupils who find themselves living in reconstituted or blended families often experience difficulty in coming to terms with their altered situations. School may be the forum in which the troubled adolescents give expression to the range of emotions triggered by changes in their young lives. Those who hold designated posts for the care element in schools are dealing with an increasing workload, and the range of difficulties that they encounter were not envisaged in the past. These developments, many of them triggered by the changing fabric of society, make the role of a teacher or a school chaplain very demanding and challenging. Schools need to have staff who have great sensitivity to the range of needs of its pupils, and who are aware of the issues that dominate their pupils' lives. Many pupils have sad personal scripts, many handle situations that are not amenable to quick fix solutions. If they feel safe and cared for in the confines of the school, their risk factors are minimised. The real challenge is for schools to help their young people to navigate the troubled waters of the adolescent period, and to set them up with a range of personal resources that prepares them for the next phase of their lives.

Teacher–Pupil Relationship

The concept of resilience is gaining in popularity among those of us who take an interest in why it is that some of our pupils succeed, despite being born into high-risk environments. It is an attractive concept in that it tends to bring a positive orientation to our thinking, rather than a defeatist of deterministic perspective.[5] There are protective factors that schools can offer their pupils. These protective factors buffer the risk that may be associated with living in areas of urban poverty, or the risks associated with growing up in a family where there may be crime, violence, substance abuse, mental illness, dysfunction or neglect. Schools have the capacity to turn around outcomes for at-risk or potentially disaffected pupils. The powerful variables within schools that are protective are: caring relationships; positive and high expectations; opportunity for pupils to participate and to contribute. The quality of the relationships is vital to the development of resilience. Relationships that are transformational for troubled youth are predicated on respect and acceptance. Teachers who model acceptance and regard tend not to take personally pupil behaviour that is in objective terms offensive. Instead, they use such an incident or piece of behaviour as a discussion point. They negotiate in a respectful, calm, firm manner. They enter into a dialogue with the offending pupil/s in a way that allows for an account of the issues to be aired by all parties. Everybody is required to listen, to reflect and to respond. Behavioural and affective aspects are considered, and possible ways forward are explored. There is no harsh judgement, no rejection, but rather a considerable time investment, based on the belief that all of us can change and grow. Pupils need some introduction to this way of resolving difficulties, as it may be in contrast to ways of dealing with hurt and offence in their out-of-school lives. They access a world that is not reliant on anger or insult or force as a means of sorting things out. Instead they have a valid place in a world that is mutually respectful and considerate, and that is tolerant of young people who are trying to find their way. The approach is not one that dilutes standards of courtesy or respect for others, but rather one that is pupil-centred in an effort to give pupils the requisite social skills and orientations that will help them to be fulfilled members of a democratic society. Personnel in schools who seek to find win/win solutions for problems that arise are not wimps or soft touches. It is not a weakness to show tolerance and patience when offended by a rude, disrespectful pupil. It is how the matter is handled that counts in the long run. Schools that invest in their relationships at all levels of interaction are safe for those who occupy them. Pupils in these schools learn to manage their anger, and negotiate rather than striking out. The work for teachers, year heads and pastoral care teams may often be uphill, but the dividends for the individual pupil and for society are unquantifiable. Schools that prioritise healthy, positive and caring relationships may contribute to breaking cycles of disaffection, despair and negativity for many of their pupils.

Empowering Pupils
Pupils who present with difficulties in schools share some characteristics. They tend to perceive themselves as failures, they are pessimistic about their futures and their perception is that they are in an inferior or disadvantaged position. Regrettably, some experiences in school may reinforce these beliefs for these disruptive pupils. It is therefore important for schools to be aware of the detrimental consequences of poor self-image and of a defeatist attitude among potentially marginalised youth. Schools need to transmit high and positive expectations for their pupils. They can help them to build a realistic vision about their future. They can work on pupil strengths, and celebrate minor victories, as these may lead on to more significant accomplishments. Pupils can be helped to set goals and to develop strategies that lead to their attainment. Teachers who empower transmit a sense of optimism and trust to their pupils rather than, as some teachers do, write them off in subtle ways. Pupils have their sensitivities, and they pick up on the messages that we send them. If we show that we believe in them and in their capacity to grow and to attain, then the self-fulfilling prophecy factor kicks in and successful experiences follow. The damage that has ensued from humiliating and oppressive experiences in the past may be turned around by teachers and caring adults who work alongside their pupils in a framework of high, yet achievable expectations. In this supportive, caring environment the pupils have a sense of purpose, a sense of autonomy and a sense of competence.

Schools that foster resilience structure a lot of opportunities for pupils to express their views, to give expression to their creativity and imagination, and to problem solve. In these schools pupils are treated as responsible individuals and are held accountable for their behaviour. Activities are structured to occur in an environment that is safe both psychologically and physically. Allocated tasks are shared, and there is the opportunity to work collaboratively and to promote pupil involvement.[6] The tasks are flexible enough to allow for participation by all. Contributions are valued, and pupils learn a range of behaviours that have applicability in areas beyond the world of school, i.e. in the local community, in the world of work. The revised curricula in our schools advocate active teaching and learning methods. There is scope to tap into the inner creativity and gifts of all our pupils and to develop their multiple intelligences. The failure identity of many of our pupils can be replaced by success identities. An 'I can' self-concept is much more preferable to an 'I'm not going to be able to do it' identity. Schools that promote pupil participation in the functioning of the school and that value pupil contributions are schools that enable the development of resilience in their pupils. The building of resilient people is a long-term process that is based on nurturing, participatory relationships that in turn are based on trust and respect and that strive towards valuable goals.

Promoting a Positive Code of Discipline

One of the recent tasks in which schools have engaged is the development of their school development plan. It is customary to devote a section of this to the code of behaviour of the school. Engaging in this task offers an opportunity for staff to reflect on the purposes of their behaviour code and to assess their practices with regard to discipline in the school. It may be that schools come to recognise that the code is outdated, and is not really implemented across the board in schools. It may be that they feel that there should be different emphases for their junior and senior pupils within the code. It may be that they perceive that the code is not in line with recent legislation, and that it leaves their school in a vulnerable position in the event of a legal situation arising in connection with a discipline matter. A review of the code may point up the reality that the code is very rules-based, and does little to develop in the pupils norms of self-discipline that will transfer to situations beyond the life of the school. So why have a code of discipline in operation at all? Possible reasons include: to allow for the smooth realisation of the core purpose of the school; to develop self-discipline in our pupils, and respect for the self, for others and for the environment; to prepare our pupils to live as responsible members of a demographic society; to be in compliance with the new legal framework in which we work.[7] The putting together of a code of behaviour provides an interesting opportunity for staff in schools to clarify for themselves their views and their values about pupil behaviour. It is not an easy task, as doubtless there will be individual variation among staff regarding what is and what is not acceptable pupil behaviour. There is the tricky task of determining sanctions and how they will be applied. There is a great need for clarity in this area. We live in a world where pupils place great emphases on their rights, but not so great emphases on their responsibilities. This focus on rights and immature dismissal of responsibility leave us open to litigation or challenges from partisan parents. So the crafting of the code must be tight enough and loose enough to cater for situations that are perhaps difficult to anticipate. Central features of a code may include the following:

» An outline of the standards of behaviour that shall be observed by the pupils attending the school
» The measures that may be taken when a pupil fails to observe those standards
» The procedures to be followed before a pupil is suspended or permanently excluded
» The grounds for removing a suspension
» The method of reporting on pupil absences from school.

It seems appropriate that the code of behaviour should chime well with a school's mission statement.[8] There should be some form of continuity between these two documents, and ideally they should be reflected in the daily business of the school. Codes work well when they are owned by as many of the stakeholders as possible, and when they are implemented across the board fairly and compassionately. Incidents of misbehaviour should be perceived as teaching/learning opportunities. It is best to try to resolve breaches of the code by including the pupils in their resolution. Pupils should be taught conflict resolution skills and peer mediation approaches. It is likely that in their academic programme they will have been introduced to problem-solving methods and to ways of working collaboratively in teams. This learning will transfer to the resolution of difficulties that may result from violations of the code. Where pupils are included in the process of addressing difficulties, they learn skills and attitudes that will prepare them for working respectfully and democratically later in the workplace, in their families and community. An approach that relies on pastoral and conflict resolution methods is much more valuable, and more developmental, than a punitive knee-jerk sanction that gives little scope for an exploration of the underlying issues that may have triggered the unacceptable behaviour. A shared approach that puts the perpetrator and the victim at the centre allows for consideration of the consequences of the misdemeanour for all concerned. In this way pupils inculcate norms of decency and altruism. They learn important listening skills and the value of compromise.

It is inevitable that the code will be reliant on rules. There are some guidelines that should be noted when drawing up rules. They should be:

- » Few in number
- » Stated positively in a way that describes the behaviour the school wishes to see
- » Reasonable and fair
- » Simple and precise
- » Explained, discussed and taught/modelled
- » Enforced and enforceable.

For the code to operate effectively, there must be consequences following a violation of a rule, and the pupils must be held accountable. The research in the area of school discipline tells us that there are variables that influence the likelihood of how discipline will play out in schools. Some schools are more deviance-prone than others. Schools that insulate themselves against major disruption tend to have some of the following characteristics:

- » They are proactive not reactive – in other words they try to work within reasonable parameters, where boundaries are clearly understood
- » The dominant ethos of the school is pastoral, with an emphasis on positive, participatory relationships, and a climate that is supportive and caring
- » There are planned routines that make for a safe and secure environment
- » There is an emphasis on rewards rather than on punishment – pupils have their efforts and their accomplishments recognised and valued
- » When breaches of discipline are addressed, it is more in the spirit of the code rather than on rigid adherence to the letter of the code. The maxim of 'seek first to understand and then to be understood' is adopted
- » Individual staff members are empowered to deal with unacceptable behaviour, and only in extreme cases is the matter referred to other authorities within the school

» Responsibility for discipline is a shared responsibility, involving the school, the pupils and the parents.

Conclusion

Working with young people today requires us to be whole and robust. Working viably and meaningfully in schools is not for the faint-hearted, as the demands therein go far beyond the enactment of the official curriculum. But in schools there is a sense of community and a sense of belonging that is difficult to create in other settings. The work is exciting, and there is the throb of being with large numbers of talented young people who will assume positions of responsibility in their families, their workplaces, their communities and perhaps nationally or internationally in the years ahead. We owe them much. In a sense they give us in large measure essential aspects of our own identity, while they struggle to find their own identity. They are unlikely to forget us whether we are positive or negative forces in their lives. Let us strive in our privileged and challenging work to be good forces in their tender lives.

Notes

1. E. Erikson, *Identity: Youth and Crisis* (New York: W.W. Norton & Son, 1968).
2. M. Totterdell, 'The Moralisation of Teaching: A Relational Approach as an Ethical Framework in the Professional Preparation and Formation of Teachers' in Roy Gardner et al. (eds), *Education for Values, Morals, Ethics and Citizenship in Contemporary Teaching* (London: Routledge, 2003), 132.
3. OECD Report online at http://www.oecd.org/edu/eag2013%20%28eng%29--FINAL%2020%20June%202013.pdf (accessed 24 April 2014).
4. M. Martin, 'School Matters: Report of the Task Force on Student Behaviour in Second-Level Schools' (Dublin: Department of Education and Science, 2006), 54ff.
5. D. Chirot and M. Seligman, *Ethnopolitical Warfare: Causes, Consequences and Possible Solutions* (Washington, DC: American Psychological Association, 2001).
6. Martin, 'School Matters', 81.
7. Ibid., 88.
8. Ibid., 70.

Forging a Path
Through Multiplicity
A Critique of Adolescent Development

Grace O'Grady

Some years ago when I asked the Kerry philosopher John Moriarty to talk to me about his developing identity as an adolescent, his reply was characteristically thought-provoking:

> I've resisted being an 'id' and an 'entity' all my life. The word 'identity' imprisons and needs to be forced apart.[1]

To stand outside the moulding dominant discourses on identity may have been an extremely difficult position for Moriarty to maintain over a lifetime. However, in doing so he pre-empted the position taken up by the contemporary movement to critically scrutinize the givens of development. Identity has achieved contemporary centrality because, according to Paul du Gay and his colleagues, 'that to which it is held to refer is regarded in some sense as being more contingent, fragile and incomplete and thus more amenable to reconstitution than was previously thought possible'.[2]

This chapter proposes to critically review some orthodox theories of identity development in adolescence – ideas that informed much of my previous writing on the subject[3] – and to examine the assumptions behind these kinds of model building. It asks how they compare with contemporary theorising about the self and finishes by pointing to new practices in developmental work with young people and presenting a short summary of a psychosynthesis programme for adolescents.

Adolescent Identity – From Plurality to Unity
In attempting to deconstruct the notion of identity, let us look briefly at some inherited notions of identity development. A point of confluence for many of the developmental theorists is that adolescence is a journey through confusion and contradiction to unity and cohesion. While the foundations of 'I' are formed in infancy through relationships with the primary carers, most theorists converge on the idea that adolescence is a time, at least in western society, when one is confronted with the enormous task of self-definition. In

the process of defining themselves, teenagers are forced to grapple with a proliferation of multiple selves: in moving from primary to second-level schooling, the young person's world opens to a wider population of people and so they need to differentiate the self in these relational contexts. As they move into middle adolescence, some of these selves can appear contradictory and cause the young person anxiety.[4] This is exacerbated by what has been referred to as the gap between real and ideal, true and false selves[5] and the pull towards possible/potential selves.[6]

While the differentiation of the self into multiple selves is viewed as a developmental advance in adolescence, there is widespread agreement among theorists that a related developmental task remains: to integrate these multiple self-concepts into a unified, consistent theory of self. Erik Erikson writes:

> The self of childhood, derived from significant identifications
> with important others, must during adolescence give way to
> a self derived from yet transcending those foundations – to
> a new whole greater than the sum of its parts.[7]

While Erikson was the first to assert that identity formation involves an 'integration' in late adolescence of earlier subselves, it has been a recurring theme throughout the developmental literature. W. D. Wall posits that central to the whole process of adolescent development is the 'acquisition of a series of identities or selves, unified by a general concept of who one is and by what standards one is prepared to live by'.[8] This theme was developed by James Marcia, who viewed the 'identity achieved' individual as having undergone three previous identity stages: diffusion, foreclosure and moratorium, and now is capable of making commitments to self, others and to a vocational path.[9]

In short, developmental theorists view adolescence as a journey in search of self. Defining who one is in relation to multiple others and discovering which of one's many selves is the 'true self' are seen as the normative developmental tasks of this period. The search is often punctuated by conflict, contradiction and confusion as the teenager tries to integrate the multiple self-concepts into a consistent, unified self-portrait.

What is being Assumed?
It is taken for granted that this self, the object to be arrived at, is the centre of experience, a coherent whole, a synthesis of former selves. It is assumed that plurality and inconsistency are characteristic of a

'stage' in the development of this 'authentic' self and that consistency and unity are the mark of maturity. Adjectives such as 'unified', 'integrated', 'achieved', 'consistent' are used liberally to describe the self of the older adolescent. The presumption is that society and cognitive processes turn individuals into mature citizens and that this process is natural, giving rise to regular patterns of change which have a clear directional trend. By late adolescence the conditions are ripe for the young person to begin to consolidate their notion of self. Plurality from this point on is viewed as either infantile or pathological.[10]

Contemporary Theorising About the Self

In a world characterised by multi-fragmented social positionings and the deconstruction of absolute truth the notion of a unified self begins to stand out like a relic from a bygone era.[11]

The deconstruction of the psychological subject has been conducted within a variety of disciplinary areas, all of them in one way or another critical of the notion of an integral, originary and unified identity. There are several converging themes in the multiple positionings of the critical movement. I will discuss just one of these here. A major argument is that psychological models of the self are inevitably culturally and historically contingent, dependent on certain kinds of social practices. The assumptions on which modern western society is based − for instance, the concept of the self as the centre of experience/the one true self − may be peculiar to this period in history and this type of society.[12] What psychology discovers may not be universal features of selfhood but may instead be an elaboration of the conventional ways people are described in a particular society.

In a modernist world characterised by universals such as 'one man, one job',[13] the 'grand narrative' of development (the story of a movement towards an integrated, autonomous self) appears to make sense. However, in a postmodern world characterised by diversity and change, the notion of a centred/unified self becomes less plausible. The discourses of leading edge theories in philosophy, psychology, social science and physics increasingly support pluralism as a foundation principle of contemporary epistemology.[14] According to Kenneth Gergen, the postmodern self owes its condition to the barrage of imagery and information generated from communication technology. In his book *The Saturated Self*,[15] Gergen observes that with advances in air travel, electronic and express mail and mobile phones, individuals have been forced to contend with a wider circle of social, multiple relationships. For Gergen, these changes have profound implications for self-development, in that they necessitate the creation of multiple selves across a variety of different contexts,[16] rendering impossible the notion of unity and integration by late adolescence:

> As social saturation adds incrementally to the population of the self, each impulse towards well-formed identity is cast into increasing doubt, each is found absurd, shallow, limited or flawed by the onlooking audience of the interior.[17]

There have been many attacks on Gergen's views and social construction theory in general. Kristjan Kristjansson argues that they represent an unjustified radical relativism undermining fundamental beliefs in human progress:

> Despite overtures to the social, postmodernist self-talk remains entrapped in an abstract language game, making the shared understandings for human understanding ultimately mystifying.[18]

James M. Glass highlights the insensitivity to the pain of personal fragmentation in the postmodern celebration of 'subjectivity in slippage'.[19] I agree with Mick Cooper and John Rowan[20] in suggesting that a major challenge for today's psychologists is to find a way of embracing contemporary critical thinking without losing the human being in the process.

A Critical Approach to Development

If we take on board the insights of the critical movement in psychology, we are challenged to look at the positions our young people are forced to take up. Much of our understanding of the young person in late adolescence is informed by the orthodox theories of development. Hence our expectations of them and the corresponding educational structures we have built demand that the student 'gets it together' by their final year in school. If we accept the postmodern construction of self as plural across the lifespan, how can we continue, for example, to subject our young people to crystallizing vocational choice to a 'first preference' on the CAO form? We must also interrogate much of our practice in school in terms of guidance psychometric measurement testing which 'categorise' identities and abilities based on an understanding of the person that has its roots in the humanistic/developmental model. As teachers, chaplains, guidance counsellors, we continue to locate ourselves in this cultural discourse of self and so we can often essentialise the young people we work with, thereby limiting the possibilities open to them.

From a postmodern perspective it may be possible for the young person to position herself or be positioned differently in a variety of situations. So, rather than 'stage developments', Marcia's identity statuses may be construed as different ways of 'going on' at different moments in the same person. Hence, with a group of teachers the 'late adolescent' may operate out of a status of diffusion; in relation to vocational choice, she may flounder in a moratorium of indecision; sexually she may have a definite orientation and be committed to a single partner; and with parents or peer group she may introject many of their values unquestioningly. While this perhaps sounds iconoclastic, Baumgardner and his colleagues contend that in the postmodern era, 'simultaneous pluralism' will become widely acknowledged.[21] Citing observational evidence, Rom Harre argued twenty years ago that all of Kohlberg's moral 'levels' can be found simultaneously in children of school age. They are situationally governed, and represent aspects of interactional style rather than some inherent developmental sequence.[22]

Harre claims that a set of stages becomes a set of alternatives. Once a certain range of relatively stable alternative selves is delimited and becomes familiar, Baumgardner argues, the person becomes free to shift from one to the other, and/or consciously to negotiate priorities across the range of alternatives as circumstances may warrant. I will return to how this process may be facilitated in the next section.

The critical approach involves the critical scrutiny of developmentalism and the search for systematic alternatives. John Morss cautions us that developmental arguments have a way of continually seeping back into new formulations. One way of establishing a critical distance, he suggests, is to treat developmental explanation as discourse.[23] Ian Parker defines discourse as a coherent system of meaning that is historically situated and that reproduces power relations.[24] Attention would be focused on developmental statements, that is, on particular claims appealing to developmental explanation. Developmental statements can be made about individuals (Mary should be settling down this year because she's in Leaving Cert) or about populations (Leaving Certs are a very mature bunch). In a discourse approach, both statements would be looked upon as having been produced: produced in particular circumstances, for particular reasons and perhaps in the interest of particular persons or groups. The co-author of *Changing the Subject*, Valerie Walkerdine makes the point that children's 'development' cannot be described except by reference, explicit or not to social conditions and practices.[25] Children are treated in certain ways by educational systems and, according to Walkerdine, this treatment has the effect of regulating those children, their parents and their teachers.

Morss describes developmentalism as hegemonic and must be seen as violently suppressing alternative ways of being. He reaffirms John Moriarty's position in stating that hegemony is threatened only by resistance. From this perspective, the high level of disaffection from third level institutions in Ireland might well be construed as a resistance, however unconscious, to the dominant discourse on identity.

Practices of Resistance and Release

Drawing on the work of Vygotsky, the psychologist Lenora Fulani argues that development is not something that happens to us as we go about constructing a 'Kantian world', nor is it a prerequisite for learning, as it is for Piaget. She claims that development and learning are sustained revolutionary activities – 'a dialectic unity in which learning leads development'.[26] She gives the example of the babbling baby who becomes a speaker of a language by participating with his caregivers in creating environments in which he learns in advance of his development. In other words, we cannot know what developmental activity is; we have to perform it. Working with African-American teenagers in disadvantaged areas, Fulani encourages them to resist the identity of the inner city youngster as having 'nothing to give' and supports them in creating their development through the activity of 'performing beyond themselves'.[27] They experiment with different roles on and off stage as part of a twelve-week programme. In this process they create multiple possibilities for who and how they want to be.

From a totally different methodological stance, the research work carried out by Gilligan and Brown on adolescent American girls highlighted that developmental progress went hand in hand with evidence of loss of voice.[28] Like Fulani, as female psychologists deeply conscious of patriarchal norms, values and societal structures, they developed a practice that would be both responsive to others' voices and yet resistant to the dominant voices – 'the cultural overlays that serve to drown out, mute or distort the voices of those with less power or authority'.[29] They developed a method called the 'Listener's Guide' – a voice-sensitive way of working that allowed them to follow and record girls' thoughts and feelings and to hear girls' struggle at adolescence. To encourage their resistance to the established story of a white middle-class heterosexual woman's life, Gilligan, Brown and their colleagues worked with the girls to help them listen to the cultural discourses in their personal stories and to experience being received in a safe group environment.

Mary Watkins[30] contends that it is through dialogue with the other, the stranger, the imaginal other, that liberation can occur. As such dialogue occurs, whether it is performative, imaginal or in a shared group setting, there is a shift from the 'ego' as a monolithic, heroic centre – one which in our postmodern world is under severe pressure – to an 'ego' which seeks to mediate the multiplicity of any given situation.[31] Here, Watkins feels the need to retain the word 'ego', which is of course an artefact of the developmental/psychodynamic/analytic discourse on self/identity. Because it has entered popular lexicon it has become 'common sense' and therefore needs to be made visible as a cultural construct, part of the palimpsest of ways of understanding the self. Cooper and Rowan, while positioning themselves similarly, advocate a path of 'authentic pluralism' characterised by an openness towards multiple worlds and dialogue.

Psychosynthesis

Psychosynthesis as an approach to education and personal development provides us with the wherewithal to walk the path of 'authentic pluralism'. Roberto Assagioli, founder of this approach, describes psychosynthesis as:

> first and foremost a dynamic, even a dramatic conception
> of our psychological life, which it portrays as a constant
> interplay and conflict between many different and contrasting
> forces and a unifying centre that ever tends to control,
> harmonise and use them.[32]

While the very word psychosynthesis (a synthesis of the different parts of the psyche) appears antithetical to the postmodern assault on the 'essentialised', unified modern self, the Irish psychologist Micheal O'Regan affirms that 'the movement and direction of a life, a psychosynthesis, is towards a polyphony rather than a single monotheistic note'.[33] The words 'unify', 'control' and 'harmonise' need to be put under erasure (*sous rature*)[34] in this theory as the programme seeks to contemporise the psycho-educational approach of Assagioli with the insights of the postmodern, critical movement. In focusing on 'personal psychosynthesis' I am aware of the vast reservoir of potential I leave untapped in this expansive transpersonal theory which draws on many psychological and spiritual traditions from Jungian psychoanalysis, Buddhism and Jewish mysticism.

Subpersonality Model
The psychosynthesis approach puts forward a *subpersonality model* as a way of perceiving our multiplicity and provides us with the skills to work with our disparate selves. Subpersonalities are psychological identities, co-existing as a multitude of lives within one person; each with its own specific behaviour pattern and corresponding self-image, body posture feelings and beliefs.[35] We can easily perceive our plurality by noticing how often we modify our outlook on life, our self-image, our perception of others and our behaviour towards others.[36] As we have seen, according to Gergen, Harre and others, these 'multiple partials' are constituted by a shifting 'coalition of voices' echoing the sometimes dominant, sometimes nurturant and often contradictory discourses in which we are enmeshed.[37] The subpersonality model fosters the identification with and disidentification from several relevant 'internal' voices that might otherwise be subordinated to the demands for a falsely 'unified' conception of self.

One of the aims of this work with young people therefore is to prevent the person from becoming dominated and limited by available identities. When the student recognises a subpersonality, they are helped to identify fully with it and then to step outside it and observe it. In psychosynthesis this process is called identification and disidentification. Assagioli writes:

> Given the sometimes negative reactions to their own development ... it is a great relief to adolescents if they can discover that their identity is more than different conglomerations of feelings, thoughts or sensations. Gaining psychological distance from the intense swings of emotional life is essential.[38]

The Psychosynthesis Programme
The twelve-week programme was carried out with a group of ten fifth year students in a school in the west of Ireland in 2005, and aimed to help the young people participate more creatively and actively in their own development; to experientially understand how they position themselves in cultural/institutional storylines and how these category positions (male/female, son/daughter, intelligent/ weak, heterosexual/gay, popular/marginal etc.) both serve and limit them; and to facilitate the experience of creatively standing outside available identities. As speaking/symbolising subjects we can invent, invert and break old structures and patterns and thus speak/write/ symbolise into existence other ways of being.[39] It is possible to be one and many, whole and multiple, deep and shallow, distant

and warm, practical and utopian, sexual and spiritual, strong and vulnerable, yet we have no language to describe the paradoxes that we all live. This fact underlines the extent to which our dichotomies (artificial productions of the mind) are mirrored in the words we use, and how these words in turn perpetuate these same cleavages.[40] Art breaks through linguistic dualisms and opens up 'lines of flight' to imagine oneself otherwise.[41] Hence, the methodologies used in the programme were arts-based methods: guided imagery work, free drawing, collage-making, relaxation and journaling. Throughout the workshops I facilitated relaxation and guided visualisation exercises inviting the young people to imagine themselves as they interact in their world of school, home and social groups. As they creatively constructed and dialogued with multiple portraits of themselves, they were helped to hear not only their 'personal' voice but how that voice is constructed in sometimes invisible cultural stories – the stories they tell themselves about teachers/students and style of pedagogy they receive, gender norms, the values and assumptions of the home/workplace/society etc. I found it helpful in promoting this kind of critical reflection to ask the students to consider the following questions after they completed a creative self-portrait and to write their responses into their journals:

» What do you see? What story is the image telling?
» Where did you hear that story? (raising awareness of cultural/institutional discourses)
» What is it like to be in that image – body, feelings, thoughts? (awareness of effects of discourse)
» How does that image/story serve you? (encouraging reflexivity/distance)
» How does that image/story limit you? Does it exclude others? (making visible the discursive construction of power)
» What image/s, if any, have been blocked out or erased? (making visible abject categories)
» Why did you choose that image and not another? (raising awareness of audience/context and the fluidity of identity)
» What changes, if any, would you like to make to the image/s? (underscoring non-fixity of identity).

Arts-based research methods challenge empirical forms that reduce human experience to knowledge claims of certainty and truth, rather seeing truth and knowledge as contextual, contingent and always in process.[42] Arts-based inquiry encourages the expression of multiple truths and problematises the relationship between knowledge and power, exposing knowledge as socially constructed, creating open texts that give expression to the marginalised voices within/out.[43]

Selection process

A class presentation was made to all fifth year students as an initial means of recruiting a target population. At these information meetings research aims, content of programme, expectations on research participants in terms of time-keeping and commitment were outlined and explained. Thirty students presented for selection to the group. Their names were then divided on the basis of gender and a sample of five males and five females was randomly selected. Ideally, there might have been an ethnic mix in the sample of students. Watkins advises that 'we must challenge our perspectives by placing ourselves in the company of others whose experiences bring into focus our assumptions and practices'.[44] However, there were no international students attending this school, so it was not possible.

Consent and ethical considerations

In line with recent research recommendations vis-à-vis children's right to participate in research as competent informants, I sought informed consent prior to parental permission.[45] Fully informed consent is not possible when we embark on research that involves unfolding processes. Following Etherington, I relied on 'process consent', ensuring that at each stage, participants were still willing to be involved and reminding them of their right to withdraw at any time.[46]

A central ethical consideration was to create a safe, trusting group environment for the students to engage in creative/critical reflective processes. I drew on my teaching and counselling skills to facilitate the unfolding stories as the young people shared their creative self-portraits in the group, and afterwards in the one-to-one creative conversations which were carried out at the end of the workshops. These individual conversations provided the participants with a private space to articulate any aspect of their creative stories that they felt constrained to do during the workshops. Much of the material from these conversations as well as the workshops served as a way of evaluating the programme and its effects on the participants.

Programme evaluation

As the participants constructed and dialogued with their self-images they became aware of multiplicity and fluidity in identity construction and how institutional (family and school) stories and social contexts validate certain identities. Some of the contributions below underscore this:

> I can be different types of me throughout the day. I am not just a happy person all the time or a confused person. I think it is a good thing to be aware of how I can have different identities with different people and in different situations. (*Tina, 17*)

> In this school I would not be seen as bright because I'm not good at Irish, but in my last school I was, like, kind of ok. That's why I drew my last school. So yeah … it depends on what the school promotes, and all the students then have an idea of where they fit in. (*Anne, 17*)

> I'm always called the boss at home because I'm the oldest. So my first portrait kind of reflected that. But then in the collage I drew myself standing outside the group. I didn't speak about it in the workshop because I felt embarrassed, but I suppose I can feel left out with the gang. Like, I don't like to see myself as an outsider, but I can be at times. (*John, 18*)

The students became conscious of some of the dominant discourses that shaped their identities to date and the effects of these discourses. One female participant insightfully said that it was new to her to discover that her 'good girl' side could sometimes make her feel exhausted. She added, 'People always expect me and maybe most girls to be like that so it makes it difficult to not get tired sometimes'. A male participant shared his image of being in a warrior's body-armoury and experiencing its unbearable weight. This young person felt that the pressure on 'lads' to be self-contained and to 'go it alone' was 'tough'. Closely linked to this was the creative narrative of another male participant who felt deep shame when he imaged 'a sheep' as part of his identity. During the programme he explored some of the cultural discourses about what it is to be a male adolescent (male as 'macho', 'rebel', 'athlete' etc.) and to locate the shame in its cultural context. He said this was 'an eye-opener in one way but also kind of obvious' that how he viewed the self-portrait images was informed by society. Therefore, he concluded, 'The way we view ourselves and other people is through the stories that are pedalled in our culture' (Mark, 18). The female participant who felt conflict between her 'warm, kind person' image and her 'need to be alone' identity also benefited from exploring how girls and women are positioned in her immediate social world, in the media etc. and how that in turn informed her reading of these identities.

To experience de-centring from fixed identities was freeing for many in the group. They expressed this in terms of the experience being 'something new', giving them a chance to look at how they identify themselves as being this or that and moving back from it. Others had difficulty imaginatively letting go of positions that they had identified with for so long, even when they became aware of how limiting these could be. Martin's image of a huge 'ear' symbolised his usual position as listener:

> This is the way I am. I am like this in every situation, at school, with family. It serves me well because I don't get into trouble but it also keeps me out of things a bit. When I turned the drawing sideways the ear became a large mouth. It looks like it might have a lot to say but I also feel a bit sick when I look at it. I am a listener really, that's what I called the portrait. (*Martin, 17*)

The students found that as they tried out different positions in the group, their identities (who they took themselves to be at that moment) changed. One person had experiences of feeling at times dominant and at times the underdog and powerless as she engaged with different members of the group throughout the twelve weeks. These identities were also creatively constructed in her self-portraits. The effects of this attention to the 'performance of self'[47] was for some participants a loosening of a fixed idea of self/identity. Throughout the programme, the students reported and recorded in their journals that in their daily lives they became more conscious of identity positions they were taking up. Martin became more conscious of standing back and seeing himself as 'patronising' at times.

The young people reported becoming more critically aware of the popular discourses in the school and in the media regarding appearances, gender-appropriate ways of behaving and age-appropriate behaviour. So statements such as, 'What would you expect of second years!', 'First years don't know any better', 'By sixth year, students are ready to move on' were starting to be more visible as discourses rather than *givens* and were viewed as stories that could be challenged. A critical eye was also thrown on the constant media barrage of perfect, air-brushed female images, the words 'attractive' and 'pretty' always uttered in the same breath as 'thin/slim', gender as fixed and sexual intimacy as heterosexual. Much of this knowledge was produced during the collage-making exercises.

> I've started noticing that even in our textbooks the images of the girls and boys are always thin, like, the message is that this is normal, that if you're fat you should be ashamed or something. (*Louise, 17*)

> I wonder what gay people read? Like all the books in the bookshops are about people like us. Like the magazines we used didn't have anything in them, you know ... I know none of us in the group were gay. And like on television you never really see gay couples. (*Carol, 17*)

The young people in the research programme were given the space to develop their capacity for critical awareness as they explored identities available to them in their culture, liberating their multiple voices through creative imaginal work and deep interpersonal receptivity. The programme enabled them to respond, to decentre and become aware, through artwork and dialogue, of the dominant identities available to them, to *perform* different identities/selves and experience this action as *performative*.

Conclusion

This chapter briefly presented the jarring positions of adolescent developmental theory and postmodern critical theories on self and development. In highlighting pluralism as a feature of selfhood in a technological, rapidly changing world, contemporary thinking challenges the modernist notion of an integrated self and thus of the young person developing a unified, integrated identity by the end of adolescence. Critical writings view the developing child/ adolescent as a product of a particular kind of discursive enterprise and not an independently pre-given object about which psychologists make discoveries.[48] According to John Morss, critical psychology of development as it now stands makes possible but does not yet constitute an alternative to developmental psychology. In this lacuna there are many developmental theorists and psychologists whose work speaks to the 'interpenetration of imaginal, social, cultural, natural and spiritual domains',[49] in terms of the development of critical/ dialogical capacities. We have touched on some of this practice above. Decentring and creatively reorienting in dialogue helps us to invite other voices in from the margins of our own minds and worlds. This type of work can be promoted as a curricular programme in discrete subject areas like SPHE (Social Personal and Health Education) or Religion, but more importantly, it seems to me, the insights of the critical movement in psychology need to be *capillaried* across the entire curriculum in terms of *how* we teach, counsel and advise our students. An openness to deconstructing inherited dominant stories about the person and a critical stance towards all knowledge production would be an essential first step 'perhaps towards the spectacular promise of what Derrida (1998/1994) called the "democracy to come"'.[50] This has implications for teacher education and guidance counsellor and chaplain education and training, which are to a large degree rooted in developmental theoretical discourses.

I join with the many theorists mentioned above in willing the postmodern vision, and the spirit of performance and resistance to which it gives rise, to continue to infect and inform our developmental practices with young people. In a characteristically iconoclastic but penetrating way, the philosopher Moriarty dialogues across the moulding, dominant, fortified discourses of the modern world:

Happy Christmas, Oedipus.

Happy Resurrection, Oedipus.

Happy Ascension Thursday, Oedipus.[51]

Notes

1. Conversation with John Moriarty, Clifden, 2005.
2. P. du Gay, J. Evans and P. Redmond, *Identity: A Reader* (London: Sage, 2000), 2.
3. G. O'Grady, 'The Adolescent Self: The Story of Multiplicity and Unity' in *NCGE News Supplement*, 04/2004, Section 1.1.7.1.
4. S. Harter, *The Construction of the Self* (New York: Guildford Press, 1999).
5. C. Rogers, *On Becoming a Person* (London: Constable, 1961).
6. H. Markus and P. Nurius, 'Possible Selves' in *American Psychologist*, 41, 9 (1986), 954–69.
7. E. Erikson, *Identity: Youth and Crisis* (New York: W.W Norton & Son, 1968), 161.
8. Cited in M. Grimmitt, *Religious Education and Human Development* (Great Walkering: McCrimmon Publishing Company, 1987), 155.
9. J. E. Marcia, 'Identity in Adolescence' in J. Adelson (ed.), *Handbook of Adolescent Psychology* (New York: Wiley, 1980).
10. K. Kristjansson, *The Self and its Emotions* (Cambridge: Cambridge University Press, 2010), 70.
11. M. Cooper and J. Rowan (eds), *The Plural Self* (London: Sage, 1999), 1.
12. J. Potter and M. Wetherell, *Discourse and Social Psychology: Beyond Attitudes and Behaviour* (London: Sage, 1987).
13. Cooper and Rowan, *The Plural Self*, 1.
14. Ibid.
15. K. G. Gergen, *The Saturated Self* (New York: Basic Books, 1991).

16. Harter, *The Construction of the Self*, 62.

17. Ibid., 73.

18. Kristjansson, *The Self and its Emotions*, 223.

19. J. M. Glass, *Shattered Selves: Multiple Personality in a Postmodern World* (London: Cornell University Press, 1993).

20. Cooper and Rowan, *The Plural Self*, 2.

21. S. Baumgardner and L. Rappoport, 'Culture and Self in Postmodern Perspective' in *The Humanistic Psychologist*, 24 (1996), 116–40.

22. R. Harre, 'The Step to Social Constructionism' in M. Richards and P. Light (eds), *Children of Social Worlds* (Cambridge: Polity Press, 1986).

23. J. R. Morss, *Growing Critical* (London: Routledge, 1996), 48.

24. I. Parker, *Discourse Dynamics* (London: Routledge, 1992).

25. J. Henrique, W. Holloway, C. Urwin, C. Venn and V. Walkerdine, *Changing the Subject: Psychology, Social Regulation and Subjectivity* (London: Methuen, 1984).

26. L. Fulani, 'Race, Identity and Epistemology' in L. Holzman and J. Morss (eds), *Postmodern Psychologies, Societal Practice and Political Life* (New York: Routledge, 2000), 155.

27. Ibid., 157.

28. C. Gilligan and L. Brown, *Meeting at the Crossroads* (USA: Harvard University Press, 1992).

29. Ibid., 15.

30. M. Watkins, 'Pathways Between the Multiplicities of the Psyche and Culture: The Development of Dialogical Capacities' in Rowan and Cooper (eds), *The Plural Self*, 254–67.

31. Ibid.

32. R. Assagioli, *Psychosynthesis* (Amherst, MA: Synthesis Centre Publishing, 2000), 26.

33. M. O'Regan, 'Psychosynthesis and Transpersonal Theory' in E. Boyne (ed.), *Psychotherapy in Ireland* (Dublin: Columba Press, 1995), 42.

34. *Sous rature* is a strategic philosophical device originally developed by Martin Heidegger (1889–1976). Usually translated as 'under erasure', it involves the crossing out of a word within a text, but allowing it to remain legible and in place. Used extensively by Jacques Derrida, it signifies that a word is 'inadequate yet necessary', that a particular signifier is not wholly suitable for the concept it represents, but must be used as the constraints of our language offer nothing better. I do not use this technique here to emphasise the inadequacy of the words but to underscore their discursive constitutive effects on us. We continue to view unity, self-control and harmony as indicators of maturity and pathologise plurality.

35. D. Whitmore, *Psychosynthesis Counselling in Action* (London: Sage, 2000).

36. Ibid.

37. B. Davies and S. Gannon, *Doing Collective Biography* (Berkshire: Open University Press, 2006).

38. R. Assagioli, unpublished paper (1962).

39. B. Davies and S. Gannon, *Shards of Glass: Children Reading and Writing Beyond Gendered Identities* (New Jersey: Hampton Press, 1993).

40. P. Ferrucci, *What We May Be* (London: Thorsons, 1995), 215.

41. Davies and Gannon, *Doing Collective Biography*, 87.

42. E. W. Eisner, 'The Primacy of Experience and the Politics of Method' in *Educational Researcher*, 26, 6 (1988), 4–9.

43. Ibid.

44. M. Watkins, 'Seeding Liberation: A Dialogue Between Depth Psychology and Liberation Psychology' in D. Slattery and L. Corbett (eds), *Depth Psychology: Meditations in the Field* (Einsiedelin: SW, 2002), 23.

45. R. Leitch, J. Gardner, S. Mitchell, L. Lundy, O. Odena, D. Galanouli and P. Clough, 'Consulting Pupils in Assessment for Learning Classrooms: The Twists and Turns of Working with Students as Co-researchers' in *Educational Action Research* 15, 3 (2007), 459–78.

46. K. Etherington, 'Researching Trauma, the Body and Transformation: A Situated Account of Creating Safety in Unsafe Places' in *British Journal of Guidance and Counselling*, 33, 3 (2005), 299–313.

47. C. K. Riessman, *Narrative Methods for the Human Sciences* (London: Sage, 2008), 106.

48. Henrique et al., *Changing the Subject*.

49. M. Watkins, 'Pathways Between the Multiplicities of the Psyche and Culture: The Development of Dialogical Capacities' in Rowan and Cooper (eds), *The Plural Self*, 254–67.

50. L. Richardson and E. A. St Pierre, 'Writing A Method of Inquiry' in N. K. Denzin and Y. S. Lincoln (eds), *The Sage Handbook of Qualitative Research* (London: Sage, 2005), 92.

51. J. Moriarty, *Nostos* (Dublin: Lilliput Press, 2001), 161.

An Introduction to Counselling in Schools

Noreen Sweeney

The purpose of this chapter is to explore some of the areas and issues common to all counselling work done with adolescents. It is hoped that this chapter will give a flavour of and some exposure to the world of counselling adolescents. It provides an overview of what constitutes counselling, the adolescent stage of development, adolescent issues, counselling approaches for working with adolescents, the practice of counselling adolescents, crisis counselling, counselling skills, the spiritual dimension, care of the counsellor, personal and professional characteristics of the counsellor and supervision.

The school chaplain or guidance counsellor uses counselling skills in their work with young people and normally has been professionally trained in the use of counselling skills. The counselling aspect of the chaplain's role in schools ranks among the highest of all their activities.[1] Many of the issues presented by the student in a session with a chaplain will be similar to those presented to a trained counsellor. The chaplain brings an extra faith dimension to the encounter with the student. The nature of the chaplain's or guidance counsellor's helping role in terms of counselling can be termed 'pastoral counselling'. This is a supportive role for adolescents experiencing problems in their life. The pastoral counsellor works in a more informal setting to that of a psychotherapist and refers clients who have deep-seated issues to others. The pastoral counsellor uses counselling skills and strategies that help meet the student's needs. In this chapter the term 'counsellor' refers to all professionals who use counselling skills in working with adolescents, including the school chaplain and guidance counsellor. It is worth noting that research shows that the majority of school chaplains in Ireland are qualified counsellors and as such are positioned to offer both spiritual and pastoral counselling in a way that other members of staff are not able to.[2]

Counselling is a contracted relationship between the counsellor and the client where they agree to meet for a set number of sessions. It is a supportive relationship that enables clients to explore issues freely, to understand themselves more fully and to take whatever action is necessary if they wish to change their problem situation. Responsibility for change rests with the client. The counsellor does not give advice nor tell the client what to do.

The Adolescent Stage of Development

In the school setting the chaplain and guidance counsellor deal with adolescents. During their time in second-level schooling the young person progresses from childhood to adulthood and from dependency to independence and autonomy. A successful conclusion to this stage of human development requires a parent or carer to recognise, allow and facilitate the adolescent to move out of the dependent role of a child in the family towards independence, autonomy and maturity. Children introject the social and moral values and ways of behaving of their families. Adolescents start to question this imposed value system and it becomes important to them to be in line with their peers rather than be in line with their parents. They search for an identity and a value system of their own. Many adolescents wish to, and need to, belong to a peer group with some level of common ideology and group identity. This need is related to the need for security and acceptability. Adolescents need the support of peer groups at this time of uncertainty and change.

During adolescence young people undergo rapid and extreme biological, physiological and social change. It is a period filled with anxiety for many adolescents. There is a noticeable difference in the rate of growth and sexual development in any group of adolescents. Sexual awareness and interest is high in this stage of the young person's life. Anxiety about their appearance can become an obsession for some. They are also making value judgements about their sexual behaviour. In early adolescence young people tend to form close relationships with friends of the same sex because they feel secure with them.[3] This is also part of their process of moving away from their parents and family.[4] By late adolescence there is a move towards heterosexual relationships for most young people. Some young people explore their sexual desires at this stage with regard to homosexuality.

During adolescence the rise in sexual hormones may influence the adolescent's emotional state. Hormones act in conjunction with the other major changes that are happening in the young person such as social relationships, changes in beliefs and attitudes and changes in self-perception.[5] At this stage of development cognitive changes are also occurring. The adolescent develops a capacity for abstract thinking, finds out how to think about relationship issues, discusses new ways of processing information and learns to think creatively and question critically.

Adolescents are egocentric, a trait that develops more fully in mid to late adolescence. They feel everyone is watching them, as though they were on stage. They may have the idea that they are unique and this makes it difficult for them to believe that another is capable of understanding them or how they are feeling. This has important implications for counsellors working with them. They learn to think critically about interpersonal issues and about other people. Learning to make sense of things helps them to make decisions about how to interact with others.

The most important task for the adolescent is the formation of a personal identity that in turn leads to effective psychological functioning. The process of socialisation is a balance between individuation and the formation of personal identity on the one hand and integration with society on the other.[6] Unless this balance is achieved, there are likely to be personal crises for the young person that may result in the need for counselling or other professional help.

The adolescent stage of development is characterised by emotional reactivity and a high intensity of emotional response. A disruptive emotion of early adolescence is shame and adolescents tend to develop strong defence mechanisms like denial, projection and regression to cope with situations and to interact with others. These are areas that counsellors may have to work with in the school context.

Society's expectations pose a challenge for adolescents. Some will find the challenges too much and feel alienated from society because they cannot meet those expectations. Those who feel overwhelmed by society's expectations may revert to antisocial behaviour. This has implications for counsellors and others in the helping professions.

The family is one of the most effective vehicles for promoting values in adolescence, helping adolescents to be successful in school and to have confidence in peer relationships. Steinberg and Steinberg found that the common link between successful adolescents is that they generally have positive relationships with their parents. So an important challenge for the adolescent is to maintain positive relationships with their parents while achieving their developmental goal of separation and detachment from them, which is hard to achieve.[7] Research discussed in *USA Today* shows that boys spend less time with their families than girls and girls are more likely to talk about personal issues with parents than boys.[8] Adolescents are more likely to talk when it suits them and when they can take the lead. These traits of adolescents have great significance for counsellors.

Adolescent spirituality is often demonstrated through the adolescent's search for meaning in life's daily experiences. Fowler says that in early adolescence the emphasis is on symbolism rather than knowing factual truth whereas in later adolescence personal experiences, symbols and rituals can play a major role in the development of spiritual beliefs for the adolescent.[9]

When an adolescent is unable to negotiate and confront a developmental challenge successfully there are likely to be unhelpful psychological, emotional and behavioural consequences. Counselling can be useful in helping the adolescent find new ways to proceed adaptively along the required developmental journey.

Adolescent Issues

Unresolved childhood issues impact on the adolescent. Early attachment problems have an effect on the adolescent's later experiences and influences how they deal with stressful situations. Unsatisfactory attachments during childhood have been linked with later substance abuse,[10] eating disorders,[11] early sexual activity and high-risk sexual behaviour[12] and poor self-image[13] in adolescents. Counsellors need to recognise that some maladaptive behaviours in adolescence may be partly the result of poor attachment relationships with primary figures during childhood.

As has been referred to elsewhere in this book, unhelpful parenting has a major influence over child and adolescent development and irresponsible parenting may result in antisocial and aggressive behaviours being passed down within a family. Neglect can result in behaviour problems, poor school attendance, weak academic grades and generally low achievement. Children who have been neglected can carry into adolescence angry feelings towards the neglectful carers and are likely to have issues around personal safety, trust, fairness and responsibility.

Adolescents who experience emotional abuse as children often present in counselling with behaviour problems. Children and adolescents exposed to physical abuse may develop symptoms similar to those of post-traumatic stress disorder and many have activity profiles similar to those of children diagnosed with attention deficit hyper-activity disorder (ADHD).[14]

Children who have been physically abused and continue to be abused may express their feelings by acting out in antisocial ways with high aggression or may internalise their feelings with the consequent development of depression or suicide ideation. Sexual abuse can often be found in the histories of young people with severe mental health disturbances. For children who experience loss, the grieving process may extend into adolescence and influence their emotions and behaviours. It is important for adolescents to work through the grieving process so that their adolescent journey is not affected by grief. Adolescents who suffer the loss of a parent by death report greater shock, disbelief and a sense of loss than those experienced by adults. They also reported more anger at the deceased, sleep disturbances, dream activity and irritability than adults.[15] When counselling adolescents, it is necessary to examine the impact of early childhood experiences on their ability to negotiate the developmental tasks of adolescence.

Factors such as the family's style of functioning, parenting style, parental relationship, separation and divorce, an alcoholic parent, domestic violence and cultural issues have the potential to cause stress for the adolescent. It is the adolescent's personal responses to the environment that will finally determine the extent of their success.

Theoretical Approaches to Counselling Adolescents

Counselling adolescents is different from counselling adults. Counsellors need to tailor their counselling approaches to engage the adolescent directly and actively and to use strategies which will specifically address their needs in a manner that is acceptable to them. The adolescent's internal emotional and psychological needs are best addressed through individual counselling. Family therapy primarily addresses interpersonal relationship issues of adolescents within the family.

The counsellor uses an approach to counselling which helps meet the adolescent's needs as well as a range of counselling skills and strategies. The Person Centred Approach, based on the work of Carl Rogers, lends itself well to working with adolescents who, through their experience of the core conditions of empathy, positive regard and congruence offered by the counsellor, are better able to mature and develop. The emphasis here is on the relationship between the counsellor and the client. The counsellor enters the subjective world of the client and communicates that understanding (empathy) to the client. This allows the client to become more open and honest. Feeling safe in the relationship as a result of warmth and caring (unconditional positive regard) of the counsellor, the client reflects this greater openness in deeper levels of self-disclosure. Rogers says that empathy is a healing agent in itself as the client feels that there is at least one other human being who has some understanding of their problem.[16] As the counsellor remains congruent, the client becomes congruent. On counselling adolescents, intense raw emotions can surface and the challenge for the counsellor is to be able to walk alongside the adolescent as they explore confusion, rebellion and failure. Holding clients in unconditional positive regard means being able to separate the person from the behaviours and this allows clients to confront themselves. The counsellor needs to note that congruence is distinct from self-disclosure, which is an inappropriate sharing of the counsellor's personal life. A counsellor's self-disclosure is a burden for all clients, including adolescents.

The Existential Approach to counselling is pertinent to working with adolescents. This approach assumes that people need to find ways of making sense of life before they can make sense of their problems. Existential counselling is an exploration of the adolescent's being in the world and how they relate to and understand that world. This approach relies on a questioning attitude to the way one lives life, as well as an acceptance of the need to explore one's relationship to the world. This approach is very appropriate to the adolescent stage of life where there is a search for meaning. The adolescent is helped to explore their 'world', which consists of the natural world, the public world, the private world and the ideal world. The counselling process is an examination of all these interconnected worlds.[17] Meaning helps us to relieve and deal with anxiety that comes from facing a world that does not have a fixed and comforting structure. Meaning gives a framework to the way we live life and helps us develop values that augment our sense of meaning. In a world where people find meaning through striving, creating and achieving, there is no time to contemplate the purpose of life. There is no time to be, it is all about doing. Young people have to come to terms with who they are and how they want to live life as pressure comes from all sides to achieve and succeed. Finding meaning allows the adolescent to engage with life rather than with meaninglessness.

Developed by Albert Eilis, Rational Emotive Behaviour Therapy is useful when counselling adolescents. The basic assumption of this approach is that people contribute to their own psychological problems as well as specific symptoms by the way they interpret events and situations in life. A reorganisation of one's self-statements will result in a corresponding reorganisation of one's behaviour. The focus in sessions is to help clients change their cognitions which in turn produces changes in affect and behaviour. Through the therapeutic process clients learn skills that help them identify and dispute irrational beliefs that have been learned and self-constructed. Focus of work is on thinking and acting rather than on feelings. The client learns the need to accept themselves despite imperfections and to stop blaming others. 'Shoulds' and 'oughts' are replaced by preferences like 'I choose to'. Unrealistic beliefs create dysfunctional behaviours.

Egan's Three Stage Helping Model is a problem-focused way of working with clients.[18] The model or framework breaks down the counselling process into three stages. In the first stage, the client is encouraged to explore their situation and identify problem areas. In stage two the adolescent explores what life might be like if some of the issues could be resolved and goals could be set. In stage three the adolescent is encouraged to develop action plans and strategies for achieving the goals set in stage two.

In working with adolescents the counsellor can use a particular approach or use an integrative approach, depending on the adolescent's needs.[19]

The Practice of Counselling Adolescents

The counselling environment should be a place of safety, security, dependability and consistency. A basic requirement of any counselling work is a room that is both private and free from interruptions. In a school environment, this means somewhere discreet away from the noise of the main thoroughfare. The counselling room should be reasonably soundproof so that noises and voices in the corridor will not interrupt the counselling work. The room should be free of distractions. For the protection and safety of all, it is advisable to have a door with a glass panel so that the counsellor can sit in the room where they can be seen from outside. This is normal practice for school chaplains and guidance counsellors.

The process of putting in place the counselling contract with an adolescent is important, but can also have its difficulties. The counsellor takes the time to present the contract clearly while ensuring that the adolescent is a willing and equal partner. Adolescents need to be told that the counsellor does not provide solutions but will help them explore issues and that they will, in turn, find their own solutions. The counsellor will inform them that they have choice around what they want to bring to the session and about how many sessions they want. This will set the tone for the rest of the counselling work. It is good to hear why the adolescent has come for counselling and if they are there on a voluntary or involuntary basis. If they are there on an involuntary basis, it would be important to explore how they feel about being 'sent', how they are now that they have arrived and how they would like to use the time.

The counsellor needs to give the adolescent time to understand what is on offer and what is expected of them in the counselling relationship. The freer the adolescent is to say no to counselling without risk of criticism, the more likely they are to stay and use the time well. Confidentiality and its exceptions need to be explained to the adolescent.

Keeping and making appointments is more of an issue with adolescents than other client groups. Some chaplains have a drop-in service and others have a mixture of appointments for a number of sessions and also a drop-in service. A drop-in provides a taste of what it is like to talk about a problem and allows adolescents to be seen in an emergency or crisis. They can discuss their problems, express feelings and look at options. Ongoing support can be negotiated for a number of sessions. Some adolescents do not like open-ended contracts so they can be offered a contract of a set number of sessions including a review session. Many adolescents do not turn up consistently for sessions and it is an area to be addressed by the counsellor, as absenteeism can be used to express their doubts or concerns about counselling.

Adolescents feel that power in society rests with older people so it is difficult for them to perceive that they will be listened to and that their beliefs, ideas, feelings and opinions will be accepted by an adult, including the counsellor. Counsellors and other people in the helping profession are often handicapped by the adolescent's low expectation of any interaction with people from a different age group. It is only by experiencing the counselling relationship that the adolescent will learn to trust and open up. For some this will be a very slow process.

Some adolescents will try to shock and challenge the counsellor. Many will act out within the counselling relationship the challenging and confronting behaviour that is a part of growing up and yet is experienced as negative by so many of the adults with whom adolescents come into contact.[20] Counsellors need to be aware of this and of their own responses to it. In working with adolescents it is vital to be responsive rather than reactive. This is asking a lot of the counsellor but supervision plays a very important role here in helping the counsellor separate the personal from the professional and ensuring that an effective service can be provided to the adolescent. Many adolescents respond by going into themselves and by being silent, so the counsellor needs to be comfortable with silence as out of it new awareness can emerge. Some adolescents are withdrawn in the counselling situation because they feel out of their depth in the sphere of feelings and expressing their emotions. Some believe that their feelings will not be believed or valued so it is only by allowing them space and allowing trust to build that a therapeutic relationship can be developed. For others silence is the only way of being in control in the world. For a few it is a way of expressing resentment and aggression.

Another kind of challenge presented by adolescents is to challenge the counsellor and see them as not on their side. The counsellor needs to separate the person and the behaviour, and to challenge the behaviour and not the person's being. Counsellors of adolescents need to avoid acting in a parental way with their clients. Being aware and having an understanding of the cultural and social context of the adolescent is essential for the counsellor. The pressure to conform to peer group norms is great for the adolescent so an appreciation of these issues is essential for the counsellor.

Young people live in the moment. What is a crisis today is soon forgotten about. Counsellors need to be able to understand and tolerate how adolescents can be notorious for missing appointments and failing to get in touch. Much of the work done with the adolescent is short term, often crisis intervention work, so the counsellor needs to stand back and trust the process and the adolescent's right to choose when they will address their issues.

Crisis Counselling

Crisis situations are presented to the counsellor, particularly chaplains, in the school context on a regular basis. A stressful event can become a crisis depending on the response of the individual. Stressful events can be divided into two categories.[21] Category one pertains to developmental changes in a person's life. The transition from one stage to another can cause emotional uncertainty, bringing the need for change. The second category of events that can precipitate a crisis consists of probable life events for us all, including bereavement, illness, examination failures, relationship difficulties and other less probable events like accidents and assault. The first category can be a more ongoing type of difficulty and will need to be dealt with over a period of weeks or months. The second category is characterised by suddenness and urgency within the experience. No two people will react to any of these events in the same way. What is manageable change for one person may result in a crisis for another. The crisis lies in the person's perception of and reaction to the event rather than the event itself. When the two categories of events coincide within a person's life, the possibility of crisis reaction increases.

The important thing for the counsellor to do in a crisis is to remain calm. By absorbing the panic and grounding the distress, the counsellor can be a calming presence in the midst of chaos. This calmness will help reduce the impact of the crisis and make possible the start of a response to the crisis. A crisis cannot be postponed. It is present now and expects a response now. The counsellor needs to attend to the physical response of the person in terms of a relaxation exercise and/or a drink of water. Next the counsellor's focus is directed on the immediate crisis and the feelings of the person. The discussion will give an indication of what triggered the crisis. All counselling skills are needed to explore the client's perception of the event. The helper next focuses on the support system that may be helpful to the person. Throughout the crisis the client has lost control of their ability to cope with what is going on around and within them. If the counsellor can entertain and convey hope for the client, then that can enable the client to entertain hope for themselves. Self-awareness by the counsellor is vital with crisis work where there is a more intense state of distress in the client. There is a need to be mindful that in a crisis there is neither a simple correct answer nor a perfect solution. While aware of their own limitations, counsellors can help as much as is in their power, knowing that they may be the only person available right now. Medical expertise may also be available to the counsellor.

The quality of the counselling relationship is critical in influencing outcomes and client satisfaction. For a successful outcome it is desirable that the following qualities be present: an authentic adolescent–counsellor relationship, the presence of warmth and empathy, understanding and acceptance on the counsellor's part. These qualities are achieved by the way the counsellor and adolescent work together. Where a relationship has difficulties, the counsellor can use supervision to identify reasons and to resolve personal issues around the relationship. The world of the adolescent is uncertain so in order to help the adolescent, the counsellor needs to be congruent, open, honest, sincere and respectful. The presence of these qualities helps create an authentic relationship.

Adolescents strive for acceptance in the world outside the family and believe that no one understands them. The counsellor has to be able to convey to adolescents the message that they are heard and understood and that they are accepted as persons regardless of their behaviour. The presence of empathy and warmth allows the adolescent appreciate that the counsellor is working to understand their world.

Adolescents are generally restless persons who need to be actively engaged. They can quickly become bored and impatient so the counselling relationship needs to be dynamic. The counsellor needs to use skills and strategies in response to the adolescent's immediate needs as they are identified at any point of time during the session. The counsellor should be active, lively, spontaneous, creative and flexible. It means being able to respond quickly and actively so that opportunities are not lost.

Use of Counselling Skills

The counsellor, by making use of a wide range of counselling skills, can engage the curiosity and interest of the adolescent. Skills are used either in direct responses to the needs of the counselling process or in conjunction with any of the strategies and approaches already discussed. The list of skills used includes attending, active listening, reflecting back content and feelings, giving feedback, questioning, summarising and challenging.

Observation is an ongoing activity. Being aware that external presentation does not always match what is happening internally is vital. The counsellor in accepting what is presented is creating trust and the adolescent will feel safe in showing what is behind their facade. The counsellor also observes general appearance, behaviour, feelings, speech and language throughout the work.

The skill of *attending* refers to the ways in which the counsellor can be with a person both physically and psychologically. It means paying attention to the person. It tells the other person that one is in a position to listen carefully to their concerns. Attending includes facial expression, eye contact, gaze, gestures, posture, physical proximity and time.

Listening means listening actively, accurately and for meaning. It involves listening to the client's experiences, behaviours, feelings, points of view, the context of their story, to what is not being said and observing non-verbal behaviour. It is an activity that requires work. Good listening can comfort, ease suffering, heal psychological wounds, act as a catalyst for moving forward and empower the adolescent being listened to. Effective listeners put the talker at ease, limit their own talking, are attentive, do not interrupt, get a sense of the other person's world and are aware of their own biases. Good listening is essential to the counselling process.

Reflection of content and feelings are skills identified by Carl Rogers as being essential to the counselling process.[22] They let the client know that the counsellor is trying to understand them. The counsellor does not repeat what the client has said but picks out the most important information and, using their own words, feeds this back to the client.

The counsellor matches the adolescent's language. Adolescents will often talk metaphorically. The metaphor might by used to describe feelings, and where the adolescent uses a metaphor it is helpful if the counsellor uses it too. Feedback includes giving compliments when it is wise to do so and affirmations to reinforce a personal truth that has been described by the adolescent and shared with the counsellor.

Apart from using reflection to feed back information, the counsellor can give feedback through affirmations, cheer leading, normalising, reframing and statements. 'Cheerleading' is a skill used in solution-focused therapy.[23] It uses questions and statements to encourage the adolescent to continue describing the changing process, for example: 'How did you do that?', 'That must have been difficult to do'. This kind of response enables the adolescent to take responsibility for and feel good in the success of achieving change.

'Normalising' is helpful when working with adolescents who are experiencing high levels of feelings which are new to them. Normalising is useful in cases where unacceptable responses and behaviours are not minimised. 'Reframing' is particularly useful when working with adolescents. It is useful to help the person see the bigger picture, and the adolescent is invited to see their picture as part of the bigger picture.

'Probing' is another skill which makes use of a variety of questions to get clarity and bring focus to the counselling process. Questioning needs to be used sparingly when counselling adolescents, as they can be questioned frequently by their parents for information. It is a good idea therefore to limit the number of questions asked and instead make use of other counselling skills which are more likely to encourage the adolescent to open up freely. Open questions are useful in all kinds of counselling, as are questions that heighten the adolescent's awareness, e.g. 'what are you feeling right now?' or 'what is happening inside you right now?

'Circular questioning' is a non-threatening way of getting information from an adolescent. Instead of asking the adolescent directly how they feel, the counsellor could ask how someone else in the family is feeling, like, 'I wonder what your brother thinks or feels when your parents argue?' Often having answered the circular question the adolescent will continue to talk about how they think, feel and behave because they want to make it clear whether they agree or disagree with the person mentioned in the circular question.

'Choice questions' help with the exploration of choices and consequences and prepare the person for future situations, for example, 'What would have been a better choice?', 'What would you like to do now?' 'Guru questions' allow the adolescent to stand aside and give themselves some advice, for example, 'Imagine for a minute you were a guru and you could give advice to someone like you – what advice would you give them?' 'Miracle questions' allow the adolescent to use their imagination to explore what would be different if their situation changed for the better, for example, 'If the problem was solved miraculously, what would life be like?'

'Summarising' involves feeding back in the counsellor's own words a brief and concise summary of what the client has said. It lets the client know that the counsellor has heard and understood and also helps the client to clarify and identify what is most important.

Challenging should be done in a way that invites the adolescent to question what they have said, what they are doing or what they believe. Adolescents are usually direct in challenging each other in peer relationships so the counsellor can be direct in a non-threatening way.

The Spiritual Dimension in Counselling

Spirituality is a personal and subjective concept. Bergin is one of many researchers who believes that being open to spiritual/religious values will result in a change in the focus of treatment towards more general lifestyle changes.[24] Spirituality is a component of mental health and its inclusion in counselling practice makes the therapeutic process more effective.[25] Spirituality should be addressed if it is a concern for the client. It can be a force that can help the person make sense of the universe and find reasons for living. It can be a source of healing and can give strength in times of crisis, while also helping the adolescent ponder on the questions 'who am I' and 'what is the purpose and meaning of my life?' School chaplains through their professional training and personal faith commitment are particularly well suited to include this dimension in the counselling they offer.

Care of the Counsellor

For many counsellors, the danger of what is referred to as 'burnout' is a reality. While counsellors cannot always control stressful events, they can control how they interpret and react to them. There is a price to pay for always being available as counsellor and for assuming that one is able to control the lives and destinies of others.[26] The counsellor can develop a strategy for keeping themselves healthy personally and professionally. The strategy may consider the following: evaluating goals and expectations and checking to see if they are realistic; having other interests besides work; bringing variety to one's work; monitoring the impact of stress on the job; paying attention to one's health, exercise programmes, diet, meditation and relaxation; developing some friendships that are characterised by a mutuality of giving and receiving; learning to ask for what one wants, knowing that one may not always get it; learning to work for self-confirmation as opposed to looking externally for validation; avoiding taking on burdens that are the responsibility of others; keeping up to date in the counselling area; rearranging work schedules to reduce stress; learning to know one's limits with others; engaging in hobbies that bring pleasure; arranging time for spiritual growth; and seeking personal therapy as an avenue to personal development. Two useful questions for the counsellor to ask regularly are, 'What do I have to offer others who are struggling with their life?' and 'Am I doing in my own life what I would want others to do in theirs?'.

Personal Qualities of Effective Counsellors

The willingness to endeavour to be a more therapeutic counsellor is crucial. The list of qualities that follow is intended to stimulate the counsellor to examine their ideas of what kind of person can make a difference in the lives of others.[27] Effective counsellors know who they are and what they are capable of and have a sense of identity. They appreciate and respect themselves. They accept their own power and allow others to feel powerful with them. They are willing to leave the security of the known if they are not happy with what they have and are open to change. They are sincere and honest. They commit to living fully rather than settling for mere existence. They are willing to learn from their mistakes. They live in the now and are able to be present with others in the now. They value others and have an interest in the welfare of others. They are able to keep healthy boundaries, they know when to say no and are able to keep a balance in their life. They have a sense of humour.

Professional Qualities of the Ideal Counsellor

Effective counsellors recognise that the client is the most important instrument in the counselling process. They are willing to use existing skills and acquire new ones. They recognise that their learning is ongoing. They are able to enter the world of the client and stay with their frame of reference. They do not impose on clients their view of reality. The client's needs come first. They are able to deal with a wide range of client feelings, thoughts, behaviours and experiences. They are flexible in applying strategies in the counselling process. They get support through adequate supervision and personal therapy. They suspend judgements and values during the counselling process. They take the risk of being self-aware. They constantly strive to be reflective practitioners. They keep professional boundaries and work in an ethical way. The ideal counsellor is aware of the importance of working values which include the following: do no harm, do not take sides, become competent and committed, keep the client's agenda in focus, value the client, value client empowerment, do not over-emphasise the role of the counsellor, avoids defensiveness and challenge one's own blind spots.

Counselling Supervision

Supervision is considered essential for all who counsel adolescents. Inskipp and Proctor define supervision as a working alliance between a supervisor and supervisee in which the latter presents an account of their work, reflects on it and receives feedback so as to learn to work more effectively with clients.[28] The purpose of supervision is to learn and to enable the supervisee to grow in ethical competence, confidence, compassion and creativity and therefore give the best possible service to clients. Supervision facilitates the personal and professional development of the counsellor and provides a personal support system for the counsellor whose work is confidential. Given the nature of the problems presented in the counselling context, the counsellor can become over-involved. So supervision is the forum where the counsellor can offload and deal with the issues and feelings arising from the work.

Working with adolescents can be anxiety-provoking, where adolescents are at a vulnerable lifestage and difficulties can become crises. Counsellors need help in containing their own anxieties so that they can contain those of adolescents whom they counsel. Ethical issues around the work can be explored in supervision. Good supervision and management reduces the risk of the development of unprofessional relationships, and supervision is an arena where counsellors can continue to learn from reflecting on their practice.

Group supervision provides insight gained from other members and peer support. One of the advantages of it is that other counsellors' cases can raise issues in one's own practice that might otherwise remain unrecognised, whilst generating support among counsellors. Group supervision is more cost effective than one to one supervision, and the volume of it should be in proportion to the volume of counselling work undertaken.

Conclusion

Those who are engaged in counselling such as the school chaplain or guidance counsellor need to keep themselves skilled by attending counselling workshops and undertaking further training. Ideally, chaplains and guidance counsellors are members of their professional associations and abide by codes of ethics and receive regular supervision. The world of counselling is one where the counsellor is always learning. While learning can be gained from reading and training, the most effective learning of all comes from the experience of facilitating the counselling process. The experience of the counselling process is our greatest teacher as counsellors and we learn so much from it through our own reflection and the use of supervision.

Notes

1. J. O'Higgins Norman and P. King, *School Chaplaincy Activity Rating Study*, A Research Report (Dublin: Dublin City University, 2009).

2. Ibid.

3. P. Blos, *The Adolescent Passage: Development Issue* (New York: International University Press, 1979).

4. K. Geldard and D. Geldard, *Counselling Adolescents* (London: Sage, 1999).

5. Ibid.

6. G. R. Adams and S. K. Marshall, 'A Developmental Social Psychology of Identity: Understanding The Person-in-Context' in *Journal of Adolescence* 19 (New York: Elsevier, 1996), 429–42.

7. L. Steinberg and W. Steinberg, *Crossing Paths: How Your Child's Adolescence Triggers Your Own Crisis* (New York: Simon and Schuster, 1994).

8. *USA Today*, 127, 2622 (1997), 8 (2).

9. J. Fowler, *Stages of Faith* (Melbourne: Dove, 1981).

10. J. Gerevich and E. Bacskai, 'Protective and Risk Predictors in the Development of Drug Abuse' in *Journal of Drug Education* 26 (Amityville, New York: Baywood, 1996), 25–38; D. Burge, C. Hammen, J. Davilla and S. Daley, 'Attachment Cognitions and College and Work Functioning Two Years Later in Adolescent Women' in *Journal of Youth and Adolescence* 26 (New York: Klewur, 1997).

11. Burge et al., 'Attachment Cognitions and College and Work Functioning Two Years Later in Adolescent Women'; J. Salzman, 'Ambivalent Attachment in Female Adolescents: Association with Affective Instability and Eating Disorders' in *International Journal of Eating Disorders* 21 (London: Wiley, 1997), 251–9.

12. C. Smith, 'Factors Associated With Early Sexual Activity Among Urban Adolescents' in *Social Work Journal* 42 (1997), 334–46.

13. J. O'Koon, 'Attachment to Parents and Peers in Adolescence and their Relationship with Self-Image' in *Journal of Adolescence* 32 (New York: Elsevier, 1997), 471–82.

14. C. Glod and M. Teicher, 'Relationship Between Early Abuse, Post-Traumatic Stress Disorder and Activity Levels in Pre-Pubertal Children' in *American Academy of Child and Adolescent Psychiatry* 34 (Washington, DC: 1996), 1384–93.

15. C. Meshot and L. Leitner, 'Adolescent Mourning and Parental Death' in *Amiga Journal of Death and Dying*, 26 (1993), 287–99.

16. C. R. Rogers, 'Rogers, Kohut and Ericson: A Personal Perspective on Some Similarities and Differences' in *Person Centred Review* 1 (Boston, 1986), 125–40.

17. Geldard and Geldard, *Counselling Adolescents*.

18. G. Egan, *The Skilled Helper* (Pacific Grove, CA: Brooks-Cole/Wadsworth, 2002).

19. I suggest *Theory and Practice of Counselling and Psychotherapy* by Gerald Corey for detailed study approaches or theories of counselling (Pacific Grove, CA: Brook–Cole/Wadsworth, 2001).

20. J. Mabey and B. Sorensen, *Counselling for Young People* (Buckingham: Open University Press, 1995).

21. U. O'Farrell, *First Steps in Counselling* (Dublin: Veritas, 1993).

22. C. R. Rogers, *Client Centred Therapy: Its Current Practice, Implications and Theory* (Boston: Houghton Mifflin, 1965).

23. J. Walter and J. Peller, *Becoming Solution-Focused in Brief Therapy* (New York: Brunner/Mazel, 1992).

24. A. E. Bergin, 'Values and Religious Issues in Psychotherapy and Mental Health' in *American Psychologist* 46 (Washington, DC: American Psychologists Association, 1991), 394–403.

25. G. Corey, *Theory and Practice of Counselling and Psychotherapy* (6th ed.) (Pacific Grove, California: Brook-Cole/Wadsworth, 2001).

26. Ibid.

27. Ibid.

28. F. Inskipp and B. Proctor, *Making the Most of Supervision, Part I* (Twickenham, Middlesex: Cascade Publications, 1993).

Caring About Parental Involvement in Schools

Siobhán O'Reilly

In 1932, Willard Waller argued, 'The fact seems to be that parents and teachers are natural enemies, predestined each for the discomfiture of the other. The chasm is frequently covered over, for neither parents nor teachers wish to admit to themselves the uncomfortable implications of their animosity, but on occasion it can make itself clear enough'.[1] There is no question nor doubt about the benefit to the child and their learning experience when parents and teachers find effective ways to work together. This has been documented in a range of studies and most recently in the European Commission's Includ-Ed five-year research project.[2] However, despite legislative frameworks and a policy commitment at national level to home–school partnership, it can be argued that this is one of the more challenging elements of the teacher's role.

Eighty years on from Waller's assertion about teachers and parents being 'natural enemies', there has undoubtedly been progress in the acknowledgement of the importance and value of the home–school partnership. In Ireland, it seems that we promote teacher and parent as 'natural collaborators'; however, we don't really talk about how best this can be achieved or what are some of the challenges inherent in this important collaboration for the child. We can however see the progress since Waller's time through the policy commitments to parental involvement in terms of the statutory status given to it and the development of formal structures to facilitate representation both at the level of school policy development and at school governance level.

This chapter outlines the why, who, what and how of parental involvement in schools with an emphasis on 'caring' within that. It identifies the importance of thinking about why schools should proactively encourage parental involvement, who should be part of the team facilitating the involvement, what parental involvement is and how it can be delivered effectively.

The Why?
It appears that a main motivator for schools to involve parents in their work is that legislation and policy tells them to. Schools are also evaluated on parental involvement under Whole School Evaluation

inspections. So what does Irish legislation and national policy say about parental involvement in schools?

First, the role of parents in the education of the child is supported by the Constitution. In the 1937 Constitution, parents are acknowledged as the primary educators of their children:

> The state acknowledges that the primary and natural educator of the child is the Family and guarantees to respect the inalienable right and duty of parents to provide, according to their means, for the religious and moral, intellectual, physical and social education of their children. (Article 42.1)

We do however need some discussion and debate regarding a clarification of the meaning of the word 'primary' in this context. Does 'primary' mean first or most important? There are obviously implications for the role of the parent in the education process of their child depending on how we interpret 'primary'.

Historically neither the Church nor the state made purposeful or systematic efforts during the 1940s and 1950s to involve parents in policy-making, consultation or the administration of schools.[3] It was not until the 1960s that the public interest increased in relation to education and there was more scope for stakeholder groups, e.g. teachers, parents and students, to express their individual opinions. In 1975 the governance structures of schools were changed with boards of management, including teachers and parents working alongside the patron's nominees, being established for the first time. Parents associations and councils have been the main formal structure for parental involvement, with the National Parents Council being established in 1985 as a national support structure for local associations and councils.

The White Paper on Education, 'Charting Our Education Future 1995', which formed the basis for the Education Act of 1998, emphasised the partnership element of the educational process. It identified the learner at the centre of this process with parents, teachers, patrons, local community and the state as the partners in learner's education. The acknowledgement of the parent role brings both rights and responsibilities, i.e. the right as an individual to be consulted and informed on all aspects of the child's education and as a group to be active participants in the education system at a school, regional and national level. It also brings the responsibility to nurture a learning environment, cooperate with and support the school and other educational partners and fulfil their special role in the development of the child.[4]

Statutory recognition was given to parents associations/councils in the Education Act in 1998.[5] At a local level, parents were given the right to establish parents associations. According to the act, the role of these parents associations would be to 'advise the Principal or the Board on any matter relating to the school' and to 'adopt a programme of activities which will promote the involvement of parents, in consultation with the Principal, in the operation of the school'. The Education Act (1998) also identifies that schools are to involve parents in school planning and that all parents are to be given a copy of the school plan. Parental representation on school boards of management was consolidated in the act and boards were given the responsibility of developing procedures about informing parents regarding their child's education.

The Education Act (1998) was intended to foster home–school links by improving the information flow to parents regarding their child's progress specifically and school policy generally. This was following the White Paper's (1995) emphasis on the importance of the development of dynamic and supportive links between home and school.

Following a review by the Department of Education and Skills of its national programmes addressing educational disadvantage, an action plan for social inclusion, DEIS (Delivering Equality of Opportunity in Schools), was published in 2005.[6] DEIS is now the framework for all programmes historically aimed at addressing disadvantage and promotes a more integrated approach to the issue of educational inclusion. DEIS has identified that 'a renewed emphasis will be placed on the involvement of parents and families in children's education'.

In Ireland, in areas designated as disadvantaged[7] and categorised then as DEIS schools, a specific role of Home School Community Liaison (HSCL) co-ordinator is resourced to target and develop relationships between parents and the school. The purpose of the scheme is to increase cooperation between school, parents and community organisations in the education of children and young people. The scheme focuses on home visiting, running courses for parents and the development of a local committee to include all stakeholders. This HSCL co-ordinator is a teacher from the school and is based in the school. As of 2009, 340 primary school and 203 post-primary schools were involved in the scheme.

It is worth noting some of the findings in relation to the evaluations of the HSCL scheme. Ryan[8] identified that while the brief was to include liaison with teachers and community organisations, an examination of the actual workload identified that two thirds of the

HSCL co-ordinator's time was spent on direct work with parents. This involved parental attendance at courses, e.g. child's education related course, personal development, parenting and home management. Ryan identified that the scheme had built-in evaluation mechanisms from its initiation which did indicate some positive impact. The HSCL co-ordinators and teachers did identify improved personal development among parents with a higher involvement in schools. Impact at primary level was stronger than at post-primary. However, the programme's positive effects were generally with parents who were actively involved in activities and were those parents who, from the teachers' perspective, were in least need of the scheme. A survey with uninvolved mothers indicated that they experienced greater socio-economic disadvantage (coming from unemployed households, were single parents or had a lot of children) than those who were participating in the scheme. One of the main aims of the scheme was to counter educational disadvantage among the children by involving their parents in school life. Ryan's report indicates that co-ordinators saw positive effects on some pupils, e.g. attendance, behaviour and positive attitudes to school; however, few teachers identified any immediate effects.

Other policy initiatives and strategy documents addressing the area of parental involvement include the DES statement of Strategy 2005–2007, which emphasises the promotion of partnership in policy development at both national and local level and the importance of information flow to parents, as well as referring to the role of parents as partners and/or consumers of education; while the NCCA has identified the importance of forging strong links between schools, parents and teachers to enable as successful an education as possible for the child.

The on-going and increasing commitment in Ireland to identifying the importance of parental involvement in schools is clear from a policy perspective. Other countries differ in the extent to which parents are regarded as partners in the education process rather than external to the school system.[9] Therefore the opportunities for formal parental involvement in education vary across countries. In the US the majority of states in the country have enacted laws calling for family engagement policies in schools. However, there is variety in relation to the substance of these laws. Most states seek to encourage family engagement through legislation emphasising public school policy. Similarly in the UK, government policy promotes the importance of parental involvement in a child's education and schooling, with proposed benefits for pupils, teachers, schools and parents.

From an educator's perspective, perhaps the more important and convincing rationale for us to talk about, strategise about, promote and facilitate parental involvement is that research has demonstrated time and time again that when parents are involved and have a positive orientation towards their child's school, children's experiences of learning and their learning outcomes are better. As teachers it is therefore inherent in our role as educators to facilitate and ensure that this involvement occurs. As teachers however, it may not always be obvious how this can be achieved, particularly in curriculum-filled days or with parents who appear disinterested or may in our view appear to be somewhat lacking in capacity.

The Who?
Schools obviously work with as wide a range of parents as those groups represented in Irish society. This calls for teachers and schools to adapt their strategies of working with parents based on the needs of the different parental groupings. The groupings' needs can be different, and again research has shown that it is when schools make conscious and proactive efforts to reach out to parents that the most effective partnerships can be established. In my research on parental involvement in schools, it was evident that there can be various reasons why parents find it daunting and/or difficult to enact their right to be involved in schools. These reasons range from socio-economic or cultural issues to being uninformed about their rights, responsibilities and the benefits to their child being involved. For example, with some parents having had less than positive experiences at school and perhaps being early school leavers, they do not possess the 'cultural capital' to inherently know how they can be involved, how to navigate the system or how best to support their child through the formal education process. In terms of the multi-cultural society Ireland has become, there are some cultures where the role of the professional is viewed as something not to be interfered with and where the parents have not experienced their role being emphasised and a partnership sought. I would argue that schools need to be proactive with *all* parents so that they know they are welcomed and invited to be involved. I would also argue that in cases where there is a lack of involvement that the school, based on the needs of the parents, develop effective outreach strategies to engage the parent. Joyce Epstein's research demonstrates that this works. The motivation for this for the school, given their very busy curriculum agenda, is that it is undoubtedly in the best interest of the child and how they will experience and 'perform' in the education system. I propose that it is part of a teacher's role to

work collaboratively with the school staff team to design strategies to facilitate interest, to ignite passion and to reach out to those parents who for an array of reasons may appear to educators as disinterested or as if they may not value education. In twelve years working in areas of designated disadvantage, while parental behaviour could be interpreted in this way, all of the parents with whom I have worked have wanted a positive school experience and a positive educational outcome for their child. They may not always know how best to make that happen, and if difficulties begin to emerge the school and its staff can either play a pivotal role in facilitating and resolving matters, or their approach can further alienate and lead to more disengagement. This view is also advocated by Annemiek Veen when she, in discussing parent–teacher communication, identifies that 'school as the professional partners is the initiator in this. Schools must demonstrate supportive behaviour towards parents so that parents behave in an educationally supportive way towards the school'.[10]

Teachers in schools and the school leadership need to work together to facilitate effective and positive parental involvement. The National Parents Council (NPC) can offer support and training to schools for those that have an affiliated parents association. Other community organisations and services may also be able to support teachers and school leaders with engaging parents. In identifying a strategy and an implementation plan around parental involvement, key partners can be identified, e.g. parents, teachers, principal, HSCL, family resource centre, local addiction service, community development project, NPC.

The What?

So what is 'parental involvement'? Studies have varied in their focus on their definitions of the term from 'helping with homework', 'helping around the school' to 'representation on formal decision making structures' to 'emotional support with challenges in the learning environment'.

Joyce Epstein has spent twenty-five years researching the area of parental involvement in the United States. She identified that when thinking about parents and schools, we need to think about the three contexts that influence the child's learning and encourages us to think about what she calls the 'overlapping spheres of influence'

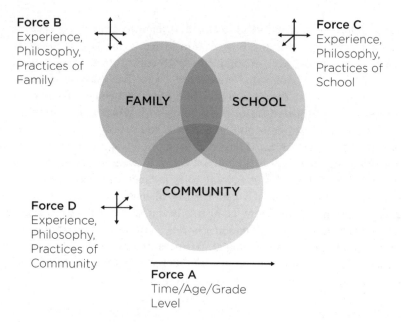

Epstein's overlapping spheres of influence

Here is the idea of the school viewing the learner as child and not merely student in school and then of the family viewing the child as student as well as child in the family and all the time operating in overlapping spheres of influence, i.e. family, school and community. The identification of the other factors at play within, outside of and between those spheres of influence having an input to the actual influence, e.g. experience, philosophy, practices, age of child, time etc., emphasises and reiterates the importance and the potential of recognising the connectedness (and potential points of tension) of the social structures surrounding a child's learning. It also identifies that as the child gets older, less interaction occurs.

There is no one clear definition of parental involvement despite a legislative and policy commitment to it and structures for 'representation' to occur. Despite the formal structures that exist to secure parental involvement, studies in this area have demonstrated that the existence of formal structures for parental involvement does not in itself ensure a 'voice', since many parents feel their involvement is limited to practical rather than policy issues.[11] It has proved challenging in Ireland for parental involvement to meaningfully move 'beyond the tea-making'. This also appears to be the case at European level.

Parents can be informally involved in their child's education through supporting their learning, helping with homework and study, advising on educational choices and providing general encouragement in relation to school and regarding educational choices post-compulsory participation.[12] Interestingly, while the formal involvement of parents is more 'visible', research has indicated that informal involvement has a greater influence on children's outcomes.[13] Some studies have identified the 'affective' support element to this informal involvement. Both O'Hara[14] and O'Brien[15] discuss the 'emotional labour' for parents involved in supporting their child's learning. This informal support, while ensuring positive outcomes for the child's learning, may not facilitate parental 'voice' at school level.

Epstein's research-based 'Framework of Parental Involvement' is really useful to help us think about how parents can be involved. It clearly identifies six types of parental involvement.

Type 1	Parenting
Type 2	Communicating
Type 3	Volunteering
Type 4	Learning at home
Type 5	Decision making
Type 6	Collaborating with the community

Epstein's framework of six types of parental involvement
Epstein has also identified challenges and redefinitions from traditional practice for all six of these areas based on her research, e.g. under the Communicating strand, this is not just a one-way stream of school to parent but a two-way and sometimes maybe even a three-way stream of dialogue and feedback between parent, school and community. This is described further below under the 'how' of parental involvement.

As part of the application of her research, Epstein worked with schools, and a number of synonyms for 'caring' emerged as matching the six types of involvement. Underlying all six types of involvement are two defining synonyms of caring: trusting and respecting.

Type 1	Parenting	Supporting, nurturing and child-rearing
Type 2	Communicating	Relating, reviewing and overseeing
Type 3	Volunteering	Supervising and fostering
Type 4	Learning at home	Managing, recognising and rewarding
Type 5	Decision making	Contributing, considering and judging
Type 6	Collaborating with the community	Sharing and giving

One school actually named its partnership programme the 'I Care Programme'. It developed an 'I Care Parent Club' that promoted support and leadership of families, and the 'I Care Newsletter' and many other events and activities. The commitment to the caring element of parental involvement is paramount in terms of the 'intent' with which it is approached at school level. If all six type of parental involvement are operating well in a school's programme of partnership, then all these caring behaviours could be activated to assist children's learning and development. If the partnership is not operating as well as it could, the commitment to 'caring' could be the motivator and guide in terms of reviewing practices to getting things back on track.

In her work Epstein[16] talks about schools having choices in terms of the approach they take in involving parents in schools and in their children's education. One emphasises difficulties and conflict and views the school as a battleground. In this kind of environment the conditions and relationships guarantee power struggles and disharmony. The other approach emphasises partnership and views the school as a 'homeland'. The conditions and relationships in this kind of environment invite power-sharing and mutual respect, and facilitate energy to be directed towards activities that promote student learning and development. Even when tension and conflict emerge, the partners are motivated to work through this to restore harmony and an environment for development to thrive.

Epstein and Sheldon[17] identified a set of principles to help researchers in building on Epstein's vast research on parental involvement. One of these principles was that 'school, family and community partnership' is a better term than 'parental involvement'. However, given the Irish context and framework and the lack of research in this area in Ireland, it appears that to retain the term 'parental involvement' is currently more appropriate.

The How?
There are two elements to the 'how' of parental involvement. One relates to the very practical things and is connected to the 'what' we actually do, the other relates to our values and philosophy in committing to a programme of parental involvement. In thinking about the 'how', I think it is important that we connect to the 'why' and the intention with which we approach it. This will dictate whether as schools we take the 'adversarial' or 'collegial' approaches as described by Epstein. It will also influence what we count as success. Currently one of the indicators in Ireland is an operating parents association. In 'ticking this box', schools may have a group of four to five parents meeting and 'helping out' in activities for the school. This is a

success in the context of the intention encouraged under Whole School Evaluation. It might however be very school-led with a very small group of parents and may never involve outreach work with those who do not feel they are in a position to contribute and participate.

Schools and parents need to collectively identify values and principles that will underpin and inform their work with each other. These could explore and discuss things like 'respect', 'being inclusive', 'power-sharing', 'communication styles' etc. With this solid foundation established, the partnership can then move on to using some of the research-based strategies, e.g. Epstein's work on the practical plan of how parental involvement will be addressed in the school and link it to the 'what'. A school may decide to focus on types 2 and 5 for one year for example, or they may decide to dip their foot into each type.

From my own research, communication within the school is really important in terms of highlighting how the school is approaching involving parents, what is happening and how things are going. To include parental involvement as an item on the staff meeting agenda would facilitate some organisational thinking and awareness also. Teachers may be reliant on the school leadership to suggest these types of things. I would encourage teaching staff to propose parental involvement as an agenda item in order for it to become part of the architecture of the school. However, this needs to be part of an overall plan identifying clear actions and outcomes at learner, parent and teacher level.

The 'overlapping spheres of influence' and the 'six types of parental involvement' have both been informed by Epstein's research work in the area of parental involvement over twenty-five years. Having applied these models over a five-year period, Epstein subsequently identified through data collected that progress on partnerships is more likely when there are eight essential elements:

1. Strong leadership
2. Good teamwork
3. Annual written plans
4. Well-implemented activities
5. Adequate funding
6. Thoughtful evaluations
7. Strong collegial support
8. Continuous planning for improvement.

Epstein et al.[18] have provided redefinitions of the areas of involvement to facilitate successful design and implementation of the six types of involvement, e.g. Type 4, Learning at Home, 'Homework', to mean not only work done alone but also interactive activities shared with others at home or in the community, linking schoolwork to real life. 'Help' at home, to mean encouraging, listening, reacting, praising, guiding, monitoring and discussing – not 'teaching' school subjects. This last one is very important in ensuring that the boundaries of the professional educator and the role of the parent support effective partnership.

As I mentioned earlier, Epstein's research clearly demonstrates that the most successful parental involvement occurs when schools plan and make concerted efforts to engage with parents. Tett identifies that if parents, particularly those from disadvantaged communities, are to fully participate in the educational process, 'some of the control that professionals have imposed on schooling for so long will have to be released and parents would need to be regarded as people with important contributions to make as collaborating educational partners.'[19] This is really important in terms of the 'how'. Schools need to be open to learning about and from the parents and communities they are working in as well as bringing all of their professional knowledge about pedagogy and curriculum. Learning in this context is a two-way thing – the teachers bring their professional expertise and knowledge and the parents bring their experience and knowledge of the child and the surrounding community.

The Irish policy context would suggest that there is already a statutory recognition and support for a framework like Epstein's to be adapted for the Irish context. However, there is no comprehensive formal element in teacher education that informs and supports schools, school leadership and teachers around developing and engaging with parental involvement strategies. The NPC have been exploring Epstein's work and have used it to adapt some of their training.

A sample of Epstein's work below maps out a 'how' in terms of Type 2, Communication. She identifies sample practices, challenges, a redefinition of communication and corresponding caring synonyms.

Epstein's Type 2 Involvement: Communication

Type 2 Involvement – Communication: definition and challenges

Parental Involvement: Type 2 Communicating	Design effective forms of school to home and home to school communications about school programmes and their children's progress
Sample practices	» Conferences with every parent at least once a year with follow-ups as needed » Language translators assist families as needed

Sample practices contd.	» Weekly or monthly folders of student work sent home for review and comments » Parent–student pick-up of report cards with conferences on improving grades » Regular schedule of useful notices, memos, phone calls, newsletters and other communications » Clear information on choosing schools or courses, programmes and activities within schools » Clear information on all school policies, programmes, reforms and transitions
Challenges	» Review the readability, clarity, form and frequency of all memos, notices and other print and non-print communications » Consider parents who do not speak English well, do not read well or need large type » Review the quality of major communications (e.g. the schedule, content and the structure of conferences; newsletters; report cards and others) » Establish clear two-way channels for communications from home to school and school to home
Redefinitions	'Communications about school programmes and student progress' to mean *two-way, three-way and many-way channels of communications* that connect schools, families, students and the community

Emphasis in implementation on 'caring' synonyms	Communicating: *relating, reviewing, overseeing*
Underlying all six types of involvement are two defining synonyms of caring: *trust and respecting*	

In the Irish context there are some questions that schools could pose and consider in establishing the 'how' of parental involvement:

1. Why are we committing to a parental involvement programme?
   Underlying values and beliefs in approaching this:
   Being honest and open about our motivation – is it really just about that WSE tick box? If it is, are we open to challenging ourselves as a staff team on that and exploring the benefits of parental involvement for the children, the school community and the wider community?

2. What are we going to focus on for this academic year?
   Potentially using Epstein's framework, work through different elements.

3. Who is involved?
   Identify strategic national level/community level partners, school staff, parents and their roles.
   How are we reaching out to those that feel they can't be involved/feel like they don't want to be involved? Who has the skill set to do that?

4. What do we hope we will achieve for students, parents and teachers by the end of the academic year?
   Outcomes, progress, movement demonstrated:
   These should be 'inclusive' in their focus, identifying progress through outreach strategies alongside achievements of the PA or a joint parent/staff sub-committee.

5. What are the structures that will help us have these conversations throughout the year?

Agendas at parents association, school staff meeting: what is the link between the two, so conversations can be joined up?
Boards of management: what is their role and what is the communication structure?

6. Who will write this up into a plan so that we can be clear about our intention and review/monitor our progress?
   Is it possible for a subcommittee of the PA and the staff meeting to work on this?
   Can it be presented at PA, staff meeting and BOM?
   When will we review what happened, what worked well, what we could improve?
   How will we use the learning for planning for next year?

Conclusion

While there is a solid and firm commitment to 'parental involvement' at a policy level in Ireland, the UK, at European level and in the United States, the evident gap between policy and practice is proving slow to fill. It is as if we have expected schools, teachers and parents to 'just know' how to work together collaboratively and effectively just because we have identified the positive outcomes of this for the child and identified at a national level that this partnership 'should be' happening. Caring about parental involvement is the first step; caring because the values and principles of our work as educators underpins inviting, accepting, reaching out for, facilitating and supporting parental involvement rather than because policy tells us to or because the school can 'tick that evaluation box'. Parents, schools and teachers can collaboratively create the 'what' of parental involvement through their conversations – some of which could be challenging, but therein lies the potential for change. The 'what', however, will only be effective and meaningful depending on the value base of the 'how'. When thinking about parental involvement, if we are ever to move beyond what could be currently termed 'a silent partnership',[20] we need to remember 'it's not what you do, it's the way that you do it!'

Notes

1. W. Waller, *The Sociology of Teaching* (New York: John Wiley, 1932).
2. European Commission, INCLUDE-ED Strategies for inclusion and social cohesion in Europe from Education, Project 6/WP22: Case analysis of local projects working towards social cohesion, Priority 7: Citizen and Governance

in a knowledge-based society, 2011. http://www.ub.edu/included/docs/4.%20 D.22.3.%20Working%20papers.%20Case%20studies%204th%20round.pdf (accessed 21 July 2014).

3. J. Coolahan, *Irish Education: History and Structure* (Dublin: IPA, 2000).

4. Government of Ireland, *Charting Our Education Future: White Paper on Education* (Dublin: The Stationery Office, 1995).

5. Government of Ireland, Education Act (1998) (Dublin: The Stationery Office, 1998).

6. Department of Education and Science, 'Delivering Equality of Opportunity in Schools: An Action Plan for Educational Inclusion' (Dublin: The Stationery Office, 2005).

7. The definition of educational disadvantage found in the Education Act (Ireland, 1998, 32[9]) is as follows: 'the impediments to education arising from social or economic disadvantage which prevent students from deriving *appropriate* benefit from education in schools.' There are many of us who believe that we should be operating from schemes underpinned by concepts linked to equity and inclusion or that if we must operate from a definition of disadvantage that it at least should be that proposed by Boldt and Devine (1998, 10) which refers to educational disadvantage as the 'limited ability to derive *equitable* benefit from schooling compared to one's peer by age'.

8. S. Ryan, 'Home-School-Community Liaison Scheme: Final Evaluation Report' (Dublin: Educational Research Centre, 1994).

9. OECD, *Parents as Partners in Schooling* (Paris: OECD, 1997).

10. Annemiek Veen, Research on the relationship between migrant parents and primary schools, European Research Network About Parents in Education, 1999.

11. B. Mac Giolla Phádraig, 'An Examination of the Values and Perceptions of Parents and Teachers in Relation to Parental Involvement in School Policy Formulation', *Irish Educational Studies*, 22, 2 (2003), 37–46.

12. C. Desforges, *The Impact of Parental Involvement, Parental Support and Family Education on Pupil Achievements and Adjustment: A Literature Review* (Nottingham: Department for Education and Skills, 2003).

13. A. Harris, and J. Goodall, *Engaging Parents in Raising Achievement: Do Parents Know They Matter?* (London: Department for Children, Schools and Families, 2007).

14. P. O'Hara, *Partners in Production? Women, Farm and Family in Ireland* (Oxford: Berghahn Books, 1998).

15. M. O'Brien, 'Mothers As Educational Workers', *Irish Educational Studies*, 24, 2–3 (2005), 223–42.

16. J. Epstein, M. Sanders, B. Simon, K. Salinas, N. Jansorn and F. Voorhis, *School, Family and Community Partnerships, Your Handbook for Action* (2nd ed.) (California: Corwin Press, 2002).

17. J. Epstein and S. Sheldon, 'Moving Forward: Ideas for Research on School, Family and Community Partnerships' in C. F. Conrad, and R. Serlin (eds), *SAGE Handbook for Research in Education: Engaging Ideas and Enriching Inquiry* (Thousand Oaks, CA: Sage, 2006), 117–38.

18. Epstein et al., *School, Family and Community Partnerships*.

19. L. Tett, 'Parents as Problems or Parents as People? Parental Involvement Programmes, Schools and Adult Educators' in *International Journal of Lifelong Learning*, 20, 3 (2001), 188–98.

20. S. O' Reilly, *The Silent Partners? Leading Parental Involvement in Primary Schools in Areas Experiencing Educational Inequality*, unpublished Doctorate thesis (Dublin: DCU, 2012).

Care of Asylum Seekers and Refugees in Schools

Patrick J. Boyle

Migration is a normal phenomenon that has existed for millennia and is part of human experience. People continue to move within and outside geographical and political frontiers for economic, social, political and religious reasons. Ireland is no stranger to migration and a quick review of our history reveals how migration has contributed to our evolution as a society. More than one Irish chief or prince claimed descent from the pseudo-historical figure of Milesias who had supposedly led his people of Spain to settle in Ireland. Later on, in the eighth century, the Norse seafarers came and settled in our coastal towns, before the Cambro-Norman invasion of the twelfth century, which itself led to the plantation of Ireland by settlers from England and Scotland in the fifteenth and sixteenth centuries. Indeed much has been written and researched by academics, government and international agencies on the affects of migration. Nevertheless what lies behind these lessons, theories, statistics and administration are people's stories and lived experiences. When shared and made known, these stories can help us connect to the 'other' and recognise our common humanity.[1]

In an age of globalisation, the reasons for migrating and the types of migration that occur have acquired a new complexity. Alongside this a tension co-exists, something that is deeper in terms of building relationship with those who we perceive as different. No longer can it be assumed that a *céad míle fáilte* awaits every new immigrant to Ireland.[2][3] Not alone this but many men, women and children continue to risk their lives in search of a better life, freedom and safety. Indeed many man-made barriers such as stricter immigration controls can increase the risks for people, including those who may fall prey to opportunistic criminals involved in people trafficking or other forms of human abuse.[4] Therefore the personal experience of individual migrants for whatever reason can have significant emotional consequences.

In terms of understanding what pastoral care is, Flannagan and Thornton argue that it is characterised by elements of relationship, empowerment and liberation. They go on to argue that the pastoral care experience is transformative and life-giving for both caregiver and recipient.[5] In exploring pastoral care, these authors remind us of the importance of understanding the context of a situation as well as the need to acquire pastoral skills and knowledge so as to be able to offer care that is appropriate and helpful in a variety of situations.[6] Furthermore, I would argue that rather than confining individuals to narrow frameworks of care, the type of pastoral care offered by a professional must be based on the needs of the person being cared for. This sometimes means going beyond a minimalist concept of duty of care and being willing to go the extra mile while remaining within professional standards.

Pope Francis provides an example of this understanding of pastoral care. It is highly significant that in June 2013, as a practical and meaningful gesture of pastoral leadership, Pope Francis on his first visit outside of Rome as pope chose to visit the island of Lampedusa in Italy. This island continues to be the scene of much human suffering. Many thousands of men, women and children have drowned in the area attempting to migrate to Europe in search of a better life. Standing on a platform fashioned from the broken wood of wrecked boats that was found in the surrounding waters and holding a crozier carved from the same wood, Pope Francis simply asked: 'Where are you? Where is your brother?' For those of religious faith and none, the symbolism and meaning of the Pope's visit and his words raised important questions about human solidarity and respect for each other, regardless of race, religion, class or culture. Both questions present us with a challenge to reflect on our approach to those who are immigrants in our midst. Do we see them as neighbours? Do we empathise and show them solidarity? Do we consider their humanity as worthy of care and respect?

This chapter aims to raise awareness and inform school staff about some of the challenges and barriers that many asylum-seeking children may experience. These will be presented mostly in the context of my experience of working closely with families who live in the current system of 'Direct Provision and Dispersal' (DP). It will first explore the general nature of how Ireland's demographics have changed in recent years with particular focus on asylum seeking. Second, it will focus on the concept of interculturalism as an ideal, in working with migrant children and the importance of engaging in this process in caring for asylum-seeking children. With the aid of a case study from my own experience, I will outline some specific issues that asylum-seeking children may experience that can impact their school life and their wider social development and integration.

Asylum Seeking and Migration

For some individuals and families, migration is voluntary, an informed decision made with preparation, hope and ambition for a better life elsewhere. For others, a 'forced' migration occurs in search of long-term safety and security. The origins of such a journey are often the result of circumstances beyond one's control, such as the need to flee conflict, war or persecution in their homeland. Many of the national, European and international laws and instruments that govern immigration, protection and human rights are complex and difficult to understand. For people migrating to seek protection, this can compound anxiety and lead to further despair. The interpretation and implementation of these laws vary from place to place, thus increasing the vulnerability of migrants in the very places they chose to seek assistance and refuge.[7] In general, when we consider the terms migrant/asylum seeker and/or refugee, they often conjure up images and understandings of the adult experience. We tend to forget that children and adolescents find themselves within the migration process. Perhaps this is because in the main, children tend to have little sway in the decisions made by parents or guardians, and in some ways they remain invisible and voiceless. In an effort to support and welcome people as they navigate their way to a better life and future in places that are sometimes unfriendly and hostile towards them, we must reach out and attempt to understand the human experience of migration and its affect on the whole person.[8]

In 2009, the United Nations High Commissioner for Refugees estimated that 44 per cent of the world's refugees and asylum seekers were children below the age of eighteen. Of course most of these children live in the developing world, including regions and areas bordering countries of conflict.[9]

An asylum seeker is a person who seeks to be recognised as a refugee in accordance with the terms of the 1951 United Nations Geneva Convention relating to the status of refugees and the related 1967 Protocol. This provides the framework for the international system of protection of refugees, of which Ireland is a signatory. The definition of a refugee in Irish law is:

> a person owing to a well-founded fear of being persecuted for reasons of race, religion, nationality, membership of a particular social group or political opinion, is outside the country of his or her nationality and is unable or owing to such fear, is unwilling to avail himself or herself of the protection of that country; or who, not having a nationality and being outside the country of his or her habitual residence, is unable, or owing to such fear, is unwilling to return to it ...[10]

In short, an asylum seeker is somebody who has applied for refugee status and whose case will be investigated and adjudicated by the relevant agencies. Contrary to popular misunderstanding, an asylum seeker is a person with a recognised legal status in their own right and not a person who is 'illegally' resident in a country. However, in the main, asylum seekers are afforded little or no citizenship rights. Indeed it is widely understood that asylum seekers as a specific cohort are not considered within official government integration strategies and therefore face further risk of isolation and social exclusion.[11]

In Ireland, in accordance with international and domestic law, the system of the application process for refugee status is administered by two independent authorities: the Office of the Refugee Application Commissioner (ORAC), which considers applications for declaration as a refugee at first instance; and the Refugee Appeals Tribunal (RAT), which considers applications for a declaration at appeal stage. These authorities make recommendations to the Minister for Justice and Equality on whether such status should be granted to a person.

There has been a significant reduction in the number of asylum applications in Ireland, from a peak in 2002 of over 11,000 applications that year. The Report of the Office of Refugee Applications Commissioner indicated that a total number of 956 applications for asylum were made in 2012. This represented a 25 per cent reduction on the 2011 figures, and the lowest annual total since 1996. It is impossible to explore the factors for such reductions within the scope of this chapter, however some may pertain to changes in Irish domestic law, European Union laws, the impact of the global economic recession, tighter European Union (EU) border controls, and mechanisms for resettlement and repatriation. According to the Reception and Integration Agency (RIA), the top five countries of origin for application for declaration as a refugee in 2013 were Nigeria, Pakistan, Democratic Republic of Congo, Zimbabwe and Malawi. Conversely, as people who require protection must be able to access it, statistics that demonstrate a reduction in numbers seeking asylum can be a cause for concern and requires careful critical observation and interpretation. It is fair to say that statistics alone are a poor indicator of the reality and needs of some asylum seekers and the subsequent response required from services. Although actual numbers are comparably lower in recent years, our specific work in community health and social care demonstrate an increased level of complexity and need in terms of health and social care supports of newly arrived asylum seekers.[12]

The most recent population census of 2011 has demonstrated that a significant percentage of non-Irish nationals live and make their lives in Ireland.[13] This demographic change has resulted in opportunities for a richer experience and understanding of ethnic, religious and cultural diversity in schools in Ireland. As schools in Ireland can be envisaged as microcosms of wider Irish society, new multicultural experiences, interactions and relationships are evolving and developing on a continuous basis in schools. Consequently staff in the Irish education sector are in a unique position to influence positive intercultural social change and provide education in a caring environment.

Direct Provision System
As mentioned briefly, asylum seekers are mostly accommodated in a system called Direct Provision (DP). The RIA, a unit within the Department of Justice and Equality, oversees the running and standards of this system. Up to March 2013, almost 5,000 people were living in the DP system. It comprises thirty-five residential centres spread throughout sixteen counties in the Republic of Ireland. The accommodation centres vary in size and type, ranging from guest houses to trailer sites, former hotels, colleges or nursing homes. Some centres accommodate large amounts of people; for example, Mosney Centre in Co. Meath has a capacity for over 600 residents, while smaller centres are accommodating up to thirty people. The RIA allocates centres as either family, single-male or single-female accommodation centres.

Although certain basic needs and a limited amount of safety and security are available to people living in the direct provision system, the negative affects of living in such an institutional environment over long periods of time can become barriers to integration.[14] For example, if people are prohibited access to full-time work, full-time education, freedom of movement or family reunification, this can increase vulnerability in many different aspects of their lives. Over many years I have observed people living within the DP system for long periods of time becoming increasingly demoralised and disempowered. What can begin as a material poverty for some people within the system, can become a poverty of spirit, hope and will. Children and adolescents living with parents and guardians in this system are not immune to these effects.[15]

As DP was established with no specific legislative authority or foundation, it has drawn significant attention and been under much scrutiny by social research and human rights advocates, as well as the media, since its inception. To date some residents and many campaigners have questioned its legal foundation, claiming it contributes towards the violation of people's human rights. Indeed it has been argued that DP lacks transparency and fairness and is exacerbating social exclusion of asylum seekers as asylum seekers are not included as a target group in official government anti-poverty and social inclusion strategies. As a point of interest at time of writing, the legality of the direct provision system is being challenged through the Irish High Court (April 2014).

Multiculturalism and Interculturalism

The concepts of multiculturalism and interculturalism have come to the fore in social and political debate in recent times in Ireland. I will now offer a brief explanation on the subtle but important difference that exists between the two as I understand it. Multiculturalism in itself is minimalist in its conceptualisation of different cultures as it only acknowledges the existence of many cultures. Consequently in discussing issues in relation to cultural diversity, the concept of interculturalism is more appropriate and has replaced the concept of multiculturalism in cultural diversity discourse in Ireland.[16] Interculturalism is a concept that calls for more than tolerance of difference. It recognises the acceptance not only of the principles of equality of rights, values and abilities but also a development of policies to promote interaction, collaboration and exchange with people of different cultures, ethnicity or religious beliefs.

The Education Act (1998) and the Education (Welfare) Act (2000) recognise the state's responsibility in promoting the overall development of the pupil. This includes the spiritual and cultural dimension of education. Furthermore, Ireland's obligations under the UN Convention on the Rights of the Child (1992) emphasise that education should be directed to the development of respect for children's cultural identity, language and values. The National Council for Curriculum and Assessment (NCCA) has outlined specific guidelines for addressing interculturalism in the primary and secondary educational systems.[17][18] It is disappointing that as a consequence of the economic recession and a lack of political commitment, the necessary level of resources for the implementation of such guidelines has been inadequate to date.[19] However, the aforementioned legislation and guidelines provide a strong legal and moral framework for an ethos of interculturalism to develop and in which to promote social integration.

Asylum-Seeker Children in School

As this section will focus on asylum seekers and the school environment, it is of interest to note that children (ages 0–17 years) accounted for 37.5 per cent (1,666 children) of the asylum-seeking population in direct provision in Ireland in December 2013. Of that cohort, 59 per cent (980 children) were of school-going age (5–17 years). Therefore it is fair to assume that many schools, both primary and post-primary, around Ireland are involved in educating children who live in direct provision accommodation. This is not to say that only pupils of ethnically diverse backgrounds in Irish schools are predominately refugees or asylum seekers.

Historically there has been cultural and ethnic diversity in the school population of Ireland for many decades. In addition to the experience of Irish Travellers, Ireland continues to work towards meeting our international humanitarian legal obligations in association with United Nations High Commissioner for Refugees (UNHCR) by resettling families in need of protection. A significant component of this permanent resettlement programme is access to education for these children. To date Ireland has facilitated the resettlement of programme refugees from Hungary in 1956, Vietnam in 1979, Bosnia in 1992 and in more recent years from Myanmar, Somalia, Iraq and Afghanistan. Following on from these early resettlement programmes, as well as the later wave of migrants and asylum seekers who came from the mid-1990s onwards, it is important to remember that many children and adolescents in Irish schools may now self-identify as first and second generation Black Irish, Asian Irish or of other mixed ethnicity. Therefore the intercultural experiences for staff and pupils are now intergenerational, a phenomenon not experienced in Ireland in any large detail until now.

This social shift within the Irish school sector requires particular attention in helping to build a positive intercultural society where the experiences of identity for pupils can be negotiated and constructed safely. In addition, this demographic change provides many opportunities for teachers, chaplains and pastoral care workers to address social justice issues in a safe and informed way. Global issues that impact locally on school life such as migration, human rights, asylum seeking, can be addressed competently based on experiential and empathetic approaches that students and staff can identify with. However, apart from personal and professional commitment by staff, what is also required is a commitment by government and school management to resource all disciplines within schools to tackle and engage with these important issues.[20]

From my own experience of working with asylum-seeking families in community care, I continue to witness the significant value placed by parents on their children's education. However, I have also observed the negative social and sometimes emotional affects experienced by parents (mostly mothers) when sending their children to school from asylum accommodation centres. These issues ordinarily relate to barriers associated with parenting and opportunities for participation in the full school life of their children while living in DP accommodation, an environment which is not a normal family environment nor suitable in the long term for raising children.[21] These issues are also felt by their children, although they may not manifest their anxieties and concerns overtly in school. For some children and adolescents, these may impact on their personal development, their school life and their relationships with peers, staff and others. Such experiences ideally require professional pastoral care interventions by informed, interested and experienced staff. Examples of these types of issues will be outlined in more detail later.

Few would doubt the stresses associated with migration, and research demonstrates negative effects of ethnicity and culture shock on health and well-being.[22] Acculturation – the process of adjusting to a new culture, often reluctantly adapting and adopting aspects of it in order to fit in and survive – can be altogether more demanding and damaging both psychologically and physically to young people in school.[23] For asylum-seeking children and adolescents, this process can be further compounded, as in addition to living in direct provision they also have to contend with adjustment to peer groups and school life in new and unfamiliar surroundings. However, it must also be acknowledged that it is of equal importance to understand and utilise their resilience and motivation in safe and sensitive ways, in achieving positive relationships and successful integration where possible in schools.[24]

Despite the existence of domestic and international laws and other conventions, such as the United Nations Convention on the Rights of the Child (1989), children continue to arrive in Ireland that have embarked on journeys that are sometimes life-threatening. Of note and more worryingly is that some children arrive alone, thus increasing their vulnerability.[25] Although difficult to accept and comprehend, some migrant children, child asylum seekers and refugees continue to face uncertain levels of protection and attainment of rights.[26]

In a recent research study in Irish schools, although pastoral care is not explicitly named but indeed implied, the study concludes that by taking into account a broader understanding of how schools, teachers and children all play active roles in articulating discourses of engagement, empathy and equality, outcomes can be more fruitful.[27] When working with migrant children in schools to create space where people feel valued, respected and more importantly safe and secure, a core component of this process must be the application of pastoral care.

Awareness and Observation: Children in School

The importance of access and participation in schools for the children of asylum seekers and refugees cannot be understated. Through attending schools, meeting staff, parents, other pupils and community members, children can be helped to 'normalise' their lives after the trauma and bereavement experienced by leaving their homelands. For many newly arrived asylum seekers today, the provision of education continues to be a vital element in enabling their families to integrate into society. However, school staff may not always be familiar with the everyday living environments and circumstances experienced by asylum-seeking children. I will attempt to outline some basic issues that may face children and school staff which will almost inevitably require a pastoral response.

Some asylum-seeking children may manifest behaviour and signs of anxiety or disharmony in school as a consequence of their pre-departure experience in their country of origin or a transit country, or their asylum-seeking experience in Ireland. For example, if coming from a tense conflict area or war zone, I have observed children fearful of the sound of air traffic overhead, knocking on the door of their rooms, fear of darkness, fear of strange adults/others, or fear of being separated momentarily from their parents. While issues such as separation anxiety and adjustment are not unique to asylum-seeking or refugee children, they do warrant particular sensitivity and understanding in the context of their reasons for fleeing persecution.

Although asylum-seeking children can avail of primary and post-primary education and are encouraged to do so by the authorities, at times the transient nature of the asylum process may cause interruption and delays in their education. In addition I have worked with some parents whose children demonstrate a fleeting regression in certain behaviours due to disruption and the transient nature of their lives as asylum seekers. Younger children, for example, may regress to bed wetting, poor eating and diet, emotional outbursts or poor sleeping patterns, due to communal-type living and disruption, factors that school staff may not ordinarily consider when working with asylum-seeking children. While these issues are not unique to asylum-seeking children, they should be dealt with sensitively. Solutions ought to be informed by an understanding of the specific migration circumstances experienced by the parents.

For older children the stress of acculturation can result in fear, lack of confidence or withdrawal from collective activities within the school or in extra-curricular activities. Other factors should also be considered by school staff such as low income. Asylum seekers (adults) receive 19.10 per week per adult and 9.00 per child, and are not entitled to other statutory social protection payments. It is clear that this payment, in place since 2002 with no legal recourse to review, falls far below the poverty threshold. Therefore poverty can be a significant barrier to integration and socialisation for asylum-seeking families and also affects full participation in school activities. I have observed that some older children and adolescents are embarrassed about living in DP. It impedes normal peer activities for them such as having friends visit for normal family and interaction activities. It also results in social isolation when school activities require payment, or can lead to a perceived stigma felt by children and parents that can be inadvertently exacerbated by simple experiences such as a school assignment.

Case study

Claude (not his real name), a sixteen-year-old boy from a West African country, came to the health centre for his voluntary health assessment three days after his arrival in Ireland. On meeting Claude, his demeanour displayed a shyness and politeness that could also be interpreted as a slight anxiety. Claude was travelling alone, having left those remaining of his family at home in his country. A family friend had arranged for him to escape from the appalling circumstances in which he and his family were living. He had witnessed the murder of some of his family and neighbours as a consequence of the ethnic conflict in his country. The oldest boy in his family, Claude was doing well in second-level school prior to the start of the conflict in his homeland and had ambitions similar to any child of his age. He was told that he was going to another country and that he had no choice in this. Claude had no idea where that country would be and he had been very frightened. However, he explained to me that, like many of those who seek asylum in Ireland, he had a strong Christian faith and that this faith would see him through. He stated that he was already grateful to God that he had arrived safely and had this opportunity to seek refuge. On arrival in Ireland Claude was initially placed in adult accommodation. Following intervention Claude was later accommodated in a facility more appropriate for his age, as a separated or unaccompanied minor as defined by the UNHCR. He was now happier to be living with peers of his own age. He was also happy to have sourced a school and resumed education. In addition, he was further motivated to make contact with other supports such as church, choir, homework club etc.

About twelve months later, Claude came to visit the health clinic again. During this visit he explained how he was getting on in Ireland. Claude stated that although he was attending school over the past year and that he felt supported to some degree by staff members, he still felt lonely. He found it difficult to make friends. He was more conscious of his 'colour' than ever before in his life and felt that it was a barrier to his forming relationships with other pupils. His loneliness he attributed to a number of reasons. First, he was alone. He had no family in Ireland. He had left all he had known at home. He had experienced the loss of his family, friends, community, his language and his way of life. He stated he had no close, 'wise' adult figure to guide him. Simple everyday things like food, music, communication and weather became factors that began to get him down. He stated he was feeling increasingly sad. Other issues that were more serious like the lack of privacy in his accommodation, uncertainty with his refugee status and other normal adolescent peer pressure issues, became major obstacles for Claude. He stated he was doing his best to be a good person but was experiencing a range of difficulties that included thinking about his people back home, grappling with pressure from peers about dating, smoking and drinking alcohol and, more seriously, his not knowing if his future in Ireland would be secure. Claude has been waiting over two years for a decision on his refugee status and he remains apprehensive. In the past few weeks Claude had stopped attending school and his church choir – something he had previously been proud of and enjoyed very much. It was all too much for Claude and he decided to opt out for a while.

Pastoral Care Response to Social and Personal Needs of Asylum-Seeking Pupils

This case study clearly illustrates how asylum-seeking children and/ or children of ethnic minority in a new country can experience difficulties due to the challenges posed by the acculturation process and asylum procedures. However, it is worth bearing in mind that the experiences of social exclusion by asylum-seeking children and families in Ireland are to a considerable extent akin to those of many children from indigenous communities in a number of respects. What is unique to the emerging problems for asylum-seeking children is the fact that they are more likely to experience poverty and social exclusion than other groups in Irish society. This is due to a higher dependence on a non-statutory payment (direct provision allowance) which is not subject to review or change by government and higher levels of housing deprivation. It would appear that policies currently in existence for asylum seekers such as the direct provision of food and accommodation appear to be exacerbating this problem. Claude's need for privacy and personal space in his hostel was causing him great anguish, so much so that his attendance and overall motivation for school and other social activities was affected. However, the likelihood of Claude finding an alternative type of accommodation is very small primarily due to the inflexibility of such policies. There is a need for school staff to be aware of the external factors that affect children like Claude and to familiarise themselves with current statutory policies that impact on pupils in this predicament. I would suggest that further to this, some school staff are in a unique position to be able to advocate on behalf of pupils like Claude who in many ways find themselves voiceless and under-represented. Claude felt powerless and consequently excluded from many decisions about important aspects of his life.

Furthermore, it is clear that Claude needed to talk and be listened to. His situation is indeed different when compared to that of a pupil who after the school day shares the support of family and friends and all that is familiar to them (i.e. their culture). The lack of this type of support adds to the stress experienced by Claude. Claude had the added complication of being alone and trying to 'go it alone' in a strange country and culture. Adolescence in normal circumstances is a time of separation and individuation; for asylum-seeking and refugee children, further separations, losses and grief lie at the core of their experience. While a large percentage of asylum seekers will have experienced loss through bereavement, a significant proportion will have experienced loss due to other reasons. Such reasons may include the leaving behind of family members and friends, home, belongings, roles, lifestyles and to a large extent their culture. In this case, Claude identified some of these issues as the cause of his current difficulties. Likewise, many of the reports mentioned already acknowledge similar experiences and elaborate on how additional factors such as fear, financial constraints and the practical difficulties of making contact with family for some young asylum seekers compounded their feelings of loss and social exclusion. For some young asylum seekers, the manifestation of post-migratory symptoms (insomnia, headaches, abdominal pain, feelings of fear, loneliness, confusion and poor concentration) is commonplace. It is likely that a child may present with one or more of these symptoms in school. Consequently school staff need to familiarise themselves with the issues that confront asylum-seeking children in schools and be alert to those who may require intervention and special care. The National Health Strategy acknowledges the contribution of educational services to the health and social well-being of all citizens. In keeping with such recommendations, some school staff may need to develop professional working relationships with local community care staff such as social workers, community/public health nurses, GPs and psychologists.

Claude also identified that he found it somewhat difficult to make friends and made a passing but significant reference to his colour. Schools need to be alert to the possible barriers that these children may encounter in their daily lives both in school and in the wider community e.g. bullying due to racism. As school is central to the child's asylum-seeking experience, there is an onus of responsibility on the school to steer away from traditional assimilatory trends and develop more inclusive intercultural models by developing partnerships with key members of ethnic minority community groups. In addition, where anti-bullying policies exist they should be explicit in their approach to combating racism and other forms of discrimination such as homophobia.

From Claude's case we are aware that the normal adolescent concept of exploring 'identity' is proving problematic due to the many extra stresses experienced by asylum-seeking children. Claude is grappling with normal peer pressure issues and is uncertain of how to respond. While most adolescents grapple with this concept, children of ethnic minority who are removed from their own culture may experience further difficulties. For an adolescent who is an asylum seeker or refugee and alone in a different culture, it will be even more difficult. For many refugee and asylum-seeking children, constructing a new identity after their arrival in their new place of residence can be extremely challenging and difficult. If a child has had a traumatic encounter as a consequence of their seeking asylum (e.g. experienced the death of a loved one, witnessed or experienced torture or endured a lengthy and dangerous journey to 'freedom'), then the process of escape also intensifies their awareness of change in self, others and the outside world. On the other hand, it may also be the case that they perceive that their own culture has failed them, is now irrelevant and no longer their own. The greatest threat to identity in refugee adolescents then is not the feeling of belonging to two cultures but belonging to none.

Claude's case is specific to his experience as a separated minor. However, it is helpful to bear in mind the circumstances of other child asylum seekers and refugees who are living with parents in accommodation centres. These children too can experience difficulties and burdens not expected of children; for example, having to assume the role of carer for younger siblings, or interpreting and translating for parents with low English proficiency. This is the conflict 'role reversal', and can take place when children have a degree of fluency and comprehension of the spoken language of the host country that the parents do not have. In effect, children become 'cultural brokers'. This added dependence by parents on their children for communicating needs can result in prolonged stress for the children. This stress may manifest in adolescents by the exhibition of anger or resentment towards their parents, and can result in children blaming parents for their own difficulties with school and social integration. Indeed some of the contexts in which children are exposed to are not appropriate for their age and may instil fear and anxiety in the adolescent, as they worry about their future or that of their parents. A general rule of thumb is that children should never be asked to interpret for adults or professionals. Ideally in the school context children should not be interpreting for the school or their parents in matters that require adult solutions and professional input.

In many respects Claude is no different from any other sixteen-year-old male adolescent. Adolescent development at the best of times can be complex and harrowing. Negotiating and confronting changes from the physical and intellectual to the emotional and spiritual, the adolescent finds themselves in a whirlwind of uncertainty and change. Therefore it is acknowledged that adolescents will require resolve but also support from those around them. For asylum-seeking children, including other migrant children, these years can be very difficult, particularly if they are facing such formative years alone, as their normal adolescent development can become hampered by their refugee experience and the acculturation process. In Claude we have a clear illustration of how an asylum-seeking pupil may experience these stresses.

Schools can provide a safe and secure environment where learning and negotiation can take place. The emerging dynamic among pupils, staff and the wider community will be multifaceted, involving changes in values and attitudes, not to mention the development of skills and knowledge for all involved. In the school context this may require additional funding, extra personnel and a change of or renegotiation of school policies and practices. It may even require a re-examination of the school culture and ethos. In addition to this, our understandings and definitions of education and the purpose of school may also need to be further explored.

Conclusion

It is essential that while working with refugee and asylum-seeking children in schools we acknowledge the resilience and resourcefulness that these pupils display on a daily basis. Claude's case illustrates a number of issues requiring attention for those working in schools. The need for school staff to fundamentally redefine their understandings of what it means to educate pupils has to be considered. Encountering diversity in all its forms challenges us to confront our own biases and prejudices and to examine our attitudes and behaviours in ways that can help us contribute to social inclusion and not discrimination. It presents for all concerned the dilemma that can exist for some staff between where the teaching role ends and the caring role takes over. The duty of care in advocating on behalf of more vulnerable pupils has traditionally been associated with the Irish education system. As global conflicts continue to impact locally on Irish schools and the Irish education system through the arrival of more asylum seekers and refugees, there will be a continued need for staff who care in our schools and who are willing to understand their specific context. Furthermore, the professional skills and knowledge of pedagogy and teaching methods may also need to be combined with pastoral skills training and education in order to serve the future pupil populations of Ireland in the twenty-first century. The emergence of Ireland as an intercultural society will continue to be a vibrant and welcome phenomenon.

Ireland has changed significantly in the past ten years and the tide of change for migration has again reversed to mass emigration. Although I never expected it when I commenced my job as a nurse specialist for asylum seekers in community care, I have been fortunate to work with many caring school staff, including secretaries, year heads, chaplains and principals, to try to make life a little easier for asylum-seeking pupils. I have been privileged and humbled to have worked and developed relationships with so many enlightened people from the refugee community whose resilience and courage can teach us so much. Despite frustration and disillusionment on occasion, I have not lost hope for a better and more inclusive society. In the course of my work, I have seen hopelessness turn to hope, sorrow to happiness and enemies become friends. I have discovered, somewhat inadvertently (and I must say reluctantly at times!), that my role is inclusive of a pastoral care approach. It must continue to be practised this way, remaining mindful of our limitations and our need to work together. It is by reaching out to others that we become transformed, where we see the 'other' as brother and sister and we journey with them in our common humanity.

Notes
1. M. van Manen, *Researching Lived Experience: Human Science for an Action Sensitive Pedagogy* (Washington, DC: The Althouse Press, 2007).
2. B. Fanning (ed.), *Immigration and Social Change in the Republic of Ireland* (Manchester: Manchester University Press, 2007).

3. R. Lentin and R. Mc Veigh (eds), *Racism and Anti-Racism in Ireland* (Belfast: Beyond the Pale, 2002).

4. C. Zimmerman et al., 'Migration and Health: A Framework for 21st Century Policy Making' in PLoS *Medicine*, 8, 5 (2011); http://www.ncbi.nlm.nih.gov/pmc/articles/PMC3101201 (accessed 14 November 2013).

5. B. Flannagan and S. Thornton (eds), *The Bloomsbury Guide to Pastoral Care* (London: Bloomsbury, 2014).

6. K. Egan, 'Pastoral Care Today: Widening the Horizons' in Flannagan and Thornton (eds), *The Bloomsbury Guide to Pastoral Care*, 9.

7. Z. Bauman, *Liquid Times: Living in an Age of Uncertainty* (Cambridge: Polity Press, 2007).

8. B. McCabe, 'Navigating the Landscape of Exile' in Flannagan and Thornton (eds), *The Bloomsbury Guide to Pastoral Care*, 34.

9. http://www.unicefusa.org/mission/emergencies/conflict/syria (accessed 14 March 2014).

10. Government of Ireland, The Refugee Act (Dublin: The Stationery Office, 1996).

11. UNHCR, Mapping Integration: UNHCR's Age, Gender, and Diversity Mainstreaming Project on Refugee Integration in Ireland (2009).

12. P. J. Boyle et al., 'The Complex Health Needs of Asylum Seekers', *FORUM Journal of the Irish College of General Practitioners*, 25 (2008), 10–12.

13. Central Statistics Office, Profile 6 Migration and Diversity (Dublin: The Stationery Office, 2006).

14. Free Legal Advice Centre, *One Size Doesn't Fit All: A Legal Analysis of Direct Provision Ten Years On* (Dublin: Free Legal Advice Centre, 2009).

15. Irish Refugee Council, 'State-Sanctioned Child Poverty and Exclusion: The Case of Children in Accommodation for Asylum Seekers' (Dublin, 2012).

16. Fanning (ed.), *Immigration and Social Change in the Republic of Ireland*.

17. Government of Ireland, Intercultural Education in the Primary Schools (Dublin: NCCA, 2005).

18. Government of Ireland, Intercultural Education in the Post-Primary Schools (Dublin: NCCA, 2006).

19. R. Tormey and J. Gleeson, 'Irish Post-Primary Students' Attitudes Towards Ethnic Minorities' in *Irish Education Studies* (May 2012), 31, 2, 157–73.

20. Government of Ireland, *Intercultural Education in the Post-Primary Schools* (2006).

21. AkiDwA, *I'm Only Saying It Now: Experiences of Women Seeking Asylum in Ireland* (Dublin: AkiDwA, 2010).

22. Zimmerman et al., 'Migration and Health: A Framework for 21st Century Policy Making'.

23. M. Tilki, 'Human Rights and Health Inequalities: UK & EU Policies and Initiatives Relating to the Promotion of Culturally Competent Care' in I. Papadopoulos (ed.), *Transcultural Health and Social Care: Development of Culturally Competent Practitioners* (London: Churchill Livingstone, 2006).

24. Tormey and Gleeson, 'Irish Post-Primary Students' Attitudes Towards Ethnic Minorities'.

25. Ombudsman for Children Office, *Separated Children Living in Ireland* (Dublin: Ombudsman for Children, 2009).

26. G. Shannon, *Child Law* (2nd ed.) (Dublin: Round Hall, 2010).

27. Tormey and Gleeson, 'Irish Post-Primary Students' Attitudes Towards Ethnic Minorities'.

II. Programmatic Pastoral Care

Supporting Bereaved Young People in School

Michelle Y. Pearlman

Death and bereavement are topics that are often difficult to talk about and comprehend, for adults and children alike. Nevertheless, many young people will experience the death of a relative or friend at some point in childhood or adolescence.[1] In fact, it is estimated that one out of every twenty young people will face the death of a parent before they turn eighteen, and that at least three out of every four young people will face the death of a relative or close friend.[2][3][4] By understanding how children and young people comprehend and cope with loss, trusted adults such as school chaplains, guidance counsellors and teachers will be better able to provide support and guidance during times of grief.

Young people vary widely in the way they respond to loss and grief, depending on a multitude of factors such as the child's age and temperament, their relationship to the deceased, and the role or function the deceased person played in the young person's life prior to and following the death. Given the wide range of responses that bereaved children exhibit, it is worth noting that there is no single timetable or series of stages that grieving children necessarily follow, but that there are common patterns of experience and behaviour.[5][6]

Age-Related Reactions to Loss and Grief

Children's reactions to grief are largely based on their age and cognitive understanding of death. The following section outlines some general patterns based on research as well as clinical observations among young people.[7][8][9] Understanding age-related normative reactions is an important part of knowing what to expect and how to provide support for young people who experience loss and grief during school years. Although the focus of this book is on young people who attend post-primary schools, I am including here reference to younger children because the way a child's grief is handled can have a lasting effect into post-primary school years and even beyond that into adult life.

Preschool age and younger

Infants and children under two years are not cognitively able to understand the concept of death or permanent loss. Because children do form attachments during this sensitive time of development, however, it follows that they would demonstrate reactions to a significant loss such as that of a primary caregiver. Normative reactions to this type of loss in early childhood involve searching behaviours, confusion and a regression to earlier behaviours (such as increased crying, difficulty self-soothing and changes in sleeping or eating patterns). Given that young children respond not only to changes in who is caring for them, but also to changes in the caregiver's way of providing for them (including their emotional state), consistency of routine and the presence of familiar faces is imperative.

Children aged approximately three–five years are most likely to respond to the way in which loss impacts their daily lives (i.e. who cares for them, takes them to school, puts them to bed, etc). Children in this age group are not likely to understand the finality of death, and they may repeatedly ask questions about where the deceased loved one is and when they are coming back. They may also believe that the death is caused by something they did wrong, and wonder who will die next. Like toddlers, preschool children may exhibit regressive behaviour (such as increased crying, separation anxiety or clinginess, tantrums and bathroom accidents) at school and home. Children this age will benefit greatly from reassurance about who will be taking care of them and what aspects of their life will stay the same (such as where they live, where they will go to school, etc.). A regular daily routine is an important part of providing that reassurance. School chaplains and counsellors can help surviving caregivers by encouraging them to maintain consistency at home and by helping them to answer children's questions about the loss in concrete, age-appropriate ways.

Early school age
By the ages of six or seven years, children are more likely to have the cognitive capacity to better understand concepts such as the finality of death. They will, however, continue to have questions about what happens to the person who has died, and about what will happen to themselves and their loved ones following a loss. Children from the ages of six–nine may become fixated on specific details such as the burying of the body, for example. They may also become more fearful about future losses and exhibit increased mood fluxes including anger/ irritability alternating with playfulness and acting as if nothing had changed. It is helpful to provide these children with a safe place to ask questions and to express their changing feelings, and it is always helpful to answer their questions in the clearest and simplest way possible. If there is to be a change in the home or school structure, the child should be told what to expect and have an opportunity to express their feelings.

Middle school age
From the ages of approximately nine–twelve years, children tend to be more capable of abstract thinking which enables them to have a more mature and clearer understanding of death as part of the life cycle. They are also more likely to understand why and how death occurs, but like younger children they may continue to blame themselves or have excessive fear about their own death or the loss of other family members. Some may react with intense emotion, while others may try to show how unaffected they are. Like children of all ages, they will benefit from reassurance about the health and safety of their loved ones and about how they will be taken care of. They may also require support adjusting to feelings of social isolation or feeling different from their peers. School chaplains, counsellors and other school staff can help by taking notice of the bereaved child's social behaviour and by helping them to re-connect with their classmates and the wider school community.

Adolescents
Like adults, adolescents are likely to vary in their responses to loss. They may show emotional distress ranging from sadness to anger to shock, or they may choose not to talk about their feelings at all. They may take on more responsibility at home such as helping to care for younger siblings, or alternatively they may act out through increased risk-taking behaviour. Chaplains, guidance counsellors and teachers should be watchful of substance abuse and increased promiscuity among bereaved adolescents. They can also help by talking with caregivers about how to handle changes in the family without putting excessive responsibility on the bereaved adolescent.

How to Help Bereaved Youngsters in School
The following guidelines for chaplains, guidance counsellors, teachers and other school staff may serve as a foundation for helping bereaved children and adolescents in a school setting.

1. Understand normative responses to grief
When faced with the death of a loved one, children and young people respond in a variety of ways. For example, some may find it helpful to talk openly about the person who died, while others prefer to grieve more privately. Bereaved children may also present with a myriad of emotions, from sadness and anger to relief and contentment. These various feelings may be evident from young person to young person, or even within one young person depending on what they are experiencing at home and at school on any given day. These

differences may be completely normal, and in that situation there isn't a healthy or preferred response.

Bereaved individuals from childhood through adulthood can experience feelings of yearning and sadness which may ebb and flow over time. These feelings may be described as 'coming in waves', referring to alternating periods without very strong feelings related to the loss, followed by a seemingly sudden period of intense grief and longing. The feelings of grief during these waves may be as strong as they were during the time immediately following the death itself. Waves of grief are often triggered by a reminder of the person who died, such as a birthday, an anniversary of the death, a holiday or other special occasion, or even engaging in an activity that used to be enjoyed with the deceased loved one. These waves may be particularly stressful for young people who are unprepared for their seemingly sudden onset, and they may lead to further guilt over having resumed normal activity, or frustration that they are still experiencing these types of grief-related feelings.[10]

Another common aspect of the bereaved young person's experience is the tendency for the loss of a family member to have a ripple effect in creating several changes and additional losses in home and school life. For example, the loss of a parent may lead to several changes in children's daily routine, from who wakes them for breakfast and takes them to school to who helps with homework and gets them to bed. Relocation and changing schools is also not uncommon. Naturally, many of these changes impact the child's functioning in school and can potentially lead to academic difficulties (such as excessive absences, declining school performance and difficulty concentrating). School chaplains and counsellors have a particular role in mediating between home and school during these times and can liaise with teachers to make them aware of all of the ways in which a bereaved child's life is changing so that they know how to help. For example, a teacher who notices that homework has become a struggle can offer to meet with the child to assist with organising the week's assignments.

2. Create a safe and supportive environment in the school
When a young person is experiencing significant change and loss at home such as occurs in the case of the death of a parent or parental separation/divorce, school can come to represent routine and security and a reprieve from uncertainty. School staff can facilitate a sense of security and support by being available to listen and by showing empathy and understanding. Chaplains, guidance counsellors and teachers can make themselves available to bereaved children for

private talks at lunchtime or in the morning before class. When trying to provide support, staff members should follow the bereaved child's lead, allowing the child to express themselves without trying to either limit their sadness or push the young person to talk more than they want. School staff can also help bereaved students to feel connected by offering reassuring statements such as 'I am here if you want to talk', and by being watchful of behaviour from the student or their classmates which may be isolating in nature.

Teachers and staff can help the bereaved student adjust in smaller ways too. In the weeks following the loss, assignments should be briefer and more structured.[11] While grieving children may not be able to focus on homework like they did before, it may in fact be helpful for the student to see that they can handle and accomplish small tasks such as a few math problems or a short reading assignment, for example.

3. Include caregivers in creating a plan to help

In order to best know how to help any individual child, it is necessary for school personnel to work collaboratively among themselves, with community agencies and particularly with caregivers to find out what is happening at home and how the school can best respond to the specific needs of the young person experiencing loss and grief. Caregivers should be asked about what strategies or services they would like to see implemented at school, and they should be informed about what reactions the staff are observing in the young person. The child's family should also be specifically asked about whether they prefer to have the child's classmates visit the home, attend funeral services, or show support in other ways. School chaplains will have a particular role to play regarding the young person's spiritual needs during and after a time of loss, while the counsellors will be able to provide opportunities to listen. When school staff and caregivers work together to form a partnership, interventions are more likely to be consistent at home and school, and all of the adults are better able to serve the best interests of the student.[12]

4. Communicating with others

Some losses, such as that of a teacher or a student, affect the whole school as opposed to an individual loss that primarily affects one child or family. One of the first steps in school-wide losses is to notify the students and staff about what has happened.

The announcement of a death that impacts the student body as a whole needs to accomplish two important tasks – convey what has happened, and do so in a sensitive way that will contain its impact. Whenever possible, the principal would notify the staff first, who could then prepare for how to notify their students. This is preferable over telling the student body and staff together via public announcement. Telling the staff first allows them to experience their own reactions and to prepare themselves, before turning to their role of notifying and comforting their students. Chaplains will usually have prepared a bereavement plan and will be available to advise staff on how to best communicate the news to the students. This order also ensures that the information given is accurate and consistent from classroom to classroom.[13] The following example illustrates how a teacher might notify a class about the loss of a school staff member:

> As many of you know, our music teacher Miss N. was suffering from cancer for a long time. I am sad to tell you that Miss N. died last night. I'd like for us to take a few minutes this morning to talk about Miss N. and about how we would like to remember her.

When there is a death in a student's family, their classmates should be similarly informed. Notifying the student's peers will prepare them for what they might hear about the death from others, and it will also prepare them to support the student during the funeral and later upon their return to school. A chaplain may be on hand when the sad news is being communicated and can provide ongoing spiritual support while the teacher attempts to maintain as normal a routine in the classroom as is possible. Whoever communicates the sad news to the bereaved student's peers may rely on a text like this:

> I have some very sad news to share with you today. Patrick is out of school because his father died in a car accident yesterday. I do not know the details about what happened, but I do know that Patrick will be out of school for the next few days. We can talk about what Patrick may be going through and how we might be able to help him and his family.

It is also important to remember that the bereaved student's closest friends may not be in the same class group and that there may be students in other classes that will be affected by the news. Fundamentally, it is important that every teacher acknowledges the loss that has occurred, otherwise students may interpret a teacher's silence as a lack of concern.

5. Assign roles and responsibilities

Whether a tragedy affects one student or the entire student body, certain steps may be taken by various key school personnel to help the bereaved and others who may be affected to adjust. Ideally, these roles would be laid out in a crisis plan before any traumatic event occurs.[14] The crisis plan would cover the roles of the principal (which will include communicating with the parents and media if applicable), the chaplain, guidance and/or counselling team, the teachers (who will be responsible for recognising the needs of their individual students) and other staff (such as classroom assistants, caretakers, secretaries and school nurses). Even the simple act of informing the staff about their roles will help them to help their students.

School chaplains will be responsible for providing spiritual support and comfort and for liaising with local churches. The counsellors will be responsible for identifying and reducing emotional distress among the students, staff and parents. Both chaplains and counsellors should also systematically determine which students are most in need of individualised support, and which students may be better served by meeting in small groups. The role of each teacher will be to let the students know what has happened and to support their understanding of what will happen next. If someone in the school has died from an illness like cancer, then the teacher will want to reassure the students that cancer is not contagious.[15] Similarly, if a child or teacher has died as a result of a violent act, the teacher should reassure the students that they are safe by letting them know what steps are being taken at school and in the community to reduce the risk of further violence.

Depending on the circumstances of the loss and the age of students in a given class, teachers may also want to lead a discussion to help the children understand the event and explore how they feel about it. These discussions can also help the students learn how to support each other. Such a discussion may begin with questions such as:

» How many of you have had deaths in your families?
» How many of you have had some serious losses, perhaps a divorce, an illness in the family, moving residence, or changing schools frequently?[16]

These types of classroom talks can also help teachers identify those children who are in need of further attention or individualised support.

6. Create ways of honouring and memorialising the deceased

Following the classroom discussion, the chaplain in conjunction with other staff may help the students and staff choose an activity to remember the person who died and/or to help those who are bereaved. School-appropriate activities which promote positive remembering of a deceased member may include a liturgy of remembrance, creating a sign or sculpture, starting a new activity or club in honour of the deceased, planting a tree, writing letters to the deceased person's family, showing support and writing letters to the deceased person him or herself including things they wished they could have said while he or she was still alive.

If the deceased person was not known by all but was a family member of one of the students, the chaplain may lead the class in choosing ways of showing support to their bereaved classmate. Examples include writing letters to let the classmate know that they are being thought of, and preparing students for what to say and do (such as asking the young person to sit with them at lunch and telling them that they are sorry for their loss) when they return to school. The class and/or school may also honour the deceased by raising money in a walk-a-thon type event for an organisation that works to limit the person's cause of death or that was meaningful to the students in some way.

One significant way to memorialise a loved one is through a memorial service. When a student, staff member or other person who was close to the school dies, it is often helpful to have an age-appropriate memorial service at the school, separate from any funeral or memorial service given by the family. Students who were particularly close to the deceased may play a key role in planning and creating the service with the chaplain. This process of participating in the planning of the service itself helps to provide a feeling that they are able to do something at a time when they otherwise feel helpless. Speakers may include local clergy, the principal, trusted teachers and affected students who feel that participation would be helpful. Family members of the deceased may be invited to attend, but they should not plan the programme nor should they play a dominant role in the service as they may be too vulnerable to do so. The focus of the school memorial should be on remembering the positive impact that the deceased had on the school, staff and students. After the service, students should be given the opportunity to express their feelings in their individual classrooms.

7. Watch for signs that additional help or intervention may be necessary
Following the loss of a loved one, young people may experience feelings of confusion, sadness, anger and worry. These feelings typically lessen over time, particularly when children have the support of trusted adults and peers with whom they can talk. Other young

people seem to have a more difficult time, experiencing psychological distress that persists over several months.

The most common emotional disturbances among young people who are bereaved are depressed mood, irritability and significant worry about the health and safety of surviving family members.[17] [18] [19] [20] There may also be behavioural problems, social withdrawal and a decline in school performance related to problems with paying attention and difficulties thinking and concentrating.[21] It is thought that 20 per cent of bereaved children are likely to exhibit significant problems which require clinical intervention.[22] When teachers or other staff members notice these types of problems among young people who are bereaved, they should speak to the school chaplain or counsellor and set up a plan to connect the child with appropriate support services. In addition to the emotional problems that may be seen among young people who are bereaved, they may also exhibit social problems stemming in part from their changing social context.

One of the most common challenges voiced by young people who experience bereavement is the way in which peers and even adults may not know how to interact with them in a supportive way. Those who experience bereavement often feel isolated and different from their peers, who additionally may treat them differently following the loss, either at school or in social settings. These challenges may be further complicated and exacerbated by the young person's loss of the person to whom they may have previously turned in these types of situations. School staff can help by giving the bereaved student a counsellor to meet or speak with, setting up a lunch buddy system for the class, and trying to get the child to stay involved (or get involved) in one or more school or community activities that may be of interest to them.

8. Be prepared to help the students with particularly sensitive issues
Certain situations, such as the death of a fellow classmate, require particular sensitivity. Children and adolescents may have a hard time understanding how someone their own age could die. In these types of cases, it is even more important for chaplains, counsellors and other school staff members to facilitate discussions which provide a forum for students to express their feelings, voice their concerns and have their questions answered. It is advisable to begin such discussions in an open-ended way (e.g. 'Today we are going to spend some time talking about Charlie'), to reflect back what the students are voicing ('I hear a lot of you expressing sadness and also the feeling that it's unfair that Charlie died so young'), and to answer questions as concretely as possible ('Charlie died in the hospital yesterday morning, and his parents were with him').

If a student in the school is facing the end of a terminal illness, it may be helpful to talk with the class to prepare them for the impending death. Such a discussion might begin with a chaplain, counsellor or teacher asking the students what they have noticed about their sick friend, and then letting the children know that the student is very ill. Depending on the situation and what the school has been told by the sick student's family (including what they have specified to share with the students), the children may then be told that their classmate is very sick with a disease from which some people die.[23] It is important to differentiate how this type of illness is different from the typical illnesses that all young people get, like colds or 'flu. It is also important to remember that the young person who is dying will also have spiritual and emotional needs. Chaplains will need to be confident here in approaching the student's family to ascertain how best they can offer spiritual support to the young person.

Conclusion

Grief is an ongoing process that does not end in the weeks or months following the loss of a loved one. Likewise, support for a bereaved student should not be limited to the immediate time period following the death. Remarkable levels of resilience have been demonstrated by young people who are bereaved,[24] and school staff can work to foster this resilience by staying involved in the bereaved student's day-to-day life. For example, counsellors can work with bereaved students to identify their areas of strength and positive coping, sources of social support and activities that encourage a sense of belonging and purpose. By understanding the experiences and needs of bereaved students, school chaplains, counsellors and other staff members can help them cope with and make meaning of their loss, move forward and thrive.

Notes

1. L. Harrison and R. Harrington, 'Adolescents' Bereavement Experiences: Prevalence, Association with Depressive Symptoms, and Use of Services', *Journal of Adolescence* 24, 2 (2001), 159–69.

2. Ibid.

3. N. Garmezy and A. S. Masten, 'Chronic Adversities' in M. Rutter, E. Taylor and L. Hersov (eds), *Child and Adolescent Psychiatry: Modern Approaches* (Oxford: Blackwell Scientific, 1994).

4. Social Security Administration, 'Intermediated assumptions of the 2000 trustees report' (Washington, DC: Office of the Chief Actuary of the Social Security Administration).

5. R. Weiss, 'The Nature and Causes of Grief' in M. S. Stroebe, R. O. Hansson, H. Schut and W. Stroebe (eds), *Handbook of Bereavement Research and Practice: Advances in Theory and Intervention* (Washington, DC: American Psychological Association, 2008), 29–44.

6. C. B. Wortman and R. C. Silver, 'The Myths of Coping with Loss Revisited' in Stroebe et al., *Handbook of Bereavement Research*, 405–30.

7. J. E. Baker and M. Sedney, 'How Bereaved Children Cope with Loss: An Overview' in C. A. Carr and D. M. Corr (eds), *Handbook of Childhood Death and Bereavement* (NY: Springer, 1996), 109–30.

8. New York University Child Study Center (2006), *Caring for Kids After Trauma, Disaster and Death: A Guide for Parents and Professionals* (2nd ed.), retrieved from http://www.abourour kids.org/file/articles/crisis_guide02.pdf (accessed 14 August 2014).

9. M. W. Speece and S. B. Brent, 'The Development of Children's Understanding of Death' in Corr and Corr, *Handbook of Childhood Death and Bereavement*, 29–50.

10. M. Y. Pearlman, K. D. Schwalbe and M. Cloitre, *Grief in Childhood: Fundamentals of Treatment in Clinical Practice* (Washington, DC: American Psychological Association, 2010).

11. S. Petersen and R. L. Straub, *School Crisis Survival Guide: Management Techniques and Materials for Counsellors and Administrators* (San Francisco: Jossey-Bass, 1991).

12. M. A. Health and D. Sheen, *School-Based Crisis Intervention: Preparing All Personnel to Assist* (New York: Guilford Press, 2005), 55–6.

13. Petersen and Straub, *School Crisis Survival Guide*.

14. Ibid.

15. Ibid.

16. Ibid.

17. A. Abdelnoor and S. Hollins, 'The Effect of Childhood Bereavement on Secondary School Performance', *Educational Psychology in Practice*, 20 (2004), 43–54.

18. J. Cerel, M. A. Fristad, J. Verducci, R. A. Weller and E. B. Weller, 'Childhood Bereavement: Psychopathology in the Two Years Postparental Death', *Journal of the American Academy of Child and Adolescent Psychiatry*, 45 (2006), 681–90.

19. L. Dowdney, 'Annotation: Childhood Bereavement Following Parental Death', *Journal of Child Psychology and Psychiatry*, 41 (2000), 819–30.

20. J. L. Genevro, T. Marshall, T. Miller and Center for Advancement of Health, 'Report on Bereavement and Grief Research', *Death Studies*, 28 (2004), 491–575.

21. L. J. Luecken, 'Long-Term Consequences of Parental Death in Childhood: Psychological and Physiological Manifestations' in *Handbook of Bereavement Research and Practice: Advances in Theory and Intervention* (Washington, DC: American Psychological Association, 2008), 397–416.

22. Dowdney, 'Annotation: Childhood Bereavement Following Parental Death', 819–830.

23. Petersen and Straub, *School Crisis Survival Guide*.

24. G. A. Bonnano and A. D. Mancini, 'The Human Capacity to Thrive in the Face of Extreme Adversity', *Pediatrics*, 121 (2008), 369–75.

Companioning Adolescents Into Adulthood

Secondary Schools as Communities of Care and Growth

Theresa A. O'Keefe

Growing up in today's world is not as easy as many teens[1] endeavour to make it look. In fact, it is perhaps harder than it was just a generation ago. This is mainly due to an increasingly globalised and market-driven culture that directs a great deal of attention at teens, and greater isolation in teens' day-to-day lives. These two factors contribute to the challenge today of growing to adulthood that is felt by almost all students in secondary schools regardless of where they are in the world, and so is a prevailing issue for those in chaplaincy, pastoral care and counselling. In this chapter I argue for the value and necessity of the wider school community being a united body attending to the care and guidance of all adolescent students as they navigate their way to adulthood.

Perhaps the most challenging task of adolescence is learning to think like an adult through a growing awareness of and engagement in the wider world. This growth is ushered in by changes in the adolescent brain, which helps make possible an increased complexity of mind and meaning-making. Developmental theorist Robert Kegan has looked at how growing complexity in meaning-making is not automatic, but more likely when supported by environments of *support* and *challenge*. The greatest aid to adolescents maturing in their meaning-making, such that they take on a sense of life mattering and their lives mattering, is the presence of adults modelling those very concepts. Secondary schools can be communities of support and challenge which help growing adolescents learn to think like adults, to see that life and learning matter, but also that their own lives matter.

A World of Expectations

Adolescents are functioning within a globalised social world, regardless of their location in an urban or rural setting. It makes itself present in the lives of students through radio, television, print media, social media and other internet access, as well as through the markets and international travel.[2] The impact of this reality is dynamic and multifaceted, and both positive and negative. Teens find themselves, consciously or unconsciously, navigating multiple value worlds in the course of their daily lives, including family, school, religious community – among whom there may be some cohesion. They also navigate the value worlds of peer groups, regional and national governments, as well as racial expectations and ethnic social norms. Lastly, there are the values of the marketplace and popular media, much of which is directly targeted at them.[3] The adolescent is frequently in the crossfire of these competing value worlds, with conflicting expectations for their young lives.

Teens are expected by the adults around them to maintain a consistent sense of identity and ethics while traversing these diverse arenas. Furthermore, adults within religious communities also expect teens to take on and live out the values of religious faith in daily life, and are frequently frustrated when teens fail to do so or seem not to care. Recognising the conflicts and contradictions embedded within and among these various interests is a challenging task for a *mature* adult; it is even more daunting for an adolescent only just beginning to see meaning and value. It is likely teens sooner *feel* rather than understand that there are conflicting demands made on them. It is evident to them in the disappointment that they see in those around them – family, teachers, friends, ministers, coaches, bosses, guidance counsellors; but it is also evident in their own dissatisfaction with their choices. The outcome for many adolescents is stress.[4] The stress comes from trying to figure out how to respond to all these competing interests, trying to please as many parties as possible, especially parents, but at the same time, trying to please themselves.

This task is made more challenging when teens perceive that they have to figure this out without the aid of caring and able adults. They perceive that part of the task of coming to adulthood is figuring out how to do this all alone. Recent studies conducted among US teens tell of real and perceived isolation felt by teens. Real isolation grows out of the fact that most teens spend the majority of their time separated into age-peer groupings, a fact since they were young children. The primary instance of this is found in schools, but also in clubs, sports and through social media.[5] For many teens, this real isolation is accompanied by a *perceived* isolation. According to Chap Clark, many teens find that the only adults around them are those paid to be there (teachers, coaches, counsellors, therapists) and so teens assume that no adult is there for them because they *want to be there*.[6] This must mean, they infer, that they have to look out for their own interests; that no one trustworthy cares for them, and they have to raise themselves. According to Clark, teens feel they are left 'to band together and create their own world'.[7]

However, Clark holds that 'adolescents need adults to become adults, and when adults are not present and involved in their lives, they are forced to figure out how to survive life on their own.'[8] The validity of Clark's observation comes from the fact that this is *what teens perceive* rather than what the adults in their lives intend.[9] In response to this sense of abandonment, teens look to their age-peers or online sources for answers, neither of which are reliable guides. Teens need the companionship and guidance of mature adults to learn their own way in the world. Teens also need to learn that many adults *are* trustworthy and helpful guides who care about the teen for the teen's sake.[10]

For those who wish to help adolescents find their way in adulthood, the challenge is two-fold. The first is to help teens learn to navigate a complex and contradictory world and live amid its competing expectations. The second is to overcome teens' perception that they need to figure out how to do this alone. Secondary schools are well positioned to do this, but the effort does not fall within the purview of any single agent within the school. Rather it calls for a coordination of efforts among multiple players – teachers, pastoral care, counsellors, chaplains, but also parents, alumni and other school community members.

Secondary Schools – Communities of Care and Learning
The work of secondary schools is multifaceted. Obviously it concerns the education of youth in various subject areas – sciences, languages, histories, vocational skills – which are largely determined by state or national boards and accrediting agencies. Outside of these academic pursuits the schools may offer co-curricular activities, such as sports, drama productions, clubs and associations. Many schools also have a religion curriculum, the framework for which may come from the national or regional religious bodies or state agencies. Frequently secondary schools see worship and prayer as well as service to the world as central to the life of the school. Yet in many ways the mission of secondary schools lays in an understanding and valuing of the students as human persons. Simply stated, it is the belief that *lives matter*, particularly that the young lives of students matter for the world now and for the adult lives they will grow into. Their value is not found in their utility or exchange value, nor in their grades, exam scores, or popularity, nor their contributions to team sports. Rather the value is found in their humanity. For religiously founded schools a further theological assertion informs the mission of the school: that each student is made by God, in the image and likeness of God.[11] Likewise, internalising that lives matter means that teens

realise that God's regard is not limited to those like themselves, but that God's care and concern extends to all. In that recognition they are challenged to extend their love and concern beyond the borders of comfort, to reach out to understand and care for others. The assertion that lives matter extends to discovering how these young people become contributors to the world. The mission of the school is to assist its students to understand the world, but also to see *that their lives matter* for the life of the world. To assert this claim is not to predetermine how those lives contribute and take shape, but to live in the conviction that they do and they will.

Maintaining this perspective on a daily basis is challenging. Amid the multiple demands and agendas secondary schools face from outside forces – funding sources, accrediting organisations and even religious leadership – it can be hard to remember that it is the lives of the students that are at the heart of the educational endeavour. Similarly, agents internal to the life of the school – sports, parents, testing, homework and clubs – can contribute to a sense of competition for the students' time, attention and loyalties. Finally, with the credentialing and professionalisation of secondary school faculty and staff, it may be hard to recognise that the care of students is the work of the whole school and not the compartmentalised work of certain members, namely chaplains, counsellors, or campus ministers.

Secondary schools can help adolescences learn that life matters and *their* lives matter by offering support in three areas: making connections across fields of study to understand how they contribute to a wider and connected view of the world; recognising values embedded in behaviours, decisions and efforts so as to make decisions for life in light of values; and learning to predict and imagine for long-term consequences, especially unseen consequences. I name these qualities of *thinking like an adult*, but stress that it is not simply an effort to master rationality. Rather it is the capacity of meaning-making that requires attention to and interconnection of emotions, values, relationships and ideas.[12] The school can help the teen learn to think like an adult, being able to see that *things matter* with greater clarity and make decisions that reflect that awareness. This work is not best done by teens in isolation where they have only their peers for guidance, but among mature adults who are about the same work. A communally conceived approach to adolescent formation – something like communal apprenticeship – has not been the prevailing pattern of the past century, so needs new warrants to undergird it. I offer two: recent work in adolescent brain growth; and constructivist-developmental psychology.

The Task of Adolescence – Learning How to Think Like an Adult

Since the early twentieth century, adolescence has been recognised as a period of dynamic movement. G. Stanley Hall's two-volume work *Adolescence* set the stage for conceiving this as a period unique from what precedes (childhood) and what follows (adulthood). Hall's evolutionary-based framework saw adolescence as a time of learning to control the primitive animal nature of childhood and corralling that energy to more useful, reasoned engagement in the adult world.[13] Hall named it as a time of 'storm and stress' and so imaged adolescence as a period of battle and confrontation wherein the young person learned to control their unruly nature and suppress it in favour of the more reasoned demands of adulthood. Over time Hall's conceptual framework contributed to the development of educational and ministerial programming that served to suppress or control the youthful energy and enthusiasm, channelling it in more socially appropriate avenues. More significantly for our purposes in this chapter, Hall's view may have contributed to a sense among the adult community of 'waiting out' this period until the adolescent was deemed mature enough to suitably enter adult company; as a result, over the past one hundred years we have seen teens increasingly sequestered away from where adults gather.[14]

New tools on board

Recent theorists have offered a somewhat different image of adolescence. Rather than mastery of a primal nature, they see adolescence as a time of developing capacities – particularly capacities of the brain and the ability to make meaning. Recent neurobiological studies of children and teens have found that the human brain continues to grow and become more organised over the second decade of life.[15] While the human brain reaches 90 per cent of its adult size by age six, a new burst of growth and organisation takes place from age ten into the early twenties. Of particular note, a growth of grey matter in the frontal cortex and other lobes of the brain prior to puberty and a subsequent development of the linking white matter throughout the teens and early twenties have been detected. These changes allow for new abilities of perception and cognition not possible in younger children. With the development of the frontal cortex the young person is more able to recognise time past and time future. That allows for the development of long-term cause and effect, as well as a sense of history and imagination. It also makes ideation possible and the ability to see oneself as *seeing* and *being seen* (self-consciousness). As teenagers come to depend more on their frontal cortex, they are able to be less dependent on the amygdala, the emotional centre of the brain, for making decisions. As a result they are more capable of greater reflection in the decision-making process and less tied to emotional or gut responses.[16] Similarly the linkages across the brain grow during this time, making communication among spheres of the brain more sophisticated and supple. There is also evidence of an eventual decrease in grey matter that follows the increase and organisation; those linkages that are made and used become stronger; those that are not used are pruned away.[17]

This last point is important because it suggests there is nothing inevitable about the maturation of the human brain. The 'use it or lose it' principle coined by these theorists recognises that environmental considerations seem to play heavily on the development of the brain at this stage in life. Those neural pathways that are used become stronger; those that are not used are lost over time.[18] Correspondingly, it takes time to develop more coordinated thinking. Similar to the body's need for practice to master movement, new brain patterns require repeated usage to become fluid. This neurobiological research should not be assumed to answer all of our questions on the developing adolescent. However, it does help us recognise the lively changes, previously unseen, happening within the brain at this stage of life. Simply put, the adolescent brain is newly able to see more and make new sense of what it sees.

An expanded frame of reference
Similarly, behavioural science has recognised adolescence as a time of developing greater cognitive ability and complexity. Since Jean Piaget, cognitive-developmental theorists have recognised a newfound capacity for ideation among teens, moving from simple concrete operational thought to seeing concepts and values previously unrecognisable to the child. Robert Kegan refers to this as a shift from 'durable categories of knowing to cross-categorical knowing'.[19] It is a slow process that may take one well into adulthood. To understand the nature of the shift, it is helpful to see what is meant by 'durable categories', and appreciate it as a major accomplishment for growing children. The stage of durable categories means that a child, starting at about age seven, is able to recognise the world as learnable and navigable.[20] Things (objects, points of view, persons) exist for real – rather than within her imagining. As learnable things, the child can navigate around them for her survival. She can figure out what her parents want; what teachers expect; how games, tools, or objects work and function in the world. She can appreciate that she has feelings, perspectives, likes and dislikes, which endure over time and are not

just momentary sensations. She can appreciate that she has a point of view. She can work for rewards, like good grades or popularity, and she can avoid consequences, like punishment or disappointment. She can see things as predictable, both in herself and in the world, and she can learn to work around those things for her self-interest.[21] These things can be known as durable categories.

As great an accomplishment as this is for the child, it is insufficient for adulthood because the world expects more of adults.[22] Cross-categorical knowing is needed. The adult is expected to see and act beyond his own self-interest but also be able to take into account and make decisions based on other's concerns and perspectives. Likewise he is expected not only to see how things work, but also to recognise the values and intentions behind them. He is expected to make connections across areas of learning – politics and economics, history and social sciences, language and culture – and see influences functioning across these areas. Similarly he is expected to take into account the long-term and non-tangible effect of actions – trust, honour, care, responsibility – rather than just their immediate and obvious consequences – grades, rewards, punishments, bonuses and salary. All of these reflect an ability to negotiate among durable categories and see and make sense of larger frames of reference within which they function. These are the capacities of cross-categorical knowing. This greater complexity in meaning-making is demonstrated in the ability to subordinate 'self-interest to the needs and values of a relationship'.[23] This is also demonstrated in the ability to recognise values behind behaviours and themes behind ideas. It is the ability to hold one's point of view in dialogue with that of someone else, learn what has given rise to both, and make determinations across them. It is the ability to recognise and predict long-term consequences to actions, and to make decisions based on those distant outcomes rather than on immediate self-interest. Kegan names the task of adolescence as this 'gradual transformation of mind' which they accomplish as they move through their teens into their twenties.[24] Unfortunately for teens, adults usually expect them to have mastered these abilities as soon as they enter adolescence; they *look* more like adults, they should *think* more like adults. In reality teens are only just confronting the limitations of durable-categories and are generally confused by what is expected of them.

The brain's growth during this period of life is dynamic, creating new possibilities for a young person's increased capacity to make sense of the world within more complex frames of meaning. That includes beginning to see ideas and values, and making connections across seemingly diverse realms of interest. Yet achieving a more complex capacity of meaning-making and connection is not automatic, but requires repeated patterning of seeing and making new sense of what is seen. This takes time and patience for both adolescents and those surrounding them. David Elkind writes, 'It is important to remember that young people are as unfamiliar with their expanded thinking abilities as they are with their reconfigured bodies. Moreover, to become proficient in, and at ease with, thinking on a higher level takes a lot of practice.'[25] Kegan posits that if we imagine our culture as a 'school', then the curriculum of our culture provides multiple and constant opportunities for challenging adolescents:

> At home, at work, in school, and even in many of their peer
> relationships, adolescents experience a continuous demand
> for cross-categorical consciousness … On these grounds our
> culture as school may deserve the highest grade when it
> comes to the criterions of providing challenge.[26]

But Kegan goes on to write that the culture is frequently not supplying the necessary supports to meet those challenges.[27] He suggests that growth is best able to happen in 'holding environments' that offer a sufficient balance of support and challenge for the adolescent.

The bottom line is that teens need help learning to think like adults. They are only becoming able to do this as adolescents and will not master it until they mature into adulthood. Yet they are living in a very conflicted world and so often face very adult concerns with very serious consequences for their lives. The gap between their ability and life's demands creates stress for their young lives. Let me include one more factor as we add up the bottom line. Teens need the modelling of adult thinking by people they believe care about them and who they can trust as guides; also they need caring and trustworthy companions in the process. Secondary schools can provide adolescents with support in three areas: making connections across fields of study to understand how they contribute to a wider and connected view of the world; recognising values embedded in behaviours, decisions and efforts so as to make decisions for life in light of values; and learning to predict and imagine for long-term consequences, especially unseen consequences.[28] Cross-categorical knowing holds within it an appreciation that things – relationships, intentions and values – are real and matter for something. As stated above, to think like an adult means being able to see that *things matter* with greater clarity and make decisions that reflect that awareness.

Spurring the Imagination: Some Recommendations for Schools

While secondary schools have been critiqued as one of the places that contribute to teens' sense of isolation,[29] secondary schools are well-positioned to help break down those barriers and enable students to move into the cross-categorical meaning-making needed for adulthood. Secondary schools can help students appreciate larger frameworks of value; they can help students make connections across subject areas; and they can bring together mature and caring adults to mentor adolescents in the meaning-making processes. This final section offers suggestions of how schools might bring students and adults to think and learn together. It is a limited list intended to spur the imagination of what might be possible and profitable.

A community of care and consideration: Learning to predict and imagine for long-term consequences, especially unseen consequences

A challenge of adult thinking is making decisions that reflect values that an adult wishes to live out of and uphold. Mature adults do this all the time, usually unaware that they are working across or amid competing values and agendas. Sometimes adults have to make decisions that seem contradictory or at cross-purposes, but are necessary in a given moment to serve less obvious needs. Teens, newly able to see how values undergird actions, may name this as hypocrisy. Adults frequently become embarrassed, angry, or defensive at that charge and discussion is closed off. Rather adolescents would benefit from seeing how adults make these complex decisions for their lives. This is not something easily taught, but it is something that can be modelled when adults 'think out loud' in the company of teens. Such modelling should not be limited to the classroom curriculum but exhibited in and through broader school interactions whereby teens can engage with a wide variety of adults.

Secondary schools can find various ways to surround teens with thinking, caring adults, who demonstrate what it means to live amid the challenges of the contemporary world. Attention should be given to the composition of these communities of care and consideration by including a variety of adults around students, intentionally moving beyond the 'usual suspects' – paid faculty and staff. Include, rather, older and younger alumni, parents and other adult family members and community members – drawing them in for different events and functions. By engaging with the issues of the world, adults can demonstrate how they think about life decisions, vocational concerns and relationship issues, and so model cross-categorical thinking.

Possible examples for demonstrating this are to:

» Invite teams of older adults and youth to work together on issues that impact the whole school community (e.g. bullying, use of new technologies). Allowing the space for mutual learning and development of solutions invites the teens into the thinking process – offering a very valuable perspective – but makes the adult consideration of broader issues (e.g. funding, donors, community-wide concerns) more transparent to the teens. Thereby teens' insights and contributions are valued and adult problem-solving is modelled.

» Offer community-wide forums on topical issues. They could be connected to the school curriculum whereby students serve as hosts and moderators, inviting knowledgeable community members to inform the discussion. For example, the political science class offers a forum on the European debt crisis, or a presidential election process, inviting an expert to interact with the audience (adolescents and adults) on the topic.

Pointing to a broad framework of meaning: recognising values embedded in behaviours and decisions

Secondary schools in general are well situated to offer teens an expansive framework of meaning since they offer subject areas that take on a more global scope than is generally possible with younger students, for example: political science, economics and religious studies. Thus each subject introduces a framework through which students might learn how circumstances and decisions reflect and are impacted by values embedded in those systems.

However, religiously affiliated secondary schools are additionally at an advantage since the whole school attempts to express a framework of meaning – that life matters because God is its source and end. A religious framework provides a challenge to the values of a global marketplace culture, which are much more self-interested and short-sighted.[30] A religious perspective conceives of life (all life) within the frame of reference of God's love and hope for the world. This means that love is not just about caring for those who I like or who are like me. Nor is it simply avoiding behaviours for which punishment might be expected. These I suggest reflect *concrete operational* capacities. Rather it calls for rethinking and reassessing the influence of immediately perceivable elements (wealth, popularity and poverty) from a boarder framework of meaning (care, justice, dignity and responsibility) and making judgements based on that broader framework. This is a move towards cross-categorical knowing. By integrating a religious or ethical perspective on life, the adolescent is able to gain a larger frame of reference for how their lives matter, and for what.

Possible means of expressing this are, briefly:

» Involving adult members of the community in service projects, not as chaperones, but as participants.
  This demonstrates that these things are not simply 'requirements' fulfilled for resumes or for graduation, but are part of valuing life in community. It demonstrates how adults continue to make connections to the wider world, their convictions, and to God.
» Involving adult members of the community to participate with students on retreats and worship. Joint planning would be valuable, where both youth and adults are seen as contributors, not as a token presence.
» Naming the values behind religious actions and perspectives. This is certainly the work of any ethics or religious education curriculum in the school. Yet for religiously sponsored schools it is potentially more influential in school-wide projects, wherein school leadership articulates the rationale behind initiatives. This demonstrates that those values are held by the adult leadership and how these values shape daily life and community actions.
» Inviting local business owners who demonstrate values of justice as employers and community members to discuss how such values add to their business model.

Making connections across disciplines: contributing to a wider and connected view of the world

Too often school subjects are taught as discrete pursuits, disconnected from each other, or from the world in general.[31] Adolescents frequently see school learning as just about that – what teachers want to teach, and not about making sense of a complex world. However, secondary education should communicate that learning matters, and not simply as discrete pieces of information, but as fields of knowledge that are interconnected. History and social sciences are connected; mathematics is connected to sciences and to economics; economics is connected to politics and history; social sciences are connected to languages, cultures and politics. Secondary education is a time for preparing for adult vocations, either leading right into employment or further education, that the skills of learning are valuable throughout life. Being able to see the connection between current school studies and the complex dynamics in the world is an important challenge for the adolescent mind. Secondary schools might be places intent on making connections across subject areas for the sake of such meaning-making. Those connections include: connections across academic disciplines so as to see how the discrete learning is about something bigger; pathways towards the adult world; and the connection of school learning to life beyond so as to see how time within the school is about broader realities. All of these connections support the ability of teens seeing their own lives within a larger frame of meaning and purpose. Math, languages, history, religious studies and sciences are not subjects taught for their own interest, but as means of engaging in and making sense of the world. Learning is about something; potentially it should be about everything.

Possible means of expressing this are, briefly:

» Team teaching by faculty with specialties in seemingly unrelated areas so as to demonstrate how the fields connect, for example, English literature and history; economics and technology; religion and social studies. The collaborative effort among colleagues also demonstrates regard, respect and problem-solving between adults in different disciplines.
» Inviting older alumni to talk about career paths as a means of demonstrating how choices made as young men and women do chart paths for the future, but do not necessarily lock one in for life.
» Inviting younger alumni to talk about life a few years out of secondary school. It allows for students to see how school experience is connected to later life pursuits.
» Inviting community employers to talk about the kinds of skills and qualities they value in employees, such as responsibility and care for the organisation.

By bringing a diversity of caring adults into the company of teens in regular and various ways, the many ways adults 'think' is made more visible. These examples suggest how community members can contribute to adolescents learning by sharing their own seeing and making sense of the world. This is not to suggest that they must all agree in their thinking. In fact that would be counterproductive. Rather it can be a means of demonstrating how those with differing perspectives can learn from and move towards shared goals – just one more advantage of thinking like an adult. Finally, if the relationships are sustained over time – ongoing service projects, committees, or retreat work – they allow for students to get to know the adult members better and learn to trust them.

Secondary schools are well positioned to assist teens in learning to think like adults by offering broad frameworks of meaning and by companioning adolescents into adulthood. Through multiple avenues, secondary schools can communicate to teens that life matters and their lives matter. Recent research identifies adolescence as a time of tremendous possibility for deeper and wider awareness of the world. However, the culture of isolation and the demands of competing value worlds both challenge that potential for teens. Secondary schools may serve the healthy growth of teens by providing multiple adult companions who can share with teens how best to understand and navigate the world as adults. Such consistent and caring guidance is not the work of single specialists within a school community, nor is it work that is limited to the classroom. It is best demonstrated across the adult community connected to a school – a community that thinks together and cares about that thinking.

Notes

1. Throughout this chapter, the terms adolescent, teen, teenager and youth are used interchangeably to refer to persons between the ages of thirteen and nineteen years.

2. While travelling in Rwanda in 2007 I found that even students in rural Rwandan secondary schools had intermittent internet access. Similarly, with the proliferation of such projects as *One Laptop Per Child* (OLPC), one can expect such access to increase in time. http://one.laptop.org/about/mission.

3. That children and teens are the major focus of significant marketing dollars and attention is the finding of Juliet Schor, in *Born to Buy* (New York: Scribner, 2004).

4. There is not enough space in this chapter to name the multiple ways adolescents are feeling the stress and anxiety of growing up in the contemporary western world. However, I offer a brief list of valuable sources on the topic in the US scene: David Elkind, *All Grown Up and No Place to Go* and *The Hurried Child: Growing Up Too Fast Too Soon* (3rd ed.) (Cambridge, MA: Perseus Publishing, 2001); Michael Kimmel, *Guyland: The Perilous World Where Boys Become Men* (New York: Harper, 2008); Rodger Nishioka, 'Violence, Boy Code, and Schools' in *Children Youth and Spirituality in a Troubling World*, Mary Elizabeth Moore and Almeda M. Wright (eds) (St Louis, MO: Chalice Press, 2008); Rachael Simmons, *Odd Girl Out: The Hidden Culture of Aggression in Girls* (New York: Harcourt, 2002).

5. Social technology researcher Danah Boyd has found that teens connect in social media mostly with peers already known to them through actual encounters (e.g. school, sports). Danah Boyd, 'Why Youth <3 Social Network Sites: The Role of Networked Publics in Teenage Social Life' in *Youth, Technology and Digital Media*, David Buckingham (ed.) (Cambridge: MIT Press, 2008).

6. This is the assertion made in the second chapter of his book. Chap Clark, *Hurt: Inside the World of Today's Teenagers* (Grand Rapids, MI: Baker Academic, 2004), 49.

7. Ibid., 44.

8. Ibid., 42–3.

9. When this finding is shared with adults, especially parents, they are usually shocked and upset. What Clark fails to take into account is that adolescents are notoriously bad at correctly interpreting adult motivations. Such is the finding of Deborah Yurgelun-Todd; increased accuracy interpreting adult emotions comes with age and the ability to read nuance in facial cues. *Frontline*, 'Inside the Teenage Brain: An interview with Deborah Yurgelun-Todd', PBS, 2000. http://www.pbs.org/wgbh/pages/frontline/shows/teenbrain/interviews/todd.html (accessed 25 October 2011).

10. I am in no way suggesting that *all* adults who appear to demonstrate care for youth are not in fact primarily concerned with the youth but with their own interests. Rather the adult community, listening closely to the youth in their care, need to create and maintain trustworthy communities.

11. This religious perspective would be drawn from and informed by the spiritual traditions of the school's founding religious community: Jewish, Methodist, Anglican, Lutheran, Ignatian, Benedictine, de La Salle, Xaverian, etc.

12. While using this phrase, I am not arguing that all adults are able to think like this.

13. Hall saw individual growth paralleling the evolution of the human person over time. The growth of the young child towards adulthood was similar to humans' evolution from primitive ancestors to modern human beings. The mature adult was understood as the fully evolved modern human, and adolescence was seen as the time of mastering and evolving beyond our primitive nature. He lays out this basic premise in the preface of his work. G. Stanley Hall, *Adolescence*, 1 (New York: Arno Press, 1969), vi–viii.

14. David White makes this critique of Hall's influence on public schools as well as Protestant youth ministry efforts in the United States through the twentieth century. In both instances, adolescents have been physically separated from adults, except those 'experts' trained to work in the presence of this population. David White, *Practicing Discernment with Youth: A Transformative Youth Ministry Approach* (Cleveland, OH: Pilgrim Press, 2005), 35–40.

15. These findings are from a body of research conducted over the past two decades. A leader in this work is Jay N. Geidd at the National Institute of Mental Health in Bethesda Maryland. Jay N. Geidd et al., 'Brain Development During Childhood and Adolescence: A Longitudinal MRI Study', *Nature Neuroscience*, 2, 10 (October 1999), 861–3. Jay N. Geidd et al., 'Adolescent Maturity and the Brain: The Promise and Pitfalls of Neuroscience Research in Adolescent Health Policy', *Journal of Adolescent Health* 45 (2009), 216–21.

16. This is not to suggest that emotions become unimportant in decision making. Rather, it becomes possible for emotions to inform the decision-making process, rather than drive it.

17. Rhoshel K. Lenroot and Jay N. Giedd, 'Brain Development in Children and Adolescents: Insights from Anatomical Magnetic Resonance Imaging' in *Neuroscience and Biobehavioral Reviews* 30 (2006), 718–29.

18. This phrase is used by Jay Giedd in an interview for the *Frontline* programme, 'Inside the Teenage Brain' (2002). http://www.pbs.org/wgbh/pages/frontline/shows/teenbrain/ (accessed 24 October 2011).

19. 'The capacity to subordinate durable categories to the interaction between them makes [adolescents'] thinking abstract, their feelings a matter of inner states and self-reflexive emotion ("self-confident", "guilty", "depressed"), and

their social-relating capable of loyalty and devotion to a community of people or ideas larger than the self.' Robert Kegan, *In Over Our Heads: The Mental Demands of Modern Life* (Cambridge, MA: Harvard University Press, 1994), 29, 32.

20. Ibid., 20–5.
21. Here 'self-interest' is not to be read in a derogatory way, but as a healthy and necessary tool for surviving in the world.
22. This is the major thesis of Kegan. It is not that orders of knowing are 'less than' but that there is a point at which the world's 'curriculum' demands more of the growing person. *In Over Our Heads*, 37.
23. Kegan, *In Over Our Heads*, 24.
24. Kegan identifies this as a shift from second to third order knowing. *In Over Our Heads*, 37.
25. David Elkind, *All Grown Up and No Place to Go: Teenagers in Crisis* (rev. ed.) (Cambridge, MA: DeCapo Press, 1998), 26.
26. Kegan, *In Over Our Heads*, 42.
27. 'If, as a culture, we expect people to operate out of the third order of consciousness as soon as they enter adolescence, then we are designing a "school" with an admirably challenging curriculum but a shameful lack of the sympathetic coaching appropriate to the gradual outgrowing of a way of knowing the world. The experience of challenge without support is painful.' Kegan, *In Over Our Heads*, 42–3.
28. Teens need lots of different kinds of support in adolescence. This list of three areas is not intended to limit the discussion but to offer a framework to further the conversation.
29. Clark, *Hurt*, chapter five. White, *Practicing Discernment with Youth*, chapter 2. John Taylor Gatto in *Dumbing Us Down: The Hidden Curriculum of Compulsory Schooling* (Philadelphia, PA: New Society Publishers, 1992).
30. This is not to suggest that religious beliefs or communities are free of the influences of the world or dynamics of power and control. However, most religious traditions contain prophetic elements that attempt to correct or challenge the community when it loses sight of its ends.
31. This is the first and major critique of John Taylor Gatto in *Dumbing Us Down*. He argues, as a school teacher, that the first great lesson on schools is 'confusion'. 'Everything I teach is out of context. I teach the un-relating of everything'; 2.

Affective Education in Post-Primary Schools

Patricia Mannix McNamara

The National Council for Curriculum and Assessment (NCCA) is the statutory body responsible for national curricula, syllabi, guidelines and frameworks for school in Ireland, similar to the recently created Standards and Testing Agency in England, and the Australian Curriculum Assessment and Reporting Authority. The broad and holistic aim of education outlined by all of these bodies provides a comprehensive agenda for an education system. For example, the aim of education in Ireland is defined by the NCCA as 'the development of all aspects of the individual, including aesthetic, creative, critical, cultural, emotional, intellectual, moral, physical, political, social and spiritual development, for personal and family life, for working life, for living in community and for leisure.'[1] Inherent within such a definitive statement is not only attention to the intellectual development of young people, but also cognisance of a much more holistic approach encompassing the education of the whole person, physical, personal and affective. The educational aims espoused by governments in Ireland, England and Australia provide a mandate for a broad and holistic programme of education in schools. In Ireland this mandate is rooted in the 1995 White Paper, *Charting Our Education Future* (the national policy consultation document on education which preceded the 1998 Education Act), which identified the school as providing the opportunity for students to learn 'basic personal and social skills which will foster integrity, self-confidence and self-esteem, while nurturing sensitivity to the feelings and rights of others.'[2] The Education Act (1998) in Ireland is similar to that of England in 1996 in that curriculum, school policy and practice are locally governed and nationally standardised. Given then that holistic and personal development features strongly in national and international education policy, one might assume that the integration of affective education curricula could be implemented in schools with relative ease. Ireland, England and Australia have all adopted a discrete curriculum approach to the teaching of health and well-being by introducing specific subjects such as Social Personal and Health Education (SPHE) (Personal Social and Health Education [PSHE] in England)[3] and Relationships and Sexuality Education (RSE) (Sex and Relationship Education [SRE] in England) and Health and

Physical Education (HPE) in Australia.[4] However, the development of curriculum alone is simply not enough. One might think that the introduction of a curriculum that engages with the personal and social development of young people and that specifically deals with relationships and sexuality education in response to the changing nature of society and the increasing pressures that young people experience[5] would be broadly welcomed and actively implemented by schools.

In Ireland, since the formal introduction of RSE in 1995[6] and SPHE in 2000,[7] there has been limited research of a comprehensive nature on their implementation. Published research that does exist suggests that the implementation of SPHE and RSE in Irish post-primary schools have been less than optimal.[8] In particular, issues such as lack of parity of esteem for SPHE and RSE, resulting in limited teacher engagement and exacerbated by challenges to integrating personal and social education into the practices of the school, have hampered its success.[9] Less discussed and potentially the most significant factor that has adversely impacted upon implementation is the prevailing culture of exam performativity that permeates post-primary schooling in Ireland. There is an inherent dichotomy between on the one hand, a school system that culminates in a terminal exam (the outcome of which determines one's future career path) and on the other, the development of the creative, aesthetic emotional, moral, spiritual and social development espoused in educational legislation and policy. This chapter will discuss the importance of affective education in Irish schools and will critically examine the potential clash of values that exist in attempting to promote affective education in a culture where knowledge reproduction and exam success dominate.[10]

Affective Education
Affective education is an important, often largely ignored dimension of the educative process. Lang offers a definition of affective education as 'all work (individual, group and programme) that is concerned with the student's feelings, emotions, and personal and social development, the positive encouragement offered by schools and the support they provide when difficulties are encountered in this area'.[11] This is clearly commensurate with the creative, aesthetic emotional, moral, spiritual and social development of young people. The SPHE curriculum is an affective curriculum in that the core aims are the social, personal and health development of students. Described as an 'enabling curriculum',[12] the aims are cognate with the philosophy of affective education in that they seek to enable students to develop personal and social skills; to promote self-esteem and self-confidence; to enable students to develop

a framework for responsible decision-making; to provide opportunities for reflection and discussion; and to promote physical, mental and emotional health and well-being.[13] Similarly RSE is also affective in orientation in that it is described as a lifelong process of acquiring knowledge and understanding and of developing attitudes, beliefs and values about sexual identity, relationships and intimacy. The curriculum is also described as enabling students to form values and establish behaviours within a moral, spiritual and social framework.[14]

Affective education has its own pedagogical approach in that it is a values-based pedagogy that seeks to facilitate personal development in order to better equip students to engage with their worlds and to be able to make meaning in those worlds in a way that is healthy and sustainable. The centrality of the experiential leaning model[15] in the SPHE curriculum requires teachers to adopt an approach that is often quite different from their traditional classroom pedagogy. SPHE requires more interactive and reflective pedagogies that are not always commensurate with traditional didactics and that require close attention to interpersonal and intrapersonal development of students. Affective education is not limited to curriculum but rather has a much broader focus. The pastoral care of students is integral to affective education in schools. Therefore, affective education is in reality interwoven into the fabric of the school via the formal curriculum, formal school structures (head of year, chaplain, guidance provision) and informal student welfare and support. While few would dispute the need for personal and social development of students, SPHE and RSE suffer from a distinct lack of parity of esteem comparable to other subjects in Irish post-primary schools. Some teachers are reluctant to teach SPHE, even more so RSE, and recent political decisions with regard to reducing guidance and counselling provision in schools appears to reinforce the relegation of affective education in the face of economic and ideological pressures. Yet the types of concerns that prompted the creation of curriculum such as SPHE – for example earlier maturation of children, the types of contexts within which young people acquire health information, the changing roles of men and women in society, health issues and the communications revolution – remain ever more pertinent issues that reinforce the need for affective education. Indeed, similar issues to those that motivated the creation of affective education curricula continue to challenge our young people, arguably in ever-increasing intensity.

The Changing Needs of Students

There is little doubt that young people in schools face increasingly diverse challenges. Navigating the diverse pressures that young people experience as part of their development requires an environment that is supportive and that can provide a facilitative space for reflection and help-seeking. Increasingly school children are gaining their information on health and emotional well-being from less formal and unsupervised contexts. Never before have school children had such immediate access to information as they now have via the internet. While internet access brings with it immediate access to global information, the veracity and appropriateness of this information is problematic. Being able to access accurate information requires maturity and critical thinking skills. It is naïve to assume that these life skills develop as a matter of course during the maturation process. Children need to be supported in the development of these life skills and in their personal and social development. The world of the student has become a much noisier place. Cyber traffic, information overload and social networking means that access to global communication is virtually never absent. There is a prevailing 'always on' culture of communication, and the increasingly voyeuristic nature of many social networking websites means that many students are under pressure to 'keep up' with their peers.

E-communication in social networking sites has a positive influence in increasing social interaction and is a quite a useful tool for young people to maintain friendships with peers they may not meet every day in school.[16] However, children also risk unwitting disclosure of personally sensitive information.[17] While bullying is a perennial issue in schools, the proliferation of cyberbullying is a growing issue that schools are now challenged to understand and contend with.[18] Because the uses of web technology evolve with such rapidity, it is increasingly difficult for teachers and parents to keep pace with the changing nature of technological bullying. Children need to be supported to develop understanding about privacy and self-management in e-communication as those who have had exposure to this form of education are less likely to get into difficulty or to make sensitive disclosures online.[19]

The challenges that students face are not limited to issues of technological communication. Students have also articulated interest in learning more about health and personal development. Through the international Health Behaviours of School Children study (HBSC), they have cited a desire for education in alcohol, puberty, drugs, drunkenness, smoking, fighting, general health, body image, physical and emotional health, happiness and friendships.[20] This study points to the need for affective education. This also suggests that more exposure to SPHE and better quality SPHE delivery is necessary in order for schools to be more responsive to current health needs. Schools are encountering added pressure to assume more responsibility for mental health promotion. Because of decreased mental health, increased incidences of distress among young people and limited skills in help-seeking amongst children, schools are under pressure to respond.[21] Schools have much work to do to promote inclusive cultures that prioritise mental and emotional well-being at the heart of their endeavours. Conversely, many schools have been identified as housing a pervasive culture of homophobia, which facilitates the emergence of homophobic bullying.[22] Being able to effectively respond to the complex and diverse range of student needs is a challenging task and lack of adequate teacher preparation for affective education exacerbates this challenge.

The Place of RSE and SPHE

In such challenging times for young people, affective education that fosters the development of positive self-esteem, healthy decision-making, mental and emotional well-being is crucial. While schools may aim to provide safe and facilitative learning environments for their students, they are not always successful in doing so. Ask teachers if they have a role in terms of the welfare of students and the response will generally be affirmative. Teachers are for the most part interested in the well-being of their students. Pastoral care of students, meeting their personal, social and learning needs is important, as is the promotion of well-being; building of quality relationships that enhance learning; and creating caring school ethos and cultures.[23] Where pastoral care systems are embedded into the practices of the school, the year head plays a significant role in the welfare of students and generally does so with real commitment.[24] SPHE and RSE are advocated as intricately linked to the pastoral care functions of the school, yet when probing post-primary teachers' involvement in SPHE more deeply, the results are less positive. The uptake of professional development in SPHE has been disappointing and even more so RSE in-service attendance.[25] After initial in-service provision fewer teachers are becoming involved in SPHE and RSE, opting to limit their teaching to areas that are more commensurate with their professional identity and their subject expertise instead.[26] While SPHE and RSE were designed to be integrated into the school curriculum, a whole school and cross-curricular approach was also intended, which would mean that all teachers in the school would contribute to the aims of the curriculum when opportunities arose. In Ireland, the Department of Education and Science explicitly stated that 'every teacher is a teacher of SPHE'[27] and yet the reality is that many teachers do not perceive themselves in this way, indeed many actively state they have no role in SPHE whatsoever.[28] The ideological assumption that all teachers are teachers of SPHE is utopian. It also lacks real understanding of the professional lives and identities of post-primary teachers, which is inextricably linked to subject expertise. Simply deciding that all post-primary teachers will identify with affective education and perceive it as core to their role is somewhat antithetical to some forms of initial teacher education programmes which predominantly focus on subject knowledge and subject pedagogical skill. It is little wonder perhaps that many graduates go on to develop teacher professional identities based on subject expertise.

There is little doubt that the decision to introduce curriculum such as RSE and SPHE in Irish schools demonstrates responsiveness to the needs of young people. The introduction of affective education curricula to be given space on the already full school timetable evidences real commitment that education needs to engage with holistic education, health and personal development. Ireland has led the way in the development and implementation of affective education curriculum. However, having a discrete subject for affective education is not a panacea. It also has some pitfalls such as the reality that in many schools, affective education has become the preserve of the SPHE teacher. This has meant that social, personal and health education is now predominantly catered for in the SPHE classroom. Other teachers can in effect abdicate their role in terms of social and personal education.[29] SPHE, RSE and pastoral care should not be the preserve of teachers who may have a stronger ontological disposition to care; they should be integral to the role of all teachers. The health and well-being of students is as central a concern as content learning. Promoting the health and well-being of students is linked to better educational outcomes. International literature points to the link between better health gains for students as having a real impact on their educational success.[30][31] Yet even though the articulated needs of children point to the importance of affective education and the international evidence shows that improved health of students leads to better educational success of students,[32] SPHE, RSE and pastoral care still struggle to gain parity of esteem in post-primary schools. While balanced affective and cognitive education in our schools is optimal in terms of educational provision, the reality is sadly divergent. Several factors impact upon the limited integration of affective education in schools. Not least of these are related to the hierarchical structure of subjects and the pervasive culture of exam performativity.

Subject Hierarchy

The current model of schooling functions predominantly on discrete curricular/subject areas. Generally, initial teacher education for post-primary teachers is dominated by education in subject expertise (content knowledge) and pedagogical expertise (subject specific teaching strategies). Not only do discrete subjects dominate the post-primary curriculum, but these discrete subjects operate within distinct hierarchies. This hierarchy is evident in the subjects that are esteemed by teachers themselves and by the whole school community including principals, students and parents alike. This hierarchy is manifest in other ways also, not least of which is how subjects are prioritised on the timetable. Schools teach far more than the content of their curriculum. They also socialise students through their engagement with the school and very quickly students absorb the messages implicit in how curriculum is appropriated and prioritised by schools. The 'hidden curriculum' denotes the informal yet no less influential messages that students pick up about what is valued in schools. Emile Durkheim prompted educators to note that there is 'far more taught in schools than the established curriculum'.[33] Later Vallance was more specific, identifying the hidden curriculum as the 'unstudied ... latent curriculum ... what schooling does to people'.[34] While much research on the hidden curriculum has focused on the reproduction of social and gender inequalities,[35][36] the impact of the reproduction of underpinning ideologies behind subject rationalisation is less studied and yet has a deep impact on the nature of education. In all modern industrialised societies, the same subject/discipline hierarchy exists.[37] Mathematics, languages and the sciences are at the top of the subject hierarchy; some way down are the humanities and the arts.[38] Affective education is positioned even further below the arts again. This hierarchy functions to serve the needs of industrialised economies,[39] in that the subjects that have currency in the production of social and economic capital for the knowledge economy become esteemed, while liberal education has lost currency and is devalued, losing its place in schooling.

Irish post-primary teachers' professional identity is inextricably linked to their subject. Initial teacher education tends to encourage subject expertise and appropriate subject pedagogies for obvious reasons. How balanced teacher education is in promoting holistic and affective education is arbitrary and dependent on the ethos of the institution in which the programme of teacher education is housed. The academic culture of universities has tended to push aside activities that involve the heart, body and the senses; therefore it is little wonder that teacher identity is driven more from subject and pedagogical expertise. The trend that teachers who graduate from traditional universities are less inclined to agree that pastoral care is an integral part of their role is cause for deep concern.[40] It raises questions as to the prioritisation of subject expertise in initial teacher education programmes for post-primary teachers in these institutions. What is vital is that all teacher education graduates have a balanced perspective on their professional identity, which incorporates both subject expertise and the education of the whole person. Ideally, all teachers should perceive their role as a teacher of children first and then as an expert in their discipline. Thus, in school cultures where many teachers may already be ambivalent about having a role in pastoral care and where affective education struggles to be esteemed, it is somewhat naïve to expect that the introduction of subjects that deal with affective education like SPHE will be met with widespread enthusiasm on the part of teachers. It is even more naïve to expect that a policy statement that 'all teachers are teachers of SPHE' will have much impact. The reality appears to be that those teachers who are committed to the education of the whole person have embraced SPHE and those more driven by subject expertise have largely ignored it.

Since the introduction of SPHE and RSE, implementation has been challenged by low levels of attendance at in-service training, and quite gendered uptake of training. In an already feminised profession, SPHE and more particularly RSE have become predominantly the preserve of the female teacher. A further challenge has been for SPHE to be given space on the actual school timetable, the result being that exposure to SPHE classes decreases from first to third year, due to the constrains of timetabling in an increasingly exam-focused system.[41] Academic, personal and social pressure increases for students as they progress through school, yet actual exposure to the type of education that can support them at this time decreases or in many cases vanishes totally from the school timetable. The fact that an overcrowded timetable is the main reason given for lack of exposure to SPHE classes shows the relegated positioning of affective education curricula in school planning. This coupled with the lack of progress in senior cycle SPHE implementation suggests lack of optimal educational provision for school children.

Exam Performativity

Examinations hold a particularly dominant role in Irish post-primary schooling. SPHE has a lower status comparable to examination subjects,[42] and as a result insufficient time is given to the subject. Some would argue that making SPHE examinable would solve the status issue and result in increased teacher engagement. The culture surrounding school subjects and what counts as legitimate knowledge means that it is not that simple; for example, art is an examined subject and yet the status of art as a subject continues to fare less well than the sciences. What we do know is that the low status of SPHE has quite a negative impact, resulting in SPHE often being avoided or overlooked by teachers.[43][44] Subject status is influenced by a deep-seated ideology about the nature of what counts as legitimate knowledge. High status subjects in schools tend to have an academic orientation in common and are primarily concerned with theoretical knowledge.[45][46] The dominant ideology of economic instrumentality is pervasive[47] and has had a significant impact on Irish post-primary schooling,[48] resulting in subjects that are considered to have a practical and less theoretical orientation becoming less valued. Space for a broader educational and more liberal agenda that includes affective education has become more and more constrained. Indeed liberal education is struggling for its very survival[49] in the ever-enveloping culture of instrumentalism and knowledge commodification.[50] The pressure on education to respond to the demands of the economy has resulted in an increasing drive towards performativity. Exams now loom large, fuelling the development of a technicised and cognitive culture.[51] The summative exam in the form of the Leaving Certificate dominates senior cycle education.[52] In effect the points system for university entry has resulted in knowledge becoming reduced to numerical currency that can decide one's future studies and career.

In this type of product-driven approach to knowledge it is unsurprising that there is little progress on affective education in senior cycle post-primary schooling. Yet it is perhaps most cogently needed at this stage of studentship as the Leaving Certificate years form a distinctly pressurised time for students. The review conducted by the Points Commission highlights the negative implications of such an exam-focussed and points-driven system, not least of which is the negative impact on students' personal development and teaching to the exam at the cost of the aims of the curriculum which becomes narrowed in order to focus on exam performativity.[53] This prevailing, measurement-driven and performance-oriented model dominant in Irish education has led to a 'teaching to the exam' ideology.[54] This is not limited to senior cycle. The discrete subject construction is so embedded in school organisation that very early in the students' post-primary journey, they must make choices as to which subjects they will choose for their junior cycle studies. These choices have an impact on their senior cycle options, so at thirteen or fourteen years of age children are making significant choices about the subjects they will continue to study for the next four years, and which possibly have a bearing on career choice and professional education later on. The Junior Certificate exam is no less daunting for the fifteen year old than the Leaving Certificate is for the eighteen year old. Hence exams are present in post-primary education to a significant and dominant degree. While we are on the cusp of change in terms of the Junior Certificate, much awaits to be seen in terms of real educational change in this regard.

Clearly in the midst of such pressures the need for affective education is evident. Yet in the clash of values between knowledge production for exam performativity and personal development, SPHE performs less than favourably. The current emphasis placed upon standardised testing and content standards and accountability means that the need for pedagogy that balances the intellectual and personal development of children seems greater than ever.[55]

Conclusion

There is little doubt that schools are under pressure to meet the diverse needs of students and to manage the pressures of exam performance. Teachers have articulated a growing sense of disempowerment in the current educational climate, often highlighting feeling ineffective and untrained on the one hand and feeling pressured to raise school standards, deal with time constraints, and experiencing the decline in their pastoral role on the other.[56] The increase in expectation of exam performativity and the ever-growing demands for education to meet the needs of the 'knowledge economy' are presenting a huge challenge to those who advocate for holistic and affective education. It is imperative that educators are critically aware of the impact of neo-conservatism and instrumentalism in schools. The social environments that children grow and mature in are ever-changing, and require a responsive education system willing to meet the changing needs of children precisely because of this variable environment. Education systems that prioritise intellectual and cognitive development over the education of the whole person are clearly not good enough. Schools and teachers do not knowingly decide to reproduce such a dichotomy; in most cases it is fair to say they are responding to the pressures placed upon them as best they know how. However, there are significant systemic challenges for educators as a result of the current dichotomisation of intellectual and affective education, not least of which teacher education plays a key role. Greater attention to the types of teacher professional identities that graduates are encouraged to foster is essential, particularly in more traditional university teacher education provision. It is essential that every post-primary teacher actually perceive their educative role as a teacher of children (of the whole person) first, and in so doing blends their professional identity as an educator of the whole person and a subject expert effortlessly together. Teachers need to be supported in this regard. There is urgent need for a stronger discourse and greater advocacy for affective education that challenges the dominant ideology of productivism and instrumentalism in our schools.

Notes

1. National Council for Curriculum and Assessment, *Social Personal and Health Education* (Dublin: Government Publications, 2001), 1.

2. Government of Ireland, *Charting Our Education Future* (Dublin: The Stationery Office, 1995), 161.

3. See Department for Education and Skills, *PSHE in Practice: Resource Pack for Teachers in Secondary Schools* (Nottingham: DfES Publications, 2005).

4. Australian Curriculum, Assessment and Reporting Authority, *Health and Physical Education*, 2013.

5. T. Geary and P. Mannix McNamara, *The Involvement of Male Post-Primary Teachers in Relationships and Sexuality Education* (Limerick: University of Limerick, 2007), 3.

6. *M4/95 Relationships and Sexuality Education Memo to Authorities of Second Level Schools* (1995).

7. *M22/00 Memo from the Department of Education and Science to Management Authorities of Second Level Schools* (Dublin: Department of Education and Science, 2000).

8. See Dáil na nÓg, *Life Skills Matter – Not Just Points: A Survey of Implementation of Social Personal and Health Education (SPHE) and Relationships and Sexuality Education (RSE) in Second-Level Schools* (Dublin: Office of the Minister for Children and Youth Affairs, 2010).

9. T. Geary and P. Mannix McNamara, *Implementation of Social Personal and Health Education at Junior Certificate Level: National Survey Report* (Limerick: University of Limerick, 2003), 28.

10. J. Hennessy, C. Hinchion and P. Mannix McNamara, 'Poetry and Pedagogy: Exploring the Opportunity for Epistemological and Affective Development within the Classroom', *Literacy Information and Computer Education Journal*, 1 (2010), 178–85 at 178.

11. P. Lang, 'International Perspectives on Pastoral Care (affective education)' in R. Best, P. Lang, C. Lodge and C. Watkins (eds), *Pastoral Care and Personal-Social Education* (London: Continuum Press, 2000), 271.

12. National Council for Curriculum and Assessment, *Social Personal and Health Education*, 2.

13. Ibid., 5.

14. National Council for Curriculum and Assessment, *Resource Materials for Relationship and Sexuality Education* (Dublin: Government Publications, 1998), 6.

15. See D. Kolb, *Experiential Learning* (Englewood Cliffs, NJ: Prentice Hall, 1984).

16. K. Subrahmanyam, S. Reich, N. Waechter, G. Espinoza, 'Online and Offline Social Networks: Use of Social Networking Sites by Emerging Adults', *Journal of Applied Development Psychology*, 29 (2008), 420–33, at 421.

17. Z. De Souza and G. Dick, 'Disclosure of Information by Children in Social Networking – Not Just a Case of "You show me yours and I'll show you

mine"', *International Journal of Information Management*, 29 (2009), 255–61 at 260.

18. J. O'Higgins Norman and J. Connolly, 'Mimetic Theory and Scapegoating in the Age of Cyberbullying: The Case of Phoebe Prince', *Pastoral Care in Education*, 29, 4 (2009), 287–300.

19. De Souza and Dick, 'Disclosure of Information by Children in Social Networking', 260.

20. See P. Doyle, C. Kelly, G. Cummins, J. Sixsmith, S. O'Higgins, M. Molcho and S. Nic Gabhainn, *Health Behaviour in School-Age Children: What Do Children Want to Know?* (Dublin: Department of Health and Children, 2010).

21. D. Rothi, G. Leavey and R. Best, 'On the Front-Line: Teachers as Active Observers of Pupils' Mental Health', *Teaching and Teacher Education*, 24 (2008), 1217–31, 1220.

22. J. O'Higgins Norman, 'Straight Talking: Explorations of Homosexuality and Homophobia in Secondary Schools in Ireland', *Sex Education*, 9 (2009), 381–93 at 383.

23. P. Mannix McNamara, E. Devaney, T. Geary, C. Sibbett and W. Thompson, *A Cross-Border Exploration of the Professional Development Needs of Heads of Year in a Sample of Comprehensive Schools (Republic of Ireland) and Integrated Schools (Northern Ireland)* (Armagh: Centre for Cross Border Studies, 2008), 26.

24. Ibid.

25. P. Mannix McNamara, T. Geary and D. Jourdan, 'Gender Implications of the Teaching of Relationships and Sexuality Education for Health-Promoting Schools', *Health Promotion International*, 26 (2011), 230–8 at 231.

26. P. Mannix McNamara, S. Moynihan, D. Jourdan and R. Lynch, 'The Experiences and Attitudes of Undergraduate Students Towards the Teaching of Social Personal and Health Education', *Health Education*, 112 (2012), 199–216 at 202.

27. National Council for Curriculum and Assessment, *Social Personal and Health Education*, 6.

28. Geary and Mannix McNamara, *The Involvement of Male Post-Primary Teachers in Relationships and Sexuality Education*, 37.

29. Mannix McNamara, Geary and Jourdan, 'Gender Implications of the Teaching of Relationships and Sexuality Education for Health-Promoting Schools', 235.

30. See S. Stewart-Brown, 'What is the Evidence on School Health Promotion in Improving Health or Preventing Disease, and Specifically What is the Effectiveness of the Health Promoting Schools Approach?' (Copenhagen: World Health Organisation, 2006).

31. L. St-Leger, L. Kolbe, A. Lee, D. McCall and I. Young, 'School Health Promotion: Achievements, Challenges and Priorities' in D. V. McQueen and K. Jones (eds), *Global Perspectives on Health Promotion Effectiveness* (St Denis: Springer, 2007), 107–24.

32. See C. Vince-Whitman and C. Aldinger, *Case Studies in Global School Health Promotion from Research to Practice* (New York: Springer, 2009).

33. E. Durkheim, *Moral Education* (New York: Free Press, 1961), 148.

34. E. Vallance, 'Hiding the Hidden Curriculum: An Interpretation of the Language of Justification in Nineteenth-Century Educational Reform', *Curriculum Theory Network*, 4 (1973), 5–21 at 5.

35. H. Giroux, *Ideology, Culture and the Process of Schooling* (Philadelphia, PA: Temple University Press, 1981), 2.

36. See B. Hooks, *Teaching to Transgress: Education as the Practice of Freedom* (London: Routledge, 1994).

37. K. Robinson, *Out of Our Minds: Learning to be Creative* (Chichester: Capstone Publishing, 2001), 60.

38. K. Robinson, *The Element: How Finding Your Passion Changes Everything* (London: Penguin, 2009), 13.

39. Ibid.

40. J. Norman (ed.), *At the Heart of Education: School Chaplaincy and Pastoral Care* (Dublin: Veritas, 2004), 23.

41. Geary and Mannix McNamara, *Implementation of Social Personal and Health Education at Junior Certificate Level: National Survey Report*, 20.

42. S. Nic Gabhainn, S. O'Higgins, M. Galvin, C. Kennedy and M. Barry, *The Implementation of SPHE at Post-Primary Level: A Case Study Approach, Executive Summary Report* (Dublin: Social Personal and Health Education Support Service, 2007), 26.

43. Dáil na nÓg, *Life Skills Matter – Not Just Points*, 34.

44. R. Burtenshaw, *Report from the Review of Social Personal and Health Education at Junior Cycle by the SPHE Support Service Post-Primary* (Dublin: Burtenshaw Kenny & Associates, 2003), 22.

45. See P. Morris, *The Hong Kong School Curriculum: Development Issues and Policies* (2nd ed.) (Hong Kong: Hong Kong University Press, 1996).

46. See I. Goodson, *School Subjects and Curriculum Change* (Bristol: Falmer Press, 1993).

47. I. Stronach and H. Piper, 'Can Liberal Education Make a Comeback? The Case of "Relational Touch" at Summerhill School', *American Educational Research Journal*, 45 (2008), 3–37 at 6.

48. See J. Gleeson, *Curriculum in Context: Partnership, Power and Praxis in Ireland* (Oxford: Peter Lang, 2010).

49. Hennessy, Hinchion and Mannix McNamara, 'Poetry and Pedagogy', 179.

50. See J. Smyth and G. Shacklock, *Remaking Teaching: Ideology, Policy and Practice* (London: Routledge, 1998).

51. E. W. Eisner, 'What Can Education Learn from the Arts about the Practice of Education?', *International Journal of Education and the Arts*, 5 (2004), 1–12 at 3–4.

52. J. Hennessy, C. Hinchion and P. Mannix McNamara, 'The Points, the Points, the Points: Exploring the Impact of Performance Oriented Education on the Espoused Values of Senior Cycle Poetry Teachers in Ireland', *English Teaching Practice and Critique*, 10 (2011), 181–98 at 187, 191.

53. See Government of Ireland, *Commission on the Points System: Final Report and Recommendations* (Dublin: Commission on the Points System, 1999).

54. Hennessy, Hinchion and Mannix McNamara, 'The Points, the Points, the Points', 184.

55. S. Ferguson, 'A Case for Affective Education: Addressing the Social and Emotional Needs of Gifted Students in the Classroom', *Virginia Association for the Gifted Newsletter* (2006), 1–3 at 1.

56. D. Rothi, G. Leavey and R. Best, 'On the Front-Line', 1220.

Leading Inclusion

Audrey Halpin

Providing equal education and life-enhancing opportunities for all learners requires that we fully accept and respond to them in our schools and throughout the education system. Although there are many layers in this provision, from national policy to choosing suitable destinations for school trips, one of the most important dimensions for informing and implementing processes that keep people and their humanity at the heart of education is that of pastoral care. This chapter will demonstrate the crucial role that pastoral educators have to play in the effective inclusion of students with special education needs in our mainstream post-primary schools. Inclusion as an approach for accommodating naturally occurring societal diversity in our schools is outlined and some erroneous beliefs about young people who are deemed to have special educational needs are discussed. Some possible implications for pastoral care educators are suggested.

Increasing Diversity

In recent years there have been a number of major reports that emphasise the importance of engagement[1] for success at school and it is well established that a good relational school climate promotes engagement.[2] The pastoral dimension in education is central to the creation, maintenance and, when necessary, renovation of a positive school climate. Absence of the climate that facilitates engagement will ultimately affect retention rates, which has major implications for life success.[3] Some noted developments in recent times have been the increasing complexity of our schools[4] and the gradual move towards inclusion.[5] As our mainstream schools are considered to be increasingly more complex places and much discussion is taking place around managing the increasing diversity of our student population,[6] a unifying force is needed within each school so that its core purpose of facilitating the learning of all its students[7] can be pursued. With so much emphasis on difference,[8] however, there has emerged a sense that incorporating so much diversity in our schools may be a very cumbersome and difficult chore rather than a source of richness and cause for celebration.

This is not surprising because much of the public and professional discourse on diversity at school has been based on the different[9] things that need to be done, and this can imply much additional work of an arduous nature.[10] Although embracing diversity does entail a range of distinctive responses, rather than expecting uniformity, what is needed is more a paradigmatic shift towards providing what we have always offered in schools to a varied population than a dramatic move to acquire a whole new set of skills and practices.[11] Some individuals will need accommodations that are quite different to what is currently common practice at our schools but the overemphasis on these has reinforced the idea that mainstream teachers do not know how to use effective inclusive teaching strategies[12] and exacerbated fears of inadequacy among educators who do not have specialised training. There are two major precepts that underpin the work in a school that accomplishes the modern challenge of being diverse: 1. Most of what all students need is to be accepted as they are, and to be supported in our existing school programmes. 2. Many also need adaptations of various kinds in order for them to be successful so policy makers need to ensure capacity for these through providing sufficient time, resources (human and material), expertise and laterality of judgement to schools. Results of publicly funded research conducted to inform policy[13] consistently indicate the need for the latter and it is hoped that these will be heeded. School pastoral care[14] and pastoral care professionals have at their core what is needed to lead in the former.

Inclusion
Competence in diversity is a dimension of all school activity and our education legislation[15] publicises inclusive approach and setting as the usual practice in our schools. Current interpretations of inclusion acknowledge that addressing students at risk of exclusion from education according to discrete categories of inequality including but not limited to social, economic, ability, language, culture and ethnicity, has had limited success, and recommend instead building rich environments that respond to individuals as required, ones that do what it takes to facilitate the presence, participation, acceptance and achievement of all pupils.[16] In Ireland, however, we still have many different programmes and initiatives to deal separately with different factors that increase students' risk of exclusion, and 'inclusion' is still strongly associated with its (opposite) acknowledged predecessor: special education. Using the term 'special educational needs' (SENs) to describe learning characteristics of some students falsely implies some homogeneity of discrepancy, and drawing any further attention to difference and deficit is in itself problematic. Nevertheless SEN is a commonly understood term that is used to describe the way in which some young people learn. Special educational needs are an

accepted set of descriptors for now, and students who share certain learning characteristics (arising from disabilities, impairments or other significant differences from established norms) are considered in our system to have SENs. This chapter will go on to address how we can better understand this agreed (albeit alienating) language in working pastorally with young people and then use this understanding to reclaim competence in educating all children who attend our schools.

Successful inclusion is a topic that has generated a lot of reaction and media attention for a variety of reasons, and there is a growing acceptance, at least in principle,[17] for its implementation. There remains a sense that it is a very difficult and somewhat overwhelming task that is sometimes feared to be incompatible with the simultaneous pressure to increase performance in traditional academic criteria.[18] Effective inclusion is indeed a multifaceted issue that commands ongoing international debate[19] so detailed analysis of its components is well beyond the scope of this chapter. While acknowledging the density of the inclusion task and the need for professionals who have dedicated time to co-ordinate its layers, it is important that we do not succumb to the disproportionate emphasis that is typically placed on the difficulties experienced by some individuals. This deficit approach can cause educators to believe that reaching students with SENs is beyond their capacity. If pastoral educators experience such disempowerment it can render vital engagement in school living and subsequent life chances diminished for many young people.

Debates are ongoing in Ireland between the various partners to the education process around levels of resourcing and what is (im)possible to achieve for groups and individuals.[20] There is also understandable alarm at the potential loss of particular supports[21] and on-going discussions about the most appropriate provision for particular students.[22] While differences exist between policy makers and practitioners, and not all inclusive measures have resource implications,[23] it is fair to say that it seems unreasonable to expect that schools will do better in terms of meeting diverse demands with less and fewer types of resources, as students in need of inclusion continue to attend our schools every day. It has been shown elsewhere that internal dynamics at schools can allow for more inclusive practice to emerge[24] while national policies are still being negotiated. Since our current national approach to inclusion is somewhat fragmented, the humanistic, pastoral aspect of education is a radical[25] approach for realising inclusivity. This is not to suggest that merely embracing students with special educational needs will be enough, nor to advocate any additional workload for particular educators, but to offer possibilities for keeping all our students in the fold of our school communities so that students have the best possible chances now while we await more favourable arrangements.

Belonging

Some young people need more support[26] than others to achieve their potential, some require significantly different help[27] and somebody with the appropriate expertise[28] needs to deliver effective parts of the response to diverse needs if we are to be inclusive. The starting place for effective inclusion, however, is in approaching all young people regarding their shared goals/needs (e.g. of belonging,[29] developing, succeeding). Starting with differences and deficits, although well-intended, can serve to set students apart from processes and peers before they have had a chance to become a part of the school. While categorisation of need and provision of particular supports according to categories was not intended to negatively stigmatise young people,[30] a certain depersonalisation occurs if this is the main/only information shared when individuals are first encountered or introduced. Young people with SENs entering our mainstream schools are first and foremost young people who have the same broad goals and aspirations as their non-SEN peers,[31] and so we need to greet them with this in mind. Although it is not inclusive or equal to treat everyone the same, it is essential to consider everyone as belonging[32] in their equal capacity as a person within the context of knowing that all difference is an aspect of the human condition. Recent research indicates that belonging and connection at school is problematic for students with special educational needs[33] so addressing this at the base of our school structures may be one of the most important considerations,[34] since engagement is so highly correlated with success.[35]

Form tutors and year heads have a particular role to play here in the very consideration of all students within their classes as primarily belonging to that main peer grouping rather than to other assemblies of students who share a categorical description or a support service.[36] This has particular implications for the social and peer relationships that are so important for engagement and ultimately success at school.[37] The implicit messages that are sent (to the students with SENs and their classmates) when the tutor or year head develops an equal relationship with all students in their group (rather than, for example, leaving the staff-student part almost completely to a special needs assistant)[38] have long-term inclusive implications for peer interactions throughout the cycles at post-primary level.[39] Fully belonging to the form class and to the year group can also have inferences for inclusion across mainstream classes, particularly in the initial stages of first year or in whatever year a student with SEN joins the school. It is very helpful if administrators can give time to tutors and specialist staff[40] (who are more likely to have received the initial information and details around particular students' additional needs) to engage and develop an inclusive understanding in advance of the first school day or another joining date. This collaborative inclusion[41] of embracing[42] all students can help to ensure a person-centred[43] approach to belonging at the school rather than a system-focused style that, although designed to provide for additional needs, can be excluding[44] rather than inclusive. Then the student(s) can proceed through the regular tiers of school life with the backing of an informed tutor (who has enough detail to provide and promote meaningful inclusion) and the additional support of specialists as appropriate rather than needing all basic information to be shared from/through a specialist. In this way, while all aspects of the individual are acknowledged and addressed openly, it is done from within the accepted structures rather than constantly being reinforced as a difference/deficit that is somehow awkward, problematic or other. This of course has time flexibility[45] implications and is another aspect where administrators/managers can facilitate inclusion[46] by considering how best to use and share additional time allocated to the school for this purpose.[47]

Misconceptions

Having considered all students as belonging in our form classes/year groups, we can then go on to provide them as best we can with what they need to achieve their individual goals from within the staffing and other resources available to us throughout the school.[48] For some students with SENs, this may entail more detailed attention than providing for those without SENs but, contrary to some commonly held misconceptions, what the majority[49] of these students need lies within the normal range of teaching and learning activities.[50] Including any students at our schools mainly involves recognising how much of what (from that range) is needed at various times. Some provision from outside this range is needed for some students at some times but that is not the focus here. The fact that additional resources to educate students with SENs are allocated to schools solely according to individual degrees of deficit[51] reinforces the notion that these students are separate from the main student body and that their additional needs are mainly to be met separately by staff members who have been allocated additional time or responsibility for them. There are guidelines for developing more inclusive practice[52] and good examples exist around the country of pooling all available resources to provide inclusive education,[53] but it remains the case that the very systems designed to help schools include students with SENs can have the opposite effect.[54] The over-emphasis on difference and difficulty has perpetuated some particularly alienating beliefs about diverse learning needs and how these are best met. The three main misconceptions that will be presented here as particularly relevant to pastoral systems and for pastoral educators are: a) that there are different need-specific pedagogies that work for groups of students who share a particular label; b) that individual education plans (complex but effective documents) are mainly intended to achieve the goal of remediating students; and c) that all students with special educational needs have requirements that are best addressed through additional/individual instruction.

Special pedagogies
In fact there are no established specific pedagogies or strategies that have been found to work universally for students who have particular categories of special educational need.[55] Although there is evidence that particular practices work for some students in certain areas of learning at various times, these are all carefully chosen applications from the full continuum of teaching and learning approaches rather than a set of fixed and different tactics for different people.[56] Even among different groups of teachers with designated support roles there are differences in perception regarding specialisms and what category of student should be supported by whom.[57] The success of students is known to be more attributable to the amount of appropriate school adjustment/support they receive when needed than to any specific methods associated with category of need.[58] Due to these widespread misunderstandings, the most frequent question from teachers who want to include but believe they do not know how is based on this notion that there is a set of tips that can be implemented successfully and somewhat uniformly for students who have the same categorical needs.[59] In fact students with SENs (just like all students) need us to be familiar with the full range of what is possible in teaching and learning, to take the time to figure out what they need to learn in different subject areas at different times and to provide this.[60]

It can be useful of course to know what there is to know about highly publicised but also widely contested evidence-based practices[61] and for specialists[62] to share this information where helpful, but a major problem throughout schools is the persisting belief that SEN specific pedagogies exist. Rather than being empowered with an understanding of the individual, and equipped with the knowledge that the best strategy for every student is to select from what is available, non-specialists believe their skills to be inadequate[63] and fear an excessive learning load involved in changing this. Naturally specialists who have worked with large numbers of students who have additional needs across a wide variety of subject disciplines have a significant input to make here in expediting the inclusion process by working collaboratively with subject teachers. There is also a significant role for pastoral care professionals in helping to increase awareness of the pedagogic reality through the network of relationships they weave in schools.[64]

Individual education plans

Individual Education Plans (IEPs) have long been considered the instrument through which students who might otherwise fail to learn will be provided with what they need.[65] The original intent of these plans was to bring together the thinking and collaboration necessary for individuals to achieve, and this remains a sound basic approach. The documents themselves, however, have largely been found to be cumbersome paper exercises[66] arising from highly bureaucratic processes[67] that can serve to highlight only the differences between students who are entitled to them and those who are not rather than guide the overall education and achievement of young people.[68] These plans often reduce the vision for individuals to measurable and timed (SMART)[69] targets for which educators can be held accountable rather than guiding a young person towards maximum participation in goals held for all students. Since staying in school and achieving certification of learning (particularly the Leaving Certificate in Ireland)[70] enhance the life chances for young people, then these common goals are the main ones for all students. The most helpful individual education plans for students with SENs therefore would be to specify what individuals need from the full range of what is available within schools in order for them to achieve as many post-primary goals as possible. While there is also a need for some additional and/or different goals for particular students, it is not helpful in mainstream schools for the main emphasis to be on these. The need for subject teachers to have ownership of IEPs has been established elsewhere[71] so simplicity of plans that can be meaningful and deliverable is recommended. Detailed guidelines for the writing of IEPs with samples for individuals who have categorical needs[72] certainly contain suggestions that can be helpful to educators but have not been widely successful in enhancing inclusion or long-term outcomes.[73] Preoccupation with corrective tasks and focus on measurable components can cause distraction from the ultimate aims, lead to unnecessary segregation, be very time-consuming with little end result[74] and make it very difficult for all educators to understand

and perform their duty to these young people. As well as their questionable complexity and benefit, the existence of IEPs as separate documents, rather than as a part of overall planning, can contribute to the flawed belief that individual plans should outline a separate programme (often delivered in withdrawal settings) for individuals and so usual practice in their mainstream classes can continue undisturbed. A single plan that encompasses all the accommodations, adaptations, modifications and considerations that will be used to facilitate inclusion (with contributions from the student and all staff members) is more likely to be followed and to be effective.

Pastoral needs as main concern
Recent studies estimate conservatively that around 12 per cent of young people in post-primary schools experience emotional and behavioural difficulties as their main need.[75] Although prevalence rates vary greatly and there are issues with identification as well as with disparity between the experience of difficulties and the recognition of same,[76] it is widely accepted that this type of diverse need is significant. Relationships with teachers and engagement at school are key elements in managing, ameliorating and reducing the long-term impact of these difficulties[77] and are crucial elements of planning for effective inclusion. Educators with expertise in relational aspects of teaching, emotional literacies and pastoral roles throughout the school are probably best placed to be leading the inclusive approach for this population.[78] Since a high proportion of the additional teaching time allocated to schools is on behalf of students whose SENs are recognised as being of an emotional and behavioural type, it is recommended that tutors, year heads, chaplains and guidance counsellors be allocated suitable amounts of this time[79] so that they can provide for the main needs of these pupils through spending contact time with them, advocating on their behalf, promoting emotional and social well-being for all students[80] and sharing their emotional/relational expertise with mainstream and support teachers. If this collaborative approach can be developed it has potential to be used for enabling more effective inclusion of students who have emotional and social needs arising from other SENs[81] as well.

Conclusion
Just as it is not possible or appropriate to prescribe for students who have special educational needs, there is no set list of recommendations that pastoral care educators should follow in order to enhance the effective inclusion of these students in our schools. Some suggestions have been included above as simple illustrations of how certain

considerations might be undertaken. The main role of pastoral educators is that of leading in creating learning communities that respond to all their members[82] rather than chase the impersonal and elusive possibility of having a set of specialised pedagogies to address differences that have been traditionally understood as SENs. In addition to the above ideas, which fall mainly into the humanistic dimension of pastoral care, seeking to provide for understanding and human rights of students, there are many implications for the programmatic and spiritual aspects. Young people who are considered to have special educational needs have the same social and emotional needs as their peers, and have been found to have increased sources of stress.[83] Recent research suggests that these young people are more likely to be unhappy at school than other students,[84] and although belonging is not enough, it is an essential ingredient for success. As pastoral educators, we are well positioned to lead the way in changing this.

Notes

1. D. Byrne and E. Smyth, *No Way Back? The Dynamics of Early School Leaving* (Dublin: Liffey Press/ESRI, 2010).

2. B. Nye, S. Konstantopoulos and L. V. Hedges, 'How Large are Teacher Effects?', *Educational Evaluation and Policy Analysis*, 26, 3 (2004), 237–57. David B. Estell and Neil H. Perdue, 'Social Support and Behavioural and Affective School Engagement: The Effects of Peers, Parents and Teachers', *Psychology in the Schools*, 50, 4 (2013), 325–39.

3. L. Bond, H. Butler, L. Thomas, J. Carlin, S. Glover, G. Bowes and G. Patton, 'Social and School Connectedness in Early Secondary School as Predictors of Late Teenage Substance Use, Mental Health and Academic Outcomes', *Journal of Adolescent Health* 40, 4 (2007), 357, 9–18. E. Smyth and S. McCoy, *Investing in Education: Combating Educational Disadvantage* (Dublin: ESRI Research Series, 2009).

4. A. Hargreaves and M. Fullan, 'Mentoring in the New Millennium', *Theory into Practice*, 39, 1 (2000), 50–6. P. McKenzie, P. Santiago, P. Sliwka and H. Hiroyuki, *Teachers Matter: Attracting, Developing and Retaining Effective Teachers* (Paris: OECD, 2005). K. Holmes, J. Clement and J. Albright, 'The Complex Task of Leading Educational Change in Schools', *School Leadership & Management*, 33, 3 (2013), 270–83. OECD (2013) *Education Policy Outlook: Ireland* (Paris: OECD, 2013).

5. Department of Education, Report of the Special Education Review Committee (1993). Government of Ireland, Education Act (1998). Government of Ireland, Education (Welfare) Act (2000). Government of Ireland, Education for Persons with Special Educational Needs Act (2004). Department of Education and Science and The Equality Authority, *Schools and the Equal Status Acts* (2nd ed.), Dublin (2005). W. Kinsella and J. Senior, 'Developing Inclusive Schools: A Systemic Approach', *International Journal of Inclusive Education*, 12, 5–6 (2008), 651–65.

6. M. Clarke and S. Drudy, 'Teaching for Diversity, Social Justice and Global Awareness', *European Journal of Teacher Education*, 29, 3 (2006), 371–86. E.

Smyth, M. Darmody, F. McGinnity and D. Byrne, *Adapting to Diversity: Irish Schools and Newcomer Students* (ESRI, 2009). M. Shevlin, H. Kearns, M. Ranaghan, M. Twomey, R. Smith and E. Winter, *Creating Inclusive Learning Environments in Irish Schools: Teacher Perspectives* (Trim: NCSE, 2009).

7. A. Lodge and K. Lynch (eds), *Diversity at School* (Dublin: Institute of Public Administration for the Equality Authority, 2004). G. Jeffers and U. O'Connor (eds), *Education for Citizenship and Diversity in Irish Contexts* (Dublin: Institute of Public Administration, 2008).

8. Meeting diverse needs requires that we acknowledge and respond to individual difference, but overemphasis on differences is problematic; e.g.: D. Devine, 'Welcome to the Celtic Tiger? Teacher Responses to Immigration and Increasing Ethnic Diversity in Irish Schools', *International Studies in Sociology of Education*, 15, 1 (2005), 49–70; C. Coates, and P. Vickerman, 'Let The Children Have Their Say: Children With Special Educational Needs and Their Experiences Of Physical Education – A Review', *Support for Learning*, 23, 4 (2008), 168–75.

9. Emphasis on some of these differences highlighted in J. Travers, T. Balfe, C. Butler, T. Day, M. Dupont, R. McDaid and A. Prunty, 'Addressing the Challenges and Barriers to Inclusion in Irish Schools: Report to Research and Development Committee of the Department of Education and Skills' (2010) (online at http://www.spd.dcu.ie/main/academic/special_education/documents/StPatricksCollegeSENReport2010.pdf; accessed 21 July 2014).

10. E.g. differentiation is often presented as a prohibitively time-consuming process that requires extensive additional preparation, whereas it is actually an approach that is most effective when simple tailorings suited to the individual's present and the task at hand are woven into teaching.

11. B. Norwich and A. Lewis, *Special Teaching for Special Children: A Pedagogy for Inclusion?* (London: Open University Press, 2005). M. E. King-Sears, 'Facts and Fallacies: Differentiation and the General Education Curriculum for Students with Special Educational Needs', *Support For Learning* 23, 2 (2008), 55–62.

12. L. Florian, 'Special or Inclusive Education: Future Trends', *British Journal of Special Education*, 35, 4 (2008), 202–8.

13. For example, many references to the organisation of resources are contained in National Council for Special Education, *Implementation Report: Plan For The Phased Implementation Of The EPSEN Act 2004* (Trim, 2006).

14. 'School Pastoral Care is an approach to education which seeks to value and develop the young person at every level. It implies caring for the quality of relationships between all the partners in the school community. It involves the engagement of all school polices, processes and programmes in the development of the appropriate structures, roles and resources to support the development of the emerging adult.' Irish Association of Pastoral Care in Education (IAPCE), www.iapce.ie.

15. Education Act (1998) EPSEN (2004) (see note 4 above).

16. G. Thomas, 'A Review of Thinking and Research about Inclusive Education Policy, with Suggestions for a New Kind of Inclusive Thinking', *British Educational Research Journal*, 39, 3 (2013), 473–90. R. Opertti, Z. Walker and Y. Zhang, 'Inclusive Education: From Targeting Groups and Schools to Achieving Quality Education as the Core of EFA', *The SAGE Handbook of Special Education: Two Volume Set* (2013), 149.

17. B. MacGiolla Phádraig, 'Towards Inclusion: The Development of Provision for Children With Special Educational Needs in Ireland from 1991 to 2004', *Irish Educational Studies*, 26, 3 (2007), 289–300.

18. N. M. Ruijs, I. Van der Veen and T. T. Peetsma, 'Inclusive Education and Students Without Special Educational Needs', *Educational Research*, 52, 4 (2010), 351–90. A. Kalambouka, P. Farrell, A. Dyson and I. Kaplan, 'The Impact of Placing Pupils with Special Educational Needs in Mainstream Schools on the Achievement of Their Peers', *Educational Research*, 49, 4 (2007), 365–82.

19. S. Stainback and W. Stainback, 'Including Students with Severe Disabilities in the Regular Classroom Curriculum', *Preventing School Failure*, 37, 1 (1992), 26–30. M. Ainscow, 'Making Sense of Inclusive Education', *Examining Theory & Practice In Inclusive Education: Trinity Education Papers*, 2, 2 (2013), 2–11. G. Stangvik, 'Progressive Special Education in the Neoliberal Context', *European Journal of Special Needs Education* (2014; forthcoming), 1–14.

20. Association of Secondary Teachers in Ireland, 'ASTI Responds to Allocation of Supports to Special Educational Needs Students', available at: http://www.asti.ie/news/latest-news/news-article/browse/6/article/asti-responds-to-allocation-of-supports-to-special-educational-needs-students-1//back_to/press-releases-2/ (2013). Teachers' Union of Ireland, Feedback on Draft NEPS Guidelines and Resource Pack for Special Needs, available at: http://www.tui.ie/teaching/special-educational-needs.1707.html (2010).

21. E.g. budgetary cuts in the school guidance counselling service as described at: http://www.independent.ie/lifestyle/education/pupils-left-without-vital-help-as-counselling-hours-cut-even-further-29910016.html (accessed 21 July 2014). Management Bodies and NAPD Call for an End to Education Cuts October 2013 available at: http://www.napd.ie/cmsv1/phocadownload/management%20bodies%20%20napd%20call%20for%20an%20end%20to%20education%20cuts%204%20october%202013.pdf. (accessed 21 July 2014).

22. A. Kelly, C. Devitt, D. O'Keeffe and A. M. Donovan, 'Challenges in Implementing Inclusive Education in Ireland: Principal's Views of the Reasons Students Aged 12+ Are Seeking Enrollment to Special Schools', *Journal of Policy and Practice in Intellectual Disabilities*, 11, 1 (2014), 68–81.

23. M. Ainscow and A. Sandill, 'Developing Inclusive Education Systems: The Role Of Organisational Cultures And Leadership', *International Journal of Inclusive Education*, 14, 4 (2010), 401–16.

24. M. Ainscow, T. Booth and A. Dyson, 'Inclusion and the Standards Agenda: Negotiating Policy Pressures in England', *International Journal of Inclusive Education*, 10, 4–5 (2006), 295–308.

25. M. Fielding, 'Leadership, Radical Student Engagement and the Necessity of Person-Centred Education', *International Journal of Leadership in Education* 9, 4 (2006), 299–313.

26. E.g. pupil who has been ill, bullied, bereaved, one who has emerged from a minority culture background or one who has an intellectual disability.

27. E.g. physical supports or alternate forms of communication.

28. This depends on the type of support (if any) required in particular contexts at certain times e.g. SNAs, learning support/resource teachers, guidance counsellors, chaplains, out-of-school professionals.

29. N. Kunc, 'The Need to Belong: Rediscovering Maslow's Hierarchy of Needs' in R. Villa, J. Thousand, W. Stainback and S. Stainback, *Restructuring for Caring & Effective Education* (Baltimore: Paul Brookes, 1992). Available at: http://www.broadreachtraining.com/articles/armaslow.htm.

30. L. A. Hughes, P. Banks and M. M. Terras, 'Secondary School Transition for Children with Special Educational Needs: A Literature Review', *Support for Learning*, 28, 1 (2013), 24–34.

31. L. Casey, P. Davies, A. Kalambouka, N. Nelson and B. Boyle, 'The Influence of Schooling on the Aspirations of Young People with Special Educational Needs', *British Educational Research Journal*, 32, 2 (2006), 273–90.

32. E. J. Prince and J. Hadwin, 'The Role of a Sense of School Belonging in Understanding the Effectiveness of Inclusion of Children with Special Educational Needs', *International Journal of Inclusive Education*, 17, 3 (2013), 238–62.

33. A. Moriña Díez, 'School Memories of Young People with Disabilities: An Analysis of Barriers and Aids to Inclusion', *Disability & Society*, 25, 2 (2010), 163–75. S. McCoy and J. Banks, 'Simply Academic? Why Children With Special Educational Needs Don't Like School', *European Journal of Special Needs Education*, 27, 1 (2012), 81–97.

34. P. Lalvani, 'Privilege, Compromise, or Social Justice: Teachers' Conceptualizations of Inclusive Education', *Disability & Society*, 28, 1 (2013), 14–27.

35. J. D. Finn and K. S. Zimmer, 'Student Engagement: What Is It? Why Does It Matter?', *Handbook Of Research On Student Engagement* (USA: Springer, 2012), 97–131.

36. E.g. Individuals and groups are sometimes referred to as 'the special needs students', which serves to define them and reinforces separating them according to their deficits.

37. M. Ryzin, A. Gravely and C. Roseth, 'Autonomy, Belongingness, and Engagement in School as Contributors to Adolescent Psychological Well-Being', *Journal of Youth and Adolescence*, 38, 1 (2009), 1–12.

38. L. Tews and J. Lupart, 'Students With Disabilities' Perspectives of the Role and Impact of Paraprofessionals in Inclusive Education Settings', *Journal of Policy and Practice in Intellectual Disabilities*, 5, 1 (2008), 39–46. C. Wendelborg and J. Tøssebro, 'Educational Arrangements and Social Participation with Peers Amongst Children with Disabilities in Regular Schools', *International Journal of Inclusive Education*, 15, 5 (2011), 497–512.

39. C. Murray and R. C. Pianta, 'The Importance of Teacher–Student Relationships for Adolescents with High Incidence Disabilities', *Theory Into Practice*, 46, 2 (2007), 105–12.

40. E.g. learning support teachers, guidance counsellors and resource teachers.

41. L. T. Eisenman, A. M. Pleet, D. Wandry and V. McGinley, 'Voices Of Special Education Teachers in an Inclusive High School: Redefining Responsibilities', *Remedial And Special Education*, 32, 2 (2011), 91–104.

42. A. Dyson, 'The Gulliford Lecture: Special Needs in the Twenty-First Century: Where We've Been and Where We're Going', *British Journal of Special Education*, 28, 1 (2001), 24–9.

43. Carl R. Rogers, *Freedom to Learn: A View of What Education Might Become* (Columbus, OH: Charles E. Merrill Publishing Company, 1969).

44. E. W. Carter, L. G. Siseo, M. A. Melekoglu and C. Kurkowski, 'Peer Supports as an Alternative to Individually Assigned Paraprofessionals in Inclusive High School Classrooms', *Research and Practice for Persons with Severe Disabilities*, 32, 4 (2007), 213–27. M. Ainscow, 'From Special Education to Effective Schools For All: Widening the Agenda', *The SAGE Handbook of Special Education: Two Volume Set* (2013), 171. G. Bossaert, H. Colpin, S. J. Pijl and K. Petry, 'Truly Included? A Literature Study Focusing on the Social Dimension of Inclusion in Education', *International Journal of Inclusive Education*, 17, 1 (2013), 60–79.

45. E.g. using the learning support/resource teaching hours allocated to the school in a creative way that responds to the contextual needs of each

student rather than a rigid assigning of hours for withdrawal/instruction by individual teachers.

46. J. Ryan, 'Promoting Inclusive Leadership in Diverse Schools', *International Handbook of Educational Leadership and Social (In) Justice* (Netherlands: Springer, 2014), 359–80. G. Mac Ruairc, E. Ottesen and R. Precey, 'Leadership for Inclusive Education' in *Leadership for Inclusive Education* (Rotterdam: Sense Publishers, 2013), 1–5. E. O'Gorman and S. Drudy, *Professional Development for Teachers Working in Special Education/Inclusion in Mainstream Schools: The Views of Teachers and Other Stakeholders* (2011), available at: www.ncse.ie.

47. The deficit model of deciding on allocation of time to schools is unfortunate in terms of supporting inclusive ideology (as per DES and NCSE circulars) but the time is ultimately allocated to the school and can be used as the school decides is best for its students. It is acknowledged here that in current times educators who have (or have had) roles as tutors or year heads are not getting recognition for this work and that some very difficult choices have to be made, so the intention is to suggest good workable practice (that might be facilitated locally and nationally through timetabling that allocates some support hours to those teachers with the most inclusive impact potential in relation to the students on whose behalf time is allocated to the school) and not to enter into the broader industrial relations implications.

48. L. Florian and K. Black-Hawkins, 'Exploring Inclusive Pedagogy', *British Educational Research Journal*, 37, 5 (2011), 813–28.

49. There are exceptions for, e.g, students with significant medical and/or equipment needs in addition to educational needs.

50. G. Thomas and A. Loxley, *Deconstructing Special Education and Constructing Inclusion* (London: McGraw-Hill International, 2007).

51. E.g Resource teaching hours allocated to schools based on individual students' degree of deficit (e.g. NCSE 02/05) and various changes/reductions to allocations (e.g. DES 0009/2012) without acknowledgement that human need does not fall neatly into these categories and no facility for examining situations according to a continuum of need as naturally exists. While the necessity of fiscal responsibility is accepted, the lack of flexibility in response to actual needs of enrolled students may be a barrier to effective inclusion, especially in schools where there is a sense that their open enrolment policies result in their cumulative resource requirements being greater than a school of similar size enrolling a less-diverse student cohort.

52. Department of Education and Science, *Inclusion of Students with Special Educational Needs Post-Primary Guidelines* (Dublin: The Stationery Office, 2007).

53. E.g. as described in Travers et al. in note 9 above.

54. S. J. Pijl, 'How Special Needs Funding Can Support Inclusive Education', *The SAGE Handbook of Special Education: Two-Volume Set* (2013), 251.

55. B. Norwich and A. Lewis, 'Mapping a Pedagogy for Special Educational Needs', *British Educational Research Journal*, 27, 3 (2001), 313–29. K. Sheehy, J. Rix, F. Fletcher-Campbell, M. Crisp and A. Harper, 'Conceptualising Inclusive Pedagogies: Evidence from International Research and the Challenge of Autistic Spectrum Disorder', *Transylvanian Journal of Psychology*, 14, 1 (2013), available at: Open University Research Repository http://oro.open.ac.uk/.

56. L. Florian and H. Linklater, 'Preparing Teachers for Inclusive Education: Using Inclusive Pedagogy to Enhance Teaching and Learning For All', *Cambridge Journal of Education*, 40, 4 (2010), 369–86.

57. P. Clough and G. Lindsay, *Integration and the Support Service: Changing Roles In Special Education* (London: Routledge, 2012).
58. T. Booth, M. Masterson, P. Potts and W. Swann (eds), *Policies for Diversity in Education* (Vol. 2) (London: Routledge, 2013). J. Rix, K. Hall, M. Nind, K. Sheehy and J. Wearmouth, 'What Pedagogical Approaches Can Effectively Include Children with Special Educational Needs in Mainstream Classrooms? A Systematic Literature Review', *Support for Learning*, 24, 2 (2009), 86–94.
59. B. Norwich and A. Lewis, 'How Specialized is Teaching Children with Disabilities and Difficulties?', *Journal of Curriculum Studies*, 39, 2 (2007), 127–50.
60. Unfortunately it is usually only specialists who have the opportunity to learn this as they explore the field of special educational needs in detail, and mainstream educators who most need to know it have little chance to unlearn the misconception.
61. This is a highly contested concept in the fields of inclusion and SEN although there is a wide belief in many schools that there is agreement on what evidence-based practices are and that they are appropriate.
62. Opportunities for all teachers who have acquired new knowledge of working with young people through additional qualification education (e.g. learning support/resource teachers, guidance counsellors, chaplains, subject specialists) to share information that informs the collaborative process is ideal.
63. Most research investigating teacher attitudes towards and efficacy in inclusive education indicate that they believe their existing skills to be inadequate. While it is recognised here that all teachers would indeed benefit from the time to consider how to apply their existing knowledge to all students, it is important to address the false impressions (of different teaching) that abound.
64. E.g. 'The Core Relationships for Year Heads' in Luke Monaghan, *The Year Head: A Key Link in the School Community* (Dublin: IAPCE, Marino Institute of Education, 1998). Also the informal networks that tutors, year heads, chaplains and guidance counsellors move between in the course of their work.
65. National Council for Special Education, *Guidelines on the Individual Education Plan Process* (Dublin: The Stationery Office, 2006). National Disability Authority, *International Experience in the Provision of Individual Education Plans for Children with Disabilities* (Dublin: National Disability Authority Ireland, 2005).
66. Paul Cooper, 'Are Individual Education Plans a Waste of Paper?', *British Journal of Special Education*, 23, 3 (1996), 114–18.
67. R. Rose, M. Shevlin, E. Winter, P. O'Raw and Y. Zha, 'Individual Education Plans in the Republic of Ireland: An Emerging System', *British Journal of Special Education*, 39, 3 (2012), 110–16.
68. A. Goddard, 'The Role of Individual Education Plans/Programmes in Special Education: A Critique', *Support For Learning*, 12, 4 (1997), 170–4.
69. L. A. Jung, 'Writing SMART Objectives and Strategies That Fit the ROUTINE', *Teaching Exceptional Children*, 39, 4 (2007), 54–8. P. Lacey, 'Smart and Scruffy Targets', *The SLD Experience*, 57, 1 (2010), 16–21.
70. D. Byrne, S. McCoy and D. Watson, *School Leavers' Survey Report 2007* (Dublin: ESRI and Department of Education and Science, 2009). Byrne and Smyth (see note 1 above).
71. S. Riddell, K. Tisdall, J. Kane and J. Mulderrig, 'Literature Review of Educational Provision for Pupils with Additional Support Needs', *Scotland: Scottish Executive Social Research* (2006).

72. NCSE (see note 65 above).

73. D. Mitchell, M. Morton and G. Hornby, 'Review of the Literature on Individual Education Plans: Report to the New Zealand Ministry of Education' (New Zealand: Ministry of Education, 2011).

74. C. Robertson, 'Examining the Role of the IEP: Does It Have a Place in the Future?', available at: http://www.optimus-education.com/examining-role-iep-does-it-have-place-future (2013).

75. S. R. Forness, S. F. N. Freeman, T. Paparella, J. M. Kauffman and H. M. Walker, 'Special Education Implications of Point and Cumulative Prevalence for Children with Emotional or Behavioral Disorders', *Journal of Emotional and Behavioral Disorders*, 20, 1 (2012), 4–18.

76. J. Banks and S. McCoy, *A Study on the Prevalence of Special Educational Needs* (Trim: NCSE, 2011).

77. P. Cooper and B. Jacobs, *Evidence of Best Practice Models and Outcomes in the Education of Children with Emotional Disturbance/ Behavioural Difficulties: An International Review* (Trim: NCSE, 2011).

78. S. Tucker, 'Pupil Vulnerability and School Exclusion: Developing Responsive Pastoral Policies and Practices in Secondary Education in the UK', *Pastoral Care in Education* 31, 4 (2013), 279–91.

79. Especially in these times of financial constraint when people in pastoral roles have great difficulty accessing allocated time for these duties and might otherwise find it difficult to support these students as necessary.

80. Paul Cooper, 'Nurturing Attachment to School: Contemporary Perspectives on Social, Emotional and Behavioural Difficulties', *Pastoral Care in Education: An International Journal of Personal, Social and Emotional Development*, 26, 1 (2008), 13–22.

81. O. Peleg, 'Social Anxiety Among Arab Adolescents With and Without Learning Disabilities in Various Educational Frameworks', *British Journal of Guidance & Counselling*, 39, 2 (2011), 161–77.

82. R. Best, 'Education, Support and the Development of the Whole Person', *British Journal of Guidance and Counselling*, 36, 4 (2008), 343–51.

83. C. Murray, and M. T. Greenberg, 'Relationships with Teachers and Bonds with School: Social Emotional Adjustment Correlates for Children With and Without Disabilities', *Psychology in the Schools*, 38, 1 (2001), 25–41.

84. A. Prunty, M. Dupont and R. McDaid, 'Voices of Students with Special Educational Needs (SEN): Views on Schooling', *Support for Learning*, 27, 1 (2012), 29–36. C. Cefai and P. Cooper, 'Students Without Voices: The Unheard Accounts of Secondary School Students with Social, Emotional and Behaviour Difficulties', *European Journal of Special Needs Education*, 25, 2 (2010), 183–98.

Playing Your Part

Using Drama Strategies to Promote Well-Being and Self-Esteem Among Young People

Irene White

The core values and ethos of schools articulated in mission statements across all sectors of education commonly refer to the holistic development, personal growth and well-being of students. In addition to providing for the educational needs of its students, schools seek to nurture students' social and personal development, and largely reflect the Department of Education and Skills' mission to 'enable learners to achieve their full potential'.[1] The inclusion of such terms in their mission statements is a clear indication of the extent to which schools recognise the role they play in supporting the wider development of adolescents.

The National Council for Curriculum Assessment (NCCA) 2008 research report noted that, in terms of general well-being, emotional and mental health are as important as the academic components of education.[2] The report urges the need for schools to support the holistic development of young people and warns that failure to do so can impact negatively on the well-being of adolescents and society at large. It stresses that 'overemphasis on the academic and on achievement has an *ill-being* effect for individuals and groups of young people' and indicates that schools seeking to foster well-being must adopt an holistic approach that ensures students feel socially valued, cared for and part of a shared community.[3] The report deems well-being to be a public issue and 'not just an individual and private matter' and notes that the interdependence of young people within the school means that 'the well-being of the individual is related to the well-being of others'.[4] These findings underline an increasing need for schools to focus attention on building a positive, supportive environment and developing good relationships among all members of its community.

All teachers have a responsibility for the welfare of their students and most recognise the importance of fostering positive relationships with and among students and the effect this has on enhancing self-esteem and promoting well-being. School staff with specific pastoral care duties, such as year heads, class tutors, chaplains and guidance counsellors, play a central role in this process and as such have an even greater responsibility to focus attention on the personal and social development of their students.

Drama has long been considered to have a positive impact on personal and social development. Recent research carried out by the Drama Improves Lisbon Key Competences in Education (DICE Consortium) found several positive behaviours among students who partake in drama programmes compared to students who had no involvement in drama.[5] Included in the long list of findings is an increased confidence in communication, problem solving, creative pursuits, reading and understanding tasks and ability to manage stress. The findings suggest that students partaking in drama have a more positive perception of school and home, are more tolerant, more adaptable and more innovative than their peers.[6] Such findings suggest that drama engenders a strong sense of achievement among students, irrespective of academic ability, and also serves to highlight drama's potential impact on student well-being. The prospect of arming students with such positive, confidence-building experiences during their school years and the opportunities that such experiences create in helping students acquire lifelong skills make a compelling case for using drama as a methodology to develop self-esteem and promote well-being.

This chapter seeks first to identify contexts in which teachers, chaplains and guidance counsellors might use drama strategies as a means of promoting well-being and self-esteem among students; second, to discuss the advantages of adopting drama techniques for this purpose; and third, to recommend specific drama strategies and approaches for use within these contexts. The drama strategies included here can be used by any teacher interested in using drama to build positive relations among students and in encouraging students' active participation in this process. Many of the exercises serve a range of purposes and can be adapted to suit individual groups' needs. The chapter will include a detailed account of how a drama session might typically be conducted within a particular context.

When Might Chaplains and Guidance Counsellors Use Drama?

Drama, like any effective teaching method, serves a number of purposes and can be applied to a range of situations. There are several occasions and scenarios when drama might be a useful tool for chaplains and guidance counsellors. It is an excellent medium for exploring sensitive issues surrounding mental health, bullying, peer pressure, anger management, intercultural education and cultural diversity. It can be used to provide support at key moments in the school year when students face additional challenges; first years making the transition from primary to secondary school at the beginning of the school year; second years struggling to reconcile asserting their independence with accepting authority; Junior and Leaving Certificate students in the lead-up to mock and state exams; transition year students deciding which subjects to choose and which career options to consider. Teachers, chaplains and guidance counsellors can all turn to drama for inspiration when it comes to advising and guiding students on these matters and more.

Why Drama?

The participatory arts, and drama in particular, encompass a broad spectrum of kinaesthetic, emotional and intellectual experiences which recognise a range of intelligences and which contribute to the holistic development of the individual.[7] Drama games are generally fun, challenging exercises that require individuals to partake in a group action. They require team work and creative thinking and are a very good way to establish a supportive environment and build positive relationships. Games provide metaphors for real life situations and can be used to generate meaningful discussion on a range of matters. When used for this purpose it is important that they are followed by appropriate questioning to enable students make the connection between the lessons learned in the game and the topic in question. Drama exercises allow participants to explore sensitive issues through a fictional lens and from a range of perspectives. Experiencing the situation first-hand but at a 'safe' distance can engender meaningful responses that are unlikely to arise through discussion alone.

Starting out

There are a couple of considerations to bear in mind before starting a drama session. First, the room should be a flat space with no furniture or furniture that can be easily moved aside while still leaving sufficient room for students to move around safely and comfortably. The school assembly hall, canteen or exam centres can often be suitable for drama workshops, as long as they are private, free of interruption and do not accommodate onlookers. Second, drama requires students to work and behave in a way that may not be familiar to them, so they may need some encouragement in the beginning. It is important to be confident about adapting the games to suit the needs of the group and to choose games that will enable students achieve the learning outcomes of the session. Many of the games have several names and variations; it is up to the teacher to decide which is best suited to a given group in a given context. As with any lesson, appropriate sequencing of material is imperative. Students should be gradually guided through the process and great care should be taken to ensure that no student is asked to perform in a manner that may cause embarrassment or distress. It is worth remembering that adolescents tend to be more easily embarrassed than adults and that humiliation of any kind is counter-productive, in the extreme, to confidence-building objectives.

Drama as a means of promoting well-being among first year students
The transition from primary to secondary school is a critical phase in students' lives.[8] The first year, and the first number of weeks in particular, is a time of enormous change for first year students. The transfer can be a source of anxiety for many, and feelings of unease affect well-being.[9] In the first longitudinal study of its kind in Ireland, an ESRI/NCCA study examining the experiences of students in their first year at post-primary school found that having a positive school climate that encourages good relationships among students and between students and teachers helps students to settle in and do well at school.[10] Similarly in research carried out by the INTO Education Committee, primary teachers identified self-esteem, confidence, a positive outlook and 'the ability to mix with other students and to form relationships with teachers' as essential attributes for students to make a successful transition into second-level education.[11] Likewise, research carried out by the Research Institute for Health and Social Change at Manchester Metropolitan University found that friendships were central to students feeling good at school and that positive well-being, in general, was linked to good relationships with friends and teachers.[12]

Chaplains and guidance counsellors play a vital role in establishing positive relations with and among students and so are pivotal to making the transition from primary to secondary education a positive and pleasant experience for students. Drama's capacity for relationship building, for team-building and for confidence-building makes it an ideal starting point. The following section illustrates examples of drama strategies that are suitable for initiating first years into second level.

A Drama Programme for First Year Students
The chief objective of this programme is to create a fun, supportive and respectful environment that will help students bond as a group and get to know each other as individuals. The first step in this process is leading students through a series of ice-breaking strategies to help alleviate barriers of shyness, anxiety and apprehension. It is always good to begin with some name games so teacher and students

alike can start to learn each other's names. There are several name games to choose from, examples of which follow below. It is useful to first acquaint the students with the rudimentary responses of moving, listening and thinking involved in drama-based activities. An opening activity that is particularly effective for this purpose is the exercise 'Up Down Freeze'.

Up Down Freeze
In this exercise, students walk around the room randomly changing direction, filling the spaces and responding to various commands called out by the teacher. It is usually best to start by asking students to form a circle so that everyone can first listen to the rules and see the accompanying teacher demonstration. Examples of commands include asking students to walk forwards, backwards, to the left, to the right, jump up towards the ceiling, crouch down towards the floor and freeze, for which students stop and hold still mid-stride. Allow this to continue for three or four minutes until students are familiar with the space. Remind them to fill the spaces, keep away from each other and avoid walking in circles. A fun variation on this game and an enjoyable way to bring it to an end is to call freeze and tell students that the game will continue for one more minute but this time they must do the opposite of the command called by teacher. For example, walk to the right when 'left' is called and walk forward when 'backwards' is called. It is usually wise to emphasise that this rule only applies for the next sixty seconds!

'Up Down Freeze' is an effective introduction to the drama games that follow. It encourages students to move around the space freely, become familiar with their surroundings, become mindful of each other and become accustomed to following the teacher's instructions. It is also a useful lead into the next game 'Meet and Greet'.

Meet and Greet
In this simple but effective ice-breaker, students shake hands and introduce themselves to each other. While this is a popular ritual of social interaction among adults, teenagers are less inclined to introduce themselves in this manner. To help make it less awkward, it is helpful if the teacher places it in the context of the previous game. Students again walk randomly around the room, changing direction, filling the spaces, and when 'Freeze!' is called, students stop and introduce themselves to the person nearest them and resume walking on 'Go!' This is repeated a number of times before adding in the variation 'Silly Meet and Greet'. In this add-on, the game is played as above but this time participants must be shaking hands with someone at

all times. In other words, they cannot let go of a person's hand until someone else offers to shake hands with them. As everyone is in the same predicament, the game usually ends with participants all holding hands and at the same time trying to break away from each other which usually results in lots of confusion and laughter. This is a tremendous ice-breaker; it releases tension and nervous energy, helps put participants at ease and is generally met with enthusiasm.

A–Z Line of First Names

Ask students to form a line in alphabetical order of their first names. Designate one corner of the room as 'A' and the opposite corner as 'Z', so a diagonal line will form. If space is limited, the line can form a V shape with A and Z ending up opposite each other. Instruct students that they must organise the line without the teacher's assistance and ask if they have any suggestions on how they might approach this task. Usually students quickly realise that they will have to find out each other's names and consult with one another in order to form the line correctly. Once this has been established it can help if the teacher begins proceedings by asking students to go and stand wherever they think their letter is likely to be in the room. After that, it is important to encourage students to work together, not only because the purpose of the exercise is that they learn each other's names but also because completing the task results in a sense of group achievement. The teacher can ascertain this through questioning at the end and so highlight the benefits of teamwork and what can be accomplished when students work collaboratively as a team. Once the line is formed, ask students to take a moment to check they know the name of the person either side of them. Then, starting from the A corner, each person will call out their name, while everyone looks and listens to see if anyone needs to swap places. Once the line has been finalised, get students to call out their name again, this time asking them to remember one person's name from the line. Students should now know three names, the person either side of them and one other. A variation on this ice-breaker is to form a line of birthdays from 1 January to 31 December. This can be used as a follow-on activity from the A–Z line as students will occupy different positions in the line and so have the opportunity to learn more names. It can also be used as an alternative to A–Z if students have difficulty in arranging themselves alphabetically.

Now that students have learned at least some names, it is time to help them get to know each other a little better. The next game requires students to speak to each other through a series of tasks and helps develop students' social and interaction skills.

Group Formations

Ask students to walk around the room as before and when asked to 'find someone with ...', they must look around the room and form groups according to the instruction given. Instructions could be to find someone with the same colour hair, the same colour eyes, the same number of brothers, the same number of sisters, the same favourite television programme, the same favourite band.

Blind Trust

This popular trust exercise is carried out in pairs. Ask students to pair with someone nearby and to nominate A and B in each pairing. A closes eyes and B guides A safely around the room by placing hands on A's shoulders. The exercise should be carried out in silence and is developed by teacher instruction. Teacher encourages A to remove hands fleetingly from B's shoulders when it is safe for A to take a couple of steps unaided. Gradually build this up for longer spells, reminding B to always replace hands when A needs to be protected from obstacles. When appropriate, encourage B, through eye contact and gesture only, to swap partners with another B. This should be done as subtly as possible, in the hope that A won't realise it has happened. After a few swaps have taken place, stop the game and tell A's to open eyes and meet their new partner. A's and B's should then return to their original partnership, reverse roles and repeat the entire exercise so everyone experiences leading and being led. This exercise can be used to generate discussion around issues of trust, support and friendship.

Up to this point, the focus has been on getting individuals to connect with other individuals. It is now time to focus on team building within the group. The aim here is to encourage students to work collaboratively on a joint task.

Group Clusters

Divide the class into groups of six or eight. The teacher calls out random objects and each group must use their bodies to form that object. Any object is fine, the more challenging the better, but to start things off keep it simple by asking groups to form various letters of the alphabet and easy-to-form shapes such as square, circle, triangle. As groups become more adept, make it more difficult by calling out objects such as a car, a ladder, a bunch of flowers, a horse-drawn carriage. It is essential that this game is carried out at quite a fast pace. It does not work nearly as well if students have too much time to think. They become much more decisive and creative when working against the clock so it helps greatly if the teacher does a ten second countdown shortly after calling out each object.

Keep the Ball in the Air

This is a team-building exercise that gets the group working together. Participants huddle closely together, and using the palms of their hands, work together to keep an object off the ground. To prevent this becoming a solo exercise, one of the rules dictates that the same person cannot hit the object more than three times consecutively.

This exercise can be used to highlight the concept of teamwork and the advantages of cooperative learning. It also promotes communication and concentration skills.

Supporting Sam

This exercise is an opportunity for students to work together on issues of immediate significance to them at the start of the school year, such as how to read a timetable, how to locate rooms and areas in the school, identify school rules and answer questions that commonly arise in relation to these matters. Give students a fictional profile of a new classmate, Sam, who will be starting school in one month's time. Ask students to work in groups to put together a starter pack to welcome this student. Provide students with the relevant documents: a map of the school, a sample timetable, a copy of the school rules and any other information that may be of help. Get students to first of all draw up a list of questions Sam is likely to have on his first day. Then see how many of the questions they can answer by studying the documents.

It might be helpful to have a couple of tasks to focus attention on specific matters, such as analysing the timetable. Ask students to list the subjects that are abbreviated and to colour code the timetable for Sam. Once this is completed, they can find key information from the timetable. For example: How will Sam know what subject he has and which room to go to? How many classes are there per day? How many before and how many after lunch? What time is break and lunch? What subjects have double periods? How often will Sam have Maths/French/Geography? What day will Sam need PE gear? A similar exercise can be carried out using a map of the school to help Sam locate the library, the reception, the canteen, the practical rooms and the staff room. The teacher can design other tasks to help students work through the various induction materials that Sam will need.

When the starter packs have been completed, introduce students first to the concept of a still image and then to the idea of a role play. Use questioning to elicit ideas and establish students' prior knowledge. Once everyone is clear on what is entailed, everyone should take a moment to strike a pose that captures Sam's feelings on the first day at school. Once students have done this, call 'Freeze!' and ask students to hold the pose perfectly still as if they were in a photograph. Remaining still, students think of a word that describes how Sam is feeling at that moment. On the count of three, everyone simultaneously calls out the word they chose. Thought tracking in this manner can help develop perceptions and deepen understanding.

Then in pairs, students prepare a short role play of Sam's first day at school, with one student being Sam and the other the class representative welcoming Sam and introducing him to school life. There is no need for students to perform for each other, the role plays can all be performed simultaneously; it is better for students to experience the situation than watch it. The tasks leading up to the role play will be a helpful stimulus for the role play. It is usually best for the teacher to signal the moment when the role play begins and ends. A simple way of doing this is to freeze the moment when Sam and the class rep meet; a handshake, for example, could symbolise their first encounter. The teacher then counts down '3, 2, 1, Action!' to start the role play and calls 'Freeze' to end the piece. This ensures that students all work in role for a set period of time and are not wondering when or how the role play should begin or end. It is always important to discuss the role play afterwards. Look for feedback on how students felt during it, what they noticed, what surprised them, what they discovered and so on. A good way to end the lesson is to invite students to write down one worry Sam might have about starting school and place it in a 'worry' box for the teacher to look after. This allows students an opportunity to express any concerns they might have and provides the teacher with some useful insights and starting point for the next lesson.

Exploring issues of concern through the safety of a fictional lens enables students to ask questions and address issues that they may not otherwise broach. Moreover, it encourages them to find solutions. The *Supporting Sam* exercise is an example of how students can explore a topic of immediate relevance through a fictional lens. Distancing students from the action gives them a sense of detachment from the situation and provides a new perspective through which they can address issues they might otherwise find difficult to discuss.

Conclusion
The freedom to engage in artistic expression stimulates creativity and promotes critical thinking; it demands and, perhaps more significantly, values a personal intuitive response. The message to students that their participation, opinion and personal contribution is not only welcome but valid has a powerful and positive effect on students'

self-esteem. The drama curriculum at primary level recognises that it is 'this affirming aspect of the creative arts that makes participation such a positive experience'.[13] It is crucial that these experiences are continued at second level. Such affirmations offer the kind of reassurance that schools need to afford students if mission statements truly aspire to nurturing the holistic development and well-being of students.

Notes

1. Department of Education and Skills Statement of Strategy 2011–2014.
2. M. O'Brien, *Well-Being and Post-Primary Schooling: A Review of the Literature and Research* (Dublin: NCCA, 2008).
3. Ibid., 170.
4. Ibid., 177.
5. Á. Cziboly (ed.), *The DICE has been cast. A DICE resource – Research findings and Recommendations on Educational Theatre and Drama* (Budapest: DICE Consortium, 2010).
6. Ibid.
7. National Council for Curriculum and Design (NCCA), *Arts Education Primary Drama Curriculum* (Dublin: The Stationery Office, 1999).
8. E. Smyth, S. McCoy and M. Darmody, *Moving Up: The Experiences of First-Year Students in Post-Primary School* (Dublin: ESRI and NCCA in association with Liffey Press, 2004).
9. M. O'Brien et al., 2008.
10. Ibid.
11. Irish National Teachers' Organisation (INTO), *Transitions in the Primary School – Consultative Conference on Education 2008* (Dublin: INTO, 2009).
12. L. Sixsmith, C. Kagan, P. Duckett, *Pupils' Emotional Well-Being in School: Preliminary Report for the Healthy Schools' Team Northmoor LEA (pseudonym)* (Research Institute for Health and Social Change Manchester Metropolitan University, 2004).
13. NCCA, Arts Education Primary Drama Curriculum, 1999.

Relationships and Sexuality Education

From Policy to Good Practice

Edel Greene

The foreword to a 1995 Expert Advisory Group Report on Relationships and Sexuality Education (RSE) emphasised that 'any programme which seeks to educate the whole person must have due regard for Relationships and Sexuality Education as part of the total programme'.[1] All schools in Ireland are now required to provide some form of RSE. This chapter explores the guidelines for good practice in bringing this about. We shall be looking in turn at policy development, parent involvement, teacher training, pupil participation and current developments in the teaching of this programme.

The RSE programme's initial introduction in 1995 preceded the Social Personal and Health Education (SPHE) programme, but was always intended to be placed within the broader context of the more wide-ranging SPHE curriculum. RSE, therefore, was part of the early stages of educational reform that developed alongside whole school development planning, whole school inspection and, more recently, is subject to the legislative reform in child protection policies. Research in 2007 indicated that the implementation of the programme was making good progress.[2]

In the current climate of change and reform it will be situated within the new Junior Certificate framework and be part of the process of school self-evaluation. The principles of collaborative change remain, all school stakeholders are at the heart of the triangulation between the design, implementation and evaluation of schools' RSE policies. Consultation and communication remain central to the effectiveness of the programme in both its content and delivery. In this way, every member of the school community has a contribution to make in the process of developing the school's RSE programme whether as parents, teachers and pupils. Their different roles are defined and their contribution highlighted in the chapter. What emerges is that through dialogue the RSE programme becomes an evolving rather than a static aspect of school life as evaluation and feedback permit growth in adapting to the needs of all members of the school community. This remains a condition of the school's ability to implement the RSE programme in a satisfactory way.

All schools must strive to have an RSE policy, and its implementation has featured in many subject inspections by the Department of Education and Skills, specifically in Whole School Evaluation (WSE) and Management, Leadership and Learning (MLL) reports. The Department of Education and Skills remind schools of this task, for example:

> Circulars M4/95, M20/96, M22/00, M11/03 and M27/2008 ... These circulars require schools to develop a Relationships and Sexuality Education (RSE) policy and programme, and to implement them for all students from First Year to Sixth Year.[3]

The difference between authentically addressing the relationship and sexuality aspect of a young person's development and having a document that testifies to the idea, rather than the fact, is dependent on good practice from the start. The school policy document provides the foundation for the implementation and teaching of SPHE/RSE. In their 2007 evaluation of the challenges facing the implementation of RSE in post-primary schools, Mayock, Kitching and Morgan found that:

> Many of the findings of this study indicate that the aim of capturing and representing rates or levels of RSE implementation is highly complex. For example, RSE policy development within schools might be reasonably assumed to be an indicator of RSE implementation: in this study 60 per cent of the schools surveyed reported that an agreed RSE policy statement was in place. However, upon closer scrutiny, approximately 90 per cent of schools reported teaching RSE in first year, suggesting that a significant number of schools may be delivering RSE in the absence of an RSE policy.[4]

The development of the school policy is now a matter of urgency and schools need to move forward, immediately, with the policy committee in producing a document that defines the school policy on RSE in the context of SPHE.

It is suggested that the introduction of the policy should give a detailed description of the socio-economic background of the school, a profile of pupils (age and gender), the trusteeship of the school and the school philosophy. The partners involved in the development of the policy should be identified: parents' representatives, teachers, principal and board of management representatives. A clear description of the collaborative process, including any questionnaires to parents, teachers, or pupils used to gather information, could be referenced in an appendix. The policy should state the aims and objectives of the school's RSE programme clearly and unambiguously. A brief summary of the moral framework the school will adopt should include the mission statement and a description of the content of the curriculum for both the junior and the senior cycle. The school's stance on topics such as abortion, contraception and Lesbian, Gay, Bisexual and Transgender (LGBT) issues (for example, the government-funded 'Stand Up! Awareness Week Against Homophobic and Transphobic Bullying'), should be outlined, together with summary information on what will, or will not, be taught and guidelines for teachers and staff practices. In this way the teacher is protected by the policy and the staff understand their collective responsibility in a whole-school approach to RSE. The RSE Curriculum and Guidelines emphasise that:

> An effective programme of RSE must be supported by the school climate marked by gender equality and a healthy respect for sexuality ... In this regard every staff member has a role to play in the delivery of the school's RSE programme.[5]

The policy statement should explain how RSE will be organised in the school, a job description of the RSE co-ordinator, number of classes allocated to RSE and how the school will facilitate teacher training and in-service in RSE. The policy statement should include the school strategy for evaluating and assessing the implementation and teaching of RSE. This might well include the encouragement of reflective practice by teachers, group evaluation sessions and, if possible, a whole staff evaluation at least every year.

The suggested policy statement needs to be understood within the context of the whole-school plan. In this way it is connected to other school policies. Thus, the RSE policy requires that further policies be developed by the school and that they are referred to in the RSE policy; for instance, the school policy on disclosure and reporting sexual abuse, sexual harassment, bullying, guidance and counselling. The RSE policy should also include the school's procedures for dealing with pupils who become pregnant. This should outline how to inform the student's/students' parents (if need be), an identification of support groups who assist in crisis pregnancy, the different procedures that are followed if the pupil is over eighteen, guidelines on how teachers deal with pupils who seek their help, and the informing of staff members that a pupil is pregnant. Another area that needs to be developed in conjunction with the RSE policy is the school's approach to sexual orientation. The school must include in its policy a commitment to combating homophobia and homophobic bullying, thus reaffirming its mission and vision statement in meeting the holistic development of all its pupils. Teachers again must be provided with guidelines on how to support a young person who discloses that they are gay or lesbian. The school must protect both pupils and staff members from prejudices and discrimination on the grounds of their sexual orientation.

A whole-school approach to RSE necessitates the inclusion of the ancillary staff in the policy development, implementation and evaluation of the programme. Ancillary staff often have to deal with pupils in sickbay, the school office or in extra-curricular activities. They must be familiar with the school policy, understand all school procedures and receive some level of training to assist young people in their development. The ancillary staff, especially those in the office, handle sensitive information often disclosed by parents over the phone, or by upset pupils. This responsibility should not be ignored or overlooked. Ancillary staff need to work closely with teachers, parents and principals in meeting their own needs and the needs of the school. The school policy should recognise the role of the ancillary staff and allow for their input into the writing of guidelines and procedures and in the evaluation of whole-school approaches to RSE.

Role of Parents

The RSE programme's emphasis on cooperation and collaboration with parents empowers parents and gives them a unique role in curriculum development. Mark Morgan highlighted from the onset of RSE that:

> The parents took the view that schools and parents have complementary roles with regard to relationships and sexuality education, part of which involves consultation and partnership with parents in the development of the programme within schools.[6]

Indeed, the research of Paula Mayock et al. noted that:

> Parents felt strongly that the RSE programme needed to be introduced to students incrementally and sensitively. They were also critical of 'one-off' or sporadic approaches

to the teaching of RSE. A number of students also stated that RSE content needed to be presented gradually and then revisited at regular intervals. In many cases, students and parents placed greater emphasis on the *way RSE is approached* than the timing of RSE, *per se*.[7]

Parents should therefore be participants in the development of the school policy on RSE, right through to the implementation and the evaluation of RSE in the school. They must be informed of new initiatives that arise out of the evaluation of the programme and be encouraged to continue to give feedback to the school on the programme. It must be remembered that parents can feel uncomfortable coming into schools. Some parents have had negative experiences of school and this can make them defensive and nervous in the school environment. Some only come to the school because of their child's discipline or behaviour problems. While there are many parents who are comfortable coming into the school, the opportunity to do so is often limited and focused on events such as the school play, a graduation night or a fundraising event. It is often parents of pupils that have problems that are most reluctant to come to the school. This strengthens the argument that all schools should have a home–school liaison teacher on staff, to meet parents in their home, identify their needs and explain programmes like RSE to them. Schools need to organise information nights for parents to review resource material, discuss their concerns and opinions on controversial issues, and create provisions for their active role in policy and implementation development.

Getting a sub-committee of parents to work with a group of teachers in exploring aspects of adolescent development and examining issues that arise in teenage sexuality and relationships could enhance the development of the RSE programme. This sub-committee could report back to the parent body, and parents with professional expertise should be invited to assist on such sub-committees. Giving parents the opportunity to share their experience of dealing with teenagers in post-primary school can be a learning experience for both teachers and parents. Mayock et al. found that parents preferred a realistic and honest approach to RSE:

A large majority of parents felt that the topics of contraception, safe sex and homosexuality needed to be addressed at Junior Cycle level. More than anything, parents were clear that schools needed to address, not avoid, the real issues confronting young people in a way that enabled

them to deal with the decisions they were likely to face in
an informed, comfortable and confident manner.[8]

Consequently, school parents' associations should not be viewed
solely as fundraising bodies but as forums for parents to run
information evenings and workshops, allowing the potential for
parental involvement in RSE to be realised.

Parental support cannot be taken for granted. Schools need to
address the fears and legitimate concerns that arise out of parental
objections to RSE. Parents have the right to withdraw their children
from the RSE programme. The problem is that there is no provision
for supervision of these pupils and this raises issues in regard to
insurance cover for the school. The supervision of pupils is a
continuing issue of debate within schools and a solution to the
problem will require much serious negotiation between teachers,
school management and the Department of Education and Science.

The RSE programme encourages schools to give parents advance
warning before commencing the teaching of certain topics. Letters
should be sent to parents giving them a date when the lessons will
begin, an outline of the topics to be taught and a time to contact
the school or the teacher to discuss concerns. Permission slips should
accompany the letter for speakers or videos that will be used during
the lessons. Parents' representatives could be invited to sit in on the
speakers and report back on their assessment of the talk. Morgan's
study found that 'while parents wanted consultation they did not
consider that the objections of small minorities should result in the
programme not being implemented'.[9] But in any case collaboration
with parents is dependent upon the school's efforts to be open,
welcoming and transparent in procedures and policies. Parents' voice
on the education of their children is a right and not a privilege.

School Ethos
The RSE programme adopted by schools contains a moral framework
that is informed by the inherent values and ethos of the school. This
has to be translated into reality by schools. In a Catholic school,
for example, this means exploring the theology of sexuality and
understanding Church teaching on relationships and sexuality and
on sex education while at the same time promoting critical thinking,
tolerance and respect for diversity.

Benedict XVI elaborated, saying that: When educating on
the great questions of affectivity and sexuality … we must
avoid showing adolescents and young people ways that

tend to devalue these fundamental dimensions of human existence. To this end the Church calls for everyone to collaborate, especially those who work in schools, to educate the young to a lofty vision of human love and sexuality.[10]

Denominational schools cannot assume that teachers have been brought up in the religious tradition of the school, or that those who are religious have an informed understanding or agree with the Church's teaching on such matters. The school has to make teachers aware of how the ethos informs the values within the programme, while maintaining the teachers' right to their own personal convictions, religious belief and professional autonomy. Teachers on the staff of a denominational school need to sit down and examine the values inherent in the ethos and identify how they will teach the RSE programme. This is where religion teachers, school chaplains and Church advisors can provide expert assistance and guidance. The Resource Material for RSE must be examined in light of the school ethos by both parents and teachers. These materials often arrive into schools and become the definitive teaching resource. This is largely because ease of access and lack of time mitigate against the refining and redesigning of material to represent the school ethos. Greater effort on the part of the denominational school needs to ensure that the RSE programme is faithful to the inherent values and ethos of the school. Mark Morgan concluded that the parents in his study overwhelmingly supported a moral framework for RSE: 'there was broad consensus that RSE should be ... linked with attitudes and values.'[11]

Parents who send their children to a denominational school have the right to expect that the values of their religious tradition be endorsed. This is however not without much debate and controversy. The scandals of Magdalene Laundries and institutional and clerical child sex abuse have damaged the trust and credibility of that very tradition. Indeed, sensitivity to the sincerity of the ethos stretches to groups and organisations that may be invited into the school to present attitudes and values pertaining to relationships and sexuality. Schools must interrogate the values and attitudes they are endeavouring to promote and ensure their authentic meaning, if the true nature of the ethos is to be accepted. Parents from a liberal democratic tradition need more clarity on school ethos, to be aware of this as a reality in choosing to send their children to a denominational school, and schools for their part should make this abundantly clear.

Teacher Training

After all the policies are written and the parent information seminars are over, the task falls to teachers to teach RSE. Morgan found that teacher training was central to the successful implementation of RSE and for its endurance as a viable part of the curriculum.[12] Mayock et al. found that:

> Those who had participated in SPHE and/or RSE training provided by the SPHE Support Service were generally positive about the experience and felt that the training they received helped them to develop skills specific to the teaching of RSE.[13]

However, they pointed out that regardless of the support services available, much hinges on how the development and implementation of SPHE/RSE is prioritised by individual schools.[14]

Furthermore, universities and teacher education colleges must equip student teachers with the necessary skills and methodologies of the RSE programme. The in-service training in RSE aims to support the personal development of teachers, with regard to relationships and sexuality, so too should initial teacher education programmes. An emphasis needs to be placed on the personal development of young teachers' self-esteem, listening skills and communication skills, to name but a few, which would form an essential part of their professional education. Provision should be made in training education programmes to train student teachers how to deal with sexual abuse disclosure and other sensitive issues. *Children First: National Guidance for the Protection and Welfare of Children* has very clear guidelines for teachers, which those entering the profession have a legal obligation to know and understand:

> If a child discloses to a teacher or to other school staff that he or she is being harmed by a parent/carer or any other person, including another child, the person who receives that information should listen carefully and supportively. This applies equally where the child implies that he or she is at risk of being harmed by a parent/carer or any other person. It also applies equally if a parent/carer or any other person discloses that he or she has harmed, or is *at risk* of harming, a child. The child should not be interviewed formally; the teacher or other staff member should obtain only necessary relevant facts if and when clarification is needed. Confidentiality must never be promised to a

person making a disclosure subject to the provisions of the Data Protection Acts and the requirement to report to the HSE Children and Family Services must be explained in a supportive manner. The discussion should be recorded accurately and the record retained securely. The teacher or other staff member should then inform the designated liaison person who is responsible for reporting the matter to the HSE Children and Family Services, or in the event of an emergency and the unavailability of the HSE, to An Garda Síochána.[15]

These procedures are very specific and unambiguous, particularly in relation to the issue of confidentiality. All teachers and especially teachers in training need to be continually aware of legislation and best practice in relation to child protection. *Children First* highlights that it is the responsibility of the board of management of each school:

> to have clear procedures, which teachers and other school staff must follow where they suspect, or are alerted to, possible child abuse or neglect, including where a child discloses abuse or neglect.[16]

Consequently, the seriousness of this responsibility requires specific and specialised training in child protection for teacher on an ongoing basis. An index of support services should be made available for teachers, to access further expertise and where necessary a guide to professional advice for teachers who may be affected by issues that arise.

Where teachers have not received training in SPHE/RSE, school policy should include an introduction to the programme by an experienced staff teacher in the school's induction of new staff. This allows schools to highlight the influence of their school ethos and explain the school's tailored programme. The school should also make provision in its policy to send untrained teachers on RSE in-service courses and to ensure that newly qualified teachers are not given SPHE/RSE until they have completed formal training.

In the area of teacher education it is important to acknowledge that there are members of the school staff who have a wealth of experience and expertise in the area of pastoral development and SPHE/RSE. Teachers need to perfect and in some cases embrace the climate of collaboration fostered by the development of whole-school planning. Indeed, teachers on the staff of any particular school could be the best people to run training programmes for the new members of staff. This, however, needs to be embraced, recognised, encouraged and financed by the Department of Education and Skills. Interested teachers could attend workshops for being RSE trainers and be certified as school trainers. Professional recognition of teachers' participation in further training, in-service and in-career development programmes like RSE needs to be provided by the Department of Education and Skills through certification. Not only can the teachers within the school be utilised more effectively, so too can the teachers from neighbouring schools.

Cluster meetings of both primary and post-primary teachers should be held to enable them to become familiar with the totality of the programme, understanding how it begins and where it leads. Fostering the holistic development of pupils from junior cycle to senior cycle in RSE is imperative. A new perspective on the programme can be obtained through understanding the work of all teachers in all stages of a child's life. Community action and development projects could inform these meetings and look at the specific requirements of a given community. Input from help agencies, the Gardaí, the Rape Crisis Centre, Alcoholics Anonymous and other relevant groups, especially parents' organisations, would create a unique forum for professional advice, discussion and information.

Teachers are people with their own personal problems. They often work with pupils who have problems that affect them personally. If teachers are to effectively support pupils in crisis they need to be supported themselves. While there is the argument that this is outside the job description of a teacher and it is true that they are not counsellors, a young person spends up to fifteen years in school, and the teacher becomes a very significant point of contact with the adult world. During those years they face many life experiences that they are ill-equipped to deal with alone, for instance, the death of a parent, suicide of a friend or a crisis pregnancy. These experiences are not left at the door of the school, they are brought into the classroom and to the attention of teachers directly or indirectly. This can be happening more often in a class such as RSE because of the content of the course and the reduced provision of guidance and counselling.

Pupils' Voice

The skills necessary to develop and maintain quality inter-personal relationships are fundamental to a pupil's overall positive development and socialisation within the school environment. Pupils are therefore relational and sexual people. Sexuality is an integral part of the human person, and the school, in addressing the holistic need of the young person, must help them to comprehend their sexuality. Consequently, ascertaining the student's voice is fundamental because it 'enables policy makers to make school life more meaningful for students and informs opinions among school staff with regard to school development'.[17] An RSE policy should be made in collaboration with pupils, allowing them to voice their needs and concerns in all aspects of their learning but especially in the area of relationships and sexuality. Mayock et al. found that students recognised the importance of RSE, stating:

> There was unanimous agreement among students about the importance of RSE. In support of this assertion students referenced the following advantages of school-based sex education:
> » The need to have accurate information about sex and relationships.
> » The need for teenagers to understand the potential negative consequences of uninformed sexual activity.
> » The benefits of learning RSE alongside their peers.
> » The fact that schools have a 'captive audience' in students.[18]

Ironically, the research highlighted that there were also varying degrees of dissatisfaction with RSE from students, from the low status of the subject to the lack of explicit information and the adequacy of teacher training in the area.[19] The final consensus was that relationship and sexuality education can only take place in a safe environment that supports learning, promotes questions, removes ambiguity, fosters honest engagement with explicit knowledge, provides clarity and ongoing development of issues and topics.

Schools need, therefore, to consult pupils in developing, implementing and evaluating the RSE programme. This can be done in a number of ways: questionnaires, small focus groups of pupils, class discussions on the structure of the lessons, an anonymous suggestion/question box for pupils to ask questions that they may be too embarrassed to ask in class, consultation with pupils on their own learning, what way they like the classroom set up for RSE class, their opinion of speakers or material used, their suggestions for future classes. The RSE programme highlights the importance of the pupil by encouraging that through negotiation the teacher works out a class contract with the pupils establishing the ground rules for the class. Pupils assume ownership of the contract because they have been instrumental in designing it. Referring to the class contract and reminding the pupil that they undertook to follow the rules reinforces positive discipline. Teachers need to be aware of the level of development each individual pupil is at and to understand the influences that affect this development. Pupils are the best source of information in identifying these influences and can also be a resource in suggesting ways of combating peer pressure and handling conflict at home or in school from their own experience. Peer leadership, peer mediation, twinning (fifth year pupil mentoring a first year pupil), the prefect system and the 'pupils' council' give pupils responsibility, training and confidence to communicate as assertive young people in an environment that listens and values their contribution. All of these initiatives serve to enhance the RSE programme and allow the aims and objectives of the programme to come to fruition.

Structuring an RSE Module
In the teaching of the RSE programme, one of the drawbacks to the effectiveness of the programme is the limited time given to the lessons. The programme recommends that RSE be taught in five or six timetabled periods. While RSE is a module within the SPHE programme, not all schools have the SPHE programme up and running at both junior and senior cycle level (as per Department Circulars M4/95, M20/96, M22/00, M11/03 and M27/2008)[20] and many have difficulty finding the space on the timetable for the additional one period a week required. RSE is often taught as a module within the Religious Education programme, or the six classes are part of a pastoral care class. Six lessons of RSE in isolation from the developmental programme of SPHE are limited in their effectiveness. It is questionable that issues such as sexual development and relationships could be explored in any depth over such a short period and in a class that occurs only once a week. Although RSE has cross-curricular links, the material is often covered in isolation from other subjects with little or no cross-referencing. There is even the difficulty that pupils coming from the experience of formal learning in their subject classes are expected to adapt and be comfortable with the informal structure of the RSE class. It takes more than six weeks to get pupils accustomed to the approach of the RSE programme, the methodologies, the role of the teacher and the classroom setting it attempts to create. The very fact that it is limited to a class period per week means that pupils move from exploring their feelings and emotions, to sitting a class test or attending a subject class that is unaware of the content of the previous class. The concern is that not enough time is available to debrief pupils, and that unearthed feelings and emotions are often left for pupils to deal with alone.

One recommendation that would facilitate cross-curricular links and make teachers more aware that RSE is taking place would be for the school to identify a particular week in the school year when each year group would undertake the RSE programme. This date could be decided at the beginning of the school term and would allow the subject teachers of home economics, religion and biology to plan to cover or revisit the material that is linked to the RSE programme. Teachers in this way get the opportunity to reinforce the RSE programme during their subject time and on a pastoral level because they will be aware of the pupils' needs and sensitive issues that might arise during the week. It could also serve as a foundational week to other planned mental health initiatives and/or to the 'Stand Up!' awareness week, as examples of programmes that would benefit from the grounding of the RSE objectives.

Monaghan's definition of pastoral care provides a context for understanding the importance of attending to the pastoral dimension of RSE:

> School pastoral care ... influences all aspects of the life of the school, in particular policies, curriculum, roles and structures in order to sustain and enrich the educational experience of each pupil and consequently that of every person in relation to the school.[21]

Planning an RSE week means that parents can be given plenty of advance warning, including a list of speakers that might be booked and information nights that might be held for parents during the week. Time could be set aside for pupils to meet with the guidance counsellor, chaplain or an outside counsellor. Teachers could also be given time for planning, to see parents and evaluate the programme as it progresses. This week could work only if it is run in conjunction with the developmental work of the SPHE programme and if there are follow-up classes to continue to reinforce the skills, attitudes and values developed by the pupils.

Evaluation
A school's policy on RSE is a working document and it is envisaged that it will be reviewed and amended following the evaluation of the programme's implementation. The context for this evaluation is school-subject inspections under the Department of Education and Skills Whole School Evaluation – management, leadership and learning process and more recently through school self-evaluation. This is a collaborative process where teachers, pupils and parents

evaluate the school. Teachers are thus encouraged to evaluate their own practices, methodologies and implementation. This is done through reflective practice, collaboration with pupils and the inspectorate. The subject inspection reports of SPHE/RSE have been published by the Department of Education and Skills. The common recommendations made by the inspectorate include: outlining the importance of an assessment policy in SPHE, the requirement of the school to develop an RSE policy, the importance of implementing provision for RSE at senior cycle, the adherence of SPHE programmes with the curriculum framework, the facilitation of core planning and the training of teachers, to name but a few.

The Department of Education and Skills Inspectorate has made significant headway in the evaluation of the provision implementation and development of SPHE/RSE. In conjunction with this form of external evaluation of schools, school self-evaluation opens the way forward for internal evaluation and improvement planning. Certainly there are opportunities for schools to target RSE provision at junior and senior cycle as a priority area for improvement. RSE teachers, school staffs and boards of management need to evaluate the content and the resources used in school programmes. This would involve exploring effective methodologies for certain topics, highlighting areas where difficulties arise for teachers in dealing with a particular topic or where pupils did, or did not, respond well to the material. This information needs to be recorded, and suggested changes or improvements need to be discussed. The idea of team-teaching could assist the programme in the event that a teacher found a particular topic too difficult to teach. The evaluation of RSE should include teachers from other subject areas – home economics, religion and science, for instance – to review the cross-curricular links and to evaluate teachers' classroom practices. An overall evaluation of the whole-school approach to RSE would examine pastoral care provision, information seminars, external agencies' involvement in RSE provision, in-service attendance, allocation of resources, financial budget and staff participation in the programme. The evaluation of the RSE programme should be presented at a staff meeting, and details of the triangulation of evidence-based research findings furnished to the board of management, thus forming part of the school self-evaluation report and school improvement plan.

Conclusion

It has to be acknowledged that schools are limited institutions and that while there are high expectations from parents, the government and society in general, they are first and foremost places of learning.

The existence of the points race and the use of the Leaving Certificate for selection means that schools, in attempting to address all the developmental needs of pupils, are often forced to prioritise academic as distinct from deeper educational goals. Although SPHE/RSE is considered to be not only important but urgently required by the Department of Education and Skills, some schools are falling short of making provision for it at both junior and senior cycle level. As society continues to turn to the school for the socialisation of young people, there is a need for greater cooperation between the school and the community, and more resources are required, ironically at a time when more and more front line services to students are being cut. Professional assistance from community members such as the Gardaí, doctors, nurses, parent organisations and most especially psychological services are urgently needed. The delivery of an effective RSE programme would certainly be aided by a reduced teacher–pupil ratio, an aspiration that is continually eroded by recessionary cuts in education. Smaller classes allow teachers to give pupils more individual attention, thus establishing good interpersonal relationships and enabling teachers to understand the personal issues that might be affecting pupils. Time is the most sought-after commodity within the teaching profession. Teachers need time to meet pupils, liaise with parents, listen to pupils, plan, evaluate and train, ironically only one of which – planning – is considered accountable for additional working hours. Despite the limitations, parents, teachers and pupils are engaged in collaborative work that has produced policy documents and witnessed the training and implementation of some excellent RSE programmes. It has come from the commitment, dedication, hard work and a considerable amount of good will of people who seek to make real the belief that education embraces the heart and the mind. It comes from a conviction that young people are the future and that while debate remains as to the best way to meet their needs in the area of relationships and sexuality within the school environment, the school has an obligation to try to genuinely address these needs within an educational framework. One dynamic aspect of the RSE programme is that it encourages schools to create structures that facilitate communication which is rooted in mutual respect for all stakeholders, and attempts to create a climate of open, honest, direct and focused communication between parents, teachers and pupils. Good practices in schools are identified in the school's ability to communicate effectively and continuously with the various participants (i.e. teachers, pupils and parents). Only through such communication can it become a community of inter-personal relationships sharing a common vision and mission. In this way relationship and sex education can be promoted not simply as a class subject but as a fundamental part of the everyday life of the school.

Notes

1. Government of Ireland, Report of the Expert Advisory Group on Relationships and Sexuality Education (Dublin: The Stationery Office, 1995), 2.
2. P. Mayock, K. Kitching and M. Morgan, *RSE in the Context of SPHE: An Assessment of the Challenges to Full Implementation of the Programme in Post-Primary Schools* (Dublin: Crisis Pregnancy Agency and Department of Education and Science, 2007).
3. Department of Education and Skills, Circular 37/2010, 'To the Principals and Boards of Management in Post-Primary Schools, Relationship and Sexuality Education', September 2010.
4. Mayock et al., *RSE in the Context of SPHE*, 18.
5. National Council for Curriculum and Assessment, *Relationships and Sexuality Education: An Aspect of Social Personal and Health Education: Interim Curriculum and Guidelines for Post-Primary Schools* (Dublin: National Council for Curriculum and Assessment, 1996), 8.
6. M. Morgan, *Relationship and Sexuality Education: An Evaluation and Review of Implementation – Summary of Main Findings* (Dublin: Government of Ireland, 2000), 74.
7. Mayock et al., *RSE in the Context of SPHE*, 42.
8. Ibid.
9. Morgan, *Relationship and Sexuality Education*, 74.
10. Catholic News Agency, 2010.
11. Morgan, *Relationship and Sexuality Education*, 74.
12. Ibid., 19.
13. Mayock et al., *RSE in the Context of SPHE*, 23.
14. Ibid.
15. Government of Ireland (2011), *Children First: National Guidance for the Protection and Welfare of Children*, Department of Children and Youth Affairs, 23.
16. Government of Ireland (2011), *Children First*, 22.
17. E. Smyth, A. Dunne, S. McCoy and M. Darmody, *Pathways Through the Junior Cycle: The Experiences of Second Year Students* (Dublin: The Liffey Press in association with the Economic and Social Research Institute, 2006), 2.
18. Mayock et al., *RSE in the Context of SPHE*, 3.
19. Ibid., 25.
20. Department of Education and Skills, Circular 37/2010, 'To the Principals and Boards of Management in Post-Primary Schools, Relationship and Sexuality Education', September 2010.
21. L. Monahan, *Moving Forward with Students* (Dublin: Irish Association for Pastoral Care in Education, Marino Institute of Education, 1999), 3.

A Pastoral Response to Adolescent Youth Experiencing Emotional Disturbances

Edward J. Hall

This chapter arises out of my work in a residential care home for young adolescents in the United States of America. While I acknowledge that there will be some cultural and contextual differences, it is my hope that these reflections will assist those who work with emotionally disturbed young people in second-level schools. It is my main argument in this chapter that in meeting the challenges presented to us in schools by emotionally disturbed pupils, the young person will benefit most by a response that is underpinned by Christian compassion. Consequently, school chaplains, counsellors and teachers who work out of a Christian framework make a very significant contribution to the pastoral care of pupils who are emotionally disturbed.

The Morphology of Emotional Disturbance

What pastoral challenges do school personnel face when they meet young people who live with significant emotional pain? What kinds of empathetic strategies might be useful to help children and adolescents name and claim their personal struggles with woundedness? What praxis is most useful for engaging young people who desire healing and wholeness and who courageously face the hole in their souls? These questions are essential pastoral perspectives when pastoral caregivers pass over from clinical definitions of emotional disturbance and empower young people to envision alternative narratives.

Biehler and Snowman define emotional disturbance as:

> Personal and social problems exhibited in an extreme degree
> over a period of time that adversely affect the ability to
> learn and get along with others.[1]

The label 'emotionally disturbed' is usually applied to children and adolescents who manifest their pain and suffering through problems or disturbances in living and relating to teachers, parents, classmates and others. It is important to note at this stage that while a label such as 'emotionally disturbed' is useful as a general indicator in the description of a pattern of behaviour, no label can capture the wholeness, beauty and essential mystery that is each person. In fact, at times labels such as emotionally disturbed can accentuate the abnormal, maladaptive or problem-laden dimension of pupils who are emotionally disturbed. Consequently, great care must be taken in our use of this and other psychological labels in the school setting.[2] I would further argue that the use of terms like 'disturbed', 'psychotic' and 'disordered' needs to be preceded by the Christian affirmation that all persons share the same human condition, manifested in different ways, and all have been created in the image of God and given an inherent dignity and intrinsic value simply because we exist. Adolescents living with emotional disturbance have the same human needs for love and acceptance, affection and independence, understanding, self-identity and sexuality as others without such impairing problems within the same age group.

In my experience the roots of the suffering of emotionally disturbed adolescents tend to reside in a deprivation of some kind. This would involve neglect or abuse during infancy and early childhood from primary caregivers (usually parents) characterised by unpredictable, unstable and inconsistent fulfilment of basic needs, especially love and affection. The parental style of relating to their children tends to have been rejective in the past and usually such a style continues during adolescence. Research has shown that poor parent–child relationships can lead to behaviour problems and emotional disturbance resulting in peer rejection and sometimes isolation for the young person during adolescence. It is no surprise then that without appropriate intervention, so many emotionally disturbed children leave school early and/or identify with a deviant peer group.

Adolescents with emotional problems manifest their pain in the internal conflict(s) they experience as well as their dramatisation of such conflicts(s) in their relationships with others through particular behaviours, affects and thought processes.[3] While the following description of such styles of relating, behaviours, affects and thought processes is not representative for each adolescent, either in the sense that all apply to one individual or that any combination represent the whole person, it is somewhat indicative of the ways in which emotional disturbance manifests itself. The following five styles are regnant in contemporary dysfunctional behaviour.

1. Acting out

In their relationship with others, adolescents are often unable or unwilling to control the expression-in-action of certain impulses, primarily aggressive or sexual impulses. The tendency to dramatise or satisfy an impulse through inappropriate action is generally called 'acting-out'.[4] Bernard, a fifteen-year-old who lived in the group home where I worked, became quite angry with me when I requested that he turn off his lights for the evening; he defiantly refused to comply with my request, shouted 'F--- you!' repeatedly, and punched a hole in the wall as a way of acting out his angry/aggressive impulse. Elisa, another fifteen-year-old, acted out her sexual impulse by running away from the group home for ten days to live with a young man she was attracted to.

This type of acting out will be familiar to chaplains and teachers who work with young people who are emotionally disturbed. Simple requests such as asking them to take off their coat in class or to move to a different seat can often be met with acting-out behaviour.

2. Manipulation

Some adolescents have learned how to get what they want or need from others by manipulating them through deceitful and self-willful ways. Sixteen-year-old Billy told me that his therapist said it was 'OK' for him to leave the group home that afternoon to sit near his office and read magazines. I had talked with the therapist before Billy's appeal, and he had said nothing of this arrangement. It was clear that Billy wanted my permission to leave the house without indicating what he would be doing while away. I told him the therapist had not mentioned such an arrangement to me and that he did not have my permission to leave the group home. Billy decided to leave anyway, but on his way out the door, the supervisor of the home entered the doorway, and Billy quickly changed his story, saying he was just going outside for a cigarette. This type of manipulation can often characterise the emotionally disturbed pupils' relationships with other pupils, teachers and parents.

3. Making demands

Adolescents frequently demand (as opposed to request) the fulfilment of needs or wants with little sensitivity to the needs or wants of others. While adolescence is a time of growing egocentricity in the normal development of identity formation, the particular neediness of emotionally disturbed adolescents can often surface as a demand or assumption for attention, care and support in which the one upon whom the adolescent makes the demand is given little freedom to respond other than in the affirmative. Joel wanted someone with whom he could play table tennis, and approached me one day, saying, 'You're playing table tennis with me'. In addition to this quality of relating to others by making demands, many emotionally disturbed young adolescents are unable to give back (marginally) to others in their relationships. The pupil who only comes to the after-school club when he feels like it or if there is something happening that he is interested in can be said to display this 'demanding' quality in that he fails to see the needs of others at the club.

4. Defensive posturing

Young people employ various defences or styles of relating to themselves and others which shields them from emotional pain, hurt and unpleasant feelings, like anxiety, guilt, shame, depression or worthlessness. To avoid painful feelings, when in a new and stressful situation or a threatening encounter, the primary defences of these young people are denial, projection, misdirection, displacement and regression. When confronted with a painful feeling or event, denial protects the young person from its reality. Projection often comes across as accusation of others. For example, Ernie, age seventeen, blamed a staff member for 'making him crazy'. Another boy, Andy, said to me, following his angry outburst, 'What's the matter? Are you feeling guilty?' when it was clear that he was feeling guilty for his own behaviour.

Adolescents who want to cover one feeling can display the opposite feeling (which is more acceptable) as a defence; this is called misdirection. Bernard, age fifteen, ran away from the home, sniffed glue, returned later that evening in an intoxicated state and was sent to his room. The next morning he bragged of how proud he was of what he had done. However, in the process of counselling, it became clear that he actually felt quite ashamed of what he had done the night before and that his show of bravado and pride functioned to misdirect others from seeing his shame and regret for his previous behaviour.

5. Displacement

Displacement occurs when a feeling, usually anger or hostility, precipitated by one person or event, is transferred to another person or event. Ernie was angry when his girlfriend ended the relationship. He displaced his anger on various staff members until he admitted his anger and hurt about the loss of his girlfriend. Regression is the return to an earlier, more 'primitive' state of functioning to protect one's self during a stressful situation. For example, Joanne, age fifteen, talks like a baby (regresses) when under stress.

Thinking

Most adolescents with emotional problems have a normal to above average score on IQ scales and therefore many can function quite well in academic as well as life settings when other problems do not get in the way. Their thought processes, however, tend to be especially affected during stressful or new situations. Four processes are apposite categories of adolescent thinking:

1. *Obsessive thinking:* a particular sentence, idea or image continually presents itself in one's thinking and resists repression, avoidance and dispelling. This obsessive thinking tends to be the result of anxiety and often centres on those issues most unacceptable to the person. Young people can obsess about many things including violence, sex, food, cleanliness and other people.[5]

2. *Paranoid thinking:* Intense projection and great anxiety team together when one thinks in a paranoid manner. Paranoid thinking destroys trust and promotes the anxiety that no one is there to help; in fact, everyone is out to hurt. Wildly paranoid thinking generally occurs in episodes of extreme anxiety and rage. Bernard perceived my efforts to help him with his schoolwork one evening (help he had requested) as suspect, and wondered if I was attempting to sabotage his work.[6]

3. *Loose associations:* This is where the young person is unable to order their thoughts in relation to others. Bits and pieces of ideas and images are loosely associated, and communication is impaired. This can be further compounded for adolescents who come from a lower socio-economic grouping where research has shown that they can have a more limited vocabulary and thus find it harder to communicate complex ideas or feelings.[7]

4. *Hazy reality testing:* Under great stress, some young people have difficulty distinguishing between what they wish, fear, assume or fantasise about, and what in reality is actually happening. Their perceptions are distorted and reality testing (what is actually happening external to their thinking) is often inconsistent and hazy. Joel slapped a female resident one evening and proceeded to beat her until staff members intervened. He fully believed and asserted that the female resident had hit him first. The staff member present watched the initial interaction between Joel and the other resident and indicated that she had not hit him at any time that day, and that Joel had simply started to assault her.

Thus far I have tried to outline what it means for a young person to be described as emotionally disturbed and some of the consequences for those who work with them in schools and elsewhere. I will now explore how a pastoral response to emotionally disturbed adolescents can be realised.

Pastoral Response to Emotionally Disturbed Pupils

Many teachers, chaplains and other professionals have struggled with the question of how to respond appropriately to young people who are emotionally disturbed. A significant part of any response to an emotionally disturbed adolescent will include psychological and therapeutic interventions. However, the basic needs of these young people are no different from those of other youth. They also need to be loved, to belong, to be respected and to be supported personally. This pastoral response can be offered by any teacher or guidance counsellor; however, the school chaplain will bring an added faith dimension to help the pupil find meaning in their suffering and pain as well as in their celebrations.[8] [9]

I believe that there are two crucial qualities that pastoral agents offer young people: the first is the ability to be present and to accompany someone on their life journey. The second is the ability to affirm young people. Being present means making oneself available to others, being perceptive, listening and relating in the here and now, all of which can be inhibited by the business and daily pressures of school life. Affirmation includes unconditional valuing of others; love. As 'being present' and 'affirmation' are the keystones of any relationship of trust and pastoral response to young people with emotional problems, I will now spend some time exploring these two aspects of pastoral care.[10] [11]

Being present

Being present to those with atypical emotional needs involves the following four qualities or virtues.

1. Being available: To be present to adolescents begins with making oneself available to them, for example making time to be with them and being open to their changing needs and situations in life. Availability assumes that one is predisposed to enter into whatever situations may emerge at any given time. For teachers in schools this will include even the uncomfortable situations of conflict. Verbal battles between young people can be frequent and may require a teacher's intervention to prevent an escalation to physical confrontation. The willingness to make oneself available to adolescents in even the most confusing or anxiety-laden circumstances reveals to young persons that the chaplain or teacher cares enough for them to be there at the most critical of times.

2. *Keenness of perception:* The willingness to be available to youth is complemented by a consistent sensitivity to their needs in any given situation. Perceptivity is the ability to piece together, often from little fragments of information, what is happening with an adolescent at a particular moment. This includes seeing as well as intuiting the needs of the other and then responding to those needs. For example, a pupil may tell a teacher that they are feeling unwell and can't go to a PE class. A perceptive teacher will look for a pattern and will be sensitive to any other reasons why the pupil may be unwilling to go to the class, such as the possibility of bullying or not being able to afford the required gym equipment.

3. *Listening:* Reflective, non-judgemental, supportive and attentive listening enables adolescents to be who they are, feel deeply understood and become connected with another in a trusting relationship. In offering pastoral care, the skilled listener, the school chaplain or a class teacher will be able to set aside their own agenda and really tune in to what the pupil is saying. This can be difficult for teachers who have so many curricular responsibilities and who are tied to a busy timetable. In fact, I would say that listening and perceptiveness depend on availability and this is often something that the school chaplain and other pastoral agents will have in abundance. In addition, pastoral agents respect confidentiality. A crucial role for the chaplain is to prudently judge the appropriate level of disclosure to other staff so as to enhance their understanding of a pupil's behaviour.[12]

4. *Relating:* The former ways of being present to adolescents combine as a style of relating to them in which they may develop a healing relationship with another. Consistent, predictable and stable relationships from primary caregivers have often been absent from these young people's lives, and therefore they especially need the establishment of such relationships within other settings. Setting clear behavioural limits and expectations with these adolescents enables them to predict and understand another and it also provides appropriate boundaries which they may collide with as a way of testing intimacy. These opportunities are essential to adolescent development. The risk of revealing one's self – commitments, abilities, values, vulnerabilities – is also present in honest relating to adolescents. The chaplain, counsellor or teacher must carefully negotiate the tension between being real and yet not crossing any professional boundaries.

Affirmation
Young people need affirmation. Affirmation of the other implies a 'no

strings attached' relationship of unconditional valuing in which the other is valued as intrinsically good. The adolescent does not have to earn love in this dimension of affirmation. If that were the case, love would be reduced to simple cause–effect events and affirmation would mean a reward for doing the expected thing or proving one's self worthy. Unconditional valuing, however, means that God has already given young people worthiness by virtue of their humanity. People do not earn it or prove it. Of course, this is not to say that what adolescents do is of no concern. Certainly, there are more helpful ways of relating than others. Constructive ways need to be encouraged and destructive ways discouraged. But affirmation assumes, before one does anything, that as human beings we are valuable and lovable. Bernard often wears a t-shirt that reminds me of how needy he is for unconditional valuing and love. It reads: 'Accept me for what I am – completely unacceptable.' How much he needs to experience the giftedness of unconditional valuing and love rather than the pain of rejection and unworthiness. Among other things, love is the uniting and harmonising force of affirmation. It enables one to reach out in caring service to another. Where fragmentation, confusion and sadness seemed to have taken over, love enters to make all things cohere.

Articulation

A banner I recently saw proclaimed: 'You may be the only Gospel someone ever reads.' In my work with adolescents, more often than not I am the first Gospel they will read. I am a sign, a 'living reminder' of Jesus Christ and God's compassion in him. Therefore, it is essential that I not only recognise the God-given worth of the adolescents I work with, but articulate that recognition in ways that enable them to see their human beauty as well. Articulation involves translating into word and action the dynamic and redeeming power of God's unconditional valuing and love of the world and one's place in relation to others and God. It means uncovering the beauty which one cannot see because it is hidden by suffering and pain. It means pointing out the face of God in the midst of one's suffering and pain. The school chaplain will articulate the Gospel to adolescents by simply acknowledging their own commitment to Jesus Christ and God's compassion in and through him, by encouraging and praising them not only when they deserve it, but also when they need it, and by expressing appreciation for their presence and relationship. Of course, articulation is not a quick technique to exercise power over adolescents, something they would easily suspect anyway, nor is it an easy gimmick in 'Ten Ways to Win Friends'; rather, it is the honest and humble communication of presenting what is already given as a gift and simply begs open recognition. Sometimes a school chaplain fulfils this through leading prayer and articulating the needs of the school community.

Forgiveness

So often in our competitive society we expect to receive from others only what we produce ourselves or somehow merit as what we deserve. This utilitarian attitude also spills over into our relationships with others, and therefore when we violate or hurt another person, the most we can expect is a light punishment. Adolescents need to experience in their own relationships the reality of forgiveness. They often act in ways that elicit punishment when they are feeling guilty about acting harshly towards another. The expectation of punishment blocks them moving beyond an act that they can no longer undo except by having someone else hurt them in return. Forgiveness is the possibility of restoring a hurt relationship without further pain or punishment. It is the glad acceptances of another's regret and welcoming acceptance of another's limitations, all the time knowing that the hurt inflicted could easily have been done by oneself. Forgiveness is not cheap grace. It does not mean the justification of sin without the justification of the sinner. It does not exclude preliminary judgements about morality. Rather it leaves final judgement in the hands of God. Forgiveness enables one to be fully responsible for hurtful actions by the common recognition of such actions and opens the way for healing by providing another the free space to show guilt and regret, yet without fear of further hurt. Adolescents often expect more from themselves than do others and harshly treat themselves when they fail to fulfil often rigid expectations. Forgiveness is the way out of compulsive and self-defeating expectations. It recognises the sinful and limited condition that we all share and encourages us to move beyond it. Forgiveness must be the ultimate aim of any school's discipline approach if adolescents are to learn that not everything has to have its match, an eye for an eye.

Challenges in the Pastoral Care of Emotionally Disturbed Adolescents

There are particular challenges which one encounters in a school setting with emotionally disturbed adolescents, tensions that often get in the way of manifesting a pastoral approach. While those who work with young people who are emotionally disturbed or who have special needs will normally have a huge commitment to this type of work and the energy to match their commitment, there are costs involved in sharing the journey of these young people. One of the costs of caring for disturbed adolescents is what psychiatrist Melvin Lewis and psychologist Thomas E. Brown call the 'regressive pull'.[13] This is where seriously disturbed adolescents can tend to make others who work closely with them feel a movement towards chaotic and archaic levels of functioning characterised by anxiety in relation to a child who has lost control: rescue fantasies or unrealistic expectations for success and healing alternating with despair, and hostility in the form of punishment. It is not clear whether such adolescents intentionally cause the regressive pull as an attempt to make others close to them feel impotent and themselves omnipotent or whether it results from simply being in their presence. What is clear is that those who work closely with adolescents with emotional problems need to be supported by their colleagues and employers. One form of support is to have a weekly or monthly debriefing session in which chaplains, teachers and caregivers can discuss their experiences and focus on a common approach.

The fact that these adolescents dramatise their conflicts in relation to the adults who work with them often makes relating to them extremely frustrating and emotionally draining, even with the type of staff support outlined above. The emotional intensity of continual conflict for teachers in a school with a high number of emotionally disturbed adolescents and the great neediness of these young people can set one up for emotional burnout if efforts for personal solitude, staff communication and even prayer are not maintained. I learned quickly that compassion and pastoral care couldn't become a competition between my needs and those of the adolescent. All those who work with young people with this type of special need require an approach that recognises the importance of everyone's needs and seeks to meet them. A failure to respond to personal needs can result in them getting in the way of offering pastoral care to those in our care.

Conclusion

For many reasons, not least of all the change in family life, more young people are presenting in our schools with emotional needs. Some of these emotional needs will be short-lived and can be addressed by a caring teacher who takes time out to listen. Others will require more ongoing support from the chaplain, counsellor or psychologist. Fundamental to any pastoral approach that seeks to meet the needs of these young people is a Christian concern for the person in which the totality of the pupil is recognised. Finally, those who engage in the pastoral care of young people with emotional needs will need to find a healthy mechanism to meet their own needs either through peer support from other teachers and chaplains or through a form of supervision.

Notes

1. R. F. Bihehler and J. Snowman, *Psychology Applied to Teaching* (Boston: Houghton Mifflin, 1993), 194.
2. J. E. Ysseldyke and R. Algozzine, *Introduction to Special Education* (Boston: Houghton Mifflin, 1990), 175–6.
3. M. Burnstein, C. Stranger and L. Dumenci, 'Relations Between Parent Psychopathology, Family Functioning, and Adolescent Problems in Substance-Abusing Families: Disaggregating the Effects of Parent Gender', *Child Psychiatry & Human Development*, 43, 4 (August 2012), 631–47.
4. S. A Burt, A. M. Klahr, M. McGue and W. G. Iacono, 'Confirming the Etiology of Adolescent Acting-Out Behaviours: An Examination of Observer-Ratings in a Sample of Adoptive and Biological Siblings', *Journal of Child Psychology & Psychiatry*, 52, 5 (May 2011), 519–26.
5. D. Bolton, P. Dearsley, R. Madronal-Luque and S. Baron-Cohen, 'Magical Thinking in Childhood and Adolescence: Development and Relation to Obsessive Compulsion', *British Journal of Developmental Psychology*, 20, 4 (November 2002), 482.
6. S. Bailey, N. Whittle, P. Farnworth and K. A Smedley, 'Developmental Approach to Violence, Hostile Attributions, and Paranoid Thinking in Adolescence', *Behavioral Sciences and the Law*, 25, 6 (November 2007), 913–29.
7. D. U. Levine, A. J. Havighurst, *Society and Education* (Boston: Allyn and Bacon, 1992).
8. M. Glackin, '"A Presence in Pilgrimage": Contemporary Chaplaincy in Catholic Secondary Schools in England and Wales', *International Studies in Catholic Education*, 3, 1 (March 2011), 40–56.
9. J. O'Higgins Norman, 'Educational Underachievement: The Contribution of Pastoral Care', *Irish Educational Studies*, 21, 1 (Spring 2002), 33–45.
10. J. Coldron, '"We just talk things through and then she helps me ..." Relationships of Trust and Mediation', Paper presented at the British Educational Research Association Annual Conference, University of Exeter, England, 2002.
11. S. Murphy, 'A Study of Pupils' Perceptions and Experiences of School Chaplaincy' in J. Norman (ed.), *At The Heart of Education: School Chaplaincy and Pastoral Care* (Dublin: Veritas, 2004), 197–212.
12. J. Norman, 'Pastoral Care in Second-Level Schools: The Chaplain, A Research Report' (Dublin: Mater Dei Institute of Education, Dublin City University, 2002).
13. M. Lewis, T. E. Brown, 'Psychotherapy in the Residential Treatment of the Borderline Child' in *Child Psychiatry and Human Development* (Cambridge: Harvard University Press, 1979), 3, 9, 181–8.

III. Spiritual Pastoral Care

Addressing Contemporary Spirituality in Education
Identifying Light and Shadow

Marian de Souza

This chapter will examine the concept of spirituality as the essence of the relational dimension of being. Spirituality will be explored through the expressions of connectedness that the human person has with Self, the Social and Communal Other, the Physical Other (in Creation) and a Transcendent Other. The role of spirituality in promoting self-worth and well-being will also be explored since it may be perceived as an essential element in the processes related to chaplaincy, counselling and guidance. Further, some aspects of contemporary living will be examined to discover how these may act as impediments to the spiritual growth of children and young people. Finally, some suggestions will be offered as to how spirituality may be nurtured within the different environments where children and young people gather.

In 2011, the body of a woman in her eighties was discovered on the bedroom floor of her home in Sydney. Apparently, she had been dead for approximately eight years and no one had missed her. Her neighbours, when interviewed, became defensive and almost belligerent, perhaps generated by a sense of guilt because they had displayed no concern as to her whereabouts. The social security department had finally ceased sending a pension cheque to her a couple of years earlier, six years after she had died. The local council remained ignorant of the fact that her rates had been unpaid for eight years, and eventually her half-sister raised the alarm when she was contacted by one government agency.

Months later, I read the review of a new documentary, *Dreams of a Life*, in the Arts section of a Melbourne daily paper. It reported on the discovery in 2006 of the body of a thirty-eight-year-old woman who had been living in a council flat in North London. Her name was Joyce Vincent and she had been dead for three years. The article stated that the cause of death could not be determined because only a skeleton remained, 'resting on a couch with the television on and wrapped Christmas presents around her'.[1]

These two incidents occurred in locations halfway across the world from each other but they bear the same troubling symptom – one of disconnectedness. Certainly, when we read of such incidents, many of us are appalled. We find it hard to believe that such a thing could possibly happen in a world where communications technology and the social media provide excellent avenues to connect with others. After all, aren't people always connecting on mobile phones, in chat rooms on the internet, on Facebook, on Twitter? We even feel some level of connectedness to remote corners of the globe or, indeed, outer space when we have images and news about these places beamed into our homes or on to our phones and tablets. If we are such a connected society, we wonder, how can something like this go unnoticed? Especially in a busy, modern city street, lined with houses and apartments that are fully occupied, with endless numbers of people passing by, going about their daily lives. We are forced to ask ourselves some sobering questions. For instance, what is it that has allowed such instances of disconnectedness to occur in our communities at this point in our evolutionary process? And, what is it that persuades us, when we know that someone is in need, to choose to remain at a distance rather than get involved? Has the bystander apathy effect[2] emerged as a symptom of contemporary living? The question arises: should we view incidents that reflect such disconnectedness as the first signs of disintegration of contemporary society where an individual becomes absorbed or perhaps obsessed with the interests and desires of self[3] while remaining detached from the interests and desires of others except when they may have some relevance to or meaning for the self? Following this we need to consider the effects on the social cohesion and the well-being of communities when the essential human traits of empathy and compassion appear to have become superseded by materialistic and consumerist values.

Arguably, it is precisely these signs of disconnectedness which imply that the human journey to spiritual maturity is being hindered. In other words, the ability to live with a heightened awareness that each of us is a relational being, a part of something greater than our individual selves, has become flawed. To elucidate this point, I need to refer to my previous research studies conducted in Australia, both of which identified spirituality as a distinct human trait that is expressed through the individual's sense of connectedness to the human and non-human world.

Contemporary Spirituality

My early studies into young people's spirituality were motivated by the statement I heard from so many of my Year 12 students[4] in the late 1990s: 'I am not religious but I am spiritual.' I needed to understand what these young people were talking about. As a result, the first study[5] investigated the perceptions and expressions of twenty-two 16–20-year-olds of their spirituality. The understanding of spirituality as applied in the research study was drawn from the literature where spirituality was discussed as relational consciousness and connectedness.[6] The sample included both young people who came from a religious background and others who had no experience of a religious tradition. Their diverse educational backgrounds included private faith-based schools, government schools and alternative educational programmes as well as Transition to Work programmes. In general, the findings pointed to the fact that the participants experienced different levels of connectedness to their families and communities and this was expressed through their attitudes and behaviours. These connections also contributed to their sense of identity and self-worth. Many participants indicated that the relational dimension of their lives was mostly concerned with the 'Other' in their immediate world, and their actions for justice and their perceptions of the important times in their lives were related to issues and rites of passage within these familial and communal frameworks. Some, however, indicated more widespread levels of connectedness to the 'Other' in the wider world through their display of concern, compassion and empathy, as well as their actions for people in less fortunate circumstances, for instance refugees and victims of disasters. Finally, most spoke of their sense of a Supreme Being or a transcendent presence outside the material world, and their concern with the Big Questions was often linked to an awareness of this presence.

The second study focused on a group of tertiary students' perceptions of their spiritual journeys and sought to identify the elements that shaped their spiritual development and sense of the sacred.[7] To this end, ten fourth-year students attending Australian Catholic University volunteered to participate in the research and be interviewed to speak about their own spiritual journeys and their perceptions of the influential factors in this area of their lives. The age range of these students was between twenty-two and twenty-eight and they were at the end of their four-year degree. One further pertinent factor is that they had included Religious Education as one of their teaching methods in their teacher education programme, and yet only a very few spoke of the importance of religion in their lives. The findings revealed that all of them constantly referred to the relational aspect of their lives which inspired them to action, such as to teach others, to share their values, to help others and to act for social justice. As well, they shared a common belief that people could not live their lives in isolation if they wanted them to flourish.

Consequently, they identified connectedness as an essential factor in their spiritual well-being and in allowing them to develop the wisdom they needed to continue their spiritual journeys.

To sum up, the findings of both these studies revealed that the levels of connectedness experienced by these young people provided them with a sense of their own self-worth as well as a sense of a place within their various communities. Not surprisingly then, these aspects helped them to find some meaning in their lives, which in turn developed in them a sense of purpose. Thus, if my relationships help me understand who I am amongst others, and provide me with a distinct place within my group, the sense of belonging that I experience encourages in me a desire to contribute and work towards the benefit of the group. Additionally, my sense of belonging leads me to discover a sense of purpose and creates a framework within which I am able to make meaning of my life experiences. Further, the findings indicated that for a small minority, the beliefs and practices of a religious tradition did have some effect on their spirituality, but for all of them, the development of their spiritual lives in terms of their sense of self and place and the ability to find some meaning and purpose was clearly more dependent on the positive relationships that they formed in their early years. Indeed, despite the background and education of the second group, only one identified religion as an influential element in his spiritual growth.

From the respondents' comments in the two studies, it became apparent that there appeared to be a movement through different layers of connectedness, beginning with the relationships that were formed within the individual's immediate environment from their early years. These relationships were significant in shaping the individual's sense of identity and their perceptions and actions. With each accruing layer, the sense of connectedness was extended to the wider world and beyond, and this was sometimes achieved through their educational experiences. Each layer brought with it a learned wisdom, empathy and compassion which was expressed by the way in which the individual interacted with others and the wider world. Importantly, the movement appeared to be a spiralling motion which moved forward and outward but also could falter and fall back depending on the context of the individual's experiences and responses. As well, there was a possibility that sometimes along the journey the individual could reach a mystical state where they glimpsed and/or experienced moments of deep sacredness and transcendence in their everyday.

A logical conclusion drawn from these findings led me to describe that the forward movement that was evident for some of the participants may have had the potential to ultimately lead them to the deepest level of connectedness where an individual would experience an all-consuming oneness with the Other. In other words, the deeper and wider the level or layer of connectedness that individuals feel to someone or something other than themselves, the closer they get to a point where the self loses itself in other, that is, a point of *Ultimate Unity*. This point lies beyond relationship or relationality since it reflects a oneness of everything. To be sure, the notion of self losing itself in Other so that it occupies a state of no-self is one found in many religious and philosophical traditions,[8] as is the notion of non-duality as a foundational concept in twentieth-century physics.[9]

The findings that led to my discussion of a relational continuum as a spiritual journey towards Ultimate Unity supported Newberg's assertions in his discussion of the neurology of transcendence. He claimed that there was a movement towards *Absolute Unitary Being*, that is, when the self blends into other, and mind and matter become one and the same.[10] Newberg suggests that there is a 'unitary continuum' where, at one point, a person may interact with others and the world but experience it as something from which they are apart. However, as they move along the unitary continuum, that separateness becomes less distinct.[11]

More recently, I suggested that the relational continuum may also be aligned with Baron-Cohen's empathy continuum.[12] Baron-Cohen contends that for most individuals, the level of empathy may vary depending on circumstances and/or emotional states, but at one level an individual will have zero degrees of empathy, and as they move along the continuum their level of empathy rises. Thus, the more connected an individual is, the more empathy that individual will have with Other. The importance of helping children and young people develop empathy with Other cannot be emphasised enough given the diverse racial, religious and cultural contexts of so many classrooms in so many countries today. The first step would be to recognise that empathy is an expression generated by the relational dimension of an individual's life; therefore, it is an expression of spirituality. Finnegan sums this up aptly:

> In spirituality we encounter belief, cultural and symbolic systems, and all of them need to be understood in their webs of significance, in their interconnected and interconnecting stories, all with their local flavours and all with their global implications for dialogue and the challenge of mutual understanding.[13]

Here, Finnigan offers the notion of 'interconnected and interconnecting stories' which require 'dialogue for mutual understanding' within the diversity of the global context, thereby highlighting the relational dimension of spirituality – once again, it is about connectedness.

The thesis offered here is that there is a distinct association between the levels of connectedness a person experiences to Self and Other in the human and non-human world and the person's identity (a sense of self) and belonging (sense of place), which leads to meaning-making and purposeful living. For that reason, an awareness of living as a relational being may be regarded as the spiritual dimension of human existence, and alongside this, spiritual growth and development may be seen as corresponding with the heightening of this awareness. Consequently, it is this dimension of human life that needs to be addressed and nurtured if individuals and their communities hope to flourish, and it is this notion that has implications for the professional practice of those who work with children and young people.

Light and Shadow – The Positive and Negative Elements in Spirituality

An important consideration in any discussion of contemporary spirituality is the recognition that there are positive and less positive aspects of relationality or human connectedness. I have discussed elsewhere the spread of research into spirituality across a range of disciplines such as physical and mental health, sociology and youth work, nursing and palliative care and education.[14] Further, I have noted that in almost all these cases, the focus on spirituality is restricted to the positive elements – that aspect of spirituality that leads to human peace, happiness and well-being. For the most part, this is where individuals forge relationships that help them to grow and flourish. Thus, they have a good sense of self-worth, they live with joy, hope, wonder and a sense of community, and they look forward with expectation and anticipation as their lives unfold. Much has been written about this positive aspect of spirituality, and indeed it is important for this aspect to be identified and for strategies that nurture spiritual development to be explored and implemented in educational and health programmes.

However, the other side of spirituality also needs to be acknowledged and addressed, and this is the shadow side. It may be evidenced when relationships stifle and suffocate individual growth, thereby leading to over-dependence, a lack of confidence, an inability to trust, boredom, a sense of hopelessness, deep unhappiness, self-hatred, despair and even, in extreme cases, suicide. These often may be obsessive relationships which prevent the individual from developing into the person they are meant to be and they may be seen in many different guises in an individual's life, for instance, connectedness to other individuals, to peer groups, to particular hobbies, sports or other recreational human activities, and so on. When these expressions of connectedness become so extreme that individual traits become submerged and only the traits that are perceived to be more acceptable or desirable are allowed to be displayed, individuals begin to lose a part of themselves which may, indeed, wither away into a kind of death. Bly suggests that the socialisation process that individuals undergo from birth actually results in a polarisation of their personalities where the attractive traits continue to be displayed and developed but the less attractive traits are put into an invisible bag and hidden out of sight.[15] However, these lost traits are essential elements that are needed for a person to develop as a whole Being, so that until they are recovered and accepted as a part of the self, the individual's growth into wholeness remains stunted.

Another aspect of the shadow side of spirituality relates to a tendency in the western world for people to focus their lives on comfort and pleasure and to avoid confrontations with elements that may cause pain, discomfort or distress. Tacey discusses this tendency in western culture to strive for the lighter side of life, and offers a Jungian point of view that 'the more an individual or group strives for light, the longer and darker is the shadow that is cast'.[16] In other words, this tendency to avoid things that may cause unpleasantness, or which may be viewed as undesirable by our families and communities, has led to an imbalance in people's lives because when shadows are avoided, they grow more intense and start weighing people down, sometimes emerging as destructive tendencies. Therefore, it is important for individuals to enter into and engage with the darkness because it is only in so doing that they will learn about themselves. Such knowledge will help them to grow as a whole person rather than living their lives as a shadow of whom they are meant to be.

Some attention also needs to be given to the type of connectedness that children and young people may be experiencing. For instance, while many young people appear to be connected to their peers through the internet, texting, tweeting, Facebook and other means of social networking which are available today, much of this is a 'distant connectedness'[17] which does not involve the close proximity of past social networks, and it also allows the disguising of the identity of individuals if they so wish. A recent news article[18] referred to the urge that is evident amongst many young people in relation to this kind of connectedness at a distance. The writer, Delaney, referred to them as 'connected loners' and argued that this urge is driven by the fear of 'being by ourselves and really, truly alone'. She refers to a report in the US that claimed that young digital Americans have a pathological fear of being alone, they feel that they may miss out or be left behind – a kind of existential fear: 'If I am not online, being mentioned in tweets and having people "like" my Facebook status, then in a modern sense of the world, I do not exist.' Delaney concludes that this need to be a connected loner is actually a 'flight away from Self' and it results in 'living off the surface – constantly distracted and consumed by technology'.[19] An additional factor that needs consideration is that such connections do not, necessarily, promote self-esteem or empathy with other. In fact, the instances of cyberbullying and other deceptions that frequently come to light are some of the downsides of distant connectedness and may be regarded as the 'shadow' element in the passage to spiritual growth.

The societal features discussed here are ones which contextualise the lives of most children and young people in western cultures today, and may have some bearing on the statistics that have been generated over the past decade that have indicated the rise in the number of young people who have been diagnosed with depression and other illnesses related to mental health, alienation and marginalisation.[20] In examining the responses from professionals seeking to promote health and well-being, it is interesting to note their recognition of the need to develop amongst children and young people the qualities of resilience, belonging and connectedness.[21] These words clearly reflect the relational dimension of an individual's life and it is pertinent to further note that the term 'spirituality' has gained currency amongst many professionals who work with young people.[22]

The Role of Spirituality in the Learning and Caring Professions

Given these understandings of the nature of spirituality as a human journey towards Ultimate Unity with the individual experiencing different levels of connectedness along the way, there are clearly some implications for the design of school environments and educational programmes which will cultivate and encourage elements that would enhance and nurture the relationships that students develop. Contemporary Australian classrooms tend to reflect the classrooms in many other western countries where there is an emphasis on competition and testing so that teaching becomes focused on tests, with little attention being given to a balance between the cognitive, affective and spiritual dimensions of learning. There is a distinct pressure on students to become proficient in literacy and numeracy, so that those students whose gifts fall outside these areas have less chance of achieving success or feeling valued for what they have to offer. Not surprisingly, these practices have had a dehumanising effect on some students and have created divisive elements related to feelings of superiority and self-absorption within the class community, thereby impeding spiritual development of students. Indeed, many children and young people continue to experience a sense of frustration and alienation as a result of striving to learn within such conventional educational frameworks. Equally, it is not surprising for children and young people to lose themselves in a virtual world where they can be and do anything that makes them feel good, and it takes them away from the hurts and disillusionment of the real world.

It is an interesting observation that often the alternative programmes offered for students who are not achieving within the mainstream classroom tend to focus on the development of life skills, resilience and the promotion of a sense of connectedness. In other words, these particular characteristics are about relationality, and therefore reflect the spiritual dimension of learning and living. As well, there has been a move in some countries over the past decade towards recognising a spiritual dimension in education[23] but there has been much confusion and misunderstanding about what this may mean.[24] Nonetheless, my own research over many years has examined the theories of rational, emotional and spiritual intelligences and has developed a learning approach that recognises the complementarity of the cognitive, affective and spiritual dimensions of learning.[25] The first deals with the thinking processes of learning, the second with the feelings involved, and the third involves the inner workings of the mind which result in intuitive/imaginative/creative action. This third element complements the first two processes in assisting young people to extend their vision by learning to view things from several perspectives which, in turn, enables them to generate insightful responses as they make meaning from their interactions with their environments. As well, this third element has been identified by Merton as the 'intuitive and interior way of knowing'.[26] Del Prete adds:

> [T]o activate and grow in our capacity to know the living
> dimensions of truth requires practice in an intuitive way
> of knowing that Merton views as natural, though neglected
> in western society.[27]

Consequently, educators should consider the potential of all learning activities to not only promote knowledge, interest and participation amongst their students but that will engage students at a deeper, more personal level. Some of the factors that may lead to this are:

1. Exploring how the activity may address the relational dimension of the students' lives since it is a vital ingredient in their spiritual, emotional and, therefore, their intellectual learning. Storytelling and personal narratives are useful strategies that may allow a student's personal story to resonate with the story of another, thereby creating empathy and a sense of belonging and connectedness.

2. Ensuring that class and school community remain inclusive and open to dialogue so that differences are not merely accepted but celebrated in real and meaningful ways. This may help students develop feelings of compassion for and empathy with the 'Other' in their community.

3. Including time for silence, solitude and contemplation in the school day and introducing appropriate strategies in meditation and mindfulness which will equip students to focus on and learn about their inner selves.

4. Creating sacred spaces in the school which are prayerful, aesthetic and accessible to all regardless of their backgrounds, cultures and religious beliefs.

5. Offering opportunities for students to develop their creative imagination and to experience joy, awe and wonder. This may sometimes be achieved by using an arts approach to teach across the curriculum, as it engages the students at different levels of thinking and feeling and encourages multi-sensory learning.

6. Persuading students to recognise that their gifts and talents are to be shared for the benefit of all, to accept responsibility for one another and to commit to action for the common good.

7. Encouraging students to become aware of and respond to a transcendent dimension and/or a divine presence in their lives.

With the advances in knowledge about education and spirituality, professionals who work with children and young people would be remiss if they did not consider the implications of this new learning for the development of their programmes and the design of learning environments. They need to pay more attention to activities that promote the relational aspects of young people's lives rather than those that continue to propagate the highly charged competitive climate. The latter encourages the individual to work against their co-students, thereby detracting from positive human qualities such as individuality, empathy and compassion. Basic human virtues of love and compassion, truth, courage, humility, honour and integrity should be modelled regularly to counteract the values of greed, deceit, power, non-involvement and self-obsession that frequently dominate in the media. Learning environments for young people should develop structures that both allow students to have a voice which may encourage in them a sense of belonging and a cause for action, and create avenues which promote engagement with diversity.

Alongside this nurturing of the light side of spirituality, children and young people also need to be encouraged to face up to the shadows, whether these are the less attractive side of their personalities or the pain that may come from disillusionment, lack of success and/ or other problematic areas that make up the daily experiences of humankind. Therefore, activities that promote self-acceptance as well as acceptance of Other should be built into learning programmes. In particular, attention should be given to recognising that all human gifts are necessary for a society to function so that particular gifts are not singled out as being of more importance. As well, there should be a focus on acknowledging that individual gifts in fact belong to everyone and should be used for the benefit of all since each child is connected to Other. Of course, this is difficult to achieve given the interference in schools from powerful external bodies with vested interests. Nonetheless, in the interests of nurturing students to overcome problems and setbacks, and to develop their potential to be well-rounded, empathetic, proactive citizens of the future, prompt action that will revolutionise current educational policy and practice is needed.

Most importantly, there must be a realisation that teachers and other professionals need to nurture the spiritual dimension of their own lives if they wish to address the spiritual lives of their students. If they desire to help their students develop into whole persons with a sense of their own identity, ones filled with hope and a sense of truth and beauty, and furthermore ones who can find meaning and purpose in their everyday, they need to develop strategies that will enhance the relational dimension in their own lives as well as the lives of their students. Such vision and action will help teachers and their students make connections and learn to engage with and become inclusive of Self and Other, thereby promoting the self-esteem and well-being of the individual and the community.

Notes

1. See Craig Matthieson's review, 'Finding the Woman Who Wasn't There', *The Age*, Thursday, 13 September 2012, 18.
2. J. M. Darley and B. Latane, 'When Will People Help in a Crisis?', *Psychology Today*, 2 (1968), 54–7, 70–1.
3. In this chapter I shall refer to 'self' as the outer identity of an individual with corresponding expressions and behaviour. 'Self' (uppercased) will refer to the inner person.
4. Year 12 is the final year of schooling in Australian schools and the age of students is between seventeen–eighteen years.
5. M. de Souza, P. Cartwright and E. J. McGilp, 'An Investigation into the Perceptions of the Spiritual Well-being of 16–20 year-old Young People in a Regional Centre in Victoria', unpublished report (Ballarat: Australian Catholic University, 2002).
6. See Rebecca Nye's work in D. Hay and R. Nye, *The Spirit of the Child* (London: Fount Paperbacks, 1998) and Maria Harris' discussion in M. Harris and G. Moran, *Reshaping Religious Education* (Louiseville, KY: Westminster, John Knox Press, 1998).
7. See M. de Souza, 'Identifying the Elements That Shape Spiritual Development and a Sense of the Sacred: Tertiary Students' Perceptions of their Spiritual Journeys – Implications for Lifelong Learning', CD ROM, *Proceedings of the Lifelong Learning Conference: Reaching the Unreached Learner* (2003).
8. See, for instance, Karen Armstrong, *The Case for God* (Great Britain: The Bodley Head, 2010), or Paul Gilbert, *The Compassionate Mind* (London: Constable, 2010), or Bede Griffith, *A New Vision of Reality: Western Science, Eastern Mysticism and Christian Faith* (London: Fount, 1989).
9. See Fritjof Capra, *The Tao of Physics: An Exploration of the Parallels Between Modern Physics and Eastern Mysticism* (35th anniversary edition) (Boston: Shambala, 2010), or Ervin Laszlo, *Quantum Shift in the Global Brain: How the New Scientific Reality Can Change Us and Our World* (Rochester, VT: Inner Tradition, 2008).
10. A. Newberg, E. D'Aquili and V. Rause, *Why Gods Don't Go Away: Brain Science and the Biology of Belief* (New York: Ballantine Books, 2001), 156.
11. Ibid., 145.
12. See M. de Souza and K. McLean, 'Bullying and Violence: Changing an Act of Disconnectedness into an Act of Kindness', *Pastoral Care in Education*, 30, 2 (2012), 165–80.
13. J. Finnegan, *The Audacity of Spirit: The Meaning and Shaping of Spirituality Today* (Dublin: Veritas, 2008), 41.
14. Paper presented at the 12th International Conference for Children's Spirituality at University of East Anglia, Norwich, July 2012.
15. R. Bly, *A Little Book on the Human Shadow* (New York: HarperCollins, 1988).
16. D. Tacey, *How to Read Jung* (London: Granz Books, 2007), 55.

17. See de Souza and McLean, 'Bullying and Violence', 165–80.

18. See Bridget Delaney's article, 'Switching off may be the key to finding true connection', *The Age*, 29 July 2011, available at: http://www.theage.com.au/opinion/society-and-culture/switching-off-may-be-the-key-to-finding-true-connection-20110728-1i27e.html#ixzz1TkOnHkhI (accessed 1 August 2011).

19. Ibid.

20. See M. de Souza, 'Promoting Wholeness and Wellbeing in Education: Exploring Aspects of the Spiritual Dimension' for a brief overview of relevant reports identifying this situation. In M. de Souza, L. Francis, J. O'Higgins Norman, D. Scott (eds), *International Handbook of Education for Spirituality, Care and Wellbeing*, 2 (The Netherlands: Springer, 2009), 677–92.

21. Commission for Children at Risk 2003 (Victoria: Department of Education and Training, 2003).

22. For instance, if the words spirituality, health or mental health are googled, there are thousands of results that list conferences, journal articles and other research and professional activities in the field.

23. In Britain, the National Curriculum Council (1993) released a document entitled *Spiritual and Moral Development: A Discussion Paper*, which described spiritual growth as 'a lifelong process of encounters in which people respond to and develop insight from experiences which are, by their very nature, hard to define'. Aspects of spiritual development were further discussed in a paper from the School Curriculum and Assessment Authority (SCAA, 1995). Also, the Office for Standards and Education in Britain (Ofsted) (1994) articulated spiritual development as relating to that aspect of inner life through which students acquire insights into their personal existence are of enduring worth. It is characterised by reflection, the attribution of meaning to experience, valuing a non-material dimension to life and intimations of an enduring reality. In the USA and Canada, various educators such as Moffett (1994), Miller (2000) and Kessler (2000) have also written extensively on spirituality and education.

24. The ambiguity and lack of understanding around the concept of spiritual education is evident, for instance, in many of the articles that appeared in the *International Journal of Children's Spirituality* over the past decade.

25. See the following publications where I have presented a case for addressing the spiritual dimension of learning: M. de Souza, 'Nurturing children's spirituality in learning environments' in Derya Şahhüseyinoğlu and Dzintra Ilisko (eds), *How Do Children Learn Best?* (Turkey: Children's Research Centre, 2010). Or M. de Souza, 'The Roles of Conscious and Non-conscious Learning in Impeding and Enhancing Spirituality: Implications for Learning and Teaching' in M. de Souza and J. Rimes (eds), *Meaning and Connectedness: Australian Perspectives on Education and Spirituality* (Melbourne: Australian College of Education, 2010). Or M. de Souza, 'Rediscovering the Spiritual Dimension in Education: Promoting a Sense of Self and Place, Meaning and Purpose in Learning' in M. de Souza, K. Engebretson, G. Durka, R. Jackson and A. McGrady (eds), *International Handbook of the Religious, Moral and Spiritual Dimensions of Education*, 2 volumes (The Netherlands: Springer, 2006), 1127–40.

26. Cited by T. Del Prete, 'Being What We Are: Thomas Merton's Spirituality in Education' in J. Miller, Y. Nakagawa, *Nurturing Our Wholeness* (Rutland, VT: Foundation for Educational Renewal, 2002), 171.

27. Ibid.

The Religious Socialisation of Young People in Ireland

Conor McGuckin

Christopher A. Lewis

Sharon M. Cruise

John-Paul Sheridan

This chapter provides a review of recent data that is pertinent in helping to understand the process of religious socialisation of children and adolescents within contemporary society. For the purposes of the chapter, our focus will be young people in the Republic of Ireland. These sources of data come from a number of distinct sources, namely the 2011 Irish Census, the fourth wave of the European Values survey (2010), and the Religion and Life Perspective study.[1][2][3] These data help provide both practitioners and researchers working within the fields of school chaplaincy and pastoral care within contemporary Irish society with a greater understanding of the context in which the process of religious socialisation occurs.

In speaking about the religious socialisation of children and adolescents, the metaphor of a three-legged stool is often mentioned: in as much as one is unable to sit on a three-legged stool if one of the legs is missing, so it is with religious socialisation: without one of the three 'partners' in this socialisation, the process is doomed to failure.

> Thus primary religious socialisation in the home is of vital importance, along with continuous (or secondary) religious socialisation in church and at school. In several European countries this insight has led to close bonds between home, church and school with a view to children's religious upbringing. In recent years, however, these bonds, once so strong, have weakened. Socio-cultural processes like secularisation, pluralisation and individualisation have resulted in a dramatic decline in religious affiliation in many parts of western Europe. In consequence many parents no longer take the religious upbringing of their children very seriously.[4]

In terms of Roman Catholic social teaching, socialisation, '... the transmission and internationalisation of societal values and norms',[5] begins within the family, which is then extended outwards to include the parish and the school, and then moves out to the wider community and society as outlined in the Bronfenbrenner systems model.[6] The third leg of the stool, the parish, is heavily reliant on the other two legs. The parish's involvement in the socialisation process relies on the religious commitment of the parents. For example, when children attend church they are frequently accompanied by parents. Indeed, in rural areas young people may not be capable of attending Mass on their own, as transport is required. In Ireland, the preparation and celebration of sacramental initiation (Sacraments of Reconciliation, First Communion and Confirmation) is still very much within the domain of the primary school. Socialisation has implications for chaplaincy and pastoral care in terms of the relationship between the lived ethos of the school, manifested in the nature of pastoral care and the religious identity, beliefs and practices of the home.

In exploring the attitudes and behaviours of adolescents, we are cognisant of the important cognitive-bio-psycho-social changes with which young people are confronted. Erikson's[7] 'stage' model of developmental growth across the lifespan proposes that adolescents (Stage 5) seek to 'shrug off' the parental values that have been transmitted to them since birth. Erikson asserts that in trying to resolve this 'normative crisis' of adolescence, adolescents attempt to develop and 'try on' their own views and opinions. Thus, at a theoretical level, the concept of 'socialisation' is conceived of as being dependent upon the quality of the relationship between the individual and the socialisation agent, a point enormously relevant to practitioners in pastoral care and chaplaincy. In terms of religious attitude and behaviour, the better the quality of the socialisation, the more inclined the person is to accept and adopt the religious perspective of the socialisation agent.

Changing patterns of religious denomination in Ireland
According to the 2011 census, Ireland has a population of 4.58 million, with Roman Catholics making up the largest religious group (3.8 million), accounting for 86.8% of the population. The Church of Ireland is the second largest religious group, with 129,039 members, which accounts for 2.92% of the population. Muslims represent the third largest religious group (1.07%, 49,204), followed by Orthodox (0.98%, 45,223), Other Christian Religion (0.89%, 41,161) and Presbyterian (0.51%, 23,546). It might also be stated that the second largest 'religious' grouping is those who stated that they had no religion (269,811), and the number of Atheists increased from 929 in 2006 to 3,905 in 2011, an increase of 320.3%. Two other large

increases were Agnostics, which rose from 1,515 in 2006 to 3,531 in 2011, an increase of 132.4%, and Lapsed Roman Catholic, from 540 in 2006 to 1,279 in 2011, an increase of 136.9%. The largest percentage increases in religious groups were Orthodox (117.4%), Hindu (75.7%), Apostolic or Pentecostal (73.0%). The Methodist community had the largest decrease in population (43.7%).

Table 1 – Religions in Ireland (2011 & 2006), with changes between the Census

Population by Religion	2011	2006	Actual change 2006–2011	Percentage change 2006–2011
Roman Catholic	3,861,335	3,681,446	179,889	4.9
Church of Ireland	129,039	125,585	7,810	6.4
Muslim (Islamic)	49,204	32,539	16,665	51.2
Orthodox	45,223	20,798	24,425	117.4
Other Christian Religions	41,161	29,206	11,955	40.9
Presbyterian	24,600	23,546	1,054	4.5
Apostolic or Pentecostal	14,043	8,116	5,927	73.0
Hindu	10,688	6,082	4,606	75.7
Buddhist	8,703	6,516	2,187	33.6
Methodist	6,842	12,160	-5,318	-43.7
Jehovah's Witness	6,149	5,152	997	19.4
Lutheran	5,683	5,279	404	7.7
Protestant	5,326	4,356	970	22.3
Evangelical	4,188	5,276	-1,088	-20.6
Atheist	3,905	929	2,976	320.3
Baptist	3,531	3,338	193	5.8
Agnostic	3,521	1,515	2,006	132.4
Jewish	1,984	1,930	54	2.8

Population by Religion	2011	2006	Actual change 2006–2011	Percentage change 2006–2011
Pantheist	1,940	1,691	249	14.7
Latter Day Saints (Mormon)	1,284	1,237	47	3.8
Lapsed Roman Catholic	1,279	540	739	136.9
Quaker (Society of Friends)	925	882	43	4.9
Baha'i	520	504	16	3.2
Brethren	336	365	-29	-7.9
Other stated religions	14,118	8,576	5,542	64.6

The historical affirmation that Ireland is a Catholic society can still claim statistical support, although the actual share of Roman Catholics in the population has decreased from 86.8% in 2006 to 84.2% in 2011, although their numbers increased by 4.9% (179,889). Recent migration and immigration have simultaneously contributed to a more religiously diverse Irish society. While numbers of adherents to other religious traditions are small relative to the Catholic tradition, their growth rate has been rapid, and they have had a major impact on the religious demography of Ireland. For example, the Muslim community in Ireland has increased from a very small population of 3,875 in 1991 to 49,204 in 2011. The Christian communities in Ireland have also experienced major change and increasing diversity as a consequence of immigration and migration. A significant example is the Orthodox community in Ireland, which doubled in numbers between 2006 (20,798) and 2011 (45,223), a percentage increase of 117.4%. The Orthodox community had also doubled in number from the 2002 and 2006 census. The number of people who state they have no religion has gradually increased from 1981 onwards, from 5.3% (1981–1991), 6.9% (1991–2002), to 7.7% in the period from 2001–2006. However, the percentage difference from the 2006 to 2011 census had increased dramatically to 44.8%. The number of people not stating their religion rose by 3.7%, having been down in the previous census.

Table 2 – Census Declaration (2006 & 2011) of 'No Religion' or 'Religion Not Stated'

	2006	2011	%
No religion	186,318	269,811	44.8
Not stated	70,322	72,914	3.7

Overall, given such high levels of self-assigned religious denominational identity, religion may be viewed as having a central position within contemporary Irish society. Overwhelmingly, the largest religion in Ireland is still Roman Catholicism. What is unclear from census figures is how this religious identity manifests itself in terms of religious beliefs and practice, and how this may be changing. In order to address this question, data collected in relation to the beliefs and practices of Irish adults is required.

Changing patterns of religious beliefs and practice in Ireland –
The European Values Study
The European Values Study (EVS) is a cross-national, longitudinal study of the beliefs, attitudes and values of Europeans with regard to subjects such as life, family, work, religion and politics. It was first conducted in 1981, just before the first direct elections to the European Parliament. At that time, 1,000 people from member countries of the European Union were surveyed. The researchers were particularly interested to know if Europeans shared common values and if these values were changing. The role and place of Christianity was also of interest, and if it was being replaced by an alternative systems of beliefs and values. The study has been conducted every nine years (1990, 1999 and 2008), and the findings reported here are taken from the last survey (4th wave) conducted in 2008 in which 70,000 Europeans from forty-seven European countries were interviewed. The findings for Ireland and Northern Ireland were synthesised and published by the Council for Research and Development of the Irish Catholic Bishops' Conference under the title *Religious Practice and Values in Ireland.*

There is increasing evidence that religious observance among those living in urban areas is in sharp decline. In the 2008 EVS, 45.2% reported that they attend Mass on a weekly or more often basis, which is a sharper decline on the 1999 percentage. An additional 16% said that they attended Mass once a month. 'Belief in God' was

89.9%; 'life after death' – 71.6%; 'Hell' – 50.2%; 'Heaven' – 76.6; 'Sin' – 75.3%; 'Re-Incarnation' – 29.9%. Nearly two-thirds (63.7%) believed in a personal God and 60% prayed either daily or once a week (outside of religious services). Just over one-third (36.1%) of Catholics also stated that they had their own way of connecting with the Divine without churches or religious services.

The data suggest that commitment to Catholicism in Ireland among adults is as much about professing a shared identity and history as it is about endorsing the characteristic beliefs and doctrines of Catholicism. Inglis has remarked that Irish children '... develop a Catholic *habitus*, a deeply embodied, almost automatic way of being spiritual and moral that becomes second nature and creates a Catholic sense of self and a way of behaving and interpreting the world.'[8] For most, formal belief and commitment to Catholicism endure throughout life: birth, marriage and death are marked by religious ceremonies. Nine persons out of 10 of the Irish population are baptised and socialised into the beliefs and practices of Catholic Christianity. Moreover, the vast majority of Catholic children attend Catholic primary and secondary schools, where they receive their preparation for First Communion and Confirmation. Adherence to Catholicism remains a badge of social and national identity, even if the religious commitment that Catholicism once expressed and represented on public occasions is now more symbolic and 'romantic', in the sense of conjuring up a picture of Ireland as uniformly and conscientiously Catholic, long after 'the acids of modernity' and individualism have eroded traditional beliefs and commitments.[9] More pertinently for our purposes, the Catholic Church's traditional control over education and schooling is increasingly being challenged on the grounds that it is incompatible with commitment to social inclusion and the principle of equality, the view being that no 'private' group or institution should enjoy privilege in the 'public' realm. Some social commentators[10] regard the use of this distinction, while consigning religion to the realm of private practice, as a clear indication of the advance of the process of secularisation in a society. According to Casanova, secularisation has three particular and different concepts: '... as differentiation of the secular spheres from religious institutions and norms, secularisation as decline of religious beliefs and practices, and secularisation as marginalisation of religion to a privatised sphere.'[11] As a phenomenon, Ireland is experiencing a time of 'transformation' and 'differentiation' in the relationship between the Churches and the State. Thus, the Irish experience of secularisation encompasses each of the particular concepts: while the Churches still have something of a role with regard to education and healthcare, this role is continuing to decline;

there has been a decline in religious practice; and there has been a marginalisation of religious observance and practice.

> Being Catholic no longer permeates everyday life as it did a generation ago ... In becoming less involved in the institutional Church, Irish Catholics have become more like their counterparts elsewhere in Europe. In so far as they see themselves as belonging to a religious heritage without embodying institutional beliefs and practices, they are becoming more like their Protestant counterparts.[12]

It is important to recognise that the EVS surveys present a picture that uses broad brush strokes: it exclusively focuses on adults, and the data has been presented as an average across all ages. However, what is not clear is whether this picture is representative for young people in Ireland. What is required is careful mapping of the place of religion in the lives of young people in Ireland.

Growing Up Irish

There has been comparatively little research focused on examining some of the fundamental questions about the unique nature of 'growing up Irish'.[13] Indeed, there is comparatively little research within developmental psychology, and especially data examining the attitudes of Irish young people.[14] The research presented here focused on the place of religion and life perspectives among a sample of young people in the Republic of Ireland. A sample of 1,065 young people aged 16–20 years (average age of 17) completed measures of social attitudes as part of a cross-European study.

Research questions

The study set out to examine four key questions regarding the life experiences of young people in the Republic of Ireland. First, it was decided to examine the specific personal life perspectives and values of young people (i.e. the micro-level). Second, the young people evaluated the institutions of the meso-level. Third, attitudes towards political life were explored (i.e. the macro-level). Fourth, it was decided to examine the interplay between variables at the micro-, meso-, and macro-level, alongside a number of core variables.[15]

Findings

First, it was discovered that the dynamism (political and economic) which has come to characterise the Republic of Ireland exists alongside a life perspective of nostalgia, and a desire to secure the past.

From this it can be concluded that a rapidly developing economy, coupled with changes in political identity, may lead to young people clinging to the past rather than embracing the future. A pastoral and chaplaincy agenda can thus be drawn to ensure that young people in Ireland retain the confidence to explore the future rather than attach themselves to the past. Exploration of values demonstrated that the traditionally perceived dichotomy between work and family is not apparent among young people in Ireland. The young people in the survey reported a values orientation toward professionalism, while at the same time supporting the view that they hold a values orientation toward the family. Through the economic redevelopment of Ireland, it can be seen that traditional values have been retained and combined with economic ambition. From this it was concluded that the role of the traditional Irish family is not threatened by rapid change to the economic infrastructure of the country.

Second, the research explored the perceptions of young people with regard to their confidence in 'institutions'. It was clear that the institutions that were not readily supported were political institutions. From the findings it was concluded that there is an urgent need in Ireland for politicians to be trusted by young people – they cannot take such trust for granted. As democracy can succeed only with the consent and trust of the people, politicians should actively seek and earn such trust.

Third, having shown that political institutions are not highly trusted, it was found that the political orientation of young people represents the view that political parties are indifferent to, and alienated from, young people. These findings strengthen the conclusion reached above; that politicians need to re-engage with young people and show that young people are stakeholders in the democratic process. It was noted that parliamentary and demonstrative political actions were those favoured by the young people in the survey. However, if young people are disillusioned and alienated from the political process, how long will it be before various forms of activism are adopted? Once more it was emphasised that politicians must, as a matter of priority, reinforce the view that young people are a part of the political process. With regard to Europe, it was shown that young people are largely confident of their place in a growing Europe; a healthy outlook that reflects a successful international integration, rather than assimilation. It was concluded that young people in Ireland may be seen as having a realistic perspective on what Europe can offer, and what it can cost a nation.

Fourth, the research explored the relationship between 'Life Perspectives, Values and Political Orientation' and 'personality, xenophobia, religiosity, relevance of parents, and sex' variables. It was found that the personality factors of neuroticism and extraversion are core to the development of attitudes and values among young people. Thus, it would be wise to take into account these differences when educating young people in Ireland for citizenship. Young people who scored high on xenophobia rejected social integration, and were generally ambivalent toward politics, and displayed a propensity toward extreme politically motivated behaviours. From this it was concluded that these young people must be enabled to make their voices, generally voices of dissent, heard within the democratic political realm. While these young people had no faith in politics to recognise their needs, they may then feel that activism is the only route open to them. With the finding that young people trust the media, it becomes imperative that the media take their role of socialising young people seriously, exerting their influence over the formation of young peoples' attitudes in a responsible manner. Indeed, there may be a need for educators to recognise the influence of the media, and it may be wise for the education community to teach children about media representations and motivations.

Church attendance was shown to remain important as a predictor of attitudes and values among young people. The Church has traditionally held a role of attitude formation and the research concluded that this role remains intact in Ireland. Religious leaders may be satisfied with this conclusion, yet they would be wise to work to maintain this position and not take it for granted. The Churches still impact on Irish life, and they should be aware of the need to carefully manage this impact.

Those who had a secure perception of the relevance of parents were generally content with their past, and happy to face the future. Thus, as a means of primary socialisation, parents remain key to the formation of pro-social values.

Those who scored high on 'religiosity' valued the past, yet they were less secure about the future. It was concluded that the Churches may wish to re-cast themselves not as guardians of tradition, but as being at the cutting edge of Ireland's future.

While sex differences continued to divide young people, it is possible to see the latent effect of traditional sex roles. Females were still more likely to take pro-social roles and attitudes, whereas young males were likely to adopt a more hard-line approach in various regards. It can be concluded that it would be socially beneficial for young males to be made aware of the potential consequences of asocial behaviours, and the possible benefits of socially acceptable attitudes.

Growing Up Catholic

As part of a larger international study concerned with the 'Religion and Life Perspectives of European Adolescents',[16] the research study explored the religious beliefs and practices of a sample of 1,065 Irish 16–20 year olds (average age of 17). The results described the religious perspectives of a sample of young people in contemporary Irish society, in which religion plays an active part in their lives.

Context of study

Most countries in western Europe have seen religious adherence and practice decline in recent years,[17] and the decline in Ireland has been laid out at the beginning of this chapter. These figures, however, only partially support the idea of a possible decline of aspects of the social dimension of religious belief and practice: for example, with a modest reduction in Church attendance and a much stronger increase in the rejection of the Church teachings. There was support in the research for a consolidation of some other aspects of the social dimensions of religion at this meso-level, most notably strong support for religious services at important times of individuals' lives (e.g., births, deaths and marriages). Interestingly, there was continued support for aspects of private, or intrinsic, religion at the micro-level, including strong religious denominational identity and belief in the central tenets of core Christian belief. The data from the research provided not only clear evidence of the continuing and active role of religion within contemporary Irish society, but also of how it may be adapting.

Summary

In exploring the religious perspectives of young people in Ireland some key questions were raised, questions of interest to practitioners in pastoral care and chaplaincy: the nature of Catholicism; the transmission of religion; and the impact of religion.

What is Catholicism?

Whilst the research highlighted that young people in Ireland were predominantly Catholic, it was noted that perhaps the Catholicism of these young people is different to the official representation of Catholicism presented through the bishops. A profile was presented of a group of young people who attend religious services, who pray and who believe. Religious rituals to mark rites of passage were important to these young people. In general, the young people reported that they had been baptised and confirmed – universal elements of Catholicism that would have traditionally been found among young

Catholics. These elements are enshrined in Irish society and reflect a conservative, stereotypical view of Ireland and of Catholicism.

The young people in the survey expressed uncertainty regarding their interpretation of scripture, particularly with reference to the divine authority of the Bible. They reported that they understood the authenticity of religious experience, and desired experiences to confirm and validate their own religious outlook. The support for pragmatism as a faith perspective highlighted that these young people do not want a religion that they receive uncritically from others. Rather, they are willing to be religious, but they want to discover and explore religion and spirituality themselves.

The Church within society is seen broadly as being ubiquitous, neither good nor bad, or perhaps a little of each in equal measure. The young people generally appreciated the role of the Church in nurturing the individual. Indeed, young people viewed the Church as being relevant to modern life in Ireland, and perceived little conflict between their 'modern' lives and their religious lives.

While the Catholic Church may believe that it is the one true Church, the young people of Ireland see their religion as being one among many. They see dialogue and understanding as being the best way to understand God. Young people are willing to think about their environment and interpret their religion in the light of their observations. Theirs is a pragmatic and progressive Catholicism that truly reflects and embraces modernity.

Transmission of religion
When exploring the religious nurture that young people may experience in their homes and schools, it was found that those who had been brought up in a religious household were generally willing to accept their parents' religion. Thus, considering that the Churches are embedded in Ireland's culture, transmission of faith would appear to be safe in the hands of parents who practice their religion. However, it should also be noted that the young people reported that they would not be willing to accept the religion of their parents uncritically. It has been shown that second generation young people who are religious are those most likely to crave a sign that will vindicate their decision to accept the religion of their parents – they crave religious experience.

Young people who are not from religious families, or those who are new to religion, are most likely to report having had a religious experience. This may be explained theologically, as God revealing himself in various ways and actions, and transmitting religion to those new believers, who are not simply following parental example. It may be that young people from homes without a religious example are drawn to religion through the authenticity of their own experience of the sacred.

Among the religious young people in the sample, there was another important aspect of religious transmission. A core of young people saw religious education as being an ideal means by which they could be nurtured in their faith. Clearly some young people will not feel that their school curriculum is complete unless their religious development is taken as seriously as their intellectual development.

On what areas does religiosity impact for young people?
The multifaceted nature of religiosity in Ireland encompasses belief affiliation, outlook, practice and attitude. Together this may be seen as the super-construct 'religiosity', which impacts on a range of political and social attitudes and behaviours. It may, however, be appropriate to look at these various facets in isolation, and explore the impact that these aspects have on each other. It can be seen that belief informs behaviour and attitudes. Religious young people, while sharing their nation, live in a different world to secular young people in Ireland.

Findings
On the basis of the findings, it would seem safe to assert that the religion and culture of Ireland seem secure. Whilst on the one hand traditional and Catholic, the religion of young people in Ireland can be seen on the other hand as modern and adventurous. Young people see dialogue between religions as being the best way to understand God. This should not be seen as a reason for the Church to panic. The young people are secure in their faith and culture, and will learn more about their own position through such dialogue. Experience of 'other' religions and cultures need not weaken the strong, traditionally based faith, which for the young people is seen as relevant to modern life. The challenge to the Church is not to avoid dialogue, but rather to ensure that relevance in modernity is maintained through dialogue.

Just as the young people wish to explore other religions through dialogue, they wish to critically discuss issues for themselves in their own faith. These sophisticated young people will not accept religion blindly, rather they will undertake intellectual investigation, and refine, reject and redevelop their ideas.

Parents and Religious Socialisation
The aim of this particular study was to examine the influence of parents on the religious socialisation of adolescents across a number of markers of religiosity, in both secular and non-secular nations.[18]

Data was drawn from ten European countries,[19] including Christian, Jewish and Muslim respondents. Young people, aged between 16 and 18 years, completed measures of religiosity. The notion of 'Religious Socialisation' was operationalised into three categories: 'no religious socialisation', 'incidental religious socialisation' and 'intentional religious socialisation'. This allowed for the examination of the relationship between the one key predictor variable (religious socialisation by the parents) and four areas of religiosity: (i) religious worldview; (ii) religion in society; (iii) institutionalised religion; and (iv) religious experience. The results of the study confirmed the significant influence of parents on the religious socialisation of their children across each of the ten countries. These findings provide further support for the view of the importance of parents on the religious socialisation of their children. These findings are discussed below.

Children and religious socialisation by parents (behaviour and attitudes)

For both emotional and physical protection in their formative years, children are sheltered from the wider ecology by their parents. In doing so, children are socialised and reared according to an unquestioned ethos that is espoused by the parents. This ethos includes the moral and religious code of the parents. As children grow older, the level of physical protection provided by the parents reduces and the child gradually comes into contact with other people and institutions that may transmit a similar or entirely different ethos than that to which they were previously exposed.

Argyle reports that parental influence is greatest when: (i) there are close personal relationships between parents and their children; (ii) the children are still resident at home; (iii) the mother has a strong belief; and (iv) the parents hold the same religious belief.[20] For example, Ozorak found that family background limited the amount of change in adolescents' religiosity.[21] Those from the most religious homes became more religious while those from the least religious homes became less so. Similarly, in exploring the strength of parental influence among a sample of 900 16- to 18-year-old adolescents, Erickson found that the greatest factor was the participation of adolescents in religious activities in the home.[22] At a more direct level of social learning, children replicate behaviours that are reinforced, such as attendance at religious events. With a strong desire to keep their children in the faith, fundamentalist Protestants, and to some extent Catholics, demand obedience in relation to religious practice, and employ coercion and corporal punishment to enforce obedience.[23]

Francis explored reports of parental religious practice and determined that parental influence was important for both sexes across both age ranges in relation to religious practice.[24] The extent of this influence increased rather than decreased between the ages of 11–12 years and 15–16 years. Francis also reported that both parental and maternal practice conveyed additional predictive information, in that mothers' practice was a more powerful predictor than fathers' practice among both sons and daughters, and that the comparative influence of the father was weaker among daughters than among sons.

Findings
Of the national samples, eight were at least nominally Christian samples, one Jewish and one Muslim. To operationalise the research, the measure of religiosity addressed five research areas: (i) religious socialisation by parents; (ii) Christian/Judaistic and Christian/Muslim worldview to religious socialisation by the parents; (iii) pragmatic worldview between religious socialisation by the parents; (iv) monoreligious attitude towards the relationship between religions by religious socialisation by the parents; and (v) desire for religious experience and religious socialisation by the parents.

While there were national differences, there were clear patterns that arose across the national samples. The first and most apparent conclusion that emerged from the research was that parents can make a clear contribution to the religious formation of their children. Whether by example, or by deliberate instruction, parents have an obvious role in shaping the beliefs and values of their children. The impact that parents have on their children varied depending on national context, and on whether the religious socialisation was implicit or explicit. Some of the key trends were explored further, as follows.

1. What is the level of religious socialisation by parents?
Only a quarter of the young people perceived that their parents offered no religious socialisation. There were different ways in which parents socialised their children religiously. For example, they may actively encourage their children to adopt a religion, or they may simply lead their children by example of their own religiosity.

2. What is the relationship of Christian/Judaistic and Christian/ Muslim worldview and religious socialisation by the parents?
A consistent finding across all eight countries was that the average scores regarding the 'no religious socialisation' group were significantly lower than the mean scores of the 'incidental religious socialisation'

group and the 'intentional religious socialisation' group. Intentional religious socialisation generated traditional religious expressions among young people. Young people who were offered religious socialisation by their parents are not only more religious than the young people who did not receive religious socialisation, but they were more *traditionally* religious. Young people socialised by their parents to be religious were likely to form a traditionally appropriate religiosity. Parental influence did not promote indiscriminate religiosity, rather, it was likely to promote the religiosity of the parents.

3. What is the relationship between pragmatic worldview and religious socialisation by the parents?

Young people who received no religious socialisation were significantly more likely to hold a pragmatic worldview that posits no place for God or a higher reality. An absence of religious socialisation in the home was likely to lead to young people who seek meaning in life without recourse to traditional elements of the sacred. Parents who value religion, and who want to ensure that their children are able to relate to the spiritual dimension of life with confidence, should give clear socialisation on religious matters.

4. What is the relationship between monoreligious attitude towards the relationship between religions and religious socialisation by the parents?

The role of parents was fundamental to the value formation of young people in terms of monoreligious attitudes. Parents who provided deliberate religious socialisation gave their children certainty. These young people were influenced by their parents and were clear that the religion promoted by the parents is 'correct'. Like many other areas of socialisation, young people can look to their parents and feel reassured that they are receiving sound guidance.

5. What is the relationship between desire for religious experience and religious socialisation by the parents?

In all of the national samples, except Ireland, the number of young people who saw religious experience as being undesirable was lowest among the group who received intentional religious socialisation from their parents. However, this does not necessarily translate to the view that those young people who have received intentional religious socialisation are most likely to see religious experience as being desirable, though young people who have received religious socialisation are significantly more likely to consider religious experience to be desirable when compared with those without religious socialisation.

In summation, this international study has given clear support to the established view of the influence of parents on the religious socialisation (i.e. 'no religious socialisation', 'incidental religious socialisation' and 'intentional religious socialisation') of their adolescent children. This finding was consistent across a number of markers of religiosity, as well as across a number of nations and faiths.

Conclusion

As adults we are inclined to make assumptions about young people, in particular those for whom we might have some responsibility. These research findings should curb our prejudices and our attitudes. In terms of socialisation, the role of parents and the institutional Churches are still important in the lives and perspectives of adolescents, but again not necessarily as we adults might see them. Our approach to pastoral care and chaplaincy in terms of socialisation might see young people as having the desire to explore their religious identity and their beliefs and practices, but in a spirit of openness on our part. There may be a lacuna between their 'lay-theories' of religious identity and the 'official' notions of identity and membership, but careful exploration of that space will have a lasting benefit for the adolescents and for the Church as it faces the future.

Notes

1. C. A. Lewis, S. M. Cruise, M. Fearn and C. McGuckin, 'Ireland: Growing up Irish: Life Perspectives Among Young People in the Republic of Ireland' in H.-G. Ziebertz and W. K. Kay (eds), *Youth in Europe I: An International Empirical Study About Life Perspectives* (2nd ed.) (Münster, Germany: LIT, 2009), 151–64.
2. Ibid., 174–91.
3. C. A. Lewis, S. M. Cruise, M. Fearn and C. McGuckin, 'The Influence of the Parents on Religious Socialisation' in H.-G. Ziebertz, W. K. Kay and U. Riegel (eds), *Youth in Europe III: An International Empirical Study of Religion for Life Orientation* (Münster, Germany: LIT, 2009), 87–103.
4. P. Vermeer, 'Denominational Schools and the Religious Socialisation of Youths: A Changing Relationship', *British Journal of Religious Education* 31, 3 (2009), 201–2.
5. P. Vermeer, 'Religious Education and Socialisation' in *Religious Education*, 105, 1 (2010), 104.
6. U. Bronfenbrenner, *The Ecology of Human Development: Experiments by Nature and Design* (Cambridge, MA: Harvard University Press, 1979).
7. E. H. Erikson, *Childhood and Society* (New York: W.W Norton & Son, 1950).
8. T. Inglis, 'Catholic Identity in Contemporary Ireland: Belief and Belonging to Tradition', *Journal of Contemporary Religion*, 22, 2 (2007), 205.
9. D. Hervieu-Léger, 'Individualism, the Validation of Faith, and the Social Nature of Religion in Modernity' in Richard K. Fenn (ed.), *The Blackwell Companion to Sociology of Religion* (Oxford: Blackwell, 2001), 161–75.

10. J. Fox, 'Secularization' in J. R. Hinnells (ed.), *The Routledge Companion to the Study of Religion* (London: Routledge, 2005).

11. J. Casanova, *Public Religions in the Modern World* (Chicago, IL: University of Chicago Press, 1994), 211.

12. Inglis, 'Catholic Identity in Contemporary Ireland', 217–18.

13. Lewis et al., 'Ireland: Growing Up Irish' in Ziebertz et al., *Youth in Europe I*, 151–64.

14. For an overview, see E. Hennessy, and D. Hogan (2000), 'Twenty-five Years of Developmental and Child Psychology in Ireland: An Analysis of PsycLit and ERIC data bases', *Irish Journal of Psychology*, 21, 105–21; S. M. Greene (1994), 'Growing up Irish: Development in Context', *Irish Journal of Psychology*, 15, 354–71; S. M. Greene and G. Moane, 'Growing up Irish: Changing Children in a Changing Society', *Irish Journal of Psychology*, 21 (2000), 122–37.

15. Bronfenbrenner Systems Model, a conceptualisation of the child's ecology as a multi-layered set of nested and interconnected environmental systems, all of which influence the development of the child but with varying degrees of directness, providing a description of how the micro-level, meso-level and macro-level factors may impact on young people in Ireland. The microsystem: the inner ring involves the child's direct interactions with the important people. These include the mother, father, siblings, grandparents, friends, teachers and anyone in close relationship with the child. In the case of Ireland, this may focus on the central place of the family, patterns of child-rearing, family life, experiences of poverty, schooling and the traditional (changing) roles of men and women. However, a minority will have had different experiences from the majority of Irish children. These may include children of Irish Travellers and of asylum seekers and refugees, and children brought up in care. The mesosystem: this ring encompasses the links between different elements of the microsystem. In the case of Ireland this would include the home along with educational, religious, political intuitions and the media, and the link between them. The macrosystem: the outer ring consists of the culture-specific ideologies, attitudes and beliefs, which shape the culture's structures and practices. In the case of Ireland these include the Irish Constitution, the Catholic Church, and others aspects of Irish history and culture. However, these culture-specific factors are increasingly being influenced by the process of globalisation through children's exposure to television and the internet. U. Bronfenbrenner, *The Ecology of Human Development: Experiments by Nature and Design* (Cambridge, MA: Harvard University Press, 1979).

16. Lewis et al., 'Ireland: Growing up Catholic?' in H.-G. Ziebertz and W. K. Kay, *Youth in Europe II: An International Empirical Study About Religiosity* (Münster, Germany: LIT, 2006), 174–91.

17. P. Norris, and R. Inglehart, *Sacred and Secular: Religion and Politics Worldwide* (New York: Cambridge University Press, 2004).

18. Lewis et al., 'The Influence of the Parents on Religious Socialisation' in Ziebertz et al., *Youth in Europe III*, 87–103.

19. Germany, Poland, Great Britain, Croatia, Finland, Israel, Netherlands, Sweden, Ireland, Turkey.

20. M. Argyle, *Psychology and Religion: An Introduction* (London: Routledge, 2000).

21. E. W. Ozorak, 'Social and Cognitive Influences on the Development of Religious Beliefs and Commitment in Adolescence', *Journal for the Scientific Study of Religion*, 28 (1989), 448–63.

22. J. A. Erickson, 'Adolescent Religious Development and Commitment: A Structural Equation Model of the Role of Family, Peer Group, and Educational Influences, *Journal for the Scientific Study of Religion*, 31 (1992), 131–52.

23. H. Danso, B. Hunsberger and M. Pratt, 'The Role of Parental Fundamentalism and Right-Wing Authoritarianism in Child-Rearing Goals and Practices', *Journal for the Scientific Study of Religion*, 36 (1997), 496–511. C. G. Ellison and D. E. Sherkat, 'Obedience and Autonomy: Religion and Parental Values Reconsidered', *Journal for the Scientific Study of Religion*, 32 (1993), 313–29.

24. L. J. Francis, 'Parental Influence and Adolescent Religiosity: A Study of Church Attendance and Attitude Toward Christianity Among Adolescents 11 to 12 and 15 to 16 Years Old', *International Journal for the Psychology of Religion*, 3 (1993), 241–53.

Faith-Based Youth Work and Social Cohesion in 'Big Society'

Nigel Pimlott

In recent times, UK schools and higher education bodies have been subjected to a vast array of assessment regimes, curriculum changes and media critique. These have focussed on academic attainment, student behaviour and political debates about the most effective pedagogies for educating young people. Despite the fact that young people spend a large proportion of their time in educational settings, more holistic approaches that potentially engender wider societal benefit have, at best, taken second stage to academic considerations. This chapter explores some of these wider dynamics, namely: the role of informal education in formal settings, the value of faith-based approaches and social cohesion discussions. It does so in the context of the UK coalition's current 'Big Society' policy notion and my own research into faith-based youth work.

Context

The beginnings of the end of modernity have brought a number of significant cultural, economic and societal challenges for western societies. In the UK, there has been a developing rationale, as Philip Blond has indicated, that something has gone 'seriously wrong'[1] in British society. Phrases like 'broken society', 'moral decay' and 'binge Britain' have fuelled the sense that trust in society has broken down, respect no longer exists and all we live for is hedonistic pleasure.[2] This has been at the expense of communal and collective considerations.

As society has wrestled with these challenges, it has often been young people who have been the subject of continual criticism and demonisation. They have become the persecuted minority as society seeks a scapegoat to appease its failings. Words like 'feral', 'thugs', 'vermin' and 'yobs' have regularly been used to describe young people.[3] They were initially and exclusively blamed for being in organised gangs responsible for the riots in London in August 2011. It subsequently transpired that many involved came from lower socio-economic backgrounds, were not operating in gangs, already had criminal records, and were not teenagers.

At the same time, young people are achieving more and more academic examination success yet face an uncertain future, with record levels of youth unemployment, new university fees and the clear prospect that they will be significantly worse off than their parents. Interest in organised religion is less than it was in previous generations. Many young people remain interested in the spiritual side of life,[4] but lack the language to express or interpret any spiritual experiences.[5] Authenticity and integrity are the qualities demanded when matters of faith and belief are given consideration.[6] They appear to simply want to be happy and value friends and family highly.[7]

It is beyond the scope of this chapter to further analyse these cultural considerations other than to say that they are the context for a new approach by the current UK government, one that recognises the failure of neoliberal imperatives, promotes reciprocity and mutuality, brings people together and aspires to be open and empowering. They have called this 'the Big Society' – the 'optimal relationship between individual responsibility, local innovation and civic action'.[8]

The Big Society

The Big Society is a new expression and description of a vision for twenty-first-century Britain. What is less clear is if it is actually a new idea, and exactly what it is all about. There is no master plan nor policy document that sets out 'how to do' the Big Society. It is perhaps more apt and appropriate to talk of the Big Society as a vision, goal or outcome, rather than a set of detailed ideas and instructions, a way of looking at things rather than any fixed programme or process.

What we do know is that it is about: 1. community empowerment; 2. opening up of public services; and 3. social action.[9] It is underpinned by several key declared values. These are:

» The desire for long-term social action and change
» Public service reform
» Effective community engagement and localism
» Empowering and involving people
» Increasing volunteering
» Decentralisation of power
» Promoting transparency
» Developing civic action and responsibility
» Maximising innovation and enterprise
» Paying service providers by results.

It is also said that it is not about:

» The state or government doing everything
» Introducing top-down agendas

» Having large amounts of controlling and target-driven
  bureaucracy
» Doing things on the cheap.

It has been philosophically presented that the government (whichever
political party represented) deciding and micro-managing everything has
not been all that successful and that allowing a market 'free for all' has
also significantly failed.[10] It is generally accepted that the consequence
of these failures has been that a few people have become very rich
whilst the gap between the rich and the poor has increased markedly,[11]
seemingly having a detrimental effect upon general well-being.[12]

It is argued that a new agenda to address these issues is
required. Instead of the state determining what needs to be done
and funding these activities, individuals, communities and mutual
bodies need to do so. New models and ways of doing things need
to be established that will develop communities, increase social and
economic opportunities and open up new possibilities for enterprise,
philanthropy and innovation.[13] Whilst this chapter is not focussed
upon faith-based schools, it should be noted that the contentious
'free schools' initiative[14] (of which many such schools are faith-
based) is seen by government in the UK as one aspect of this new
approach. Supporters of the Big Society claim that it will be the
biggest political, societal and economic change that Britain has seen
in recent decades. Dissenters simply highlight that these debates have
been raging for many centuries and point to the philosophical work
of Hobbes, Rousseau and Blake as evidence.

The initiative has attracted both plaudits – who recognise the
potential of the ideals – and a number of key criticisms,[15] most notably:

» It is not 'coherent', 'lacks clarity' and is 'very
  contradictory'[16]
» Deficit reduction budget cuts undermine and destroy the
  very things they are supposed to support
» People have been doing Big Society type work for years
  – they will simply continue to do so, but not much new
  work will commence
» It is all about saving money, sacking workers and
  'employing' volunteers in their place
» The state has a responsibility to protect and work on
  behalf of the most vulnerable in society and must ensure
  that it does so in a fair, just and cohesive way – just what
  responsibilities these are and how they will be carried out
  is very unclear in the Big Society

» A contracting and tendering culture to provide services will only result in big powerful organisations dominating the market, marginalising further the poor and socially excluded

» It is not clear to whom people will be accountable when they deliver services and how things will be addressed if they don't go according to plan.

Faith groups have been quick to remind people that they have been doing Big Society type work for hundreds, if not in some cases thousands of years.[17] They have also been working with children and young people for many years. Apart from a summer programme for sixteen-year-olds, the National Citizen Service,[18] what has been largely absent from Big Society debates is consideration of the role children and young people will play.

Youth Work?

It is hard to define 'youth work'. As Mark Smith notes, 'The first thing to say is that it is helpful to think of there being different forms of youth work rather than a single youth work with commonly agreed characteristics'.[19]

It is even more difficult to define faith-based youth work and, as Ahmed, Banks and Duce reflect, 'many faith communities do not share a concept of youth work'.[20] In the UK, the beginnings of youth work can be traced back to the early Christian and Jewish men and women of compassion who wanted to do something about the impoverished state of many children and young people in society. You might say they were the forerunners for the Big Society.

Over time the nature of youth work has grown and developed, but faith-based providers still retain a high degree of prominence, facilitating weekly clubs, activities, social opportunities, specialist advice services, intervention programmes and a myriad of other expressions as well as more religious-focussed teaching, worship and prayer opportunities. Christian faith-based providers make up the largest single cohort, but Muslim, Sikh, Jewish, Buddhist and Hindu organisations represent a growing body of faith-based youth work facilitators.

Whilst recent developments have sought to bring youth work and other work with young people under the one banner of 'joined-up' approaches, I remain something of a purist! For me, youth work is a practice based upon the principles of informal education.[21] It may be planned work, but participation in it is voluntary. It might be part of a programme of work, but it is spontaneous, inclusive and democratic in nature and unpredictable in outcome. It avoids what Freire describes as 'banking'[22] pedagogies and endeavours to be transformational and emancipatory as it goes with the flow in connecting the needs, experiences and contexts of, in this case, the young people with whom it seeks to engage. Just 'being' with young people, talking with them, exploring and enlarging their experience and creating opportunities for them to reflect and think about things on their terms rather than constantly 'doing' things to them underpins the rationale.[23]

This social pedagogical approach[24] is clearly in contrast with the formal educational aspirations and settings of the school. It is *contrast* rather than *competition* as there is room for both approaches. Whilst traditionally the two approaches have taken place in different spaces, this need not be the case. The advent of the informal educating youth worker working in a formal educational setting potentially complements and enhances the educational experience for the young person. A 'both/and' combination approach offers a more holistic paradigm, meeting student needs and contributing to social cohesion in the school and wider community. It is particularly advantageous in assisting those pupils for whom school is either a frightening, threatening, or contested environment.

Policy is designed to bring together many of the educational components of work with young people, so that youth work might increasingly be concerned with more general social welfare agendas rather than purely informal education prerogatives. Maintaining the pedagogical and practice distinction enables an educational approach to work with young people that comprises the best of both worlds rather than hegemonic homogeneity.

This approach, combined with a clear rationale designed to recognise, foster and provide space for the spiritual and faith development of young people,[25] begins to encapsulate a host of possibilities promoting general well-being,[26] social capital and enhancing cohesion. This indicates youth work is a practice that creates safe spaces for young people to explore personal, social, political and spiritual choices within the context of social action and citizenship parameters.

How Faith Development Occurs

Faith-based youth work encapsulates a broad spectrum of activities that include many of the above attributes with additional implicit or explicit faith components. These range from convictions about humanity, values and the transcendent through to observance of cultural traditions and festivals; from beliefs about what is the common good to intentional acts of proselytisation – the latter deemed inappropriate in formal school settings.

Faith-based work with young people can be at its best when it involves schools, communities and faith bodies in partnership, with the common good being the overarching objective. Experience suggests that these partnerships take time to form and that trust needs to be developed. My own practice has witnessed a number of significant ventures that have been rooted in a mutual approach involving young people, schools, faith groups and community bodies. One of these resulted in a community centre being built on a redundant factory site. Others have witnessed relationship and sex education lessons (which teachers did not want to do!), inclusion work with those disaffected, social action projects that have improved the environment and organised sports activities in a public park. Youth workers have been involved in work with gangs that were causing both school and community challenges, as well as in drugs projects and strategies to reduce teenage pregnancy rates.

'Neil' lived and worked in what can only be described as a very challenging environment. His community was overwhelmed with issues associated with poverty, violence, high-rise property developments, the sex industry and endemic substance abuse. He worked with young people in his community and in the local school. Two competing drug gangs controlled his area. Assaults and intimidation were rife, with kidnappings and murder not unknown. Neil's face told you that the work he did had taken its toll. It was a tough place, but he remained committed to the people. He had talked a number of gang members out of killing other young people and no one in the community had a bad word to say about him. He had the respect of all. He managed to ensure that his actions were an authentic expression of his faith, rooted in compassion, sacrifice and integrity.

Regrettably, there has been a lack of robust research to evaluate the effectiveness of the type of faith-based youth work undertaken by people like Neil. There are many stories to tell, but these are often not drawn together in a cohesive way, subjected to critique nor supported by academic investigation to substantiate any claims made. This has tended to diminish the educational value placed on this type of youth work. This, along with general misgivings about the motivations of faith-based workers, can lead to what Muhammad Khan refers to as a 'suspicion of faith-based youth work'.[27] In order to redress this position I have begun researching[28] the relationship between faith-based work and civil society discourses.

The Impact of Faith

Along with many other western societies, 'Britain has become far more ethnically and religiously diverse than it ever has previously been'.[29] Whilst for many centuries we have been a diverse society, we are becoming more multi-cultural: ethnically, religiously, sexually, economically and as regards family norms.[30] It is not the purpose of this chapter to discuss the advantages or otherwise of these developments here, but to note the reality of the situation and that this is the culture that young people are currently growing up in.

Part of this development is that many cultures are moving away from being mono-faith to embracing plural dynamics incorporating people of many faiths and of none. For some, religion is a problem when it ventures into the public realm. Its place, purpose and merit are argued about and its position contested. Whilst Johnson affirms that 'Britain is grappling with the role that faith may play in the public sphere and how that can be managed in secular society',[31] Dinham and Lowndes question if we are actually a secular society and that 'the place of faith in the public realm is not as clear cut as might first appear'.[32] Faith is blamed for conflicts, oppression, abuse and a lack of societal cohesion whilst also applauded for undertaking social work, bringing people together, supporting the marginalised and powerless and promoting societal cohesion.

I referred previously to the 2011 riots in London. Previous riots in England, triggered by racial tensions and differences, took place in 2001. The enquiries subsequent to these riots[33] led to a plethora of ideas and initiatives designed to promote community cohesion. Attempts were made to bring people together to help them avoid living 'parallel lives'[34] that never connected with anyone who came from a culture different to their own.

The last New Labour government established community cohesion as a key performance indicator within schools, defining it as:

> Working towards a society in which there is a common vision and sense of belonging by all communities; a society in which the diversity of people's backgrounds and circumstances is appreciated and valued; a society in which similar life opportunities are available to all; and a society in which strong and positive relationships exist and continue to be developed in the workplace, in schools and the wider community.[35]

The UK Coalition government has now reduced emphasis on cohesion agendas, instead preferring Big Society notions. My research was designed to find out what faith-based youth workers thought about these things and how their practice reflected thinking. The term 'community cohesion' has to some extent become interchangeable with that of 'social cohesion', referring to 'the capacity of a society to ensure the well-being of all its members, minimising disparities and avoiding marginalisation'.[36] It is this imperative that has reflexively informed and motivated my practice and research investigation.

My research was undertaken during 2011 and involved a scoping survey of 168 faith-based youth workers and a more nuanced consultation process with thirty-two faith-based workers. Some of the key findings are as follows:

» 69% of workers were in regular contact with local authority (government) youth groups, but 75% were not in regular contact with a youth group/organisation from a faith group other than their own
» There was:
  – strong interest in community cohesion, justice and equality of opportunity issues
  – a good level of interest in learning about other faiths
  – mixed levels of interest in the Big Society
» 50% of respondents said that young people mixed well together in their area; 32% said they didn't
» 68% didn't think that young people were treated fairly
» 62% thought this generation of young people were more tolerant of different faith perspectives than their generation
» 81% indicated a positive future role for faith-based youth work in the Big Society
» There were diverse views about the Big Society, with the following factors regarded as significant:
  – Opportunities: community, creativity, responsibility, cohesion
  – Challenges: cuts, funding, inequality, uncertainty.

For some, the Big Society embraced the idea of returning to past utopian ideas of 'community', whilst for others this was too idealistic and simplistic. There was a universal sense that responsibility and citizenship needed to be promoted and that partnership was a key factor in helping achieve this. There was a hope that the Big Society would do what the vision intended – putting right all that was perceived to be wrong in the country – and that faith-based work was pivotal to achieving that objective.[37]

Whilst faith-based work was deemed to be creative, resilient and responsive, there was widespread concern that the current economic crisis would negatively impact Big Society and social cohesion work. The deficit model of working,[38] target-driven and 'tick-box' culture of statutory youth work was generally perceived negatively, highlighting the commitment to more holistic and inclusive approaches advocated previously.

Building Social Cohesion

The research pointed toward a number of recommendations designed to help people and partnerships work more effectively and build social cohesion within the context of the Big Society notion:

Develop understanding

Understanding about the Big Society needs to be developed. This should be done so that faith-based workers recognise what is happening with regards to youth work policy, engage in robust critique, decide upon responses, determine approaches and implement actions that serve the needs of young people and communities.

Be values-driven

Faith-based youth work needs to be facilitated from a values-driven perspective. Such work should be envisaged, planned, undertaken and evaluated against these values irrespective of government and other external policy agendas and outcome expectations.

Cultivate inter-faith youth work partnerships

Partnership work between faith-based groups should be developed. It should be done from a place of what is agreed on, rather than what is not agreed on.

Work intentionally

Work with young people needs to be intentional in its strategic development, focus and operation. It needs to embrace the broad ideals of informal education and faith objectives, thereby avoiding the much-criticised 'tick-box' culture.

Positively influence

It is recommended that faith-based groups don't just sit back and do nothing about the Big Society. There is an opportunity for campaigning, community organisation and continual presentation of positive views about young people and the work that is undertaken.

Share resources

It is clear that there is a vast amount of resource in the faith-based youth work world. This should be shared to avoid duplication, competition and territorial positioning and attitudes.

Cherish common objectives

Faith-based youth work is rooted in shared desires for justice, a more equal society, healing and wholeness, the common good and a counter-cultural holistic view of the world. It is recommended that these common objectives are more fully cherished, promoted and integrated into all work undertaken with young people.

Given the context of this book, these recommendations could be applied to the broader school setting and given consideration as a set of positioning statements to help chaplains, counsellors, teachers and youth workers work toward strategic capacity building for social cohesion.

Social Capital, Equality and Cohesion

Faith communities can be among the most effective bodies in helping create social and economic capital and they often do this with people in society who have significant needs.[39] When faith groups work with others, then they can be particularly effective.

It has perhaps been the work of Putnam that has done most to both recognise these dynamics and take widely held anecdotal conjectures and develop them into more concrete theoretical assertions. His seminal *Bowling Alone*[40] sets out the case that the United States has experienced a rapid decline of civil society as traditional associations between people diminish. The consequence has been a decline in cohesion and social capital. Whilst his work has an American context and is not without critique,[41] I consider that the key findings have provided a further rationale for the Big Society.

His subsequent book, *American Grace* (with David Campbell),[42] undertook further research identifying both the merits and challenges of faith in pluralistic societies. Of particular note in this context is the finding that people involved in faith communities are more generous, more likely to work on community projects and make better citizens. According to Putnam, the type of faith community people are part of is inconsequential. It is the act of being part of such a community that is the key determinant.

One of the challenges in the current context is to consider approaches that help build the type of capital Putnam advocates; the much-heralded 'glue' that holds society together in ways that are equitable and inclusive. This means crossing cultural boundaries to build 'bridging' capital that transcends economic, social, faith and cultural backgrounds. It is in this respect that faith-based youth workers, if they work inclusively, can help connect young people across communities, schools and faith groups.

The previously mentioned UK government's National Citizen Service has the same cohesive aims. Whilst this is commendable, the fact that the service is only accessible by sixteen-year-olds and only lasts for one summer holiday period is no substitute for a sustained and long-term strategy. The desire and demands for immediate results is counterproductive to the proven effectiveness of sustained embedded and supportive faith-based community work approaches.[43]

Conclusion

Most faith-based youth workers seem to have empathy with the Big Society vision. My research indicates that they are a little unsure about what it all means and are very concerned about government cuts. At the same time, there is recognition that faith-based youth work undertakes some pivotal work in enhancing community and social cohesion.

The research indicates that there is a renewed desire to work in partnership for the benefit of young people and communities. One obvious place for this relationship to gather momentum and pedagogical credence is in local schools. If faith-based organisations, local communities and schools can all work together for the common good of young people, then they will be the better for it.

This might mean that some have to step back from traditional silo mentalities and, whilst retaining distinctive pedagogies, work together more to achieve holistic outcomes that serve young people's best interests. This serving demands that success is not just assessed on exam results or faith development aspirations or ultimate material gain, but rather on life-long and life-wide learning that embeds, develops and builds sustainable social cohesion, for the common good and well-being of all.

Notes

1. P. Blond, *Red Tory: How Left and Right Have Broken Britain and How We Can Fix It* (London: Faber and Faber 2010), 1.
2. See, for example, I. Duncan-Smith et al., *Broken Britain* (London: Centre for Social Justice, 2006).
3. See, for example, Barnardos and ICM Research, *Life Story Survey: Almost half of Britons think children are violent* (2011) and D. Wiles, D. Curtin and J. Baxter-Brown, *Labels R4 Jars* (Frontier Youth Trust, Impact and Churches Together in England, 2007).
4. S. Collins-Mayo and P. Dandelion, *Religion and Youth* (Farnham: Ashgate Publishing, 2010).
5. P. Rankin, *Buried Spirituality* (Salisbury: Sarum College Press, 2005), 42.
6. S. Collins-Mayo, B. Mayo and S. Nash, *The Faith of Generation Y* (London: Church House Publishing, 2010).

7. S. Savage, S. Collins-Mayo and B. Mayo, *Making Sense of Generation Y: The World View of 15–25 year olds* (London: Church House Publishing, 2006).

8. M. Smythe in N. Seddon et al., *Building The Big Society* (London: Reform, 2011), 5.

9. Cabinet Office, *Supporting a Stronger Civil Society* (London: Office for Civil Society, 2010).

10. Blond, *Red Tory*; J. Norman, *The Big Society* (Buckingham: University of Buckingham Press, 2010); M. Bishop and M. Green, *The Road From Ruin: A New Capitalism for a Big Society* (London: A&C Black Publishers, 2011).

11. Organisation for Economic Development, *Divided We Stand: Why Inequality Keeps Rising* (OECD Publishing, 2011).

12. R. Wilkinson and K. Pickett, *The Spirit Level: Why Equality is Better For Everyone* (London: Penguin, 2010).

13. Blond, *Red Tory*; Norman, *The Big Society*.

14. See www.education.gov.uk/schools/leadership/typesofschools/freeschools.

15. For additional comment about these criticisms and others, see A. Coote, *Cutting It: The Big Society and the New Austerity* (London: New Economics Foundation, 2010) and G. Brandon, *The Big Society in Context: A Means to What End?* (Cambridge: Jubilee Centre, 2011).

16. House of Commons Public Administration Select Committee, *The Big Society*, Seventeenth Report of Session 2010–2012, Vol. 1 (London: The Stationery Office, 2011), 7.

17. Brandon, *The Big Society in Context*; Faithworks, *The Big Response: Churches Engaging with the Big Society* (London: Faithworks, 2010); Jewish Leadership Council, *The Big Society and the UK Jewish Community* (London: The Jewish Leadership Council, 2010).

18. See www.education.gov.uk.

19. M. Smith, *Developing Youth Work: Informal Education, Mutual Aid and Popular Practice* (Milton Keynes: Open University Press, 1988), 51.

20. S. Ahmed, S. Banks and C. Duce, *Walking Alongside Young People: Challenges and Opportunities for Faith Communities* (Durham: Durham University and The Churches Regional Commission in the North East, 2007), 5.

21. T. Jeffs and M. K. Smith, *Informal Education: Conversation, Democracy and Learning* (Nottingham: Educational Heretics Press, 2005).

22. P. Freire, *Pedagogy of the Oppressed* (London: Penguin, 1972).

23. For a fuller discussion of these considerations, see T. Morgan, P. Morgan, and B. O'Kelly, *Youth Work In Schools: An Investigation of Youth Work, as a Process of Informal Learning, in Formal Settings* (Bangor: Department of Education Northern Ireland, 2008).

24. For more details, see Children's Workforce Development Council, *Social Pedagogy and Its Implications For Youth Work* (London: Children's Workforce Development Council, 2009).

25. See N. Pimlott and S. Bullock, *Glimpses* (Leicester: National Youth Agency, 2008) and N. Pimlott, S. Bullock and A. Brymer-Heywood, *Glimpses for Young People* (Gloucester: Jumping Fish Limited, 2010).

26. For a more detailed critique, see S. Nash and N. Pimlott, *Well-Being and Spirituality* (Cambridge: Grove Books, 2010).

27. M. G. Khan, *Towards a National Strategy for Muslim Youth Work* (Leicester: National Youth Agency, 2005).

28. I am working towards a PhD in Faith-Based Youth Work at Staffordshire University in partnership with Oasis College and Centre for Youth Ministry. For more information, see www.pimlott.org.

29. D. Conway, *Disunited Kingdom: How the Government's Community Cohesion Agenda Undermines British Identity and Nationhood* (London: Civitas, 2009), 24.

30. For a full critique, see B. Parekh, *Rethinking Multiculturalism: Cultural Diversity and Political Theory* (Basingstoke: Palgrave MacMillan, 2006).

31. In M. Wetherell, M. Laflèche and R. Berkely, *Identity, Ethnic Diversity and Community Cohesion* (London: Sage, 2007), 24.

32. In A. Dinham, R. Furbey and V. Lowndes, *Faith in the Public Realm* (Bristol: Policy Press, 2009), 4.

33. See T. Cantle, *Community Cohesion – A Report of the Independent Review Team* (London: Home Office, 2001); T. Clarke, *Burnley Task Force Report on the Disturbances in June 2001* (Burnley Borough Council: Burnley, 2001); D. Ritchie, *Oldham Independent Review: One Oldham, One Future* (Government Office for the Northwest: Manchester, 2001).

34. T. Cantle, *Second Cantle Report – The End of Parallel Lives* (London: Community Cohesion Panel, 2004).

35. Department for Children, Schools and Families, *Guidance on the Duty to Promote Community Cohesion* (Nottingham: DfCSF Publications, 2007), 3.

36. *Report of the High Level Task Force on Social Cohesion in the 21st Century: Towards an Active, Fair and Socially Cohesive Europe* (Strasbourg: Council of Europe, 2008).

37. The full results of the research can be found via www.fyt.org.uk.

38. R. Chalk and A. Philips, *Youth Development and Neighbourhood Influences: Challenges and Opportunities* (Washington: National Academy Press, 1996).

39. Furbey et al., *Faith As Social Capital: Connecting or Dividing?* (Bristol: Policy Press and Joseph Rowntree Foundation, 1996).

40. R. D. Putnam, *Bowling Alone* (New York: Touchstone, 2001).

41. See, for example, R. Andersen, J. Curtis and E. Grabb, 'Trends in Civic Association Activity in Four Democracies: The Special Case of Women in the United States', *American Sociological Review*, 71, 3 (June 2006), 376–400.

42. R. D. Putnam and D. E. Campbell, *American Grace: How Religion Divides and Unites Us* (New York: Simon and Schuster, 2010).

43. These arguments are more fully explored in J. Pimlott and N. Pimlott, *Youth Work After Christendom* (Carlisle: Paternoster, 2008).

Chaplains in Schools
Constitutional, Legislative and
Policy Perspectives

Áine Moran

In my exploration of who defines the role of chaplain, I have examined the High Court and Supreme Court rulings of 1996 and 1998[1] to see how the role of school chaplaincy is understood by the courts, and I have considered the official inspection reports of the Department of Education and Skills to establish how the inspectorate views the role. Both sets of documents are considered through the lens of the Education Act (1998), which calls on schools to promote 'moral, spiritual and personal development of the pupil'[2] to embody its 'characteristic spirit'. The Education Act (1998) was drawn up at the same time as the court cases relating to chaplaincy were being heard and together they give a good blueprint for possible roles in school chaplaincy. In this piece I will give a brief overview of the court cases and my findings from the study of the Whole School Evaluation/Management Leadership Learning (WSE/MLL) reports.

Judicial Perspective
In 1996 a case was taken in the High Court questioning the constitutionality of the state funding school chaplains in community schools.[3] The *Campaign to Separate Church and State* v. *The Minister for Education* was taken under Article 44.2.2 of the Constitution of Ireland, which prohibits the State from 'endowing' any religion. It was the contention of plaintiffs that the State, in providing funding for the employment of chaplains in community schools, was in effect benefiting the Church and that this constituted endowment of religion. It is possible to extrapolate from the court ruling that the role of the school chaplain is based on providing a service by a school, offering a certain religious formation of students by embodying the ethos of a school and assisting parents to exercise their constitutional rights regarding the religious formation of their children. School chaplains are not in schools to advance any particular religion but are part of the educational service provided by the school.

This case was subsequently appealed to the Supreme Court, where the judges also found in favour of the State. The judgment of the Supreme Court began by examining Articles 44 and 42 and found that the payment of salaries to school chaplains is a manifestation of the principles which are recognised and approved therein. The court ruling delivered by Justice Keane deemed that 'the duties of the chaplain are, for the most part, pastoral or sacerdotal',[4] and 'by no means confined to religious instruction in the sense in which that phrase is used in Article 44.2.4.'[5] The religious education that the chaplain offers is exercised through 'personal contact with individual students, by class contact, through religious worship and by maintaining a lively interest in recreational, cultural and apostolic activities'.[6] It was the understanding of the court that the chaplain in a community school is 'called upon to play an increasing role in relation to the welfare other than the strictly spiritual welfare, of the pupils'.[7] Therefore the rights of parents to provide for religious education for their children remain the same. Neither today nor in the past were parents, under the Irish constitution, obliged to settle for mere religious instruction. The role of the chaplain today is to help to provide the extra dimension to religious education.[8]

It can be concluded therefore that the role of the school chaplain as understood by the High Court and Supreme Court is to:

» Embody the ethos of a school
» Assist parents in providing for religious formation of their children
» Provide liturgical experiences for students with due respect to the beliefs and practices of students from other faiths and none
» Meet students on a one-to-one basis and in class for spiritual guidance and experiences of prayer
» Maintain an interest in the extracurricular lives of students and provide opportunities for cultural and apostolic activities
» Care for the corporal welfare of students
» Provide an extra dimension to religious education.

Due to the timing of the Supreme Court ruling, its influence on legislation was minimal in that the contents of the Education Act (1998) had already been determined as the court was publishing its findings. However, the Education Act (1998) was not designed to radically change the provision, structure or experience of schooling in Ireland, and as such there is no contradiction between what the courts decided and what is intended by the act. Furthermore, when Section 9(d) of the act is read in the light of the Supreme Court ruling, the role of the chaplain can be easily identified with the pastoral and spiritual responsibilities of a school.

Legislation

The Education Act (1998) states that a school management board is required to uphold the 'characteristic spirit' of the school as determined by its 'cultural, educational, moral, religious, social, linguistic and spiritual values and traditions'.[9] It then leaves each school to decide how this ethos will be reflected in the way the school is managed and operates. This ability to decide on how to allocate resources gives great freedom to schools but also challenges them to live up to the values and goals that they declare in mission statements. The voluntary secondary schools and the non-designated community colleges and vocational schools have a particular freedom of choice in respect of provision for pastoral care, spiritual development of young people and building up the characteristic spirit of their school – the other three school types having full-time school chaplains who might naturally been seen as fulfilling these roles.

This act also obliges the school to promote the 'moral, spiritual and personal development of the pupil'[10] and one of the functions of the board of management, under this legislation, includes determining the moral and religious education of pupils. This obligation on the school to promote 'moral, spiritual and personal development of the pupil'[11] is the clearest legislative mandate for the work of a school chaplain within the school, as no other person within the school system is professionally trained for precisely such responsibility. The Education Act (1998) gave schools a strong legal framework in which to address the provision of pastoral care of pupils, which was further enhanced by the Education Welfare Act (2000). In 2002 the Department of Education and Science issued guidelines for school self-evaluation, reflecting the new legislation which had recently been enacted. The section on pastoral care particularly mentions the school chaplain and advises schools to reflect on 'the characteristic spirit of the school and the manner in which the spiritual development of students is addressed, with particular reference to provision for religious education and chaplaincy'. This document also suggests that part of school self-evaluation is to evaluate 'the extent to which the chaplaincy dimension is integrated into the pastoral care policy and practice of the school' and 'the extent to which staff members holding specific pastoral roles, such as class tutor, year head, and chaplain, are given access to appropriate professional development'.[12] As one of the named primary givers of care in schools, the work of the chaplain is endorsed and strongly influenced by these pieces of legislation.

Current Experience

Since the rulings of the High Court (1996) and Supreme Court

(1998) and the enactment of the Education Act (1998), there have
been no further statements from the state on the role or provision
of school chaplaincy in Ireland. In order to reflect on how they are
currently being implemented in schools, I undertook a study of fifty
WSE/MLL reports[13] published by the Department of Education and
Skills between January 2010 and December 2012. This accounted for
one fifth of the WSE/MLLs which took place during this period.
These were analysed for reference to the role of the school chaplain
in light of the Education Act (1998) and the rulings of the High
Court and Supreme Court. The aim of the analysis was to establish
the themes under which the Department of Education and Skills
acknowledge the role of the school chaplain and to get 'a feel' for
the roles the chaplains were fulfilling across the various sectors of
Irish schools. The only selection basis used for sampling was the
date of publication. This resulted in there being thirteen Catholic
voluntary secondary schools (two fee-paying) in the sample, thirteen
community schools (one with Church of Ireland patronage, eleven
with Catholic patronage), three comprehensive schools (two with
Catholic patronage and one with Church of Ireland patronage),
thirteen English medium non-designated Education and Training
Board (ETB) schools, one Irish medium non-designated ETB school
and seven designated ETB schools. Twenty-three of the schools in
the study were therefore entitled to a state-funded chaplain as a
community, comprehensive or designated ETB school. From the
reports it was apparent that a further nine of the schools in the
voluntary secondary sector had a chaplain in the school. I did not
make further enquiries as to the terms of their employment or if
other schools had a chaplain but they were not mentioned in the
report. I made the assumption that if a chaplain was not mentioned
in the report of a community/comprehensive or designated ETB
school that there was, in fact, a chaplain employed in the school in a
full-time capacity. Despite there being at least thirty-two chaplains in
the schools inspected, just over half (58% – eighteen) of the schools
had their chaplain mentioned.

Analysis of WSE/MLL Reports
Four roles for the chaplain emerged from my analysis in the WSE/
MLL reports:
1. Pastoral care
2. Spiritual guidance
3. Liturgical role
4. Promotion of ethos through the other three elements of
   the role.

1. Pastoral care
The strongest feature to emerge from the study of the inspectorate reports is the emphasis that Irish schools, across all sectors, put on care. This emphasis begins with school mission statements. Seventeen of the fifty schools studied had specific mention in their mission statements of the importance of providing strong pastoral care. These schools were a cross-section of school types – three community schools, five non-designated ETB schools, one designated ETB school, one comprehensive school (with Church of Ireland patronage) and seven voluntary secondary schools (one of which is fee-paying). Eleven of the schools that emphasised care in their mission statement have a school chaplain. This number grew to thirty-four where mention of particular emphasis being place on pastoral care in other specific schools is mentioned elsewhere in the report. A little over half of this group (eighteen) have a chaplain. Again the schools that the DES acknowledge as paying particular attention to care come from all sectors, with ten voluntary secondary schools (77%), eight community schools (62%), three designated ETB schools (43%), ten non-designated ETB schools (71%) and the three comprehensive schools (100%). These figures would appear to indicate that less emphasis is placed on care in community schools and designated schools despite there being a full-time chaplain employed in these schools. It raises the question: if there is a full-time chaplain, is the role of care delegated to this person and therefore less likely to permeate the life of the school? It also begs the question: if the chaplain is not providing care in these schools, then who is?

Who provides care?
In nineteen schools, senior management is considered key personnel in ensuring students are cared for. The reports include comments such as: 'The school's management has a very hands-on approach to student care, and given the school size is able to respond quickly on needs basis to issues as they arise' (non-designated ETB school); and 'The deputy principal plays a key role in the care and support of staff and students' (community school). In six of these schools there is a full-time chaplain employed. The year head and tutor system is also heavily relied on to provide pastoral care to students. Thirty-one of the schools were reported as using these roles in this way, although some concerns were also raised. The reports acknowledged that tutors were providing care in a voluntary capacity and many schools reported not having sufficient posts available to provide year heads to every year. Despite the erosion of posts of responsibility, some schools were still prioritising pastoral care in their post structures. One report

suggests that class tutors get continuing professional development (CPD) for class tutors to enable them to clarify boundaries between their pastoral role and discipline procedures of the school. Twenty-one schools also highlighted the role of the class teacher in the care structures. These schools were split almost evenly between those with chaplains and those without. On the other hand the role of the guidance counsellor as a provider of pastoral care was emphasised in only eight reports. Six of these schools had chaplains and out of these six schools, four of the chaplains were mentioned as working in collaboration with the guidance counsellor on care issues. This lack of inclusion of chaplains as a key person in pastoral care contrasts sharply with the 2013 Memo of the Department of Education and Skills (Memo 0025/2013) which acknowledges the significant role chaplains play in this aspect of school life. Section 5.5. of that memo states:

> In the case of school chaplains paid by the State, these posts are regarded as teaching posts, and therefore those appointed to them should be registered teachers. However, it is also recognised that the most significant aspect to the role and time of a chaplain is not teaching but the provision of pastoral care in recognised schools. Having regard to that objective, any school chaplain currently in employment who cannot gain registration with the Teaching Council will be permitted to continue in his or her primary role in pastoral care but will be prohibited from teaching. New appointees to chaplain positions must be registered teachers.[14]

It is fair to draw the conclusion that the role of the chaplain as a professional pastoral caregiver goes largely unnoticed and unevaluated in WSE/MLL reports in contrast with the significant value placed on the role in other Department of Education and Skills documents.

Despite the lack of prominence of the chaplain in the general comments on care in the school, the chaplain is cited as being a member of the care team in the school. The care team has a very important place in the functioning of most schools and twenty-eight of the fifty schools (56%) had mention made of it in their reports. The inspectorate regards it as 'core to the effective operation of the school' (community school). It is in this setting that the involvement of the chaplain appears to be most valued and in some schools the chaplain leads the team. One comment went so far as to say that 'respect was also strongly in evidence for the thoughts shared with the group by the school chaplain' (comprehensive school). The role of the chaplain in counselling students is also strongly acknowledged. Seven out of the eleven schools (64%) with chaplains in this category acknowledged the work of the chaplain in this area. The chaplain's role in counselling is seen in the context of offering spiritual advice and guidance and promoting Christian values. One reference appears to question the chaplain's role in this area, commenting 'there is a programme of educational and vocational guidance in place and counselling is being provided by the school chaplain. Best practice would suggest that personal and social guidance should be provided by the school's guidance counsellor' (designated ETB school). Given that qualified chaplains all have the same level of counselling qualifications as a school guidance counsellor, this suggestion of 'best practice' could be seen as undermining the role of the chaplain with respect to personal and social guidance. The fact that some chaplains, in the same way as guidance counsellors, avail of personal supports such as supervision and professional development is acknowledged.

2. Spiritual guidance

According to the Education Act (1998), schools are obliged to promote the 'moral, spiritual and personal development of the pupil'[15] and one of the functions of the board of management, under this legislation, includes determining the moral and religious education of pupils. Despite the enshrinement of this obligation in law, how this function of the board is being carried out would appear to be rarely evaluated during inspections. It is worth noting that this mandate is a legal obligation for all schools and not connected to a particular characteristic spirit – in Ireland, all schools must provide for the 'moral, spiritual and personnel development' of students, although it has been noted that Irish schools are coming late to the conceptualisation of spirituality as a separate experience from religion.[16]

The spiritual function of the chaplain finds prominence in literature when seeking to define the role of the school chaplain. Pohlmann, an Australian writer, quotes Burnham who describes the primary role of school chaplaincy as caring for the soul.[17] John Sullivan, reflecting on chaplaincy at third level in the UK, argues that chaplains have a role in 'finding spaces and creating opportunities ... for students to consider their inner lives ... to ask existential questions that academic courses do not address, to see themselves in a wider context than "module fodder" or as part of the intellectual production line'.[18] Literature from Irish writers identify the chaplain as having a certain professionalism in this area, but are also keen to acknowledge that they ought not monopolise the role. Kevin Egan acknowledges that while the chaplain in an educational context does not have exclusive rights to the role of spiritual guide, the chaplain does have specific training and competency in this area.[19] In fact, Monahan and Renehan are very specific that while the chaplain is an identifiable facilitator for the spiritual welfare of students and school staff, all the responsibility for spiritual well-being should not rest on them. The chaplain needs to be supported by and accountable to the school community in the exercising of their spiritual role.[20]

One might expect, therefore, that if a chaplain was referenced at all in a WSE/MLL report it would be in this context and that schools would be drawing on the resource of a school chaplain to meet some of their obligations in respect of Section 9(d) of the Education Act (1998). In fact the responsibility of the chaplain was acknowledged in only five of the thirty-two schools (16%) in the study that have a school chaplain. Two of these schools are community schools, one comprehensive school, one voluntary secondary and one a designated ETB school.

In the voluntary secondary school, the inspector commented that 'the spiritual care of students is well provided for in the school. The role of the school chaplain is significant in this regard'. Other comments were more general: 'the school's full-time chaplain seeks to respond to the spiritual and religious needs of the members of the school community'. Later on in the same report for that school some clarification is offered, that this is done through the coordination on the part of the chaplain of 'a number of activities associated with students' faith journey' (community school). Only one school specifically mentions that the chaplain is about promoting Christian values: 'the role of the chaplain encompasses the promotion of Christian values, pastoral care and counselling support' (comprehensive school).

A further three schools indicated how they were providing for the spiritual needs of their students without mentioning the chaplain's involvement, giving a total of just 16% of schools who have been evaluated for this legal obligation. All three of these schools are Catholic voluntary secondary schools; one has a school chaplain. One of the schools appears to be particularly proactive in this respect and, in keeping with the advice of Monahan and Renehan, is using a whole school approach to the provision of spiritual care. In this school, staff have engaged in a CPD in order to draw up a faith development programme, and they annually identify 'a clear set of goals to guide student formation'. The report goes on to say that 'spiritual development is taken seriously in the school' (voluntary secondary school). No mention is made in this school of the spiritual formation as belonging to any religious tradition. Of the other two schools which have their efforts at promoting 'moral, spiritual and personal development' highlighted, one made mention that this was being done in the context of the Catholic tradition.

It might be helpful if this approach was used more commonly so that non-faith schools might also begin to see the importance of spiritual development during adolescence. I agree with Kevin Egan when he suggests that if chaplaincy services were described more in spiritual rather than religious terms, it could better reach out to those who feel alienated from institutionalised religion. Spirituality, he says, 'transcends denominational boundaries [and] it does not leave one open to the accusations of proselytising.'[21] The lack of reference overall to spiritual education in the WSE reports is explained by O'Higgins Norman and Renehan, who argue that for much of the history of education in Ireland, formal learning and spirituality have been understood as synonymous activities to the detriment of spiritual education.[22]

3. Liturgical role

The job description for school chaplain as put forward by the three managerial bodies[23] for second-level schools includes praying with students. They suggest that this may be done though what is described in the documents as liturgical or para-liturgical celebrations in the school and the marking and celebrating of major feasts and the season of the Church year. All documents exhort the centrality of the Eucharist in liturgical celebrations – despite the fact that all chaplains under their auspices are not Catholic. The sacerdotal role is also highlighted in the Court rulings. This function can be understood as a means of enabling students to reflect on key life events and interpret them through symbol, poetry, music etc. The courts held that the provision of such liturgical experiences was an important means of adding an 'extra dimension' to religious education. Indeed, Monahan and Renehan suggest that the chaplain's role in the provision of meaning-making school liturgies is the link between personal development and education.[24] This is an interesting and, I think, very appropriate place to position chaplaincy in schools – integrating these two enterprises, through liturgy.

Liturgy may well be the main pedagogical tool that the chaplain uses to teach, but I can say with some definitiveness that the quality of this teaching and learning is not being evaluated by school inspectors. Only four schools (8%) had the liturgical role of their school chaplain, or indeed any other staff member, highlighted, and none of them in an evaluative manner. All four schools had full-time state-paid chaplains – two community schools, a comprehensive school and a designated

ETB school. The liturgical function, as acknowledged in the reports, consisted of 'organising prayer services and Masses' (community school) and 'promoting activities including religious services and retreats' (designated ETB school). The inspectorate saw liturgies as a means through which 'social, spiritual and holistic development' of students could be developed and their 'spiritual welfare ... promoted'. In two reports, the chaplain's work in maintaining the 'sacred space' and in one case securing a 'sacred space' is acknowledged.

This very low reporting of this role is alarming given the high percentage of time chaplains put into this aspect of their job. In the School Chaplaincy Activity Rating Study (April 2009), 100% of school chaplains reported that they coordinate liturgical activities within the school, with 85% doing so routinely. While some chaplains concentrated on the Christian liturgical calendar as the basis for the liturgies, others reported that, out of respect for students from other religious traditions and none, liturgies were often of a more 'spiritual' than 'religious' tone. In these situations liturgies were used, as suggested by Renehan and Monahan, to mark transitions and as a means of helping students at times of bereavement. Liturgies, used in this way, also helped staff and parents. This report also highlighted the significant amount of time chaplains spend with small groups of students, in the prayer room or oratory, practising meditation. The practice of meditation also contributes to a positive atmosphere in the school and contributes to the well-being of students. None of these positive aspects of liturgical work by the chaplain is reflected in the WSE/MLL reports.

4. Promotion of the school ethos
The Education Act (1998) states that a school management board is required to uphold the 'characteristic spirit' of the school as determined by its 'cultural, educational, moral, religious, social linguistic and spiritual values and traditions.'[25] The 2002 School Development Planning: National Progress Report particularly mentions the school chaplain in this context, advising schools to reflect on 'the characteristic spirit of the school and the manner in which the spiritual development of students is addressed, with particular reference to provision for religious education and chaplaincy'. Given the legal basis of this requirement on the board, and the DES suggestion that the chaplain may be of help to the board in fulfilling such a duty, I trawled the reports for any such link. Eighteen out of the fifty reports contained a reference to the characteristic spirit of the school, and a further eighteen schools had their 'ethos' acknowledged. I took these terms to be used interchangeably, resulting in 72% of the schools in the study

being evaluated for their interpretation of their characteristic spirit or ethos. Of these schools, five were voluntary secondary schools, ten were community schools, three were comprehensive schools, three were designated ETB schools and nine were non-designated ETB schools. Ethos has been defined as 'the atmosphere which emerges from the interaction of a number of aspects of school life including teaching and learning, management and leadership, the use of images and symbols, rituals and practices, as well as goals and expectations.'[26] It is not difficult to imagine how a chaplain might have a contribution to make in this area.

These figures suggest that 70% of schools studied that have a full-time, state-paid school chaplain had reference made to their school spirit. Only two schools (one comprehensive, the other community) in the study had the work of their chaplain in the area of promoting the characteristic spirit of the school acknowledged. This accounts for less than 9% of the schools with full-time chaplains in the study. For one school, the high quality of care provided by the chaplain for students is an embodiment of the ethos of the school (comprehensive school), and in the other, the links established with the local community and involvement with charitable work is seen to reflect 'the school's ethos as a community school' (community school). It is not hard to see how a chaplain would have an impact on this aspect of school life.

Given that chaplains don't feature in the reports to any great extent in the context of characteristic spirit and ethos, I decided to look at a 'catch all' phrase often used in Ireland to sum up a school's ethos – the term 'holistic education'. Monahan and Renehan make the point that any school claiming to provide such a holistic education cannot ignore the spiritual and religious dimensions of life.[27] I thought this might be another angle to see if the school chaplain makes a contribution to school life. Eighteen out of the fifty schools in my sample did indeed highlight their desire to provide a holistic education or enhance the holistic development of their students. Again these schools were representative of all the types of second-level education and included seven voluntary secondary schools (54%), five non-designated ETB schools (36%), one comprehensive school (33%), four community schools (31%) and one designated ETB school. What contributes to holistic education, according to the reports, is interesting and varied. Some schools provide for their students' holistic development through an 'in class approach' of broad curriculum, programmes and practices which enhance self-esteem, respect and tolerance, targeted interventions, PE, SPHE and co-curricular activities. No mention is made in this context of religious education. Other schools look beyond the classroom to the sports field, other extra-curricular activities, mentoring programmes, student council, pastoral care provided by tutors and the prefect system, immersion projects in developing countries and fostering a sense of community. In three out of the eighteen schools, the holistic development of students does indeed concentrate on the spiritual and religious dimensions of the person. These schools use religious services, liturgical celebrations, retreats and spiritual advice and guidance as ways of promoting the holistic development of their students. One is a voluntary secondary schools, one a comprehensive school and one a designated ETB school. All three acknowledge the chaplain's contribution to the holistic development of students. Other schools also acknowledged the chaplain's role in this area in more general terms as providing care to students. The board of management of one school (voluntary secondary school) is said to show its strong commitment to providing a holistic education programme by employing a full-time chaplain. On the other hand, one school that I know to have not only one chaplain but a chaplain for every year group (fee-paying voluntary secondary) had the resources it puts in to its 'well developed pastoral care system' which is 'devoted to the holistic development of students' acknowledged. Tutors, the care team and even the prefect system were acknowledged in this context, but no mention whatsoever was made of the chaplaincy department.

Although the role of the school chaplain is clearly supported by the two court judgments in the 1990s, and there is substantial validation of the role in the DES document on school self-evaluation, the evidence is that this does not appear to be translating into the role of the chaplain being actively evaluated or considered as part of a Whole School Evaluation/Management, Leadership and Learning report. The Education Act (1998) puts an onus on schools to provide for the spiritual development of its students; it calls on the board of management to ensure the characteristic spirit of the school is being lived out; the courts suggest that the chaplain has a key role in pastoral care and also in providing the extra dimension to religious education through spiritual guidance and liturgical experiences. These four areas could form the basis for any inspection of a chaplain. If a chaplain is not being evaluated alongside their colleagues, it may give rise to frustration among teachers and a sense of isolation on the part of the chaplain. Either chaplains are part of the educational endeavour of the school, or they are not. These reports suggest that at the moment they are not and that their specific contribution to education is not even being considered by those who undertake curricular evaluation in schools.

Notes

1. See HC *Campaign to separate Church and State* v. *Minister for Education*, 1996, 2 ILRM & SC *Campaign to separate Church and State Ltd* v. *The Minister for Education*, 1998.

2. Education Act (1998), 9(d).

3. HC *Campaign to separate Church and State* v. *Minister for Education*, 1996, 2 ILRM & SC *Campaign to separate Church and State Ltd* v. *The Minister for Education*, 1998, 3 IR 321.

4. SC *Campaign to separate Church and State*, 1998, 2 ILRM, 84.

5. Ibid.

6. Supreme Court Judgment 1998, 93.

7. SC *Campaign to separate Church and State*, 1998, 2 ILRM, 92.

8. Ibid., 101.

9. Education Act (1998), 15.2(b).

10. Education Act (1998), 9(d).

11. Ibid.

12. See Department of Education and Science, *School Development Planning: National Progress Report* (Dublin: The Stationery Office, 2002).

13. Whole School Evaluation, Management, Leadership, Learning Reports.

14. Memo 0025/2013, Department of Education and Skills, 15 May 2013.

15. Education Act (1998), 9(d).

16. J. O'Higgins Norman and C. Renehan, 'The Custody of Spiritual Education in Ireland' in J. Watson et al. (eds), *Global Perspectives on Spirituality and Education* (London: Routledge, 2014), 42.

17. D. Pohlmann, *School Chaplaincy: An Introduction* (Preston: Mosaic Press, 2013), 39.

18. P. McGrail and J. Sullivan (eds), *Dancing on the Edge: Chaplaincy, Church and Higher Education* (Essex: Matthew James Publishing, 2007), 95–6.

19. Ibid., 117.

20. L. Monahan and C. Renehan, *The Chaplain: A Faith Presence in the School Community* (Dublin: Columba Press, 1998), 14.

21. McGrail and Sullivan (eds), *Dancing on the Edge*, 115.

22. O'Higgins Norman and Renehan, 'The Custody of Spiritual Education in Ireland', 41–2.

23. Joint Managerial Body (JMB), the Association of Community and Comprehensive Schools (ACCS) and the Education and Training Boards Ireland (ETBI).

24. Monahan and Renehan, *The Chaplain*, 108; McGrail and Sullivan (eds), *Dancing on the Edge*, 117.

25. Education Act (1998), 15.2(b).

26. J. Norman, *Ethos and Education in Ireland* (New York: Peter Lang, 2003).

27. Monahan and Renehan, *The Chaplain*, 11.

The Evolving Role and Identity of Chaplains in Schools

James O'Higgins Norman

The well-being and holistic development of students is a central concern for schools worldwide. This concern with holistic development and spiritual education is not confined to recent times. However, since the publication of the Education Act (1998) in Ireland, the Education Reform Act (1988) in the United Kingdom, the No Child Left Behind Act (2001) in the USA and the Education Act (2004) in Australia, schools have had a renewed legal obligation to promote the holistic development of their students by advancing:

> the moral, spiritual, social and personal development of students and provid(ing) health education for them, in consultation with their parents, having regard to the characteristic spirit of the school.[1]

Consequently, in many western societies there has been a renewed interest in the spiritual and pastoral aspects of education. This obligation has been supported through initiatives and programmes to promote the spiritual and personal aspects of education. In this context it is not surprising that school trustees and managers have turned their attention to the role of the school chaplain as a key figure in promoting and supporting spirituality and well-being among students.

The first study of specific relevance to school chaplaincy in Ireland was conducted in 1999 and was funded by the Association of Managers of Catholic Secondary Schools (AMCS) and the Joint Managerial Board (JMB).[2] This study set out to describe current practice regarding 'the terms and conditions of employment, qualifications and training, role and functions' of school chaplains in second-level schools.[3] The second important study on school chaplaincy was published in 2002 by the Centre for Research in Religion and Education at Mater Dei Institute of Education, a College of Dublin City University. This second study sought to examine in detail the nature of the work carried out by school chaplains in Ireland in pursuance of their educational and ecclesial mandates.[4]

The findings of both of these studies made an important contribution to the recent development of school chaplaincy as a distinct professional role within education in Ireland. The first study clearly revealed the ad hoc and insecure nature of the employment of many school chaplains at that time. For example, within the voluntary secondary sector, over 40% reported that they were receiving an annual payment of less than IR£1,000 while less than 10% across all school types had a written contract of employment.[5] Regarding qualifications, the Hynes study found that while the majority of school chaplains held an undergraduate degree, the majority had no formal qualification in school chaplaincy and very few had formal training or experience in counselling work.[6]

The second study delved deeper into the nature of the work carried out by school chaplains and found that the majority spent most of their time engaged in counselling and leading or co-ordinating liturgy.[7] Considering the lack of qualifications in chaplaincy and counselling, it was worrying that so many were involved in counselling without prior qualifications or experience in the field. Both studies pointed to the need to develop better employment procedures for school chaplains and related to this the need for school chaplains to have a relevant qualification. From 2002 onwards, great efforts were made to address these issues, including the development of standardised protocols of employment for school chaplains and the development of a postgraduate qualification at the Mater Dei Institute of Education.

Research Aim and Design
The current study was carried out in 2009 to evaluate the professional qualifications and activities of chaplains in second-level schools in Ireland. In order to address this aim, the research team employed a multi-modal approach relying on both quantitative and qualitative methods. There were two strands to this project. Both Strand 1 (survey) and Strand 2 (focus group interviews) were concerned with the general nature and scope of chaplaincy services in second-level schools in Ireland.

Strand 1 – Surveys
The questions on the survey were designed to collect data specifically in relation to the:

1. Training and support for school chaplains
2. Activities of chaplaincy in schools
3. Perceptions and expectations of membership of the
   School Chaplains Association.

The central component of the survey was focused on accessing the activities of school chaplains within second-level schools. In approaching this aspect of the study the research team adapted the School Counsellors Activity Rating Scale (SCARS) instrument, which was developed at the Centre for School Counselling Outcome Research in the University of Massachusetts Amherst by Professor Janna L. Scarborough. The SCARS instrument was developed for use among school counsellors in the USA. The research team adapted this instrument so it could be used to measure how school chaplains actually spend their time and how they would prefer to spend their time in job-related activities. The SCARS instrument is a quantitative self-administered survey based around the use of a 'verbal reasoning scale' to collect perception data from research participants about how often they perform aspects of their work in schools.[8] Frequency was measured by a five-point verbal frequency rating scale reflecting how often an action is performed.[9] Respondents were instructed to rate actual performance for an item regarding whether they never do this [activity] (1), rarely do this [activity] (2), occasionally do this [activity] (3), frequently do this [activity] (4), or routinely do this [activity] (5). Similarly, on the second dimension, preferred performance, participants rated whether they would prefer to never do this [activity] (1), would prefer to rarely do this [activity] (2), would prefer to occasionally do this [activity] (3), would prefer to frequently do this [activity] (4), or would prefer to routinely do this [activity] (5). The SCARS was constructed in such a way that participants identify their actual frequency rating and their preferred frequency rating for each activity before moving to the next item. The survey was then distributed by post to 156 school chaplains based on the membership list available from the School Chaplains Association. Of these, ninety-one (55%) valid responses were returned and analysed using SPSS and these were routinely checked for statistically significant differences using Pearson's Chi-square. The findings from this survey allowed us to obtain information about the nature and scope of the practice of chaplaincy in schools in Ireland and guided the construction of the questions for the focus group interviews which took place in the next stage of the research.

Strand 2 – Focus Group interviews
The focus group interviews were conducted over two days at the School Chaplains Association's National Conference. Two focus groups of one hour each were planned. The focus groups were included as an option on the programme of workshops at the conference so that participants could self-elect to attend or not. As it happens, the numbers who elected to attend were considerably higher than expected, with fifteen and twenty participants at the first and second session respectively.

Research Findings
Profile of school chaplains
In the first report carried out in 1999, the majority (77%) of school chaplains in Ireland were male.[10] This position has completely changed, as currently 62% of chaplains who responded to this survey were female. Another significant change in the profile of school chaplains is that in 1999 just 9% were lay people with 72% being ordained clergymen.[11] In our current study we found that just 10% are now ordained, with 66% describing themselves as laity. While the number of clergy has gone down, there has been a slight increase in the number of religious sisters working as school chaplains, with 20% in schools today compared to 14% in 1999. Furthermore, in 1999 only 6% of school chaplains were married whereas today 42% of our respondents are married. Of some significance, the overall age profile of those who work as school chaplains has remained quite similar over the intervening years, with 60% of school chaplains between 30–49 years of age compared to 59% in the first study.[12] The fact that the age profile has remained the same would suggest that a high number of school chaplains have moved out of the job as they got older and have been replaced by younger chaplains.

In summary, the profile of school chaplains in Ireland has changed significantly between 1999 and 2010. While in the past the majority of school chaplains were men and ordained minsters, today the majority are female and many of these are married. The fact that the age profile has remained the same indicates that there has been a high turnover of personnel in the role, as otherwise we would have expected to see the age profile get older over a ten-year period. The question remains as to whether this pattern will continue in the future.

Qualifications
In the 1999 study the largest number of respondents had a BA followed by those who had a BD degree, with the majority of chaplains stating that they had two or more qualifications.[13] This situation has totally changed with 78% of our current respondents reporting that they have an undergraduate degree in theology compared to just 54% ten years ago. Only 19% of chaplains had a teaching qualification in 1999 compared to 82% today. Furthermore, in 1999 only 12% had a specific postgraduate qualification in school chaplaincy, whereas of those who responded to our study, 70% now have a postgraduate qualification in school chaplaincy, the majority of whom hold an MA degree from the Mater Dei Institute of Education.

While these developments in the professional qualifications of chaplains are impressive, the most surprising finding from this current study is that 72% of respondents stated that they had a certificate or diploma in counselling and/or psychotherapy. The majority of these respondents to the survey obtained their counselling qualification, in addition to a chaplaincy qualification, from a higher education institute or equivalent professional body. Basic counselling skills on a par with those of a guidance counsellor are provided as part of the postgraduate qualification in chaplaincy. However, the fact that so many chaplains have obtained additional qualifications in counselling shows that many school chaplains have taken the initiative to obtain additional training in the area of counselling, which is probably due to the high degree of involvement chaplains have in counselling work.[14] Clearly, in terms of value for money to the state, the employment of school chaplains who are dually qualified in chaplaincy and in counselling provides a challenge to the continuation of funding to guidance counsellors who are not similarly qualified.

Seventy-four per cent of school chaplains reported that they were a member of one of the two teaching unions for teachers; only 8% were members of the Religion Teachers Association. It would seem that the majority of respondents understand school chaplaincy as a distinct and specialised role within teaching and separate from religious education, a view confirmed by those who participated in the focus groups. In terms of continuing professional development, 94% of school chaplains attended professional development activities related to their work.

Planned school chaplaincy programme
The data from this survey reveals that the majority (90%) of school chaplains in Ireland coordinate and maintain a comprehensive planned school chaplaincy programme which includes 93% conducting classroom activities to introduce themselves and explain the chaplaincy programme to students. In the focus group interviews, the chaplains explained that many of them produce an annual year plan and end of year report for the board of management or school principal and that they regularly evaluate the programmes they offer. Many of the chaplains produce brochures or leaflets outlining the purpose of their role in the school and the type of activities they engage in with students. Regarding informing parents about their role and the possible interventions of a school chaplain within the context of their school, 76% of respondents said that they did this, and of those who did not, the majority would prefer to do so. Sixty-seven per cent were also involved in coordinating orientation activities for new students.

In the focus group interviews, chaplains explained that some of the other school staff might perceive them to be 'doing less' or 'just hanging around'; however, the chaplains were quite clear that their time each day was used with intention and direction. Most of the chaplains who participated in the focus group interviews described their role as being characterised by availability, confidentiality and being a 'faith presence'. However, they also seemed aware of the elusive nature of some of their work and had learned to be able to account for what they did through annual plans, evaluations and report as well as maintaining regular diaries and records of meetings with individual students. In fact, 61% of respondents said that they keep track of how time is spent on the activities that they perform, although 88% did say that they could improve this aspect of their work.

Personal and family concerns
Overall, 78% of the respondents to the survey reported that they frequently or routinely counsel with students regarding personal or family concerns, with another 17% of respondents stating that they occasionally counsel students in this way. When we analysed the results of the 'Actual' scale against the 'Prefer' scale, we found a close convergence between what school chaplains do in counselling and what they prefer to do, with 82% of respondents stating that they would prefer to frequently or routinely counsel students regarding personal or family concerns, with another 15% stating that they would prefer to occasionally do this work.

Table One: Counsel with students regarding personal/family concerns

Responses	Actual	Prefer
I occasionally do this	17%	15%
I frequently/routinely do this	78%	82%
Overall	95%	97%

School discipline
The data from the survey also shows that school chaplains play a significant role regarding student behaviour, with 55% of respondents reporting that they are frequently or routinely engaged in counselling students regarding discipline and another 26% of respondents reporting that they occasionally counsel students regarding behaviour in school. The comparison between actual and preferred activities here is interesting, with the scale increasing towards chaplains preferring to be occasionally (30%) involved in this type of counselling rather than being frequently involved (21%) or routinely involved (23%).

Table Two: Counsel with students regarding school behaviour

Responses	Actual	Prefer
I occasionally do this	26%	30%
I frequently/routinely do this	55%	44%
Overall	81%	74%

The data from responses to this question would suggest that overall school chaplains would prefer not to be as involved in counselling regarding school behaviour. The data here concurs with the focus group interviews in that school chaplains now understand their role more in terms of a 'spiritual' guide rather than as someone involved in school discipline. Furthermore, it seems that school chaplains collaborate with other school staff concerning student behaviour as 74% reported that they frequently or routinely do this and 76% reported that they frequently or routinely consult with community and school agencies concerning individual students.

Crisis and emergency issues
Fifty-six per cent of respondents reported that they frequently or routinely counsel students regarding crisis/emergency issues, with another 35% reporting that they occasionally counsel students in crisis or emergency situations. It would seem that school chaplains feel they are striking a balance here as analysis of their actual scale against their preferred scale in this regard reveals the same score on both scales (91%).

Table Three: Counsel with students regarding crisis/ emergency issues

Responses	Actual	Prefer
I occasionally do this	35%	27%
I frequently/routinely do this	56%	64%
Overall	91%	91%

Also of interest is that 71% of the chaplains reported that they coordinate a school-wide response for crisis management and intervention. Clearly school chaplains believe they have a particular contribution to make when a crisis/emergency arises in students' lives and they are prioritising this aspect of their work in accordance with this perception of their role. This was borne out in the focus groups with many chaplains reporting that they had a leadership role within their school both in developing crisis response plans and in being available to students and staff at times of bereavement and illness.

Relationships

Of those who responded to the survey, 60% reported that they are frequently or routinely involved in this type of counselling, with another 26% occasionally counselling students regarding relationships. However, there seems to be a desire on the part of school chaplains who responded to the survey to engage more in this type of counselling, with 92% preferring to engage in this type of activity. This is hardly surprising considering the typical motivations and concerns of adolescents in this regard, and school chaplains appear to be aware of students' needs on this issue. In the focus group interviews, chaplains explained that it is important for students to have someone in school who they can confide in regarding not only relationships of a romantic and sexual nature but also relationships with peers and family at home, as these relationships impact on the capacity of the student to learn at school as well as their overall well-being.

Table Four: Counsel with students regarding relationships

Responses	Actual	Prefer
I occasionally do this	26%	27%
I frequently/routinely do this	60%	67%
Overall	86%	92%

According to school chaplains, very few of them conduct small groups regarding family or personal issues such as substance abuse, however 85% of respondents indicated that they would prefer to conduct small groups regarding family/personal issues and 53% regarding substance abuse. Again, interviews revealed that chaplains were aware of the need for life skills and relationships education, but they reported that neither they nor their teacher colleagues had enough time to provide this type of support. Furthermore, 67% reported that they frequently or routinely follow up on individual and group counselling participants. While this is impressive, it falls short of what they would prefer to do in this regard, with 92% reporting that they would prefer to follow up more than they are with students. Again, in the focus groups school chaplains said that the main cause of not following up was their heavy workload and the lack of time available within the school day, with a considerable amount of this time already going towards individual counselling and 77% participating in team and committee meetings within the school.

Liturgical activities
Not surprisingly, 100% of school chaplains reported that they coordinate liturgical activities within the school, with 85% routinely doing this. From the focus group interviews we know that many school chaplains use the Christian liturgical calendar as a basis for planning and carrying out liturgies within the school. Consequently, festive seasons such as Christmas and Easter provide a focus for many of the liturgies that students experience at school. These liturgies take the form of Eucharist, meditations and themed prayer services. Other chaplains explained how due to low practice rates in mainstream churches and the arrival of new ethnic minorities in their schools, they tended to provide liturgies that were more 'basic' and spiritual rather than religious in nature. Although even those who stated that they saw themselves as being more of a spiritual than religious presence in school, when asked to explain this, they revealed a form of religiosity in their practice. They spoke about arranging liturgies at times of bereavement and loss as well as times of transition such as the beginning or end of an academic year. School chaplains also explained how in times of crisis/emergency a liturgy can often help students, other staff and parents to come to terms with the event. A significant amount of the time chaplains spent with small groups was in meditation, usually in a prayer room or oratory.

Conclusion
The data from the survey and focus group interviews reveals a picture of school chaplaincy as a highly professionalised role. The majority of school chaplains hold at least three higher education qualifications, including a teaching qualification and a postgraduate qualification in school chaplaincy. School chaplains work in an autonomous and collaborative manner. A great deal of their work involved individual counselling or consultation with students, staff and parents alike, although mostly with students in relation to personal and family issues which impact on a student's ability to engage with teaching and learning in schools.

School chaplains have interestingly been to the fore in engaging with the emerging interfaith context that characterises modern Ireland. Many school chaplains have adapted their practice to cater for those of 'other faiths' and 'no faiths' and they make a significant contribution to the school as a welcoming place for people of every faith and culture. It is interesting that many of those interviewed talked about being a 'spiritual' rather than a 'religious' presence in the school; however, finding a language to realise this self-conceptualisation still proves difficult for them and much of their practice in this regard is marked by a Christian religiosity.

Over the past fifteen years school chaplaincy has emerged as a lay and mostly female profession within Irish education and this is not surprising given the demographic changes within the wider teaching profession and the fall-off in vocations to the ordained ministry in the main Irish Christian churches. Finally, it is interesting to note the amount of time that school chaplains devote to counselling students as well as the more traditional aspects of their role, not to mention the levels of qualification chaplains typically have in this area.

Notes

1. Education Act (1998), 9(d).
2. N. Hynes, *Report on Research into Chaplaincy in Second-Level Schools* (Dublin: AMCSS and CORI, 1999).
3. Ibid., 1.
4. J. Norman, *Pastoral Care in Second-Level Schools: The Chaplain* (Dublin: Centre for Research in Religion and Education, Mater Dei Institute of Education, 2002), 8.
5. Hynes, *Report on Research into Chaplaincy in Second-Level Schools*, 12–13.
6. Ibid., 15.
7. Norman, *Pastoral Care in Second-Level Schools*, 9.
8. J. L. Scarborough, 'The School Counsellor Activity Rating Scale: An Instrument for Gathering Process Data', *Professional School Counselling*, 8, 3 (2005), 276.
9. P. L. Alreck and R. B. Settle, *The Survey Research Handbook* (Homewood, IL: Richard D. Irwin, 1985).
10. Hynes, *Report on Research into Chaplaincy in Second-Level Schools*, 33.
11. Ibid. Lay refers to the ecclesiastical state of not being ordained rather than the more secular usage of not being a professional.
12. Ibid.
13. Ibid., 15.
14. Norman, *Pastoral Care in Second-Level Schools*, 9.

Chaplain and Guidance Counsellor as Professional
Some Theological Reflections[1]

John Murray

Some people might be uncomfortable with the idea of the chaplain or guidance counsellor as a 'professional'. The term suggests high pay and status, neither of which is associated with the reality of being a chaplain or counsellor.[2] Further, the term often implies a cold, detached expertise that simply does not describe the essentially pastoral and spiritual character of what a chaplain or counsellor is and does. Taking a more positive perspective, one definition of the school chaplain sees them as 'a faith presence committed to the values of Christ, [who], on behalf of the school and church communities, accompanies the students on their journey through life'.[3] This may seem a million miles away from being a 'professional'; in fact, it might seem to be the opposite of what that term implies. Instead, chaplaincy is often seen as a spiritual *vocation* in which one is called to serve people in a very personal way. This chapter looks at how theological reflection supports and shapes the description of the chaplain or counsellor as a 'professional', in spite of this term's negative connotation, in a way that harmonises fully with the notion of chaplaincy and counselling as vocations. It does so by offering insights from the faith tradition that illuminate and support entirely *positive* definitions of a professional.

Positive Definitions of Professionalism
Positive definitions of 'professionalism' found in some recent sociological and philosophical treatments indicate several typical characteristics.[4] A synthesis of these includes the following: the attainment of specialised knowledge and skills through education or training and the use of this knowledge and skill to serve others; 'a high degree of self-control of behaviour through codes of ethics internalised in the process of work socialisation and through voluntary associations organised and operated by the work specialists themselves';[5] 'autonomy of judgement and authority restrained by responsibility in using their knowledge and skill';[6] and personal commitment to a calling or vocation to serve others.[7] A professional is concerned essentially with a person-centred service of others:

A true profession, therefore, is rooted in theory but aimed at practice – a practice that does not produce things external to persons, but a service to persons themselves. Furthermore, this service is not applied to persons who receive it passively, but facilitates those persons' own activity [...] Counsellors should not act on clients nor dominate them, but should enable them to become fully, autonomously themselves. Thus a profession cannot properly be elitist. It communicates power rather than enforces dependency.[8]

These are attractive definitions of professionalism, ones that we would be happy to apply to the chaplain or counsellor. They communicate an understanding of the professional as one with a particular commitment or calling to serve the needs of others by using one's special knowledge and skill, both individually and in the context of a community of service, in a thoroughly responsible way. Is this concept of professional supported by theology? This chapter focuses on moral theology in particular, developing an introduction to a Christian ethics of chaplaincy and counselling.

The Value of Being Specific
Stepping back for a moment from individual elements of analysis and interpretation, however, it is worth remarking that the issue of what is meant by 'theology' itself raises interesting questions concerning professionalism in chaplaincy and counselling. It could be said that chaplains (and, sometimes, counsellors) are understood at times to be concerned with merely a rather vague, non-specific 'spirituality'. Of course, a choice not to identify oneself with a particular denominational tradition could be motivated by an admirable intention to avoid alienating or seeming to exclude anyone on the basis of differences of specific faith commitments. Identifying the chaplain with a particular faith tradition might seem to be overly narrow. On the other hand, however, a vague concept of faith could be taken as an indication that the chaplain has a rather nebulous role, and that their identity is unclear. If this happens, then it can be difficult for people to grasp the difference between what a chaplain does and what a secular counsellor or social worker does. Surely if chaplains are 'professionals', they will be clear about the nature and value of their role and identity and will confidently communicate this to others in various ways, particularly in the way they carry out their specific tasks of ministry, whilst always respecting the freedom and sincere convictions of others.

To be a professional is *to stand for something*. Note the root: 'profess'. Think of the Profession of Faith prayed at Mass each Sunday, for example, or the profession of vows taken by a religious.[9] I cannot stand for something, however, if I am confused or unclear or diffident about my commitment. If I am unclear about what I stand for, what I profess, this will not help me to be focussed and professional in what I do. Nor will it help others to understand what the 'service' is that I, as a professional, offer. It should be clear who and what I am in my professional role. Honesty demands it; so too does a concern to effectively serve others.

A Faith Perspective: Specific and Inclusive

The theological reflections in this paper come from within the Catholic tradition, the writer's own tradition. It is a specific, defined faith tradition, but not an exclusive one. It acknowledges that God's truth and grace can be found in the other Christian traditions, and indeed other religious traditions too, as well as in philosophy more generally.[10] It is hoped that what is said here, therefore, will find an echo in the heart of all concerned with ethical, professional chaplaincy and counselling.

There is little value in professing interest in a vague 'spirituality' or commitment to a woolly 'faith'. The concept of 'professional' highlights the values of precision, clarity and honesty in one's commitment and work for others. This is not to deny that the faith dimension of chaplaincy involves an essential element of mystery that defies overly narrow definition and is always both within and yet beyond our grasp. Mystery is of the essence in God's self-revelation, to which faith is our free response in grace.[11] Nor does an emphasis on clarity and definiteness promote an understanding of professionalism that ignores the constant necessity for chaplains and counsellors to exercise sensitivity and demonstrate respect for freedom and conscience in carrying out their roles. One carries out one's professional service *for others* and this will mean that one must never treat others manipulatively or aggressively or impose one's convictions on them, even for the best of motives.[12] The paragraphs that follow indicate, albeit briefly, how a firm commitment to a specific faith tradition and the truth it teaches can support and guide a professional approach to chaplaincy and guidance counselling that is secure in its identity, clear in its role, open to all truth and goodness wherever they may be found, and always suitably flexible and competent in its application to varied circumstances and in its aim to serve the needs of each and every person with respect for their human dignity.

The Theological Theme of Creation

This mention of the concept of human dignity shared by all leads to the first theological heading or theme to reflect on: Creation.[13] Our focus here is especially on the beginning of the Bible, the first chapters of Genesis. These describe the 'prologue' for the story of salvation.[14] They also provide a foundation for morality and ministry. The human person is created in the image of God (cf. Gn 1:26-27 and 2:7). The foundational text of the scripture indicates that each human person has an inherent dignity and worth because they are created by God in his image.[15] All God's creation is 'good' (Gn 1:31). The human person is given a task by God. In the first chapter of Genesis this is expressed by the command to 'fill the earth and subdue it' (Gn 1:28);[16] the second chapter sees it in terms of cultivating and caring for the garden (cf. Gn 2:15). It is worth emphasising the fact that the human person is described in essentially social terms in these chapters (cf. Gn 1:27 and 2:18).[17] We also notice the situation of freedom: the human person is free to eat the fruit of any tree, but not 'the tree of the knowledge of good and evil' (Gn 1:17).

These texts can speak God's Word to the chaplain about their own self and the selves of those to be served. Indeed, we can approach *all* aspects of these theological reflections on chaplaincy and counselling with this dual focus: what we learn about ourselves as persons and professional ministers[18] on the one hand, and what we learn about those we serve in our ministry on the other. Both the servant and the one(s) served are made in God's image. And we, personally and professionally, are called by God to love our neighbours *as ourselves*. The biblical message is that all of us human persons are sacred in our human dignity, in our free will, and in our God-given vocation to care for our world and develop it. How we treat people should reflect this truth. It is because of this truth that there are limits beyond which we should not go, just as the Man in Genesis 2 was warned not to eat of the forbidden tree. The human condition is one that has built-in boundaries, so to speak, and we must not transgress these boundaries.[19] To do so results in a loss of happiness and harmony symbolised in the Adam and Eve story by their shame, their lies, their hiding from God, their passing the blame and ultimately their expulsion from the paradise that God intended as their home. These opening chapters of the Bible express an inspiring but sobering view of humanity – we have tremendous value and potential but we can abuse our freedom terribly and do great damage and harm.[20] Applying this to chaplaincy is not difficult. We are called to treat others with respect always, as equals in dignity, no matter what their status or age or popularity or wealth. We are never to treat another human person merely as a means, but always as an end in him or herself.[21] In addition, we are called to be stewards of God's creation, appreciating and using the various skills and talents we have been gifted with for others in our chaplaincy.[22]

God's Word in Creation: Natural Law

The Creation accounts in Genesis suggest another, related ethical theme: Natural Law.[23] This is a vast subject, and these present reflections can treat only a few ideas. The classical definition of natural law in the theological tradition is in St Thomas Aquinas's *Summa Theologiae*: natural law is 'the rational creature's participation in the eternal law'.[24] Briefly and put simply, this means that, by means of our natural human reasoning about what it is to be a human being (living in community with others), we can come to know what is right or wrong to choose, and what dispositions and habits/virtues to form and develop to empower us to choose what is right. Morality, in other words, is grounded in our very humanity, a humanity that we share with all other human beings. For chaplains or counsellors, this indicates that it is the shared humanity of their pupils/clients and themselves that *grounds* the ethical requirements of chaplaincy; these requirements are not imposed by external authority or law.[25]

There is a basic human equality between a school chaplain and a pupil that forbids any treatment of the latter by the former that is manipulative, condescending or harmful. To abuse the confidence of a pupil, for example by gossiping about personal details learned in counselling, would be to sin not only against a professional code of ethics, whether written or implied, but against one's own humanity as a chaplain and the humanity of the pupil too. Ultimately, it would be to sin against God, the creator of humanity, and to act contrary to his wise and loving plan for our happiness. (This is what is meant by God's 'eternal law' in Aquinas's definition above.) All that a chaplain does should be done for the happiness of the people they serve, the happiness God has created each of us to enjoy and share. The happiness referred to here is not an emotion but *integral* human fulfilment. To be happy is to be a *good* human person, to be the person you were created to be (in community with others who are also called to happiness). The chaplain's (and the counsellor's) role is to help the people they serve to pursue this goal of happiness, that is, of goodness. In this way, one is guided by the natural law, the law 'written on our hearts' (as St Paul refers to it in Romans 2:15), the natural light of practical reason given to us by God.

Participation Matters

The concept of *participation* is central to natural law thinking as championed by Aquinas in the thirteenth century (and developed by many others since). It is interesting to note that the concept of participation has been central also to recent liturgical renewal and is an important aim in education too. Natural law refers to the natural *ethical* participation of the reasonable human person in God's loving and wise providential plan for the happiness of his creation. What might this suggest for chaplaincy and counselling? One idea it suggests is related to *empowerment*. As we have already seen in an earlier definition of the term 'professional',[26] the chaplain or counsellor is called (by the nature of the humanity of the person or persons they serve) to treat the person as a *participant*, not an object or a merely passive receiver of attention. The person to be served, precisely as human, is a person endowed with reason and will, with potential for thinking and choosing, and this must always be respected. One must not minister to a person, therefore, in ways that reinforce over-dependency or passivity. Rather, one ought to be concerned to empower that person to participate in living well by choosing to pursue happiness reasonably. We must acknowledge the individuality of the person, with their personal human dignity, though not in an isolationist or narrow sense. We are persons in community always; our freedom and responsibility is always a shared freedom and responsibility. Nevertheless, one's own participation in living well is one's own task, responsibility and privilege. The chaplain or counsellor is dealing with people at a very important and often vulnerable phase of their development. Pupils are leaving childhood and entering adulthood; clients are facing difficulties and looking for a listening ear and helpful advice. The challenge of participating maturely and well in all the various spheres of existence – family, school, parish, nation, church, and so on – is a challenge to be faced by all teenagers as they grow up, and, indeed, by adults at various stages of later life too. It is a difficult challenge, and it often presents formidable obstacles.[27] No person should have to face this challenge alone. The chaplain or counsellor is a person, indeed a professionally trained and qualified person, who can accompany people in various kinds of need and context, in the light of the faith tradition of their community, on the journey to ever greater participation in all that is good and truly fulfilling. Every person, whether those of a religious tradition or those of secular convictions, can have access to the natural truth about how to be happy, or in other words how to be good and integrally fulfilled; nevertheless, the light of God's Revelation that chaplains share in through the gift of supernatural faith can enable them to facilitate each and every person they help, whether in an explicitly religious fashion or in a more implicitly religious fashion (as appropriate to the particular situation and person), in searching for and finding happiness, in finding the good.[28]

The Theological Theme of Covenant

The Creation theme in the Bible is followed by the Covenant theme.[29]

> God also spoke to Moses and said to him: [...] Say therefore to the Israelites, 'I am the Lord, and I will free you from the burdens of the Egyptians and deliver you from slavery to them. I will redeem you with an outstretched arm and with mighty acts of judgement. I will take you as my people, and I will be your God. You shall know that I am the Lord your God, who has freed you from the burdens of the Egyptians. I will bring you into the land that I swore to give to Abraham, Isaac, and Jacob; I will give it to you for a possession. I am the Lord.' (Ex 6:2, 6-7).

What might this suggest to the chaplain? This is a rich theme but only a few ideas can be treated here. Although all people are related to each other and to God by creation, or nature, as we have just been exploring, there is a more specific relationship established by God by means of the *Covenant*. At first, God called a particular People and gave them a particular land. (Later, as we shall examine below, he widened this call in the New Covenant.) He promised the Jewish people to be their God and to protect them. He called them to live in a thoroughly ethical way by the Ten Commandments given to Moses on Mount Sinai (as well as by the other laws contained in the Old Testament and oral Jewish tradition).[30] We may be tempted today to look upon the Commandments as mere rules or regulations. By seeing them in their proper context, as part of the Covenant, we can gain a more accurate and more positive understanding. They 'spelled out for the people the nature and content of their loving response to God's all-merciful and faithful loved (*hesed*), which characterised his covenant with them.'[31] Also, when we remember that they were given in the context of God's liberating act, which saved his people from slavery in Egypt, we can link the following of specific commandments to the privilege and challenge of being free. The Decalogue 'warned the recently liberated people of forms of slavery infinitely more subtle and pernicious than those experienced in Egypt'.[32] God's rules were given, in other words, to help his people to avoid becoming slaves to sin and to help them to be a truly free people, a community of faith and peace.[33]

Covenant Informs a New Appreciation of Discipline

This suggests a particular way of understanding discipline and ethics in chaplaincy.[34] The requirements of a relationship need to be specified in definite guidelines or rules so that one can be freely faithful to the relationship. Good rules are not an imposition on one's creativity or one's individuality, but a protection of them. This applies to both the code of ethics guiding the ministry of the chaplain as professional and the code of discipline of any school. It offers to the chaplain a way of appreciating the ethical requirements of their own ministry as the way a relationship necessarily shapes one's freedom, rather than as a mere formality or as authority arbitrarily telling one what to do. Just as with the creation theme as noted above, the covenant theme suggests that we can understand a code of ethics as something that is natural, in this case a natural and fitting part of a relationship of trust and commitment, a covenant. It also offers the school chaplain a way of integrating their own faith into an appreciation of the exigencies of school discipline. This can be very important for such chaplains. Even if they are not expected to be an official part of the discipline structure of a school, they will sometimes have to deal with issues arising out of problems in the area of school discipline, and will need to do so in a way that is faithful to the school and to the pupil. The positive understanding of commandment outlined above can help here.

Covenant Is Not Mere Contract

The notion of *covenant*, including particularly its focus on relationship as the central dynamic of one's identity, offers a useful reminder that ministry is more than mere *contract*.[35] Although it includes specific duties that may be listed in a contract or a code, professional ministry is better understood as a personal task or set of tasks carried out in the service of others to whom one is connected by *a relationship of trust*. God's election of his people is a sign of his trust in them; it calls for a response of fidelity. Much of the Old Testament is taken up with God calling his people back to the covenant (which they frequently broke), especially through the prophets. In Hosea, for example, the covenant relationship between God and his people is seen as a marriage, which the people have betrayed by their infidelity, and to which God, their Husband, implores and warns them to return (cf. Hosea 3:1-5, 9:1). The role of chaplain or guidance counsellor in a school is one that is characterised by trust; therefore, it calls for fidelity. In particular, a chaplain or counsellor ought never to take advantage of the vulnerability of those to whom they minister. God's care for his people in the Covenant and his ethical requirements of this relationship included a particular focus on the needs of the most needy and vulnerable – the widow, the orphan and the stranger (cf. Exodus 22:21-22; Deuteronomy 14:27-29). God calls his people to act like he acts and to care for the needy. A strong concern with respecting the trust placed in us by the vulnerable and our attempts to meet their needs are not just matters of legality; they are matters of faithfulness to one's identity as chaplain, as one called to a covenant relationship with the people one serves, a covenant relationship that requires high ethical standards, professional standards.

Covenant and Professionalism

The link between covenant and professionalism has been a major focus of the work of William F. May[36] (though not mainly from an explicitly theological perspective). The following quote from a recent work of his illustrates some of what this link implies:

> The professional's covenant, in my judgement, opens out in three directions that help distinguish professionals from careerists: the professional professes something (a body of knowledge and experience); on behalf of someone (or some institution); and in the setting of colleagues. This summary definition highlights three distinguishing marks: *intellectual* (what one professes), *moral* (on behalf of whom one professes), and *organisational* (with whom one professes). These distinguishing marks call for three correlative virtues – practical wisdom, fidelity, and public spiritedness. Professionals need these virtues to be fully themselves ...[37]

This description echoes some of the characteristics of a professional noted at the beginning of this paper, but takes them further. It is interesting that May sees the *moral mark* of the professional in terms of faithfulness to a personal relationship, rather than fidelity to an impersonal code or law or ethics.[38] This is one of the implications of viewing one's role as a minister through the lens of the covenant theme. We are reminded that morality, whether *private* or *professional*, is a matter of our response to a personal link between God and ourselves (and those we serve), shaping the requirements of our particular duties and responsibilities. It is also interesting that May sees virtue as integral to the idea of professional, virtue being understood as those personal abilities or dispositions that make it possible to be fully what one is called to be in and for the covenant relationship.[39]

The Theological Theme of New Covenant

This central idea of relationship, of right relationship to be more precise, is developed in the New Testament where the Covenant theme becomes the New Covenant theme. Christian faith leads us to believe that 'the covenant between God and the Chosen People was but the preparation for the new and definitive covenant to be made between God and humankind in and through the redemptive work of his only begotten Son, Jesus Christ.'[40] Again, this chapter can focus here on only one or two main points of this profound theological theme.[41]

With reference to the three *marks* of the professional described above, we could say that the distinctive Revelation of God's love in the Gospel provides the theological truth of God's love to be professed by the chaplain (the intellectual mark), the ethical values and wisdom of Christ to guide the chaplain's work (the moral mark), and the Church community that believes and celebrates and lives the Gospel (the organisational mark).[42] Or, referring further back to the characteristics of a professional mentioned at the beginning of this chapter, we could say that the Gospel Revelation of God's love is at the heart of the specialised knowledge the chaplain or counsellor professes to have learned (however necessarily limited that knowledge of God's mystery will be). In addition, the Gospel shapes the ethical code of chaplaincy as a life lived *in Christ* for others (who are also *in Christ*). Finally, the Gospel as it is historically mediated provides the chaplain with a communal matrix, the Church, calling the chaplain to a vocation to share in its mission to complete Christ's work on earth, thus shaping the identity of the chaplain as a minister-among-ministers.

Two Commandments of Love Compared

To unpack all that would require a book in itself. Let's simplify matters by focussing on two well-known Gospel *love-commandments*. The first is Jesus' summary of the Decalogue, at least insofar as it refers to our treatment of each other: 'Love your neighbour as yourself' (Mt 22:39). The second is his new commandment given to his disciples at the Last Supper to 'love one another just as I have loved you' (Jn 15:12).

The first can be seen as an expression of the Creation theme, of the natural law. We are called, personally and professionally, to treat our neighbour as we would like to be treated. This is expressed in the Golden Rule taught by Christ (cf. Matthew 7:12), which is found in other religious traditions too, as it expresses a moral principle of the natural law accessible to all. Note the phrase in the commandment, 'as yourself'. This implies a focus on the truth that we are all equally human, created in God's image as persons of great innate dignity, with the universal gifts of conscience and free will. This focus on equality should highlight for the chaplain the necessity of treating all with respect and sensitivity. Though strongly informed by the Christian Gospel, this love-commandment is one that can shape a chaplaincy that reaches out to all, no matter what their faith, to help them discover the goodness of their humanity and their dignity. Consider, for example, how a prison chaplain relates to prisoners not as things, not as criminals, not as people to be judged and rejected and given up on, but as people with dignity, called to respect themselves and others, to make a new start. The love-commandment can inspire and shape this commitment of a prison chaplain.

We are all called in some way to be part of God's Chosen People, though this call was first limited to the Jews before Christ's time. This first love-commandment summarises the Old Testament Decalogue, the heart of the Covenant for which we have been created and to which we are called. Our creation and call find their fulfilment in Christ and the New Covenant.

As part of this New Covenant, Christ gives us a new commandment: 'I give you a new commandment, that you love one another. Just as I have loved you, you also should love one another. By this everyone will know that you are my disciples, if you have love for one another' (Jn 13:34-35). The call to love is common to the two love-commandments: love grounds the ethical requirements of our personal and professional lives. What is *new* in the second commandment examined here, however, is the phrase 'as I have loved you'. What does this mean? What does it mean for the chaplain or counsellor?

The New Commandment: How Is It New?
The phrase 'as I have loved you' specifies morality as Christian by focussing attention on the source of morality – the love of God. This was revealed primarily in Christ's life, death and resurrection.[43] John 3:16 puts it this way: 'For God so loved the world that he gave his only Son, so that everyone who believes in him may not perish but may have eternal life.' The whole Bible, in fact, can be seen as the revelation of God's great love for us, a love that reached its greatest epiphany in Christ's salvific death. This revelation of divine love is shared with the whole world and carried forward through history by the Church's Tradition: its teachings, liturgy, martyrs and saints, and everything that makes up the living faith of the Pilgrim People of God. The essential point for ethics, including professional ethics, is that God's love provides the basis for our response of love. This

is summed up in another amazing Bible verse: 'We love because he first loved us' (1 Jn 4:9). What the chaplain is and what the chaplain does (and how they carry out this role in character) are thoroughly theological whilst being thoroughly professional: both aspects of chaplaincy are founded on the truth of God's love calling us to respond with love.

The chaplain's Christian faith enables their acceptance of the Good News of this divine love and so shapes the *content* of the service the chaplain offers those served; it also grounds the ethics that guides the *process*. Another way of putting this is to say that as chaplain, you receive your identity from your standing for Christ and all that Christ himself stands for. The chaplain professes Christ and his values. This is the faith dimension that informs all that the chaplain or counsellor symbolises and does in a school or other setting. It might be better, therefore, to revise the definition mentioned at the beginning of this paper[44] to state that the chaplain is 'a faith presence committed to Christ and his values' instead of 'a faith presence committed to the values of Christ'. The former clarifies the commitment as a *personal* relationship. Christianity is not a philosophy, but a relationship. We are called to live *in Christ*. Relationships of love are at the heart of pastoral care.[45]

Growing in the Knowledge of Christ

These theological reflections are far from comprehensive[46] and certainly too short to do justice to the mystery of the love of God, but it is hoped that they have introduced the reader to some areas for further study and prayer (or, at least, reminded the reader of what was already known). On-going development of one's knowledge is a central feature of genuine professionalism.[47] For chaplains, this means a daily effort to grow in the knowledge of Christ, who is the norm for our ministry and the hope that Christians profess. With this in mind, we can understand that being professional as a chaplain implies a dedication to spirituality and all the elements of Christian living that nourish and express one's vocation as a follower of Christ.

Conclusion

Some chaplains are not full-time but are priests with many duties in their parishes. What is written above applies to them too, although they may not think of themselves as professionals and may not, unfortunately, be seen by others as such either. Their ministry in school is shaped by the same theology outlined here. It is incumbent on such priests to use their limited time well however, and this would suggest the importance of meeting with the pastoral care team in one's school at the start of the school year (or perhaps every term if possible) to focus on the precise needs of the school and how best to use the time available to greatest advantage. Even limited time can be very valuable, and the present writer knows, having taught in secondary school for many years, that the work of chaplain priests (especially the busy ones) is much appreciated by catechists or RE teachers and other staff. The story of the disciples on the road to Emmaus (cf. Luke 24:13-35) suggests a few final theological reflections appropriate for such chaplains

Was it not helpful to the disciples on the road that the Risen Jesus joined them at first as a stranger? This allowed them to share honestly their doubts, fears and disappointments. Their religious experience seemed to them to be a total letdown; this mirrors the situation of many young people today. The priest chaplain may appear as a kind of stranger to these pupils, but maybe this is not always or fully a bad thing, though it may appear so to many priest chaplains. The fact that the ordained chaplain is sometimes not very well known to them, and, in addition, is not identified with the school institution and its procedures, may help to put pupils at their ease in talking with the chaplain about their honest concerns. (This may well be of prime importance in the school's organisation of the sacrament of penance, for example, where pupils may experience greater comfort in confessing to a 'stranger' priest than to a priest they know.)

The Risen Christ was able to explain the scriptures to the disciples, enlightening their minds and helping them to make sense of the puzzling events of the previous few days. The priest's study of theology, and subsequent knowledge of its mysteries, is a gift and a responsibility. Pupils can gain from this knowledge and should be encouraged to ask questions and expect answers.

Finally, the Risen Lord was revealed to the disciples in the breaking of bread. So too the priest enables the Mass to be celebrated in school and makes communion with Christ possible. Even the very presence of a priest in the school is a reminder to staff, pupils and parents of the wider context within which schooling occurs and is an invaluable symbol of the love of God that puts all our work, including exam work and all that goes with it, into proper perspective.

Notes

1. The author wishes to thank Sr Pat O'Donovan, Dr Alan Kearns and Dr Gabriel Flynn for their advice regarding aspects of the revision of this chapter.
2. As chaplaincy is a faith-based role and guidance counselling is not always so, this chapter's theological reflections are more directly applicable to chaplaincy. However, it is hoped that much of the chapter might apply also to counsellors,

especially when carried out in a faith-based context, such as a denominational school.

3. L. Monaghan and C. Renehan, *The School Chaplain: A Faith Presence in the School* (Dublin: Columba Press, 1998), 13. By taking out the specific references to pupils and school, and replacing them with broader terms, this definition could be used to describe chaplaincy more generally.

4. See B. Ashley and K. O'Rourke, *Health Care Ethics: A Theological Analysis* (4th ed.) (Washington, DC: Georgetown University Press, 1997), 69–73; and B. Ashley, J. Deblois and K. O'Rourke, *Health Care Ethics: A Catholic Theological Analysis* (5th ed.) (Washington, DC: Georgetown University Press, 2006), 204–10; as well as R. Gula, *Ethics in Pastoral Ministry* (New York/Mahwah, NJ: Paulist Press, 1996), 1–14, and the literature cited therein. *Health Care Ethics* (4th and 5th eds) contain many insights that are applicable to school chaplaincy and chaplaincy in general, although they focus explicitly and specifically on professionalism in healthcare; Gula deals with ministry in a general sense, including chaplaincy.

5. *Health Care Ethics* (4th ed.), 72, citing B. Barber.

6. *Health Care Ethics* (4th ed.), 72, citing W. Moore and G. Rosenblum.

7. See *Health Care Ethics* (4th ed.), 72. Gula is particularly good on the relationship between vocation and profession; see his *Ethics in Pastoral Ministry*, 10–14. There is an interesting section on whether teachers are professionals in J. Norman, 'Ethos and Education in Ireland', *Irish Studies*, 7 (New York: Peter Lang, 2003), 67–73, much of which may be more widely applied.

8. *Health Care Ethics* (5th ed.), 206. What is said here about counsellors can easily be applied to chaplains, of course, as well as other person-centred professions.

9. See Gula, *Ethics in Pastoral Ministry*, 12.

10. See Vatican Council II, *Lumen Gentium*, 13, 15–16. This document, also known by its English title 'The Dogmatic Constitution on the Church', was first promulgated in 1964. One should also look at the short but profound and innovative Vatican II document on Christianity and world religions, *Nostra Aetate*, promulgated in 1965. Both documents are available online in full at the official Vatican site: http://www.vatican.va/archive/index.htm (accessed 27 September 2011). A theological treatment of the issue of the relationship of Christianity and other religions, including both Catholic and Protestant perspectives, is found in A. McGrath, *Christian Theology: An Introduction* (5th ed.) (USA: Wiley-Blackwell, 2011), 424–43 (chapter 17), and regarding faith and reason, 152–194 (chapters 7 and 8).

11. See A. Dulles, *The Assurance of Things Hoped For: A Theology of Christian Faith* (New York: Oxford University Press, 1994).

12. See *Health Care Ethics* (5th ed.), 50–60 and 241–9.

13. This chapter draws on Gula's first chapter in the choice of three major theological themes: creation, covenant and discipleship. It changes Gula's ordering of the themes, however, to emphasise the creation theme and to invite a more narrative-shaped framework for synthesising these themes. Gula emphasises the covenant theme more than the creation theme, treating it first and giving it more space. The present writer believes the creation theme allows for a more inclusive approach to people/clients, particularly those who might seem to have little or no faith, and so it is placed first and given emphasis.

14. A slightly more developed account of salvation history and its ethical dimension is found in this author's *Issues of Justice and Peace, Into the Classroom* Series (Dublin: Veritas, 2005), 154–73.

15. See Theodore Hiebert's notes on the relevant texts from Genesis in *The New Interpreter's Study Bible: New Revised Standard Version with the Apocrypha* (Nashville: Abingdon Press, 2003), 7–8. See also the *Catechism of the Catholic Church*, paragraphs 356–361 and 1700–1715, available online at the Vatican site: http://www.vatican.va/archive/index.htm (accessed 27 September 2011).

16. All biblical quotations are from the *New Revised Standard Version* (NRSV); see previous note.

17. The sacred and social nature of the human person in Genesis is dealt with in *Ethics in Pastoral Ministry*, 21–5.

18. This chapter uses 'minister' in a broad sense, not in the restricted sense of an ordained person or official church leader.

19. The theme of respecting boundaries is a very useful one in professional ethics. Gula deals in detail with the practicalities of respecting boundaries in one's ministry in chapters 4, 5 and 6 of *Ethics in Pastoral Ministry*. Published in 1996, Gula's book treated well the issue of respecting sexual boundaries; we have come to see since then more and more clearly how important it is for anyone involved in any kind of Church ministry, and indeed any kind of professional activity, involving or for young people, to respect the rights of children and to avoid every kind of abuse or neglect of them.

20. A good treatment of the theology of the creation accounts is found in *Christian Theology: An Introduction*, 215–23 and 248–355.

21. This idea echoes a central principle of ethics as understood by the philosopher Kant. For a treatment of this that discusses the relationship of Kantian ethics with natural law ethics, see J. Finnis, *Fundamentals of Ethics* (Washington, DC: Georgetown University Press, 1983), chapter V.

22. See *Issues of Justice and Peace*, chapter 3.

23. This theme is mentioned only briefly in Gula, *Ethics in Pastoral Ministry* (at 23). His treatment of the theme in his earlier well-known introduction to moral theology, *Reason Informed By Faith* (New York/Mahweh, NJ: Paulist Press, 1989) is interesting but, in this writer's opinion, it is seriously weakened by an unnecessary bifurcation between natural law as biology and natural law as reason and Gula's rejection of important aspects of the Church's teaching on sexual ethics. A more accurate, though intellectually rather demanding, treatment of the theme is found in William E. May, *An Introduction to Moral Theology* (2nd ed.) (Huntington, IN: Our Sunday Visitor, 2003), 71–40. A very reader-friendly account is found in J. Budziszewski, *What We Can't Not Know: A Guide*, revised and expanded edition (San Francisco: Ignatius Press, 2011).

24. *Summa Theologiae*, I-II, 9:4. A translation of the *Summa* is online at http://www.newadvent.org/summa/ (accessed 27 September 2011). See also *Catechism of the Catholic Church*, paragraphs 1954–1964.

25. It should be acknowledged, however, that external authority and law have an important role in supporting natural law and natural justice and in guiding us in how to act according to the moral law. Thus, true professionals will have great respect for the law of the land as well as for the relevant code of conduct for their profession. This would apply, for example, to guidelines and laws regarding the safety of children and vulnerable adults; such laws have an indispensable role in shaping consciences, promoting and enabling accountability and protecting rights. One example of a very thorough approach to ethical aspects of chaplaincy is found on the National Association of Catholic Chaplains (USA) site: http://www.nacc.org/certification/standards-and-procedures.asp (accessed 27 September 2011).

26. See note 7 above.

27. As well as the usual universal obstacles and challenges of life, people sometimes face particular difficulties, and so need special help and accompaniment. Prisoners are one example: see R. D. Shaw, *Chaplains to the Imprisoned: Sharing Life with the Incarcerated* (New York/London/Norwood: The Haworth Press, 1995).

28. C. Rice, *50 Questions on the Natural Law: What It Is and Why We Need It* (revised edition) (San Francisco: Ignatius Press, 1999), 175–96; this details how the light of faith can and must illuminate our natural knowledge of morality.

29. Gula, *Ethics in Pastoral Ministry*, 14–21, deals in some detail with the ethical implications of this theme. Indeed, it is a central theme in the whole book, focused on the principles of trust and faithfulness. May, *An Introduction to Moral Theology*, 32–37, provides a concise discussion of the place of 'covenant' in moral thinking. A recent, non-technical treatment of covenant in the Bible can be found in B. Hegarty, *The Bible: Literature and Sacred Text*, *Into the Classroom* Series (Dublin: Veritas, 2003), 41–53.

30. The Ten Commandments are found in Exodus 20 and Deuteronomy 5, and are treated in detail in the *Catechism of the Catholic Church*. There is also a very reader-friendly treatment of them in the new Catechism for young people: C. Schonborn, *YouCat* (London: Catholic Truth Society, 2011).

31. D. Bohr, *Catholic Moral Tradition* (revised edition) (Huntington, IN: Our Sunday Visitor, 1998), 46.

32. Ibid.

33. This linkage of law and freedom is developed in depth in Pope John Paul II, *Veritatis Splendor*, 35–53. This encyclical is available online on the Vatican website: http://www.vatican.va/holy_father/ (accessed 27 September 2011).

34. See also *Ethos and Education in Ireland*, 91–4. What is said in this paragraph can easily be applied to guidance counsellors too, of course.

35. See *Ethics in Pastoral Ministry*, 14–16, 21.

36. Not to be confused with the moral theologian William E. May, referred to elsewhere in this work.

37. W. F. May, *Beleaguered Rulers: The Public Obligations of the Professional* (Louisville/London/Leiden: Westminster John Knox Press, 2001), 7.

38. This is not to dismiss the importance of a code of ethics for a profession or ministry, but rather to emphasise that any code is not sufficient in itself, but needs to be supplemented with an integral understanding of morality and humanity, as well as personal and professional integrity.

39. The area of virtue and its importance for ministry is treated in the second chapter of *Ethics in Pastoral Ministry*. A very thorough and readable treatment of moral theology centred on a virtue-ethics approach is found in W. C. Mattison III, *Introducing Moral Theology: True Happiness and the Virtues* (Grand Rapids, MI: Brazos Press, 2008).

40. May, *An Introduction to Moral Theology*, 35.

41. Gula develops this theme under the heading of 'discipleship' (see *Ethics in Pastoral Ministry*, 25–30). This chapter takes a different, though complementary, approach that follows William E. May's work on the distinctiveness of Christian ethics, a dominant issue in modern Christian ethical debate (see *An Introduction to Moral Theology*, chapter 6).

42. Of course, there is also the 'organisational mark' of belonging to a specific professional organisation of chaplains or counsellors. See, for example, the website of some such organisations in Ireland: School Chaplains' Association of Ireland (http://www.schoolchaplains.ie/schoolchaplains/Main/Home.htm),

and the National Association of Healthcare Workers (Ireland) (http://www.
nahc.ie/resources/links.html). The latter has several links to other chaplaincy
organisations, including inter-faith ones and organisations in Europe and
the USA. It also has a 2006 document detailing best practice for healthcare
chaplains: http://www.nahc.ie/pdf/Guidelines_For_Best_Practice.pdf (accessed
27 September 2011).

43. This comparison of the two love-commandments is indebted to Germain
Grisez's work; see his *The Way of the Lord Jesus, Volume Two: Living a
Christian Life* (Quincy, IL: Franciscan Press, 1993), 306–17. Grisez's work is
now online in full: see http://www.twotlj.org/ (accessed 27 September 2011).

44. See note 2 above. The point here about personal commitment to Christ is
implied in how the authors understand their own definition, but the present
revision tries to be more explicit. See *The Chaplain: A Faith Presence*, 14:
'the chaplain recognises that the most effective way to follow Christ is in the
effort to *live* the values of Christ' (original emphasis).

45. See, for example, *Ethos and Education in Ireland*, 102: 'From the *Declaration
on Christian Education* (1965) up to the latest document on education, *The
Catholic School on the Threshold of the Third Millennium* (1998), the Catholic
Church has recognised that young people are above all educated through
relationships.' Relationships play a central role in healthcare and in prison
ministry too, of course. See J. Quinlan, *Pastoral Relatedness: The Essence
of Pastoral Care* (Lanham/New York/Oxford: University Press of America,
2002). This focus on relationships, however, does not mean that chaplains
will turn a blind eye to structural and political issues relevant to the welfare
of those served; see, for example, the Irish Prison Chaplains Report 2010,
which indicates several structural issues of justice and pastoral care, online
at http://www.dublindiocese.ie/index.php?option=com_content&task=view&id
=2180&Itemid=373 (accessed 27 September 2011).

46. This chapter has had no space to treat, for example, one of the most important
areas in need of accurate theological understanding: sin and reconciliation.
Nor has it developed the area of ecclesiology, which is an important aspect
of vocation and professionalism as the Church in its different levels forms
the religious community context for chaplaincy.

47. See *Ethics in Pastoral Ministry*, 51–6.

Nurturing the Prayer Life of Children

Vivienne Mountain

Prayer exists, no question about that. It is the peculiarly human response to this endless mystery of bliss and brutality, impersonal might and lyric intimacy that composes our experience of life.[1]

This chapter is a brief investigation of the prayer life of children in Australia. I am conscious when examining this topic of three aspects of truth in my theological reflection.[2] First, there is the truth from my own experience; second, the truth from my faith background of Scripture and Church; and third, the truth from our contemporary culture of scientific research. I will briefly outline some personal experiences through teaching and learning from children. Then I will acknowledge my faith understanding. The major part of this chapter will focus on scholarly research related to children and prayer. It is my hope that this work will give teachers, chaplains, counsellors and pastoral workers a greater ability to nurture and develop the prayer life of the children in their care – an encouragement to their spiritual life in relation with the Divine.

Truth from Personal Experience

From the perspective of a parent of five lively children, there is a sense of both joy and anxiety in raising them. Children are a blessing, bringing delight, creativity and enthusiasm into a family, but at the same time there is anxiety about making wise choices whilst living in an environment of temptation and the potential for immorality and misfortune. Saying prayers with children became an important part of family life for us. Around the dining table at meal times, or on special occasions of holidays or times of trial or sadness, children and parents together searched for words to connect our lives with God. Bedtime prayers were a three-way conversation with God, using words of thanks and concern, an important ritual at the end of the day. Making the sign of the cross on a child's forehead was my ultimate prayer without words. As the children grew to be teenagers who resisted this night time routine, my prayers continued as I stood outside the bedroom door and silently made the sign of the cross.

Moving into a career as a religious education teacher and chaplain, I found prayer to be the easiest and most comfortable part of my work. Children wanted to pray. They wanted to pray their own words, they were keen to pray for others, and they wanted me as an adult to pray for them. Prayer became a place of honest connection and intimacy: we could pray our angry prayers to God, who could understand. We could tell God stories of our confusion and fear. There was also the opportunity to express thanks and re-live joyful moments.

For young children there were many gateways into prayer: lighting a candle, taking off our shoes, controlling our breathing, centring our bodies, using our hands, singing a prayer song, or becoming still and quiet. Often prayers could be expressed more easily in art. Meditation practices and creative reflection became the flipside to our spoken prayers.

In senior school, prayer continued to be an important and powerful connection point between teacher and students. Perhaps this was because in prayer we all become equal; I am no longer the teacher marking assignments and exams but, rather, a fellow traveller with the students. Students took interest in researching prayers from the past and rewriting liturgical prayers in their own language. Prayers written by students for worship, often illustrated with PowerPoint images, provided new creative insights into faith, hope and love.

In my teaching experience with children and prayer, I have been very much aware of the importance of Object Relations Theory.[3] The child comes to me with their personal god under their arm. My task is to walk carefully – nurturing the images and awareness of God already there, whilst seeking to extend and develop new dimensions of theology and faith. This is allied to the major area of investigation into children's spirituality. The interested reader is directed to further literature in this area of study.[4] In the words of Jerome Berryman, children's spirituality proposes a 'high view' of children; as we welcome them, they lead us to Jesus and the One who sent him: 'The grace children so intensely reveal is the raw energy flowing out from God.'[5]

Truth from the Tradition

When I joined the Church as a teenager, prayer became a key feature of my Christian faith. As I moved amongst many churches – Presbyterian, Anglican, Catholic, Salvation Army and Pentecostal – the practice of prayer was seen as a rich and diverse resource. My experience linked with scripture; prayer is at the centre, a visible sign of the relationship between God and humans. We can stand in awe of the depth of connection in the prayers of the Psalms or consider the prayer life of Jesus. There were so many aspects of his life and ministry where prayer was a central focus, an expression of his connection with the Father. Examples abound: from the temptation in the wilderness to the prayer in the garden, both his extreme honesty and mysterious power touch us in our need. Jesus' prayers for healing show compassion. Blessing prayers over food, bread and wine, or the blessing of the children, offer a sense of the goodness of life, an encouragement for us who follow.

The practice of prayer in private and in the worshipping community is part of the tradition. Prayer is an expression of faith that God is with us and also an expression that we rely on God's grace as we endeavour to walk in God's ways.

Truth from the Contemporary Culture

As a teacher and clinical counsellor, I have been influenced by a wide range of scholarly study and live within professional boundaries that are necessary at this point in time in western society. The culture of research and testing is a cornerstone of contemporary scientific thought. I contend that our personal faith life is validated as we engage in professional academic research. This is not easy; the requirements of research are strict and must be monitored with thorough 'member checking'. I have completed two research projects concerning children that have application for this chapter, both of which I will outline here.

Research 1. Investigating the Meaning and Function of Prayer for Children[6]

Prayer is a central element of all religions.[7] Alongside the theological notion of the importance of prayer, recognition of the psychological reality and benefit of prayer for adults has increased.[8] My research investigated the theological and psychological perceptions of prayer held by children, through an investigation of the meaning and function of prayer.

As there is little existing literature on children and prayer, the findings of that study provided valuable new understanding and proposed new aspects of theory with implication for professionals involved in the education and welfare of children. The research reported represents the first Australian research in this area.

The choice of participants in my study reflected the diverse philosophical and religious traditions found in the Australian multi-faith society. Semi-structured interviews were video-recorded with sixty participants from primary school Year Five (10–12 years of age). Five male and five female participants were selected from each of six different schools in the Melbourne metropolitan area, namely: Catholic; Independent (Christian); Christian (Parent-Controlled or Community School); Jewish; Islamic; and government schools. Students completed a drawing exercise and a written sentence completion exercise as part of the interview and the three sources of data were analysed qualitatively using the method of Grounded Theory.

The lengthy analysis process of Grounded Theory involved extensive member checking and verification. Over thirty specialists and colleagues were used in the verification process, checking for interviewer affect as well as the reliability of the analysis. Finally, the data revealed that all sixty children were found to agree on the two categories of meaning and function. The associated properties expanded the categories; these ideas were expressed by a large number of the participants. The summary of findings is reproduced in the chart below, followed by some expansion of the main concepts.

Summary of findings
The meaning of prayer is communication with the good God. The function of prayer is a personal way to perceive and respond to the experiences of life.

CATEGORY – Meaning – Prayer is communication with the good God
PROPERTIES – Understood through faith traditions with defined images of God
- › God above, Holy, Lord, Giver of life, and Judge
- › Personal God as: Lover, Healer, Forgiver, Guide, Protector
- › Known in the person of Jesus
- › Understood through personal images of God
- › Expressing social connection with the faith community
- › Expressing personal feelings and hopes
  – Praise – Grief – Need – Guilt

CATEGORY – Function – A personal way to perceive and respond to the experiences of life
PROPERTIES – Finding help through individual connection to God
- › In challenging emotional states of anxiety, loneliness, fear, anger, guilt
- › Finding social identity through communal ritual, activity and belief
- › Giving hope for the afterlife
- › In personal identity formation
- Helping others
  - › Family and friends
  - › In extreme circumstances of social injustice
- Expressing praise and thanksgiving

The Meaning of Prayer

Finding One: Prayer means connection or communication with God

The research by Hay,[9] Nye[10] and Coles[11] has suggested that spirituality – the sense of connection with the inner self, with others, with the environment and with God – is an innate human characteristic. This study supports this proposal, in that students from a variety of faith perspectives and family backgrounds report a common understanding of the meaning of prayer. For some it was entwined with their religion: 'A very important part of Islam'; 'Because they have faith in Jesus Christ'; 'A religious act showing you care'. For most participants, personal prayers were seen as deeper than the formal liturgy: 'Prayers come from within you'; 'you just know how to pray'; 'It's like a baby learning to walk, you just keep trying'; 'no one needs to teach you'; 'thinking from your heart'. For all of the participants, prayer was recognised as part of life or a way to respond to life.

Finding Two: Prayer is related to the image of God

The participants coming from schools associated with a faith tradition showed prayer associated with the image of the god of that faith tradition. The image of God as holy and above the earth was reflected in participants from the Muslim school, while participants from the Christian school spoke of God in more familiar terms of 'Saviour' and 'Friend'.

The data from those participants who professed no religion or religious affiliation is significant in that it identified the reality of prayer and the reality of the image of God. As the first generation growing up without a formal sense of 'God' *vis à vis* the recognition of God as an agreed cultural assumption,[12] a sense of 'God' was still present. This God was recognised as good, possessing attributes of healing, guidance and comfort. This is supported in the literature of Object Relations Theory. The image of God in this case is not determined by the teaching of the faith tradition but is rather viewed as a human psychic connection, an expectation of relationship and love. This concept relates to the psychological understanding of Ulinov[13] that prayer can be viewed as part of relational living, a primary human call to 'the Other'.

Finding Three: Prayer continues within the secular environment

One example of this discussion was seen as participants were asked to consider the common expression, 'Oh my God!' This expression is heard on television and films, usually in situations far removed from experiences of faith traditions. In the case of the exclamation of 'Oh my God!', the reality of secular culture comes into tension with the reality of religious faith cultures. The attention participants gave to the 'Oh my God!' expression and how it related to the meaning of prayer could be considered an indication of the capacity to hold together the seemingly incompatible ideas of tradition and the modern secular context. Many participants regarded the possibility that the 'Oh my God!' expression could be a prayer if the person who utters the expression has appropriate feelings of fear or need.

Finding Four: The meaning of prayer is an inner aspect of life related to feelings and hopes
The data from individual participants show that personal feelings and hopes are expressed as part of the meaning of prayer. For all participants, prayer was regarded as an activity where aspects of personal life could be included. Expressions of need and gratitude were the common elements within confession of sins, personal prayers about problems and illness, intercessory prayer, respect for God and thanksgiving. Within the communal experiences of prayer, participants recognised that opportunity was given for their personal prayers to be offered. Even though the participants from the Jewish and Muslim schools understood the need for a strict ritual, the words and actions were supplemented by the inner intention of the participant.

Finding Five: The meaning of prayer is affected by the environment
The data on the meaning of prayer shows considerable differences between participants involved in the different schools. As mentioned above, this is a complex situation in that the school curriculum or pedagogy should be considered as only one factor alongside family teaching and other environmental forces. Within the limitations of this study, it can be stated that the religious beliefs of the child's environment does have an effect on various aspects of prayer. Two examples can be seen in the amount of time spent in prayer, and in the type of prayer associated with the image of God as the recipient of prayer. The literature from the different faith traditions presents some variation in the perception of the being of God, which influences the type of prayer. The concept of God varies within and between traditions, including a variety of images such as transcendent and holy or accepting and immanent.

The Function of Prayer
Finding One: Prayer functions as a personal way to perceive life experiences
The word 'perceive' has been chosen in the final category emerging from the data, to represent the idea of prayer as a way in which life

experiences can be understood by the individual. The identification of the concept of personal perception is related to the finding of the expression of personal feeling as a function of prayer. The data from participants demonstrated the expression of feelings to God in prayer as the most common response. The feelings of joy and gratitude do form part of the data collected, but largely the participants identified the expression of difficult feelings such as grief, sadness, anger, fear and loneliness. A number of participants spoke of the value of prayer as a way to talk about the difficult things they couldn't tell anyone else. It is possible that prayer was valuable as a safe way to express needs and difficulties. One participant said that prayer was like talking to a favourite toy. Another said that in prayer you could 'get all of the bad stuff out'. This could be related to the understanding of the developmental need to recognise and express human vulnerability and anxiety. It could also link with the ideas of Hederman,[14] where a relationship is shown between paying attention to the 'shadow', that is the personal unacceptable attitudes, and feelings that need to be recognised in order to move through challenging times. Ulanov also used the term 'shadow', which is seen through life experiences as difficult forms of self-understanding and feeling which, when acknowledged, can lead to vitality and a new point of view. This concept is expressed in the words of Rahner: 'Once we have opened out hearts, we no longer seek to escape from ourselves.'[15] It is possible that the act of praying is a form of catharsis. Prayer may provide a safe place to express strong feelings that are often considered socially inappropriate in other contexts. From this acknowledgement that prayer provides a way to perceive or appraise life experience, prayer can be called a coping mechanism.

Finding Two: Prayer acts as a coping mechanism
From the data above, prayer can be identified as a method of coping or moving through the strong emotional states of life. As stated by Lazarus and Lazarus,[16] the fifteen recognisable human emotions are all attached to a personal pattern of meaning and belief. The emotions are grouped: the 'nasty' emotions of anger, envy and jealousy; the 'existential' emotions of anxiety, fright, guilt and shame; emotions from 'unfavourable' life conditions, such as relief, hope, sadness and depression; and emotions from 'favourable' life conditions, namely happiness, pride, love and empathic emotions of gratitude, compassion and aesthetic awe. The data shows that prayer is used as a form of response to all of these emotional states. As a way of coping with the 'nasty' emotions, there is the prayer of confession where 'it's like telling someone we really trust' and a way of 'getting everything bad out of your head'.

Participants most commonly reported the use of personal prayer to appraise and examine unfavourable life conditions and existential emotions. A few examples of this are: 'People pray if they are upset, they want something set right or they are angry'; 'Just talking to God helps you'; 'They need God's love ... they need help'; 'People with an easier life don't pray as much.' On the other hand, the emotions of favourable life experiences led to prayers of thanksgiving and praise. The emotions of empathy were expressed as intercessory prayer or praise. Although prayer could be used negatively as a form of denial or 'disavowal of reality',[17] it seems from the data that prayer acted as a positive 'distancing' mechanism, through which the perceived negative situation could be reassessed. Pargament stated the positive possibility within prayer thus: 'the religious world helps people face their personal limitations and go beyond themselves for solutions ... the most central of all qualities of coping is possibility.'[18] The data from this study supports this concept, as participants recognised prayer as a context in which many different emotional states could be brought to God, whom they recognise as good.

The idea of God as good, as someone to be trusted, as the Creator, as the One who understands, as the One who heals and, for some, as the One who works miracles, is linked in the data. It is possible that the positive image of God in relationship with participants through prayer led them to a new appraisal of their situation. With God present there was a possibility that something good could be found within the difficult feelings associated with perceived negative life experiences. In this way, the old pattern of stimulus leading to response is replaced by stimulus being affected by 'organismic variables' before the response.[19] Many forms of 'organismic variables' are possible, leading to different levels of ability to cope with the negatively perceived stimulus. Pargament suggests that various religious activities act as forms of connectedness, enhancing the coping capacity of the individual when dealing with difficult life experiences. The experience of connectedness is complex and polyvalent; it could refer to connection to the inner emotions of the self, connection to others through the faith community and/or connection to the transcendent image of God.

It seems likely that prayer acting as a link to the good, caring God, could be one way to reappraise a negative situation, looking with a different perspective at the good possibilities within that situation. This links with the major thesis of Hay who defines spirituality as 'relational consciousness'.[20] In prayer there is awareness of a relationship with the transcendent and a sense of connection that helps to reappraise the challenging experiences of human existence.

All of the sacred texts from the traditions involved in this study make reference to this aspect of faith in the God who is there and who cares for 'his' human creatures (the Bible, Torah and the Qu'ran). The participants made many references to this thinking pattern throughout the interviews, for example: 'Behind every bad thing there is always a good thing ... keep praying'; 'God has a plan ... the cycle of life ... God knows ... in safe hands'; 'When I pray quietly to myself ... it gives me a good feeling, thinking that you are really next to God, talking to him'; 'They pray because they think ... I am a person, no one can take that privilege away from me ... God is there to help me, to love me ... He's a father'.

Finding Three: Prayer functions as a personal way to respond to life experiences
As an extension of the concept that prayer acts as a way to perceive and understand, prayer was also understood by many participants as a way to respond to life experiences. These were usually the uncontrollable experiences of life; the most common experiences expressed in the data related to issues of illness, death and separation. When a participant's mother had cancer, prayer was used; when a pet dog died, the participant prayed; when a participant was injured, prayer helped. As one participant said, prayer was something to do when there was nothing else to do. This could be linked to the concept of prayer in Godin, who claims that prayer can hold both a 'manipulative aim' and an 'expressive aim'.[21] Many prayers from the participants had the manipulative aim of changing the circumstances of life, asking God to do something. This was shown through the many prayers requesting healing for family members, or the prayers from one participant who asked God to prevent his parents from separating. However, other prayers were linked to the 'expressive aim' of linking to God who could understand and in some ways share the experiences of life. One participant spoke of prayer that 'keeps me going' through his struggle with asthma, and another saw prayer as taking him through the gates of heaven to be close to God. A third participant, when talking about 'unanswered prayer', said that life 'comes from God ... we can't do anything about it ... just praise to Allah'.

Finding Four: Prayer has a community-building and identity-formation function
Prayer was shown through the data as a community activity in the majority of cases. As discussed earlier, many of the subjects from the independent and government schools indicated that they had very little contact with any form of organised religious worship,

and yet these children recognised prayer as part of Church life. For the participants from the Catholic, Christian, Jewish and Muslim schools, the experience of prayer within the worshipping community was expressed in all of the interviews.

The place of the community in defining and endorsing prayer was most obvious in the data from the participants from the Jewish and the Muslim schools, as they considered communal prayer as the 'normal' way to pray. The Jewish ritual was always conducted in Hebrew and the Muslim prayer ritual was always conducted in Arabic. The participants from these two schools expressed awareness that they were learning the language, and could only join in prayer to the degree to which the language was known. There was a common understanding that the prayers of children needed to be supplemented by the adult community, as children's grasp of the language was limited. Some participants from these groups were aware of other forms of prayer, but the family, school and worship centre combined to encourage the traditional rituals for the group. This did not mean that the prayer ritual was considered complete in itself, for individual prayer in the heart or in the mind and the proper intention were understood to be important parts of the formal ritual.

Finding Five: Expressing praise and thanksgiving is a function of prayer

Asking and thanking have been considered from the literature of the faith traditions to be two aspects of the relationship with God expressed in prayer. Thanksgiving and praise were mentioned by all participants from the schools of the Muslim and Christian traditions, with particular reference to the appreciation of the faith tradition. The idea of Jesus' love and salvation were dominant aspects of praise amongst participants in the Christian school, while praise and thanksgiving were given to Allah in his high position as Creator in the Islamic tradition. These findings agree with the literature reviewed by Rahner and Abdalati.[22] For a large number of participants from all school groups, thanksgiving formed a part of the function of prayer. A selection of quotations shows some of this understanding: 'You feel joyful inside'; 'Like talking to one of your friends ... just talking to God and Mary'; 'I love Simhat Torah ... the men dancing and singing'; 'Just thanks for the gift of life'.

It is possible that the use of thanksgiving in prayer could be associated with the coping theory. As the God to whom prayers are addressed is recognised as the good giver of life, so the prayers in times of distress (when addressed to this same God) can be appraised more easily as having some good purpose or hidden meaning. The thanksgiving function of prayer in this way fits with the perception and response to life as a totality, and both good and seemingly bad experiences can be brought together in the prayer relationship with God.

Recommendations arising from this study
– For teachers of religious education
i. Prayer should be taught and practised in religious education.
ii. Prayer should be taught with a multi-faith awareness.
iii. Pedagogy should reflect an awareness of children's spirituality.
iv. Children should be involved in aspects of ritual and symbol.

– For professionals involved in the helping professions related to resilience in children – teachers, child psychologists, welfare workers
i. Prayer is a coping mechanism.
ii. Prayer should be given greater recognition as an activity with psychological importance.

– For those involved professionally in the development of children's spirituality
i. A relationship with God through prayer is part of children's spirituality.
ii. The religious community and communal prayer are part of children's spirituality.

In closing this section, some of the words of children demonstrate their sincere and often creative ideas (with one quote from each of the different school groups):

What is prayer?
'[Like] walking into heaven ... a special thing you can do.'
'Like telling something to someone you really trust.'
'It brings you closer to your God ... great feeling of contentment ... you feel like a good person.'
'You can't exactly compare them [different religious traditions] ... they are completely different ... I think all prayers are the same, except they just say it in a different way – this is my God, I love him, he's the only one – that's what they all probably say.'
'It's something everyone does and religious people do more.'

What does prayer do?
'When you open the Sidur ... prayers float into your mind ... they hover there, then they float up to heaven.'

'Prayer probably comes off you like a thought ray … a sixth sense
… like sharks have electro-sensitivity.'
'Prayers help you spiritually … not on the outside but on the inside;
like if someone teases you, that's on the inside.'
'If we pray, our God builds up palaces for us in heaven.'
'With your problem, he just gives you a hint of how to fix it.'
'Eyes shut helps you get close to God.'

Research 2: Children and the Church

This study sought to assess aspects of the Child Theology Movement
that are considered relevant to those in leadership with children in
selected churches in Melbourne, Australia. The Child Theology
Movement[23] has arisen from the words of Jesus, 'Except you change
and become like a little child you will not enter the Kingdom of
Heaven',[24] and the associated action of Jesus placing a child 'in the
midst'. The child in the story is not special in any way; it is a child
alone without family or religious context, without reference to special
need, ability or gender. The image of Jesus with children is one of
the most common depictions, celebrated visually in paintings and
stained glass; this thesis questions the relevance of this image in the
contemporary Church. In the face of the current child abuse scandal
and the falling number of children reported as attending churches,
the Child Theology Movement stirs new interest and questioning.
As White suggests, this story of Jesus with the child is a possible
'seed' in scripture whose time has now come to shoot and grow[25] as
a new focus of theology, in some ways similar to Feminist Theology
or Liberation Theology.

In the design of this study, the churches selected were those who
employed a specialist children's pastor. These pastors came from
eight churches representing various protestant traditions: Anglican,
Assemblies of God, Baptist, Churches of Christ, Christian City
Church, Salvation Army and Uniting Church in Australia. It was
hoped that these selected leaders would provide a fundamental
understanding of the place of children in the Church. The senior
ministers in these Churches were also interviewed. The viewpoints
of the senior ministers were considered an extension of the views of
the children's pastors, and provide a wider perspective of care for the
whole Church. Using Grounded Theory, the data was collected and
analysed. The individual participant checked each interview summary,
and the final analysed data was presented to a focus group for further
correction, extension and interpretation.

Findings
Again using the careful analysis process of Grounded Theory, three findings were identified from the data:
Finding One: The Child Theology Movement has relevance for personal discipleship.
Finding Two: The Child Theology Movement has positive significance for the Church.
Finding Three: The blessing of children should take higher priority than the teaching of repentance.

Summary of Finding One
The following six supporting properties explain and amplify the category. The numbers associated with each property are an indication of the number of participants who identified this property. For example, in number 1, 2 and 3, all participants recognised some of these properties. The final numbers on the list contained properties that were identified by the majority of participants but not by all:

1. Children recognise the centrality of relationship – friendship, acceptance of others, caring, getting over it (forgiveness), relationship with God, spiritual connection of empathy with others.
2. Children are open to the new – showing qualities of trust, humility, questioning, being willing to learn, having simple faith, being open-hearted, accepting, ready for life, courageous, capable.
3. Children are open to mystery – awe, wonder, presence of the Holy Spirit, wisdom, miracles, joy, insight.
4. Children are honest – natural, simple, naïve, not cynical but innocent, focused, gifted, curious.
5. Children pray – healing, empathy, trust, expectancy, gratitude.
6. Children have imagination and creativity – seeing spiritual connection, fun and experimentation.

When considering the reported properties of this first finding, the sense of connection with God and connection with others is central. Although prayer was not mentioned specifically by all participants, the link can be seen with relationship to God, the attitude of openness to the new and openness to mystery. Many stories of children praying were related by the participants, often confounding adults with their honesty and insight, even if the children's perspectives were theologically immature at times.

Conclusion

This chapter has looked at the place of prayer for children from three perspectives: the personal experience of the author; some understanding from the Christian tradition; and from two research projects.

The first research study into the meaning and function of prayer for children led to recommendations for those teaching religious education, for those working in the secular sphere with children and for those interested in developing children's spirituality. This research highlighted the very common use of prayer by children. Of the sixty participants, twenty came from homes and schools not associated with a religious tradition, yet all of these children had prayed and all spoke quite easily and naturally about prayer. The other highlight was the use of prayer to help in the difficulties of life. Some children said, 'I don't believe in "God" but there is something up there'. Before this study commenced, the researcher had anticipated that in the increasingly secular society some children might view prayer as old-fashioned or an activity for the religious. But this was not the case.

The second research project was not specifically focused on prayer, but prayer was part of the assessment of childhood life. Relationship with God was considered a special part of childhood, and prayer was part of this relationship.

Prayer has been shown as a real part of the life of children and the Church is called to nurture and develop this aspect of faith. Much further discussion is possible, but at the very least my research findings awaken a respect for the possibilities of prayer in the life of children. The seemingly natural ways in which children reach out in communication with God could be viewed as relational consciousness, in a similar way to the child reaching out to parents. We are left with the question: is prayer an overlooked natural resource of childhood?

Notes

1. P. Hampl, *Virgin Time* (New York: Ballantyne Books, 1992), 35.
2. J. Whitehead and E. Whitehead, *Method in Ministry* (Kansas City: Sheed, 1995).
3. A. M. Rizzuto, *The Birth of the Living God* (Chicago and London: University of Chicago Press, 1979).
4. Many authors could be suggested, such as: D. Hay, *Something There* (Philadelphia: Templeton Press, 2006); R. Nye, *Children's Spirituality* (London: Church House, 2010); D. O'Murchu, *Evolutionary Faith* (Maryknoll, NY: Orbis, 2002); D. Zohar and I. Marshall, *Spiritual Intelligence* (London: Bloomsbury, 2000); M. de Souza, *How Can We Address Spirituality in Education?* (Melbourne: Australian Catholic University, 2003); T. Hart, *The Secret Spiritual Life of Children* (Makawao, HI: Inner Ocean, 2003). *The International Journal of Children's Spirituality* also provides a broad selection of articles supporting this understanding of children's spirituality.

5. J. Berryman, *Children and the Theologians* (New York: Moorehouse, 2009), 27.

6. V. Mountain, *Children's Perceptions of Prayer* (Staarsbrucken: DVM, 2008).

7. N. Coleman, *The Worlds of Religion* (Sydney: McGraw-Hill, 1999) and K. Engebretson, *Aspects of Faith* (Katoomba, NSW: Social Science Press, 1999).

8. K. Pargament, *The Psychology of Religion and Coping* (New York: Guilford Press, 1997).

9. D. Hay, *Something There* (London: Templeton Press, 2007).

10. R. Nye, *Children's Spirituality* (London: Church House, 2009).

11. R. Coles, *The Spiritual Life of Children* (Boston: Houghton Mifflin, 1990).

12. D. Coupland, *Life After God* (New York: Pocket Books, 1995).

13. A. Ulinov and B. Ulinov, *Primary Speech: A Psychology of Prayer* (Atlanta: John Knox Press, 1982).

14. M. P. Hederman, *Kissing the Dark* (Dublin: Veritas, 1999).

15. K. Rahner, *On Prayer* (New York/Mahwah, NJ: Paulist Press, 1958).

16. R. Lazarus and B. Lazarus, *Passion and Reason* (New York: Oxford University Press, 1994).

17. Ibid., 166.

18. Pargament, *The Psychology of Religion and Coping*, 86.

19. E. Frydenberg, *Learning to Cope* (Oxford: Oxford University Press, 1999).

20. Hay, *Something There*, 113.

21. A. Godin, *From Cry to Word* (Belgium: Lumens Vitae, 1968).

22. H. Abdulati, *Islam in Focus* (Indianapolis: American Trust, 1996).

23. J. Collier, *Toddling to the Kingdom* (London: The Child Theology Movement, 2009), 29.

24. From Matthew 18:1-5 and similar references in Mark and Luke.

25. K. White, *Toddling Forward* (CTM Melbourne: Victorian Council for Christian Education, 2010), 6.

Contributors' Biographies

Dr Patrick J. Boyle is a clinical nurse specialist for Asylum Seekers Health Assessment in the Health Services Executive (HSE), Dublin. He is a member of the National HSE Ethnic Minority Intercultural Governance Committee and the HSE Advisory Group on Medical Resettlement of Programme Refugees. He is an adjunct lecturer at the School of Nursing & Midwifery, Faculty of Health Sciences, in Trinity College, Dublin.

Dr Sharon M. Cruise is a research fellow in the Centre for Public Health in the School of Medicine, Dentistry and Biomedical Sciences, Queen's University, Belfast. Her recent research has focused on examining the early life determinants of health and development using secondary analysis of large-scale, epidemiological birth cohort data from Ireland and the United Kingdom. She has a particular interest in how the social environment, including parents' psychological health and health behaviours, influence the child's health and well-being.

Dr Finola Cunnane has lectured extensively in education, spirituality, theology, psychology and pastoral care throughout Ireland, Europe, USA, West Africa and New Zealand, and has undertaken considerable research in these areas. She is the author of *New Directions in Religious Education* (Veritas, 2004) as well as over one hundred articles, and is a renowned spiritual director and retreat facilitator.

Dr Marian de Souza is a former senior lecturer at Australian Catholic University. She previously spent many years as a curriculum coordinator and taught music, drama, English, history and religious education at second level. Marian has published extensively on her research into the spirituality of young people and the implications for education, with her approach recognising the complementarity of the cognitive, affective and spiritual dimensions of learning.

Edel Greene MEd is a teacher of religious education, history, SPHE, CSPE and substance abuse prevention in Loreto Secondary School, Balbriggan, Dublin. She has worked as head of the SPHE department and pastoral care co-ordinator. She was an associate trainer for religious education as an exam subject with the National Council for Curriculum and Assessment (NCCA), as well as a part-time lecturer in a number of higher education colleges. Edel is former head of the Equal Opportunities section of the Department of Democratisation in the OSCE Mission to Serbia, and continues to offer consultancy on education to the OSCE.

Dr Edward J. Hall is a member of the Passionist Community based in Ireland and the USA. He is a former director of religious education at St Thomas Aquinas Parish in the University of Connecticut, and has lectured at the Mater Dei Institute of Education, Dublin City University. He has also worked in Counselling Pastoral Education with the Government Commission on Mental Health Services at St Elizabeth's Hospital, Washington, DC, and has been a mediator for Baltimore Community Mediation in Baltimore, Maryland.

Audrey Halpin MEd MSc is a teacher educator in the Church of Ireland College of Education, Dublin, where in addition to lecturing undergraduate and postgraduate students, she is pursuing research interests in all aspects of diversity in education and the policies that influence practice in these areas. Her research considers the relational dimension of teaching with diverse student populations through mainstream and support roles in Ireland, Canada, Dubai and Kuwait.

Dr Christopher A. Lewis is a professor of psychology and dean of the Institute of Health, Medical Sciences and Society at Glyndwr University, Wales. His research interests include psychology of religion, health psychology, psychology of peace, conflict and violence, and positive psychology. He is founding co-editor of the journal, *Mental Health, Religion & Culture*, and former editor of the *Irish Journal of Psychology*. He is currently an executive board member of the International Association for the Psychology of Religion.

Dr Patricia Mannix McNamara is a senior lecturer in education in the faculty of Education and Health Sciences at the University of Limerick. She is co-director of the Research Centre for Education and Professional Practice. Patricia has expertise in both health and education and has authored and co-authored books, book chapters and journal papers spanning both fields. She has been a national evaluator for the European Network of Health Promoting Schools since 1999 and is a core group member of the Schools for Health in Europe (SHE) Research Group.

Dr Conor McGuckin is assistant professor of educational psychology in the School of Education at Trinity College, Dublin. His research interests include bully/victim problems among children and adults, psychology applied to educational policy and practices, psychology of religion, psychometrics and guidance counselling. He is an associate fellow of the British Psychological Society and the Psychological

Society of Ireland, and a chartered scientist with the British Science Council.

Dr Maeve Martin is a former senior lecturer in psychology at the National University of Ireland, Maynooth. She is a founder member of the Irish Association of Pastoral Care in Education. She was appointed by the Minister for Education and Science as chair of the National Taskforce on Discipline in Schools and authored its report, *School Matters*, published in 2006. She is a member of a number of boards in the education sector, and she acts as a panellist on some strands of the implementation of the Education Act.

Dr Áine Moran is the principal of Le Chéile Secondary School, Tyrrelstown, Dublin. She completed her PhD in education at the Mater Dei Institute of Education on the topic of school chaplaincy and holds qualifications in school chaplaincy and pastoral care, school management, theology, catechetics, economics and law. She was chairperson of the School Chaplains Association from 2010–11, and currently lectures on school chaplaincy at St Angela's College, Sligo.

Dr Vivienne Mountain has taught at primary, secondary and tertiary levels. She is currently involved in adult education as an adjunct lecturer at the University of Divinity, Melbourne, and facilitates psycho-education groups through the Lifeworks organisation. She also works as a clinical counsellor for children and families. She is the author of two books, and has contributed chapters in others and published articles in a variety of journals.

Dr John Murray is a lecturer at the Mater Dei Institute of Education, a college of Dublin City University. He taught Religious Education and English at second-level for seventeen years. He is a representative of the Irish Bishops' Conference on the Health Care Chaplaincy board and is a member of the Irish Episcopal Conference's Theology Committee. He is the author of *Issues of Justice and Peace* (Veritas, 2005).

Dr Grace O'Grady is a lecturer in the Education Department, National University of Ireland, Maynooth. She is director of the Postgraduate Diploma and Master of Education in School Guidance Counselling and co-leader of the Structured PhD programme. She teaches on all courses in the department in the curricular areas of Human Development, Developmental Psychology, Child Protection and Social Personal and Health Education, and is a founding member of the Centre for Transformative Narrative Inquiry (NUI Maynooth).

Dr James O'Higgins Norman is a senior lecturer and researcher in the School of Education Studies, Dublin City University, where he is also director of the National Anti-Bullying Research and Resource Centre. He is an international associate editor of the *Journal of Pastoral Care in Education*. He has authored a number of books on aspects of equality and bullying in schools and has presented conference papers on his research in Ireland, Australia, the UK, Finland and the USA. He is a former member of the NCCA's sub-committee on inter-culturalism in education.

Dr Theresa A. O'Keefe is an assistant professor of Practice of Youth and Young Adult Faith at the School of Theology and Ministry at Boston College, Massachusetts. She has been teaching for many years in the areas of youth and young adult faith. In her work she assists ministerial and educational leaders to read the context of contemporary culture and analyse its impact on their constituencies. Dr O'Keefe also leads the Contextual Education programme at Boston College, in which students use field opportunities to develop their praxis.

Dr Siobhán O'Reilly is executive director of FamiliBase, an NGO that works with families who need support in Ballyfermot, Dublin. She is a former teacher in the formal education sector, including a special school for children and young people with emotional and behavioural difficulties, and has also worked in an informal education context with young people at risk in Tallaght, Dublin. She has worked in Ballyfermot since 2002, initially as education co-ordinator in Ballyfermot Partnership, then going on to lead the Familiscope service. She is an adjunct lecturer at the School of Education Studies, Dublin City University.

Dr Michelle Y. Pearlman is a clinical psychologist in New York and New Jersey. She specialises in helping children and families through grief, trauma, anxiety and other stressors. She is founding director of the Trauma and Bereavement Program and the clinical director of the Institute for Trauma and Resilience at New York University's Child Study Centre.

Dr Nigel Pimlott is deputy CEO for Frontier Youth Trust. He has written a number of books and resources about youth work – particularly Christian-motivated youth work – and has worked with, and on behalf of, young people for over thirty years, combining practice, advocacy, research and academic study. His research has investigated the relationship between faith-based youth work and social policy, developing a contemporary model for such work.

Dr John-Paul Sheridan is a lecturer at St Patrick's Pontifical College, Maynooth. He served for seventeen years as an advisor for primary school catechetics in the Diocese of Ferns, and was a member of the Executive of the National Association of Primary Diocesan Advisors. He is the author of *Promises to Keep: Parents and Confirmation* (Veritas, 2004), and has written extensively, providing educational policy documents for his diocese and resources for primary school teachers.

Noreen Sweeney MSc is an accredited counsellor and supervisor working in private practice in Dublin. She also lectured in counselling at the Mater Dei Institute of Education, a college of Dublin City University. She has supervised groups of guidance counsellors in second-level schools since 2005. She worked in second-level education before taking up her present career.

Irene White MA is a lecturer in the School of Education Studies, Dublin City University. She taught English and Drama at post-primary level for twelve years. She works with Irish participatory arts organisations using drama to promote positive mental health and well-being in the community, and has directed a range of community-engaged theatre projects in Ireland. Recent projects have focused on raising awareness of issues surrounding suicide and suicide prevention among adolescents in second-level schools throughout Ireland.

Dr Kevin Williams is a former senior lecturer at the Mater Dei Institute of Education, and former president of the Educational Studies Association of Ireland. His most recent publications include *Education and the Voice of Michael Oakeshott* (Imprint Academic, 2007), *Faith and the Nation: Religion, Culture, Schooling in Ireland* (Dominican Publications, 2005) and *Religion and Citizenship Education in Europe* (2008), written as part of the Children's Identity and Citizenship Education in Europe (CiCe) project funded by the European Commission.